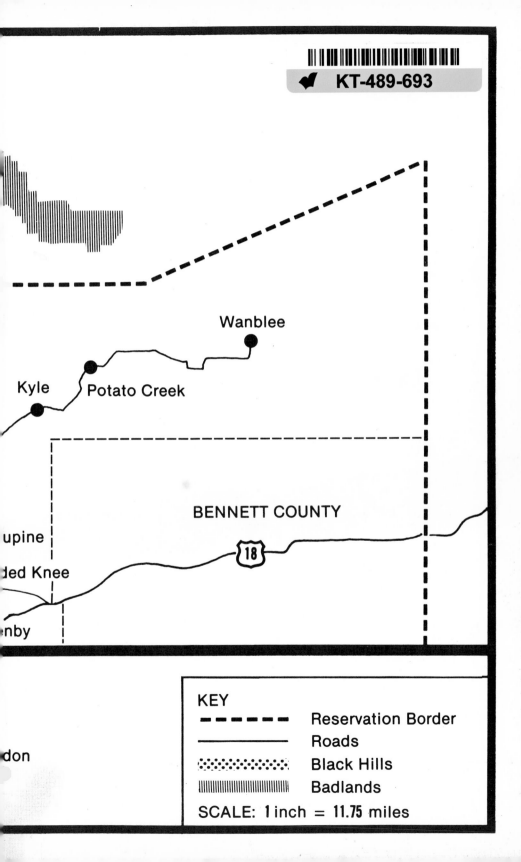

Wanblee

Kyle   Potato Creek

BENNETT COUNTY

18

upine

ded Knee

nby

don

KEY

- - - - -   Reservation Border
────────   Roads
∷∷∷∷∷∷∷   Black Hills
▧▧▧▧▧▧   Badlands

SCALE: 1 inch = 11.75 miles

Airlift to Wounded Knee

BILL ZIMMERMAN

Airlift to Wounded Knee

HE SWALLOW PRESS INC.
CHICAGO

Swallow Press—8-10-77   M3

First Edition
    Second Printing 1977

Published by
The Swallow Press Incorporated
811 West Junior Terrace
Chicago, Illinois 60613

This book is printed on recycled paper

ISBN 0-8040-0691-1
Library of Congress Catalog Card Number 76-3138

To
my father, Sid Zimmerman,
who left Austria-Hungary before World War I to escape the draft.
He fled toward the myth of America,
hoping to find a New World.

Contents

Foreword

This is not another book about Indians written by a white person. This is a book written by a white person about a project undertaken by a few non-Indian people to help a large number of Indians—those who seized and occupied Wounded Knee, South Dakota, in the winter and spring of 1973.

All the events in this book are true. The story has never before been told. I initiated and participated in the project to be described, which came to be known as the Wounded Knee airlift. Like many other acts of political dissent, the Federal Bureau of Investigation viewed this one as illegal. Consequently, some thought had to be given to protecting the identities of many of the people involved. I consulted the principal participants in the airlift, and together we decided that the action should be described regardless of the legal consequences. We firmly believed that no jury would convict us of a criminal offense if our story were accurately told. And we all felt that it might be a significant, and hopefully educational, story to tell.

As a result, in the interests of maximum accuracy and truthfulness, those centrally involved in the airlift agreed to be identified in the book. But the fact remains that the FBI and other forces in the government would take great pleasure in locking us up and at the same time disposing of all of the many others who helped us. Clearly, there is no reason to make the job any easier for them. So, despite the fact that most of those in question would be happy to be publicly identified with what we did, and given the very likely possibility that all of us will want to get together and do something like this again, some people must remain nameless.

Thus, when a person in this book is identified by first and last name, the reader can know the name is real. When only a first name is used, it is fictitious and was given to protect a person who helped us. Unfortunately, federal prosecutors would be quick to include such people among "the guilty." The only other departure from the truth is in false registration

1

numbers created for aircraft mentioned in the book. Everything else in
the airlift story is true and based upon extensive notes and taped interviews with all of the principal participants.

However, the airlift accounts for only part of the book. In order for our
story to have any real meaning, it was essential also to tell the story of the
Indians who took Wounded Knee. I would have liked to bring to their
story much more detail and depth. Wounded Knee was one of the most
fascinating public dramas of our day, and an account of what led up to it
contains much information that many Americans would be surprised to
discover. But space was too limited to do the story justice. As a result, the
reader will be directed to other sources that can provide more detailed
description, should it be desired. Wherever possible, events in this book
that took place before and during the occupation of Wounded Knee are
described through the eyes of Indian people who were direct participants.
For this, I am particularly indebted to Gladys Bissonette of the Pine Ridge
Reservation and Dennis Banks of the American Indian Movement.

Other material not obtained from eyewitnesses was taken primarily
from articles authored by eyewitnesses. These articles appeared in the
Indian newspaper *Akwesasne Notes,* published by the Mohawk Nation in
upstate New York. Their Spring and Summer editions in 1973 contain a
remarkably detailed and informative day-by-day account of events inside
occupied Wounded Knee. Interested readers can obtain copies of this
excellent Indian publication by writing to the Mohawk Nation, via Roose-
veltown, New York 13683.

By far the best overall picture of Wounded Knee and the events that
led up to it is contained in a large and beautifully reproduced book of 260
photographs, with tape transcripts, documents, and commentary edited
by four radio reporters who participated in the entire occupation. This
book, entitled, *Voices From Wounded Knee 1973,* is published by
Akwesasne Notes and can be obtained directly from them by sending
$4.95 to the address above. Other written material is available from the
Wounded Knee Legal Defense/Offense Committee, P.O. Box 2307,
Rapid City, South Dakota 57701.

Some of the historical material in this book was taken from Dee
Brown's widely acclaimed *Bury My Heart At Wounded Knee* (a Bantam
paperback). Other very useful historical works were *The Long Death* (a
Collier paperback) by Ralph K. Andrist and the first volume of *To Serve
The Devil* (a Vintage paperback) by Jacobs, Landau, and Pell. Early
Indian quotations were taken from *To Serve The Devil,* Virginia Irving
Armstrong's *I Have Spoken* (a Swallow paperback), John Neihardt's
Black Elk Speaks (a Bison paperback), and T.C. McLuhan's *Touch The
Earth* (a Pocket Books paperback). Tom Hayden's *The Love of Posses-
sion Is A Disease With Them* (a Holt paperback) develops some of the

startling parallels between the 19th century American wars against the Indians and the modern American war in Viet Nam. *The Road to Wounded Knee* (a Bantam paperback) by Burnette and Koster is a good source of background material regarding the last hundred years of reservation life in America. *Akwesasne Notes* is also valuable in this regard.

It should come as no surprise if the reader detects a bias in my interpretation of facts gained from all of these sources—a bias in favor of struggling Indians and against the government of the United States. This book takes a side. To do otherwise would be dishonest, both in the narrow sense of hiding my own beliefs and in the broader sense that genuine historical neutrality is never possible.

My understanding of reality, like everyone else's, has been formed after long experience and careful reflection. Like others, I am not able to completely put aside the filters through which I have come to see reality. But I can try to remain open to new ideas and new ways of understanding the events I encounter. I can try above all to be honest. But it would be wrong to claim that the filters do not exist. No historian or journalist can ever tell a story about conflict between real human beings in a totally neutral and unbiased way, despite the fact that many commonly claim to do so.

+   +   +

Many people helped pull me along through the whole gratifying ordeal of creating a book. To those who were advisors, helpers, prodders, agents, researchers, informants, critics, typists, editors, lawyers, and most of all friends, I want to say, thank you, especially to: Mark Amsterdam, Joan Andersson, Elinor Blake, Chris Burrill, Ron Chutter, Ken Coplon, Reine Cram, Tom Davidson, Betsy Dudley, Michael Falk, John Flym, Jane Fonda, Marvin Frankel, Ann Froines, Mike Frost, Lou Gerwitz, Eda Gordon, Linda Gordon, Bob Greenfield, Frank Greer, Tom Hayden, Marc Kadish, Caryn Kaufman, Kathy Kolman, Carol Kurtz, Miguel Lopez-Vivas, Ellen Ruby Lustbader, Bliss Mattison, Bart Meyers, Mimi Meyers, Seymour Meyers, Rickie Miller, Jack Nichol, Karen Nussbaum, Paul Ryder, Sharon Satterthwaite, Billy Schechter, Danny Schechter, Rhonda Schoenbrod, Lillian Shirley, Peggy Stewart, Cindy Talbot, Mary Jo Von Mach, Durrett Wagner, Leonard Weinglass, Charlotte Weissberg, Mort Weisman, Susan Wind, and Bill Yahrous.

There are others to thank, too, but anonymously. First, the photographers who allowed us to use their pictures without credits. Some of the people in the pictures would otherwise run the risk of the photographs being introduced as evidence against them at upcoming trials. But by our withholding the names of the photographers, government prosecutors cannot subpoena anyone able to testify to the authenticity or the date of the pictures.

Second, the people involved in fund raising. Projects like the Wounded Knee airlift depend in part on generous contributors and people who accept the tedious and frequently unacknowledged job of contacting them and asking for support. These funding networks are too valuable to expose to the scrutiny and possible interference of police agencies anxious to stop them. So, to the people who helped financially, a quiet and sincere thank you.

Third, I owe much to the people who flew with me on the airlift and to the many others (who must also remain anonymous) involved in necessary behind-the-scenes and support work. This is their story, too, and one way to thank them is to go ahead and tell it.

Finally, the help I received from the Indian people of the Pine Ridge Reservation and the American Indian Movement was essential to the development of this book. They, too, can best be thanked by the telling of their remarkable story and by some straight talk about the sources of their suffering.

Bill Zimmerman
Los Angeles

1

AIRLIFT
The Request

Tuesday, April 3, 1973
Boston, Massachusetts

At first it was hard to understand why they wanted to seize a little village on an Indian reservation where the only things "reserved" were poverty and poor health. But then almost immediately it began to sink in —Wounded Knee was no ordinary village. There, in 1890, the U.S. Army killed some 300 Indian people who were not only unwarlike but were also unarmed. It was the very last massacre of the Indian Wars, and it was the most unnecessary, the most shameful. In the age of Viet Nam, Wounded Knee was not something the government of the United States wanted in the headlines of the nation.

The tiny village was seized on the evening of February 27, 1973. Several hundred Indians participated. Most of them were members of the Oglala Sioux Tribe. They lived near Wounded Knee or in some other part of the Pine Ridge Reservation. The action was taken to protest conditions on the Reservation, which the participants felt had become intolerable. It was an interesting and important story, but one factor turned it into a sensation—the Indians were armed. By the next morning, it was on the front page of every newspaper in the country.

Soon the village was surrounded by FBI agents, U.S. marshals, and local police. The Indians inside held them all off with hunting rifles and shotguns. Strangely enough, their defiance produced a note of sympathy in some of the most conservative citizens and newspeople. Millions of other Americans, less committed to hard-line notions of "law and order,"

5

gave the action their wholehearted or grudging approval. Many anx-
iously watched the news, worried that at any moment the armed might of
the federal forces would be turned loose and the country would have yet
another massacre on its conscience.

Everywhere people were caught in the grasp of the event and painfully
reminded of America's countless crimes against the Indian people. It was
a drama of epic dimension. The country was alive with Indian ghosts
galloping across a land that would always be more familiar to them than
to anyone else. They rode from place to place over bridges of collective
guilt. Their power was sudden and immense, at once unexpected and
inescapable. Americans watched spellbound as the ghosts materialized
from the mists of South Dakota, 83 years later, on the very spot of the last
horrible slaughter—Wounded Knee.

+   +   +

Intense interest in Wounded Knee lasted for two or three weeks. Then
the real complexities of Indian problems in the U.S. and on the Pine
Ridge Reservation began to emerge. The Paris Peace Agreement, ending
direct (but not indirect) U.S. combat involvement in the Viet Nam War,
had been signed a little more than a month before. The public and the
news media started slowly backing away from the Wounded Knee story,
giving way to greater interest in the returning POWs and the tales that a
CIA agent named McCord was telling about the mysterious Watergate
burglary.

After a month of sporadic gunfights and several injuries, the Wounded
Knee situation appeared stalemated. The Indians inside would not give
up. Washington officials were reluctant to stage a military assault and
suffer the worldwide condemnation that would surely follow. Yet, the law
enforcement officers on the scene talked incessantly about doing just
that—go in shooting and damn the consequences. Sympathizers around
the country, including my friends and me, feared the worst, but we often
had to look on page five for the news. Like most Americans, we were
busy with our own work, so we read what we could and did nothing.

At that time, I was working in Boston with an anti-war organization. My
interest in the occupation of Wounded Knee was only that of a concerned
spectator. South Dakota was 2,000 miles away. Then, on April 3, 1973,
five weeks after the seizure, I returned to my desk after lunch and found a
phone message from an acquaintance of mine in New York. He wanted
me to walk to the nearest telephone booth, get the number, and call him.
Afterward, he'd walk to a pay phone in New York and call me back at the
booth in Boston.

I smiled, thinking that the Watergate atmosphere was leading to a
certain fashionable paranoia about tapped telephones. But in our case, it

was not necessarily unfounded. We were a well-known and effective anti-war group, and as it happened, I already had the number of an outdoor telephone booth around the corner, two of them in fact. We were not in the habit of doing anything illegal, but there had been other occasions when we didn't want government tape recorders overhearing our conversations.

I called New York and left the number, then strolled around the corner. It was a crisp sunny day, not yet spring, but definitely past winter. A stiff New England wind was pushing puffy little cumulus clouds across the sky. The strong breeze had cleaned the air of pollution and the sky was a clear, deep blue. I leaned up against the booth and waited. New York was a hard place to find a working telephone, and it was five minutes before I heard the ring.

The person on the other end of the line was someone I had known for years in the anti-war movement. We were never close, but there was every reason to trust him. He began by telling me that he was just back from Wounded Knee. I was surprised to hear that, not realizing how many non-Indians had gone there to offer help to the occupation. It was my first direct contact with the Wounded Knee conflict and I listened carefully to details that were not available in 60-second TV reports or short newspaper articles.

My friend said there were two major problems at Wounded Knee. One was the declining interest of the news media. Indian leaders in the village believed that the danger of an armed government assault would increase if the public began ignoring the siege. Such an attack would inevitably become a bloody disaster. The rifles and small arms in the hands of the Indians were no match for the Viet Nam-era weapons issued to federal forces on duty there. People in Wounded Knee felt their best protection against attack was the fact that so many Americans were watching on the evening news what the government did. They trusted the American people to put up the strongest possible opposition to a second unjustified massacre on the historic site of the village.

The other and more immediate problem was the serious shortage of food. When government roadblocks were thrown up around the village, the Indians organized human trains of backpackers to carry food in at night by moonlight. It was a dangerous hike over ten miles of open prairie. The backpackers had to avoid the roads and dodge federal patrols by hiding in gullies and ravines. Occasionally they were shot at. Finally, the government discovered some of their trails and began arresting them. Supplies were dwindling rapidly. Less food was getting through to the 350 people inside than was being consumed, even with daily rationing down to two meals, mostly of rice and beans. Children in the village showed signs of malnutrition. It could get worse very quickly.

As my friend prolonged his explanation of the food shortage, I got the feeling that he had an ulterior motive. "Okay, hold it," I interrupted. "You didn't arrange for us to talk on pay phones just so you could tell me all this. You want me to do something, don't you?"

"Yes, I think so. I talked to a lawyer out there who said he knew you. He said you were a pilot. Is that true?"

It was true, and I suddenly knew exactly what they wanted. The lawyer had acted on behalf of the leadership in Wounded Knee. When he heard that my friend on the telephone was going back east, he had asked him to carry a message to me, a request that I fly a planeload of supplies into Wounded Knee.

"Do you know what you're asking?" I said. "I could get shot doing that!"

"I know. You'll have to decide. But, is it possible? Could you do it?"

"If they control 2,000 feet of flat ground, it's possible. With that much, somebody could land a small plane in there and take off again—provided they weren't shot down while they were doing it. Look, there are a hundred things to check on and think about before I'd agree to do something like that."

"Why don't you start checking. I'll start raising some money. We've got to move fast or things are going to collapse out there. People here in New York will support it. How much do you think it will cost?"

It was a crazy idea, but the Indians needed help and it just might work. Landing a single-engine plane on a field or a flat road, I could bring in 400-500 pounds of food. Depending on the terrain, the size of the land that the Indians controlled, and whether or not the other side was using machine-guns, it might be feasible. Those were big "if's", but I ignored them for the moment and started thinking out loud.

"We'd have to begin far enough from Wounded Knee to avoid any kind of suspicion. No one is going to rent us an airplane if they think there's a chance it'll come back with holes in it. Denver would be a good starting point. I'd have to fly the plane some place where we could take the seats out and load the food on without being seen. Some little grass landing strip, maybe.

"It might work. I could fly into Wounded Knee just before dark and take off at night with no lights. They'd never see me. It sounds like six or seven hours of flying, up and back from Denver. Figure about $200 for the plane, another few hundred for the food, then add $300 or so to fly me out to Denver. Can you get that much?"

He said he probably could, and offered to start trying immediately. If the information I gathered indicated that the flight was too risky, it would be a simple matter to return whatever money was collected and drop the whole project.

I hung up, too excited to think clearly. Suddenly I was involved. Suddenly I had to deal with the possibility of physical danger. Wounded Knee telescoped in on me. From 2,000 miles away, it was abruptly the day after tomorrow, or the day after that. I had too many thoughts all at once. It wasn't just the risk but the legal jeopardy as well. The FBI was arresting people right and left for bringing food to Wounded Knee. I needed to push everything out of my mind and let the questions come back in one at a time. And I needed advice.

I took a deep breath, ready for the plunge, picked up the telephone, and called my old flight instructor in Chicago. We had become friends when I was working on a commercial pilot's license a few years before. He was a professional, with more flying knowledge than anyone else I knew. While my own flying experience was strictly as an amateur, he flew for a living, having done everything from crop-dusting and cargo hauling to working as a captain on a small Midwest commuter airline.

It had been six or eight months since we had seen each other. As there was no reason to assume that his telephone was tapped, we chatted for awhile and then I asked him how he felt about Wounded Knee. He and I had often disagreed politically, especially over demonstrations and other forms of protest. For a short time, ten years before, he had worked as a cop. I wanted to be certain which side he was on before revealing the reason for my call. But happily this time there was no argument. Despite their militancy, he was enthusiastic in his support for the Indians and what they were doing. I explained their need for food, the government road-blocks, and my own thoughts on how to land a plane inside Wounded Knee.

"You want to know what I think?" he asked forcefully, "I think you haven't thought this over very carefully. You've got two primary consid-erations. Number one is your own ass and hauling it out of there in one piece. Number two is delivering the biggest payload you can as efficiently as possible.

"First you need good reconnaissance. Get yourself as much informa-tion as you can about the terrain and who might be shooting at you with what. Then throw away all of that information and prepare for the worst. Figure the fields are all uneven and full of rocks. You'll have to land on a road. Then figure the roads the Indians control are either lined with telephone poles or don't have straightaways long enough to get a VW into second gear. On top of that, flying in there is going to be like walking past the wrong side of a shooting gallery."

"Well, that's great," I laughed. "What do I do?"

"Go in with the best possible equipment for what you want to do," he replied, continuing his rapid-fire advice, "not a regular old private plane. Get one of those World War II medical evacuation jobs, like the one we flew aerobatics in a few years ago. Remember? The whole side opens up for a stretcher. There's nothing inside but a canvas seat for the pilot, it's equipped for short takeoffs and landings, and it's a tail-dragger. You don't want a nosewheel up front if it's gonna get caught in some hole in the ground.

"And you won't find the right plane in Denver. If you do, don't rent it. Get one here in Chicago. I know a couple that might be available. Once you have it, I'll take you out for a day and we'll land on some fields and country roads and fly under a few telephone wires. You'd better be prepared for anything once you get to Wounded Knee.

"I don't know what to say about the shooting," he admitted, lowering his voice an octave, but speeding right along. "There's not much you can do. Come in low. Give them a target that looks like it's moving as fast as possible. But don't be so low that they can take a level shot at you. Go in at dawn or dusk. Those are the only two times. At dawn you might catch them sleeping and be able to get out before they have time to react.

"Now look, don't cut corners on this thing. I know it's more of a hassle to fly out there all the way from Chicago. But, if you're going to do this, do it right. Do it so you've got the most going for you when you start out."

It was just the kind of nuts and bolts talk that I needed, a little overwhelming but necessary to avoid recklessness. I accepted my friend's advice on every count and thanked him for taking the matter so seriously. He offered to start checking aircraft availability and, since Wounded Knee was 1,000 miles from Chicago, to arrange at least a three-day rental. Turning from the telephone, still reeling a little from the shock of my sudden involvement, I walked off toward the river to try and sort things out.

The flying part of the venture was the least of my worries. For that I needed a cunning enough plan, one that anticipated every imaginable kind of problem. But basically the flying part was a technical detail, a tool problem. There would be many people to help me solve it. That, and other tangible problems like raising money, would have hard, tangible solutions. The really pressing difficulties were more intangible.

Why did I want to get involved with the Indians in the first place? Was their struggle related to me? Was it worth participating in at the risk of my safety and freedom? All of a sudden someone on the telephone had asked me to take considerable risk for Indian people I admired from a distance but did not really know at all. I was asked to suspend my own work for a time and throw myself completely into a project that might possibly end in injury or imprisonment.

My work was important to me and was not something I wanted to leave. I was on the staff of and had helped start the Medical Aid for Indochina organization. We sent medical equipment to the people in

North and South Viet Nam, Laos, and Cambodia who were being bombed by the United States and its allies. The work consisted of raising money, communicating with the various Indochinese health services about their needs, purchasing the proper medical equipment, and trying to find ways of shipping it into the war zones. We wanted to aid the victims of the fighting. But, equally important, we wanted to unite the anti-war movement by providing a truly wide spectrum of Americans with a way of actively demonstrating their opposition to U.S. policy in Indochina. At the time I was asked to make the food flight, the Paris Peace Agreement was already two months old. My own work did not then require the same kind of emergency attention as Wounded Knee, yet I was confident that it was no less important to do.

The problem was not taking time from work. If things went well, the flight would require only a few days. But if something went wrong and I were arrested, it might lead not only to time-consuming legal problems but also to possible difficulties or adverse publicity for Medical Aid for Indochina. The organization's success, which so many people had helped to achieve, was too important to jeopardize, even minimally, without careful consideration.

The flying problems were indeed the least of my worries. Walking along, I remembered how children with malnutrition often suffer irreversible side effects. I remembered the children of Viet Nam and the awful fate being forced upon so many of them. Indian people at Wounded Knee were making a brave and desperate stand that might flounder simply for lack of enough to eat. That was an outrageous possibility. What the Indians were doing was too important to fail for such a reason. And if airplanes were the only way to deliver food, how many pilots in the whole country could be counted on to help? I was put on the spot. It was not possible to duck the responsibility. The request was made to *me*, and my answer would say something about my life and how I chose to live it. In a world where meaningful acts and meaningful work are so elusive, if I refused to take the risk, if I was not able to respond to such a request, then surely my own life would be diminished and robbed of some of its meaning.

But how are such decisions made? I thought of my friends, the people with whom I had chosen to live and work, people who had in some ways tied their lives to mine. They had a right to participate, especially when the decision might affect them in serious ways. I started back for the office. There was a lot to do, a long list of people to contact. Also, I had an intense interest in finding out more about Wounded Knee. What was really going on out there and how had it all come about?

2

San Salvador to Dakota Territory

"Yet, hear me, people, we have now to deal with another race—small and feeble when our fathers first met them but now great and overbearing. Strangely enough they have a mind to till the soil and the love of possession is a disease with them. These people have made many rules that the rich may break but the poor may not. They take tithes from the poor and weak to support the rich and those who rule. They claim this mother of ours, the Earth, for their own and fence their neighbors away; they deface her with their buildings and their refuse. That nation is like a spring freshet that overruns its banks and destroys all who are in its path."

—Tatanka Yotanka (Sitting Bull)
Medicine Man and Chief,
Hunkpapa Sioux, 1877.

Until 1973, the village of Wounded Knee, South Dakota, was known to only a handful of people as a minor tourist attraction on the Pine Ridge Indian Reservation. Few areas of the United States are more isolated.

Through the window of an airplane flying low over the tiny settlement at that time, not very many things could be seen. From 500 feet high, the most noticeable structure was a small church sitting on top of a low hill. There were few trees. Except on days when heavy snow blanketed the area, the stark white building stood out against the brown landscape. It was a conventional one-room country church with a tall, narrow steeple. Next to it, there was a very unconventional graveyard.

The square little cemetery on the rounded hilltop was clearly visible from the air. Down its center one could see the outline of a trench, about eight feet wide and as long as the church building itself. It was a mass grave. Buried in the trench were the bodies of 146 men, women, and children of the Sioux Nation. In December 1890, they and some 150 other unarmed people were butchered by the U.S. Army's 7th Cavalry. It was the last great massacre of the bloody Indian Wars and it gave Wounded Knee an unfortunate immortality.

The hilltop church cemetery overlooked a few clumps of small buildings that together were hardly enough to be called a village. There was only a single trading post/general store. It was more of a populated crossroads than anything else. Four roads came into town but were neither straight nor perpendicular to each other as they would have been in the cornfields 500 miles to the east. This country, the High Plains, was too hilly. A short distance from the houses, a creek bearing the same name as the village intersected a dry ravine. A few leafless trees could be seen out along the banks of the creek. Otherwise, except for the brown buffalo grass, nothing natural rose above the ground.

But during March and April 1973, this tiny village was under military siege. From a low-altitude vantage point, it was easy to see barricades across each of the four roads less than a mile out from the center. Next to the roadblocks were jeeps and large olive-green vehicles that looked like tanks. On the low hills surrounding the village a dozen more tank-like vehicles were scattered about. Looking more closely, it was possible to see trenches and sandbagged bunkers inside Wounded Knee and all around it. Some of the houses were barricaded and their sides reinforced. From 500 feet up, there was no question that one was flying over a very small war.

Beyond and around the miniature battlefield, the shallow hills rippled across the plains. The erosion of wind and water cut small gullies and ravines sharply into the dry land. Narrow creek beds skirted the hills. Here and there a few stunted pines lived on the infrequent water. The Pine Ridge Reservation is in South Dakota's arid southwest quadrant, just below the Badlands National Monument. In places, the reservation is 90 miles long and 45 miles wide. More than half the size of Connecticut, it has fewer than 12,000 people.

Besides Wounded Knee, there are about a dozen villages of the same size scattered across the reservation. Each contains 100-400 Oglala Sioux. Isolated houses and cabins dot the countryside. Where the thin grass grows, a few cattle and horses are grazed, but large-scale farming is virtually impossible. There is one larger town that serves as the administrative center of the reservation. It, too, is called Pine Ridge (population: 2,000). The three-story Bureau of Indian Affairs (BIA) building and the Public Health Service Hospital are there. They are the largest buildings for 100 miles in any direction. In addition to a jail, a single gas station, one supermarket, several small stores, a community center, and a few schools, Pine Ridge has a number of modest houses and acres of broken-down shanties.

The squalor in which the Pine Ridge Sioux live is almost unmatched anywhere in America. More than half of the people are out of work. Housing is substandard, sanitation facilities are poor, life expectancy is short. There are a few jobs working on the land. Most of the other work is with the BIA, as a cop or a road repairman or a clerk. The tribal government, which dispenses the BIA jobs, wields immense power.

Some people manage to keep themselves busy even without jobs, especially those who live on the land, outside the town of Pine Ridge. But others are unable to fill up their time. Some men·hang out on the dusty street corners in town. It should come as no surprise that many turn to alcohol in a vain attempt to escape the emptiness and despair. But drinking adds to their problems, and the greater frustration leads to bitterness and violence. Suicide, too, is abnormally high. As in most places in the West, guns are commonplace, and despite the lack of money, everybody seems to have one. All around, the land is vast and wide open. It's the kind of place where people think nothing of driving 50 miles for a glass of beer, at 90 miles an hour.

Most Oglalas, if they survive childhood at all, do so without electricity or running water. Diseases long neutralized in other parts of America still destroy young lives at Pine Ridge. Few children ever leave the bleak, self-enclosed world of southwestern South Dakota. If they have any experience of what lies beyond, it is often only from a glimpse at a neighbor's television set. When they quit or finish school, some leave the reservation for an equally dismal adult life in the Indian ghetto of a big city, like Denver or Salt Lake City. They rarely move back. Others, if they don't stay on the reservation, end up in Rapid City, 100 miles to the north. From there it is at least possible to return home and visit relatives.

But few find work in Rapid City. The Indian population is far higher than the available jobs. It is a small city (population: 45,000), but it is big enough to have its little version of an Indian ghetto. Unemployed men fill up the streets and the brassy white-owned bars that cater to them. It can get very demoralizing after a while, and a lot of people go back to the reservation. There the cycle starts over again, and many Oglala Sioux spend their whole lives going back and forth from the Pine Ridge Reservation to Rapid City.

The full-blood Indian children and adults on the reservation live with an additional burden. Over the years, the offspring of mixed Indian and white marriages have found it easier to get jobs with the BIA and to do business with the whites who controlled the economy around the reservation. The mixed-bloods accumulated in the town of Pine Ridge. As their economic advantage grew, cultural differences emerged as well. On the whole, the mixed-bloods assimilated to a greater extent, adopting the habits and tastes of the white culture. This made it easier for them to increase their economic advantage even more.

Eventually, the town of Pine Ridge came under the sway of the mixed-bloods who then gained control of the tribal government. Most have lost the ability to speak the Sioux language. Today they jeer at and make fun of their neighbors who still cling to it. In the schools, full-blood children with long braids and darker skin are taunted as social inferiors. Meanwhile, in the countryside surrounding the town, people remain loyal to the old ways, to what is left of the Sioux language and traditions. Chiefs and tribal headmen are still designated and sought out for advice and counsel. Medicine men are looked to as spiritual leaders.

The gulf grew wide between town and country, new American techniques and old Indian wisdom, those influenced by the whites and those trying to preserve the Sioux traditions. There is often overlap, but the split indicates that the economic deprivations of the tribe are accompanied by a clear cultural disintegration as well. Ravaged by virtually inescapable poverty, Indians like the Oglala Sioux have also to contend with the destruction of their identity as a people. Torn between the lure of white materialism and pride in themselves as Indians, many remain confused and angry.

The Oglala Sioux were not always troubled in this way or confined to the hostile land around Pine Ridge. At one time they were part of a proud nation whose land and civilization stretched 750 miles from Iowa and Minnesota westward into Wyoming. Their lives were graced with abundant food and a gratifying culture rich in song, dance, and the handicraft arts. Their society was orderly; their leadership was respected and freely followed. Crime was almost unknown and disease minimal. For hundreds of years, the many tribes of the Sioux Nation lived happily and securely on the Great Plains of North America. But that was before the coming of the white race.

Now the Sioux are reduced to several bleak reservations like the one at Pine Ridge. How they got there, how they became the people they are today, how the seizure of Wounded Knee in 1973 was related to the massacre at Wounded Knee in 1890, can only be discovered by examining the history of Sioux contact with whites. It is a long way back from South Dakota to that island in the Bahamas where the invasion from Europe first got underway. But no story about the Indian people of America, least of all the tribes of the Sioux, can be understood without going over some of that blistered and blood-soaked ground.

+   +   +

THE FIRST ENCOUNTERS

Practically everything that most of us learned about the early Indians is false. Over the years, distortions and lies were frozen into a mythology that was called history in white schools and accepted as fact in white culture. It began with Columbus, the "explorer" who presumably "discovered" the New World. Not much is known about the real man. Some historians believe he was a well-educated Italian captain who gave up the sea to marry into the lower reaches of the Spanish aristocracy. He failed as a merchant; then, in order to save himself from bankruptcy, petitioned his adopted king for a commission in the Spanish navy.

This Italian sea captain was no explorer. He was hired to bring back gold, not chart new lands and seas for the next edition of the Spanish atlas. Specifically, he was to take three ships and find for the Spanish a short cut to the riches of Asia—a sea route to the islands of the East Indies. Neither was Columbus the discoverer of America. When he landed, he had no idea where he was. He mistook the Bahaman isles for Asia, erroneously assuming that the people he met there were East Indians. But more importantly, the idea that America was *unknown* and *undiscovered* until the eyes of 15th-century white men were laid upon it is not only thoughtless but racist as well. It completely ignores the existence of primitive and advanced "Indian" civilizations already present on the continent (and presumably well *known* to the inhabitants).

When Columbus landed in 1492, there were about 600 different Indian societies in the New World, many with their own languages. They ranged from primitive tribes in southern California, who lived primarily on acorns, to fully developed nations older than Spain and every other nation then in existence in Europe. At least three of these nations, those of the Maya, Aztec, and Inca peoples of Central and South America, administered territory as large as any country in Europe. These three civilizations had continuous recorded histories older than Greece and Rome. The Mayan calendar used in 1492 was more accurate than the European one still in use today.

But there were advanced nations in all parts of the New World. The Iroquois inhabited what is now New England. They lived in wooden houses and carried out extensive farming. First five and then six nations in the area formed the politically sophisticated Iroquois Confederation that kept the peace and provided all the benefits of organized government. In the Deep South, the Cherokees and other societies built large settlements and temples and achieved far-reaching political alliances. Around the Great Lakes, Indians lived in houses and supported themselves by hunting, fishing, and farming. In the Southwest, some tribes constructed elaborate irrigation systems and farmed the desert. Others lived in large buildings with many floors and rooms. Complex societies based on fishing flourished along the Pacific Coast. And on the Great Plains there were nations, including the Sioux, which lived primarily by hunting. They evolved a complicated nomadic culture and lived in tipis, the large tent-like portable structures that most Americans still take to be the standard housing of Indians across the continent.

Among the many tribes, there were different languages, different cultural patterns, and different stages of development. Some lived in almost continuous states of minor warfare or deprivation, while others achieved a relatively permanent peace and stable economy. Some of the "savages" of the New World were able to breed wild plants into domestic crops. They understood seed selection and knew how to fertilize their land. It was the Indians who first introduced the white men to corn, white potatoes, pumpkins, tomatoes, beans, squash, peanuts, cashews, pecans, gourds, chili peppers, sweet potatoes, hominy, coffee, and a long list of other foods.

When Columbus waded ashore that October morning in 1492, it was on an island inhabited by the Taino Tribe of the Arawak people. They presented him with generous gifts and invited the men of his expedition into their homes. It was clear from the start that the Europeans were in the company of an unusual people. Later, Columbus said this of them in a letter to the King and Queen of Spain:

> So tractable, so peaceful, are these people, that I swear to your Majesties there is not in the world a better nation. They love their neighbors as themselves, and their discourse is ever sweet and gentle, and accompanied with a smile; and though it is true that they are naked, yet their manners are decorous and praiseworthy.

Despite his seemingly high regard for the Tainos, Columbus abruptly renamed their island San Salvador and declared its ownership transferred to the Spanish monarchy. Like a true European, he took the gentleness of these Indians to be a sign of weakness. Returning to Spain with ten kidnapped Tainos and a handful of their gold, Columbus announced the discovery of a sea route to the riches of Asia, a misconception he retained until his death fourteen years later.

Plans were made for the immediate exploitation of those riches. Columbus was dispatched back to the New World with 17 ships and 1,500 men, many of them gold-hungry members of the aristocracy. They came with armed cavalry and killer dogs. Upon landing, the order went out to loot the Taino and the other Arawak tribes of the Bahamas and Caribbean. Columbus, the navigator who found the wrong place, became the first European marauder and bandit to bloody the shores of the North American continent.

The island Arawak people were defenseless against soldiers on horses and attack dogs, neither of which they had ever seen before. In search of the precious metal, villages were burned and people killed. Women were brutally raped. Children were kidnapped and shipped back to Spain to be sold as slaves or exhibited like creatures in a zoo. Less than ten years after Columbus first set foot on America, thousands and thousands of Arawak people from those peaceful islands were dead. It was the first episode in the history of white American civilization, but it was only a taste of what was to come.

Jamestown, Virginia, 1607: the first English-speaking colony in America. The Indian woman named Pocahontas, who married one of the white "settlers," came from the Algonquin Confederacy, a group of tribes ranging over 200 miles of coastal land in what is now Virginia and North Carolina. But friendship between the Indians and the English was short-lived. Only two years after the first encounter, Powhatan, leader of the Algonquins, said this to the English:

> Why will you take by force what you may obtain by love? Why will you destroy us who supply you with food? What can you get by war?. . . I am not so simple as not to know it is better to eat good meat, sleep comfortably, live quietly with my women and children, laugh and be merry with the English, and being their friend, trade for their copper and hatchets, than to run away from them.

His argument fell on deaf ears. In a little more than a generation, 7,000 of the 8,000 members of his tribe were killed by English weapons.

Massachusetts Bay, 1620: the landing of the *Mayflower* and the founding of the first permanent English colony in America. By their own admission, the whites would have starved if the Indians had not given them food and shown them how to grow their crops. Seeing how few in number the English people were, the Indians reasonably concluded there was enough land and food for everybody. Their attitude has been memorialized ever since by that most American of holidays, Thanksgiving.

But the peace and tranquility did not last. Some 55 years after the first celebration, the Wampanoag Nation (among the hosts at the original event) and their neighbors, the Narragansetts, were virtually exterminated by the English. The Indian leader, Metacom, was decapitated and his head publicly displayed in the Christian town of Plymouth for the next 20 years. Ironically, Thanksgiving is celebrated today by eating turkey, sweet potatoes, cranberries, and pumpkin pie—foods first introduced to white Europeans by Indians, but foods most Indians cannot now afford to buy.

Manhattan Island, 1625: the founding of New Amsterdam, which would become the largest city in the world. Most people know the pathetic story of the Dutch colonists "purchasing" New York for 60 guilders worth of fish hooks and beads. The polite Indians revered the land and had no way of understanding how pieces of it could be bought and sold—or owned by individuals. In the beginning, however, they saw no reason not to share it with the whites and often humored them in their strange "purchase" ceremonies.

But by 1641, the aggressive Dutch had appointed a "governor" for the entire area. That year he sent troops to Staten Island to arrest members of the friendly Raritan Nation for crimes actually committed by Dutch settlers. The Raritans, at peace with the whites, had not recognized either the sovereignty of the Dutch legal system or the legitimacy of the Dutch "governor," so they simply refused to submit. The Dutch soldiers killed four of them. The Raritans had their own legal code and responded by killing four Dutchmen.

At that, the governor of the "civilized" side in this conflict ordered the extermination of two entire Raritan villages. This was done one night with bayonets while the victims slept. Babies were impaled and flung into the Hudson River. Bodies were chopped to pieces. When it was all over, a few survivors staggered into a nearby fort, and an eyewitness to the scene wrote, "Some came running to us from the country having their hands cut off; some lost both arms and legs; and some were supporting their entrails with their hands."

THE COLONIAL PERIOD

So it was at the beginning and so it was from then on, as the whites expanded out of these little pockets on the shore of the Atlantic Ocean. Each new area was settled at the cost of destroying the people who already lived there. Resistance was attempted, but intertribal rivalries frequently prevented Indian unity, as did the great distances that had to be traveled without horses or other beasts of burden. Nevertheless, as early as 1642, Miantunnomoh from Massachusetts traveled all the way to eastern Long Island to counsel with some of his old enemies:

> Brothers, we must be one as the English are, or we shall all be destroyed. You know our fathers had plenty of deer and skins and our plains were full of game and turkeys, and our coves and rivers were full of fish. But, brothers, since these Englishmen have seized our country, they have cut down the grass with scythes, and the trees with axes. Their cows and horses eat up the grass, and their hogs spoil our bed of clams; and finally we shall starve to death; therefore, stand not in your own light, I ask you, but resolve to act like men. . . . we are resolved to fall upon them.

It was a remarkable prediction of the ecological catastrophe eventually to strike the area around Long Island Sound. But Miantunnomoh was a Narragansett, and by the end of the century they were gone.

Further west, the Six Nations of the Iroquois lived by farming and hunting. They were confederated under a constitution before the white men set foot on North America. Their wooden houses could be found across an area that now includes New York, Pennsylvania, and parts of Maryland and Virginia. The Iroquois Confederacy was very likely the most advanced and organized civilization in North America at the time. Even Benjamin Franklin called attention to their high level of government in 1754, as he argued why the American colonies should join together to form a new nation:

> It would be a strange thing if Six Nations of ignorant savages should be capable of forming a scheme for such an union, and be able to execute it in such a manner as that it has subsisted ages and appears indissoluble; and yet, that like union should be impracticable for ten or a dozen English colonies, to whom it is more necessary and must be more advantageous, and who cannot be supposed to want an equal understanding of their interests.

To Franklin, the Indians were "savages," but to the Indians, Franklin and his people were no less bizarre. Indians did not understand why the Europeans stayed pent up in crowded towns and settlements. They were shocked that some whites in the towns were permitted to have more food than they could eat, while other whites in the same town had none. The Indians thought competition to be destructive. Individual profit was viewed as a crime against the tribe. Leadership based on wealth was so obvious a disaster, any child could see it. The gap was too wide. Whites and Indians each viewed the other as an inferior people. But while a distinct majority of the whites assumed that Indians were in fact a lower form of life, more like animals than humans, Indians merely looked upon the whites as childlike, ill-tempered, or plainly stupid. Ironically, the white attitude encouraged excessive violence, while the Indian attitude led to an excess of patience.

In the late 1750s and early 1760s, many battles were fought between whites and Indian tribes in western Pennsylvania and on both sides of the Ohio River. These tribes were not part of the Iroquois Confederation. Seeking revenge for an attack, the white people of Lancaster County murdered a large number of friendly Indians from a tribe that was in the Six Nation Confederation. In 1764, Benjamin Franklin wrote a pamphlet denouncing the slaughter. He told of an old Indian leader and friend cut to pieces in his bed and of young children shot and hatcheted in their parents' arms:

If an Indian injures me, does it follow that I may revenge that injury on all Indians? . . . It is well known that Indians are of different tribes, nations, and languages, as well as the white people. In Europe, if the French, who are white people, should injure the Dutch, are they (the Dutch) to revenge it on the English, because they, too, are white people? . . .

The Six Nations, as a body, have kept faith with the English ever since we knew them, now near a hundred years; and their governing body have notions of honor, whatever may be the case with the rum-debauched, trader-corrupted vagabonds and thieves on the Susquehanna and Ohio, at present in arms against us.

Franklin's point was well taken, but the Indians on "the Susquehanna and Ohio" had good reason to be "in arms against" the whites. Their land, the Ohio Valley, was claimed by both the English and the French kings. Between 1754 and 1763, the English, with the help of their American colonials, fought both the French and the native Indian population for control of the area. But the issues involved in the French and Indian War were far more complex than most history books admit.

In 1747, partly under the leadership of Lawrence Washington, the Ohio Company was organized to speculate in land west of the thirteen colonies. The King of England, who claimed control of this territory, granted them a half million acres in the Ohio Valley, which they planned to resell at a handsome profit. At the same time, Benjamin Franklin, one of the most zealous businessmen in the colonies, put together the Walpole Company, another group of land speculators with even more ambitious designs on the Ohio Valley. Franklin traveled to England in 1754 to begin negotiating with the King for the purchase of ten million acres.

When the French and Indian War broke out in 1754, the Ohio Company organized its own army to carry on the fight. They offered their troops a bonus in land out of their vast holdings in the Ohio Valley. Privates were promised 50 acres apiece, sergeants 200 acres, captains 3,000 acres, and the colonel in charge, Lawrence Washington's younger half-brother, George, 5,000 acres. Colonel Washington began laying aside capital of his own to buy up shares from his men. Many were poor and the land offered was far from their homes. George Washington planned on convincing them to sell cheap.

By 1763 the French and Indian War was over. The English were able to seize Canada from the French while their American allies prepared to move into the Ohio Valley. But the English King and his Ministers wanted to stabilize relations with the Indians who inhabited the Ohio Valley, especially Chief Pontiac and the Ottawa Nation who had earlier captured nine English forts and killed or captured 2,000 English soldiers. In a move that took the American businessmen completely by surprise, the King of England issued the Proclamation of 1763, granting the Indians owner-ship of the Ohio Valley and barring any land speculation or settlement by whites.

Washington's Ohio Company, Franklin's Walpole Company, and other similar corporations began a campaign of bribery and maneuvering in London and on the frontier. But to no avail—the Proclamation of 1763 remained in force. Eventually, these businessmen raised the cry of "tyranny" against the English King. They hid their desire for freedom to speculate beneath demands for more noble freedoms and became some of the leaders in the War for Independence a decade later. While demo-cratic idealism may have moved many of the participants, one of the hidden causes of the American Revolution was simple land hunger frustrated by the 1763 Proclamation.

Violence between Americans and Indians in the Ohio Valley continued during the 1770s. Many individual and corporate speculators, including Washington and Franklin, ignored English law, hired surveyors, and laid claim to land that belonged to Indians. The western reaches of the Six Nations of the Iroquois Confederation were affected, as well as the tribes farther west, "on the Susquehanna and Ohio." When Independence was declared in 1776, it was no surprise to find the Iroquois fighting with the English against the Americans. In 1779, George Washington ordered troops to march through upstate New York and destroy the Iroquois settlements there. The following is from an account of that march.

> The capital of the Senecas, a town consisting of sixty houses, surrounded by beautiful cornfields and orchards, was burned to the ground and the harvest destroyed. Canandaigua fell next, and then the army stretched away for the Genesee flats. The fourth day it reached a beautiful region, then almost wholly unknown to the white man. The valley, twenty miles long and four broad, had scarce a forest tree in it, and presented one of the most beautiful contrasts to the surrounding wilderness that could well be con-ceived. As the weary columns slowly emerged from the dark forest and filed into this open space . . . they seemed suddenly to be transported into an Eden.
>
> The tall, ripe grass bent before the wind—cornfield on cornfield as far as the eye could reach waved in the sun—orchards that had been growing for generations, were weighted down under a profu-sion of fruit—cattle grazed on the banks of a river, and all was luxuriance and beauty. . . . [All about] were scattered a hundred and twenty-eight houses—not miserable huts huddled together,

but large airy buildings, situated in the most pleasant spots, surrounded by fruit trees, and exhibiting a civilization on the part of the
Indians never before witnessed.

Soon after sunrise immense columns of smoke began to rise the
length and breadth of the valley, and in a short time the whole
settlement was wrapped in flame from limit to limit; and before
night those one hundred and twenty-eight houses were a heap of
ashes. The grain had been gathered into them, and thus both were
destroyed together. The orchards were cut down, the cornfields
uprooted, and the cattle butchered and left to rot on the plain. A
scene of desolation took the place of the scene of beauty, and the
army camped that night in a desert.

It was the kind of total warfare that went on against Indians for another
hundred years as the U.S. Army led the sweep across the continent to the
Pacific. Killing warriors wasn't enough for them. They killed non-
combatant men, women, and children. They burned villages and destroyed the farms, orchards, and animals that kept a civilization alive. And
after the Army had done its murderous work and been congratulated for
it by a grateful Congress (as was the case with the expedition described
above), the traders and missionaries followed in their wake.

The traders sold alcohol to Indians who had no previous experience
with intoxicants. They tried to spread white notions of commerce and the
use of money, credit, and debts. The Indians had their own ways of
distributing wealth. Unfamiliar with commercial practices, they were
cheated at every opportunity. Those lucky enough to survive the Army
became the victims of crooked deals that included everything from
overcharges on purchases to large-scale land swindles. White pockets
were filled with Indian wealth, and, more importantly, Indian people
were kept from amassing political power through economic gain.

Christian missionaries had been trying to convert the native American
population since the first days of Columbus. Some were well intentioned,
others were not. But it hardly mattered, since the net effect of their work
fit so well with the objectives of those outside the Church who sought to
divide and destroy the Indian nations. The missionaries perverted Indian
culture and religion and ate away at the fabric holding Indians together as
a separate and identifiable people.

But most Indians resisted religious conversion. Christianity preached
peace while making war and was just as absurd as the white man's
strange methods of distributing goods and selecting leaders. The Indians
had their own religions but not the same separation between religious
practices and everyday life. Indians did not understand why whites
needed a special house within which to worship, or why one day of the

week was always better for praying in the special house than the others. They were profoundly aware of the hypocrisy of Christianity, as the following speech indicates.

In 1805, a missionary came to the defeated Iroquois seeking permission to preach in their territory. Red Jacket, one of the chiefs, sent him away with a brilliant argument that typified Indian attitudes toward white religion everywhere in America.

Brother, listen to what we say!

There was a time when our forefathers owned this great continent. Their seats extending from the rising to the setting sun. The Great Spirit had made it for the use of Indians. . . .

But an evil day came upon us. Your forefathers crossed the great water and landed on this continent. Their numbers were small. They found friends and not enemies. They told us they had fled from their own country for fear of wicked men, and had come here to enjoy their religion. They asked for a small seat. We took pity on them; granted their request; and they sat down amongst us. We gave them corn and meat; they gave us poison [alcohol] in return. . . .

At length their numbers had greatly increased. They wanted more land; they wanted our country. Our eyes were opened and our minds became uneasy. Wars took place. Indians were hired to fight against Indians, and many of our people were destroyed. . . .

Brother, our seats were once large and yours were small. You have now become a great people, and we have scarcely any place left to spread our blankets. You have got our country, but are not satisfied. You want to force your religion upon us. . . .

We understand that your religion is written in a book. If it was intended for us, as well as you, why has not the Great Spirit given to us, and not only to us, but why did he not give to our forefathers the knowledge of that book, with the means of understanding it rightly? We only know what you tell us about it. How shall we know when to believe, being so often deceived by the white people?

Brother, you say there is but one way to worship and serve the Great Spirit. If there is but one religion, why do you white people differ so much about it? Why not all agreed, as you can all read the book? . . .

Brother, we are told that you have been preaching to the white people in this place. These people are our neighbors. We are acquainted with them. We will wait a little while and see what effect your preaching has upon them. If we find it does them good, makes them honest, and less disposed to cheat Indians, we will then consider again of what you have said.

for them in cornfields as they do them? Shall we wait for that moment or shall we die fighting before submitting to such ignominy?. . . . The annihilation of our race is at hand unless we unite in one common cause against the common foe. Think not, brave Choctaws and Chickasaws, that you can remain passive and indifferent to the common danger, and thus escape the common fate. Your people, too, will soon be as falling leaves and scattering clouds before their blighting breath. You too will be driven away from your native land and ancient domains as leaves are driven before the wintry storms.

But Tecumseh's eloquent speech was answered by another Indian orator, Pushmataha, the Choctaw, who argued for accommodation with the whites:

The war, which you are now contemplating against the Americans, is a flagrant breach of justice; yea, a fearful blemish on your honor and also that of your fathers, and which you will find if you will examine it carefully and judiciously, forbodes nothing but destruction to our entire race. It is a war against a people whose territories are now far greater than our own, and who are far better provided with all necessary implements of war, with men, guns, horses, wealth, far beyond that of all our race combined, and where is the necessity or wisdom to make war upon such a people? [Let us] not yet have recourse to war, but send ambassadors to our Great Father in Washington, and lay before him our grievances, without betraying too great eagerness for war, or manifesting any tokens of pusillanimity.

The Council of the Choctaw and Chickasaw accepted the advice of Pushmataha. Tecumseh traveled on to other southern tribes and after only moderate success in extending his confederacy, he returned to the Midwest and joined forces with the British in the War of 1812. The Indians and their English allies lost the war. The great Tecumseh died in battle, and his loose confederacy, built to dam the flood of white expansion into the Midwest, was broken.

As the settlers poured into the Illinois country after the War of 1812, one Sauk chief, Black Hawk, formed a new alliance of Winnebagos, Potawatomis, and Kickapoos. For the next 20 years, they fought a remarkable guerrilla war against the new settlements. A former ally of Tecumseh, Black Hawk described to his own family some of the strange fighting habits of the whites—the British and the Americans—at war with one another:

Instead of **stealing** upon each other, and taking every advantage to

> Brother, you have now heard our answer to your
> all we have to say at present.

The great Iroquois Nation did not survive. By the dawn
century, they and all the other tribes on the Atlantic coastal
either exterminated entirely, decimated and confined to piti
vations, or chased across the Appalachian Mountains into the
and South. The Sioux and other tribes of the Great Plains lived
the Mississippi River and received only scant reports of the carnage
of the Appalachians.

"WE ARE ALL GUNMEN"

American history is rich in mythology, especially with respect to the early American Presidents. Among them, the Virginians were particularly unsuited to exalted images, despite the humanitarian ideals they frequently put on paper. In real life, their fine principles were not meant for blacks whom they kept enslaved on their plantations, women whom they excluded from public and political life, and Indians. In 1806, Thomas Jefferson, the most "liberal" of the early Presidents, met with ambassadors from the Indian nations west of the Mississippi, including the Sioux. After describing the power of the United States and his desire that the Plains tribes not oppose that power, Jefferson said: "My children, we are strong, we are numerous as the stars in the heavens, and we are all gunmen."

At the time of the War of 1812, a great confederacy of midwestern and southern Indian tribes was created by Tecumseh of the Shawnees. Post-Revolutionary War land speculation had opened vast new territory for settlement. Tecumseh's alliance was formed to resist what had become a virtual flood of white migration west of the Appalachians. Tecumseh traveled widely to organize his confederacy, both through his own territory in the Midwest and into the South. There he engaged in a great debate before the combined councils of the Choctaw and Chickasaw tribes, arguing that war with the Americans was inevitable and unification of the tribes the only Indian alternative:

> Before the pale-faces came among us, we enjoyed the happiness of unbounded freedom, and were acquainted with neither riches, wants, nor oppression. How is it now? Wants and oppression are our lot; for are we not controlled in everything, and dare we move without asking, by your leave? Are we not being stripped day by day of the little that remains of our ancient liberty? Do they not even now kick and strike us as they do their black-faces? How long will it be before they will tie us to a post and whip us, and make us work

kill the enemy and save their own people, as we do (which, with us is considered good policy in a war chief), they march out, in open daylight, and fight, regardless of the number of warriors they may lose! After the battle is over, they retire to feast, and drink wine, as if nothing had happened; after which, they make a statement in writing, of what they have done—each party claiming the victory! and neither giving an account of half the number that have been killed on their own side.

The young Abraham Lincoln, no less progressive a man than Jefferson, joined the army to fight against the followers of Black Hawk. Apparently he thought that clearing Indians out of Illinois was a sufficiently important way to spend his time. Lincoln, the "Great Emancipator" of the blacks, re-enlisted for a second tour of duty against the Indians.

ANDY JACKSON AND THE DEPORTATION OF THE CHEROKEE

While Lincoln fought Indians in the Midwest, an older man, who would become President long before him, led the slaughter of thousands of Indians in the South. General Andrew Jackson attacked many nations, including the Choctaw and Chickasaw whom Tecumseh had tried to rally to resistance a decade earlier. These two tribes, along with the Cherokee, the Creeks, and the Seminoles, formed the five-nation Cherokee Confederacy, the most advanced and civilized tribes in the southern part of the United States.

The Cherokee Nation was unique among Indians in the extent to which they adapted their life style to that of the white society around them. They not only laid down their arms in the 1780s, they also gave up hunting and became farmers. In response to the wisdom they saw in the Declaration of Independence and the U.S. Constitution, the Cherokee people formed their own republic. They had a Chief Executive, a two-house legislature, a written constitution, a system of courts, and a police force. They built a capital city called New Echota. An illiterate named Sequoia invented an alphabet for the Cherokee language which the people accepted with enthusiasm. Within a short time, a majority of the Cherokee could read and write, and a high quality newspaper was being published on a Cherokee printing press.

In 1829, after a bloody career as an Indian fighter in the South, Jackson took over the White House. In 1830, gold was discovered in Georgia. It was the beginning of the end of the Cherokee. In the spring following the gold strike, the Congress of the United States, under Jackson's direction, passed the Indian Removal Act, ordering Indians of the Southeast to resettle on barren land west of the Mississippi. The bill was in direct violation of several treaties with the U.S. government. The Cherokee took their case to the Supreme Court. But claiming they had no jurisdiction in a suit involving "domestic dependent nations," the Court refused to hear the Cherokee case. The decision had a massive impact on Indians throughout America. By failing to force the U.S. government to abide by solemn treaty obligations, the Supreme Court rendered all Indian treaties meaningless, subject to violation by the government at any time.

After the decision, the Georgia legislature took advantage of the Indian Removal Act to order the Cherokee people evicted from land they had developed and lived on for decades. But the Cherokee still had faith in the U.S. Constitution. They returned to the Supreme Court with a new set of arguments and obtained a favorable decision. In the historic case of Cherokee Nation v. State of Georgia, Chief Justice John Marshall ruled that an individual state could not violate the treaty rights of Indians. The ruling was followed by an equally historic White House pronouncement in which President Andy Jackson, "the man of the people," said, "John Marshall has made his decision; now let him enforce it!" The President of the United States blatantly refused to carry out an order of the Supreme Court. The Cherokees, vindicated by due process of law, lost their land anyway. In 1835, the government ordered the Indians to remove themselves from Georgia lands by May 1838, or face forced eviction.

The Cherokee people stayed in their comfortable homes, not believing that an injustice of such magnitude would actually be carried out. But several months after the deadline passed, the U.S. Army came to move them. They were hauled out of their houses and forced to walk from Georgia to Oklahoma. Food supplies provided by the Army were inadequate. Winter started before they reached their destination, and there were not enough blankets to go around. It was a death march. Of the 16,000 Cherokee who started out from Georgia, 4,000 died on route. All the other formerly peaceful and friendly tribes of the Southeast were also forced to walk down the infamous Trail of Tears. Out of one party of 1,000 Choctaw, only 88 arrived in Oklahoma alive. News of the Trail of Tears spread across the Plains until every tribe had heard of it, including the Sioux.

"WE HAD SEEN NOTHING WHICH WE COULD NOT GET"

In 1834, the U.S. Congress, again under Jackson's direction, enacted legislation declaring all territory west of the Mississippi River, except land in Missouri, Louisiana, and Arkansas, to be "Indian country." Whites were barred from residing there, and trading with the Indians was prohibited without a license. Jackson had argued that the land would be guaranteed to the Indians by the federal government and that their relocation there was for their own protection and betterment. Like so many acts of aggression, this "final solution" to the Indian problem was made to look like humanitarian relief for its victims.

But even before the new law could be enforced, another wave of white migration poured into Wisconsin and Iowa. The "permanent Indian frontier" was hastily moved westward to the 95th meridian of longitude, which ran from Lake-of-the-Woods on the Minnesota-Canada border south to Galveston Bay in Texas. By 1840, virtually all the Indians east of this line had either been killed or forced to leave their ancestral homelands and marched to the unfamiliar Plains. Dozens and dozens of tribes that had inhabited the eastern half of the United States were completely exterminated. Others would disappear in the coming years or be reduced to remnants of their former size. The list is endless: the Chesapeakes, the Potomacs, the Montauks, the Hurons, the Miamis, the Eries, the Mohawks, the Senecas, the Mohegans, the Omahas, the Missouris, the Iowas, the Kansas, the Osages, and on and on and on. Many of these tribes had unique languages, cultural lives, and handicraft arts, all obliterated in an incalculable loss to humanity.

The toll of lost tribes numbers in the hundreds. Their ghostly names hang over America like linguistic tombstones of the dead. More than half of the fifty states of the union and the country's fifty longest rivers all have Indian names. The melodious words are one of the few concessions this country has made to the Indians ever having been here in the first place.

But white Americans today would be wrong to feel guilty about the extermination of Indian tribes, either because of their white skin or because their ancestors may have participated in the senseless slaughter of a century past. An understanding of Indian history that provokes only guilt does a disservice to Indians and to whites, since it focuses attention exclusively on events in the past which cannot be undone rather than on conditions in the present which are under our control. The truth is that there were criminal individuals on both sides of the warfare: but while the criminals were guilty, the entire races were not.

Agony and suffering were inevitable, not because the whites were more cruel or criminal than the Indians, or vice versa, but because one civilization could not exist side by side with the other. What occurred was a clash of two social organizations in contradiction to each other, two different conceptions of reality.

White western civilization defined progress in terms of advances it made in a self-proclaimed war against nature, advances in machinery and technology. It saw its destiny in conquest and wealth. Indian civilization, although it made extensive use of the circle or hoop in its imagery and its conceptions of social organization, cared so little about technology it never bothered to invent the wheel. Indians believed their destiny lay in ever greater harmony and integration with the natural world around them. Individual Indians and individual whites together were sucked into the vortex of this clash of social organizations. The whites brutally destroyed the Indians. But it must be remembered that white western civilization defined personal happiness and fulfillment in terms of material possessions and the exercise of power. Ordinary whites cannot be blamed if their vision of happiness was limited by what their civilization allowed them to see. The evil lay in the civilization and its values.

Reasons why white society could not tolerate the existence of Indian society were very complex. Possession of the land was the principal reason, inasmuch as it was the key to the twin goals of wealth and power. But, surprisingly, there was enough land for everybody. Estimates of the original Indian population of what is now the continental United States vary widely: the average figure is approximately one million. If that estimate is anywhere near correct, and only one million people inhabited an area that now supports over 200 million, it is obvious that land must have been available in overwhelming abundance. In fact, that was one reason why the Indians were so generous with it when the whites first arrived. Therefore, simple possession of the land was no reason to destroy the Indian civilizations living upon it.

The reasons lay at a deeper level. Seizing the real estate was less than satisfactory if the victims of the theft were free to wander about advertising the injustice, even if they were unable to prevent it. Thus, one reason for the destruction of Indian society was to legitimize the land claims. But there were other causes of the killing, some quite intangible.

The whites were incapable of integrating their society with the Indians and were also not willing to leave them uncontrolled. The Indians were justifiably outraged at the resulting injustices (reservations and other detention camps, forced marches, swindling, wanton treaty violation, etc.). Many Indian tribes made the "mistake" of not surrendering after they were defeated; that is, winning a battle against them did not always mean they would submit to white control or refrain from further attacks. White civilization took the easy, and profitable, way out—continued war.

For the most part, the civilization and attitudes of the Indians prevented them from accepting the strict regimentation and discipline of the settler communities and farms. Living freely in nature and drawing an easy sustenance from it, Indian civilization was capable of undermining the hard-working, self-sacrificing attitudes necessary to white civilization. In the same way, Indians were not only a psychological threat to the institution of black slavery, but they often helped runaway slaves and sometimes rendered assistance to slave revolts, thus giving whites in the South even more cause for alarm.

Later, as the Industrial Revolution got underway, white working class and newly emigrant people were forced to accept heavy taxes and fourteen-hour workdays. The vision of Indian people living within a different system of survival without that kind of work, and relatively free of material ambition, raised too many embarrassing questions about the current and coming society in America.

Sharitarish, a Pawnee chief, made this point perfectly clear during a visit to the White House in 1822. With a profound sense of loss, he told President Monroe that his people actually had fewer needs before their exposure to the whites, but nevertheless, were far richer: "There was a time when . . . we had seen nothing which we could not get."

Civilizations, whether white, Indian, or otherwise, create cultures that justify and rationalize their particular priorities. A culture fosters a variety of myths that reinforce the civilization's conception of reality. For example, it is shocking to discover that the original native population of the United States may have been as low as one million because it is important for Americans to accept the myth that Indians swarmed all over the continent.

Similarly, most whites are taught the myth that Indian people were war-like and cruel, when in fact this was true of only a minority. The remainder were peace-loving and generous. But for those individual whites who have difficulty accepting the unnatural slaughter of Indians, this myth helps ease the contradiction inherent in killing innocents. As a result of the myth of Indian savagery and its companion, the notion of a swarming native population, it "made sense" to murder the Indians.

The ultimate military defeat of the Indian societies was quite predictable. Hampered by great distances they rarely traveled and in some places by deep-seated tribal rivalries, the Indians never achieved the one goal that might have won them significant concessions from the whites—a wide-ranging united front of the various tribes capable of providing a base for prolonged guerrilla warfare. As it was, in a contest of military strength the Indians were no match for the whites. The entire thrust of white civilization was the harnessing of natural forces and the bending of those forces to its use. As a result, the musket and the cannon prevailed in the East, just as the repeating rifle and the Hotchkiss gun would in the West.

Furthermore, in a one-sided contest of strength, white civilization gave no quarter, having been instructed by its own history that mercy was everywhere inappropriate except within the four walls of the churches it so carefully separated from the real world of commercial and military affairs. It is not that individual whites were never merciful. They were. But their best instincts emerged in spite of their civilization, rarely with its cooperation. If any are to be judged guilty, it is only those few individuals who possess such massive power as to be able to redirect western civilization, but who consciously and deliberately opt for a continuation of its very profitable barbarism. It must be said, too, that some guilt rests with those who come to understand the faults of the civilization and contribute nothing, however small, toward changing it.

BIOLOGICAL CONQUEST

Wherever there was great wealth or natural resources to exploit, it made even more "sense" to kill Indians. In California, the plunder was especially brutal. The numerous mountains and deserts there formed natural barriers that helped prevent the formation of large Indian nations. Many tribes occupied only a single valley and numbered no more than a few hundred. These isolated, usually gentle people, totally un-accustomed to organized warfare, were slaughtered without reason as greedy white adventurers carved up the bounty of the state. Over fifty tribes were totally obliterated. White Californians hunted Indian men, women, and children for sport. A few even made blankets out of dozens of Indian scalps.

Many of the Indian survivors were forced into slavery, the men to work in the California mineral mines and the women to prostitute themselves in the mining camps. Thousands died from venereal disease, smallpox, measles, chicken pox, typhoid, diphtheria, cholera, and other diseases unknown before the coming of the whites. The few who lived could make no sense of what had happened to their people. Demoralized, many succumbed to alcoholism and lost the desire to live. When the Spaniards first arrived in California in the 16th century, it is estimated that 300,000 Indians lived there. At the time of the 1849 gold rush, the population was probably down to some 100,000. By 1870, it was reduced to 30,000, and by 1910, 16,000, less than 6 percent of the original number. The California genocide was very likely the worst that occurred in North America.

Prior to the invasion from Europe, the Indians of the New World lived in a state of remarkable physical health. Infectious diseases were almost unknown among them. They were noticeably taller and probably a good deal stronger than the first whites. Recent archeological evidence indicates extraordinarily low rates of cancer, high blood pressure, ulcers, and tooth decay. But when the whites came, the Indians found themselves exposed to European bacteria, against which they had never developed any natural immunities (antibodies). Epidemics, which often spared the white Europeans, raged through the tribes. Indian medicine men had no time to find herbal remedies capable of at least controlling their spread.

Despite extensive armed conflict, some experts believe that more

Indians died from smallpox alone than from all the white bullets and bayonets used against them. At the time of the Pilgrims, smallpox was the major factor in reducing the Indian population of New England. Smallpox epidemics killed Indians throughout the thirteen colonies before the Revolution. Typically, the disease broke out shortly after the first whites penetrated a new area. These epidemics were only rarely planned or intentional, despite how well they fit in with white expansion. The one well-documented exception occurred during a campaign between a troop of Royal Americans (fighting under a British flag prior to the Revolutionary War) and a force of Ottawa Indians. The white commander, Lord Jeffrey Amherst, besides giving his name to a college in Massachusetts, ordered blankets from a smallpox hospital to be given to his Indian enemies.

Epidemics on the Great Plains were as bad as any of the others. In 1837, the Mandan tribe living along the banks of the Missouri River caught smallpox from white traders. The sudden agonizing death of so many of their loved ones produced in the survivors a mass suicidal delirium. Bewildered and distraught, people hanged themselves and forced arrows down their throats. Of 1,500 Mandans in 1837, only 31 survived the epidemic.

But the smallpox spread from the Mandans to the other tribes of the Plains. Like the worst plagues of the European Middle Ages, vast and unimaginable suffering was commonplace. Half of the Cheyenne people died. Some 7,000 Crees were believed lost. A few infected Sioux were taken prisoner by the Pawnees, who were partially immunized from a previous epidemic, but their children were unprotected and a quarter of the tribe died. A white trader, missing his regular Blackfeet customers, went out to look for them on the Plains. He discovered a gruesome abandoned village putrid with the stench of death. Hundreds of decomposed bodies were lying about, and in the midst of them, two smallpox-infected old women groveled about, raving and insane.

After the epidemic of 1837 subsided, white fur trappers moved in to take over Blackfeet land. But more epidemics followed and smallpox was not the only disease to kill with such ferocity. In 1849, cholera destroyed half the Comanches and half the Kiowas. In 1870, smallpox returned to strike the Blackfeet and other Plains tribes once again. At the turn of the century, as the whites penned the Indians up in reservations and forced them to live in overheated and poorly ventilated cabins, a new wave of respiratory diseases like tuberculosis and pneumonia took its toll. Inadequate food supplies on the reservations resulted in chronic malnutrition which lowered Indian resistance to other disorders. The Indian population of the U.S. eventually dipped to less than 100,000. If one million is the correct estimate of the original native population, the loss in human life is a ghastly 90 percent. If, as some insist, the correct estimate is closer to ten million, the loss is 99 percent. Either figure is unprecedented in the modern world.

It was with obvious good reason that Indians were referred to as "the vanishing Americans." In 1900, their birth rate was less than their death rate. Some Bureau of Indian Affairs officials actually argued at the time that if the government neglected the Indians for just a few more decades, they would no longer be a problem. The population, however, underwent a recovery during the first half of the 20th century, hovering consistently around 250,000. It was not until 1955, when the Department of Health, Education and Welfare took over Indian health care from the BIA, that the Indian population began a massive and significant upward trend. By 1970, the number of native Americans in the United States was finally back to one million.

When the white Europeans came to North America, they brought death not only to the native people, but to all forms of life on the earth. They laid waste the forests, killed the wild animals, exhausted the soil, and poisoned the very water and air. One of the clearest examples of ecological catastrophe occurred in the Bahaman Islands. Today they are sand deserts unsuited for anything except an occasional coconut palm. But when Columbus first saw them, they were covered with tropical forests and vegetable gardens. First, the Europeans destroyed the native Arawak people. Then they chopped down the rich forests and built cotton plantations with African slave labor. Eventually, the plants exhausted the soil, wiping out the cotton economy. The plantation owners then took their wealth and moved on, abandoning the land to wind erosion. Without a forest for protection, the plantation lands were soon buried by sand. Most of what lived on the islands before the Europeans came was dead—the humans, the trees, the animals, the birds, the life in the soil and water. Instead of the paradise of the Arawaks, a barren wasteland was left to the descendants of the former African slaves. Today many make a living by servicing the descendants of the white Europeans who go there to vacation.

Most of the Indians of North America believed that the earth was their spiritual mother and that all things that lived upon the earth were the product of a loving union between her and some mythical male figure, like the Great Spirit or a Sun God. As a result, Indians believed themselves to be the relatives of all forms of life, each of which they held in high esteem. Most Indians believed they lived in a world of abundance, rich in food and all the necessities of life. But they respected the natural order, equally avoiding waste and excessive use. They knew a secret the whites would never learn—that America was a paradise on earth. It made it all the harder for them to understand the Europeans as they rolled across the continent, killing, spreading disease, creating filth and pollution, destroying forests and precious game, hoarding food and wealth as though they were more important than life itself.

THE FINAL CONQUEST

By 1865, the only free Indians left in the United States were on the Great Plains. All the tribes west of the Rocky Mountains and all the tribes east of the Mississippi and Missouri Rivers were either erased from the face of the earth or under the control of whites. The pattern was the same as in the previous century. After supposedly "military" campaigns against their villages and the destruction of their homes and sources of food (acts that today are known as "war crimes"), they were forced onto small parcels of land which could rarely support them. Dependent upon the government for food and tools, they became the prey of federal bureaucrats and irresponsible businessmen. Their religious practices were systematically crushed, fragmenting them from each other and separating them from a history of their tribes which might have helped make some sense of their lives.

In the end, all the native civilizations of North and South America perished. The white men, by their own hand, destroyed people who might have become their valuable allies, people who could have taught the new emigrants respect for the ecology of the land and its many creatures and plants. Such wisdom was lost to the whites. Not until a later century would its immense importance be understood. But at that time white civilization could not believe that it had anything to learn from people of color.

During the second half of the 1800s, the free Indian nations on the Great Plains were attacked as the other tribes had been earlier. They fought stubbornly and their resistance was, for a time, effective. But in the end, they were doomed. The technology of the Industrial Revolution had vastly increased the speed of white westward expansion—and the deadliness of white weapons. Hemmed in on all sides, or spread out over vast distances on the prairies, the various Plains tribes were divided and destroyed one by one.

The Indian Wars on the Great Plains officially ended in 1890, when an unarmed band of 350 Sioux people were cut down in their camp on the Wounded Knee Creek in South Dakota. But Wounded Knee was no isolated tragedy. It was unique only in that it was the most recent (one hesitates to say "the last") of the brutal western massacres. Before the Sioux fell at Wounded Knee, they had ample opportunity to see and understand the essential nature of the invading whites. Typical of the tragedies they witnessed as the whites moved closer to their territories

were those that befell their neighbors to the south, the Southern
Cheyenne who lived on the grasslands of Colorado and Kansas. Like the
Sioux, the Cheyenne hunted the buffalo, obtaining from it food, clothing,
blankets, medicine, bone tools, ornaments, skins for their tipis, grease,
oil, and many other materials.

THE CHEYENNE AT SAND CREEK AND WASHITA

In 1851, in the company of other nations on the Great Plains, including
the Sioux, the Southern Cheyenne signed a treaty with the Americans at
Fort Laramie. The land was vast and the whites were few, so the Plains
tribes freely granted the Americans the right to build roads and military
posts across their territory. They did not relinquish their own right to live
and hunt upon the land.

But, in 1858, white men discovered gold, the yellow crazy-making
metal, at Pike's Peak. Thousands of fortune hunters poured into Colorado. They had little regard for the Indians and numerous fights took
place. Within a year, the whites were building Denver City and other
settlements on Indian land. Then, in 1861, Congress committed the
outrageous act of creating the Colorado Territory on land that had been
assigned to the Southern Cheyenne and the Arapaho at Laramie in
1851. No representatives of these two nations, with whom the U.S. was
presumably at peace, were even consulted.

The Cheyenne met to talk of war. Of the 44 chiefs, Black Kettle was
among the few committed to maintaining peace with the whites. This
patient and thoughtful man argued with the other chiefs that war with the
Bluecoats could only lead to disaster. No decision was made. Black Kettle
took those Cheyenne who would follow him to the desolate southeastern
corner of Colorado, land assigned them by the white government. In
1863, he journeyed to Washington to meet with Lincoln in a vain attempt
to insure peace on the Plains.

By the following year, armed clashes with the increasingly numerous
Bluecoats were commonplace. Black Kettle sought the protection of the
U.S. Army at Fort Lyon, Colorado. The commanding officer guaranteed
the safety of the Cheyenne camp at nearby Sand Creek and gave the
young men there permission to go hunt buffalo far to the east. Then, he
sent for the Colorado militia, a force of civilian stalwarts. Some days later,
600 Colorado militiamen arrived at Fort Lyon under the command of
Colonel (also Reverend) John Chivington. With 100 federal troops and
four mountain howitzers, Chivington and his men set out to attack the
peaceful Cheyenne camped with Black Kettle at Sand Creek. Because of
the buffalo hunt, there were only 35 young men and perhaps another 65
older men in the camp. The remaining 500 people were women and
children. At dawn on November 29, 1864, the white horsemen rode in.

Only their drunkenness during the previous night's ride and their complete lack of discipline prevented the death toll from being any higher. When the awful butchering was over, 105 women and children and 28 men were dead.

Robert Bent, a half-white, half-Cheyenne rancher who was forced to guide the Colorado citizen-soldiers to Sand Creek, later testified against them at a Congressional inquiry into the massacre. Bent stated under oath:

> There seemed to be indiscriminate slaughter of men, women, and children. There were some thirty or forty squaws collected in a hole for protection; they sent out a little girl about six years old with a white flag on a stick; she had not proceeded but a few steps when she was shot and killed. All the squaws in the hole were afterwards killed. . . . Everyone I saw dead was scalped. I saw one squaw cut open with an unborn child . . . lying by her side. . . . I saw the body of White Antelope with the privates cut off, and I heard a soldier say he was going to make a tobacco pouch out of them.

To their enduring credit, three Army officers disobeyed direct orders and refused to take part in the well-organized massacre. One, Lt. James Conner, corroborated Bent's testimony. He told investigating Congressmen that he had "heard of numerous instances in which men had cut out the private parts of females and stretched them over the saddle bows and wore them over their hats while riding in the ranks."

Black Kettle was among those who escaped from Sand Creek, but the insane attack left him with little influence. As was often the case, the actions of the whites discredited the leaders among the Indians most prepared to work for peace. The Cheyenne turned to their war chiefs who counseled moving north to join the much stronger Sioux. Black Kettle, still determined to live peacefully, led a small group of women and children, old men and wounded warriors further south into Kansas, away from the predatory Americans.

A year later, in 1865, the whites came looking for him, this time with pen and ink. Because of the Laramie Treaty of 1851, the Cheyenne formally owned the land under the thriving city of Denver, as well as all the land claims of all the settlers and miners in Colorado. With no safe place to go and no ready source of food, Black Kettle was forced to sign a new treaty. It nullified all Cheyenne claims to the Territory of Colorado in exchange for some government issue supplies, a new and even more desolate parcel of land, and the promise of everlasting peace. His trials, though, were far from over.

In the autumn of 1868, Black Kettle moved his people even further south to avoid new outbreaks of fighting in Kansas. He went all the way to

Oklahoma and set up a small village next to the Washita River. But soon even Oklahoma began to fill up with Bluecoats. Black Kettle asked the commander at Fort Cobb to protect his band, but the officer was already aware that General Phillip Sheridan had other plans for the peaceful Cheyenne. (It was this same Sheridan who said during a ceremony in which a band of Comanches surrendered to him, "The only good Indians I ever saw were dead." The remark evolved into the peculiarly American proverb—The only good Indian is a dead Indian.) Sheridan ordered one of his crack battalions, the 7th U.S. Cavalry, to attack the Washita village at dawn on November 27, 1868.

When they galloped in, Black Kettle rushed out of his lodge struggling to see through the morning fog. The soldiers of the United States Army charged the camp from four directions. It must have seemed impossible to Black Kettle, nearly four years to the day after Sand Creek, that he was in the midst of the carnage once again. But this time, there was no escape. In a matter of minutes the cavalrymen killed 103 Cheyenne, eleven of whom were warriors.

Later that day the Bluecoats left Washita carrying the scalp of the gentle Black Kettle. Back in their base camp they showed the gruesome "souvenir" to Gen. Sheridan. He congratulated the 7th Cavalry's commanding officer, George Armstrong Custer, for "efficient and gallant services rendered." Custer would be repaid in kind eight years later by the Sioux at the Little Bighorn, but fourteen years after that, the 7th Cavalry would have the last word at Wounded Knee.

By consistently degrading the humanity of Indian people, officers like Sheridan, Custer, and Chivington made it easier for the men under them to carry out extraordinary acts of barbarism. The degradation of the Indians was as systematic and wilful as the slaughter. Occasionally, men of principle like the three Army officers at Sand Creek, refused to take part. But the racist dehumanization of the Indians was sanctioned by the authorities and perpetuated by civilian leaders and officers of high rank and public stature.

For example, when Chief Black Hawk died in prison in 1838, the governor of Iowa Territory took the trouble to obtain his skeleton and display it in his office. When General George Crook, in charge of all of Arizona, was unable to apprehend an Apache named Delshay, he offered to pay a reward for the Indian leader's head. Two cutthroats eventually appeared, each with a severed head identified as Delshay's. Gen. Crook stated, "Being satisfied that both parties were *earnest* in their beliefs, and *the bringing in of an extra head was not amiss*, I paid both parties." (emphasis added) The heads went on display at the general's parade grounds. When Kintpuash, the leader of the nearly exterminated Modoc people of northern California, was hanged, officials allowed his body to be stolen and secretly embalmed. Soon afterwards it was on display for a dime in carnivals back east.

It is no mistake to reflect on this nameless madness. It is part of who we are as a nation. Perhaps today clues can be found in this history to help us understand the racism and casual brutality that are so much a part of America. But there is another reason to remember the savagery, a very compelling reason. The grandchildren and the great-grandchildren of its victims are alive today. They do not forget the past. And when they come together to make a desperate statement to this nation, as the Oglala Sioux Tribe did at Wounded Knee in 1973, how shall we understand them if we allow ourselves to forget?

THE SIOUX IN VICTORY

The story of the Sioux people is the last chapter in the history of the free Indian nations. After winning more military victories against the whites than any other tribe, in the end, at Wounded Knee in 1890, they suffered the same cruel defeat.

Before 1850, the people of the Sioux Nation inhabited land in the present states of Minnesota, Iowa, North and South Dakota, Nebraska, Colorado, Wyoming, and Montana. The nation was divided into three principal branches, the Santee, the Yankton, and the Teton, or, in their own language, the Dakotas, the Nakotas, and the Lakotas. Each branch consisted of several independent tribes. The Teton Sioux were the westernmost. They were horse Indians who lived on the Plains by hunting buffalo and other game. By the end of the Civil War in 1864, the Tetons were the only Sioux still living freely on their own land. The tribes of the Teton, or Lakotas, were the Oglala, the Brulé, the Hunkpapa, the Minneconjou, the San Arcs, the Two Kettles, and the Blackfeet Sioux. The tribes, in turn, were composed of several smaller bands.

The Teton Sioux (Lakotas), along with the Cheyenne, Arapaho, and other Plains tribes, signed the treaty at Fort Laramie in 1851 permitting the Americans to build roads through part of their territory. The Sioux had purposely excluded from this agreement that part of eastern Wyoming that lay between the Black Hills and the Bighorn Mountains, the valley of the Powder River. The roads of the white men gave rise to Army forts, and the roads and forts encouraged traders and eventually led to full-scale white settlements. By 1865, the valley of the Powder was the only hunting ground left to the Sioux that was still rich with game and free of white men. Then, without prior consultation, the U.S. Army sent three columns of soldiers to establish a fort on the Powder. At the same time, a group of white civilians entered the valley to build a road across it to the Montana gold fields.

Outraged at the invasion of their last hunting ground, the Sioux went looking for the advancing troops. Before they made contact, an Army detachment destroyed a peaceful Arapaho village in an early morning surprise attack. The Cheyenne massacre at Sand Creek had taken place less than a year before. The time for talk was past. Sioux tribes rose up to fight the Bluecoats. They selected two principal war chiefs. One was Red Cloud of the Oglalas, the largest Lakota tribe. He was a great chief, famous across the Plains for his skill as a leader. The other was a much younger and lesser known man, Sitting Bull of the Hunkpapas.

Under the military leadership of these two men, the whites were successfully cleared from the valley of the Powder River. The following spring, in 1866, the defeated Americans invited the Sioux chiefs to come into Laramie for treaty talks. Spotted Tail of the Brulé was the first to arrive. He told the treaty commission:

> It has been our wish to live here in our country peaceably, and do such things as may be for the welfare and good of our people, but the Great Father has filled it with soldiers who think only of our death. . . . It seems to me there is a better way than this. When people come to trouble, it is better for both parties to come together without arms and talk it over and find some peaceful way to settle it.

Shortly afterward, Spotted Tail was joined by Red Cloud and some of the Oglalas. But eight days after the formal treaty proceedings began, the Sioux learned that while they sat talking to the American commissioners, a U.S. Army infantry regiment was simultaneously moving back into the Powder River country to build forts. The outraged chiefs immediately left Laramie and began raiding. Within two months, Red Cloud had raised an army of 3,000 warriors. His Oglalas were joined by Sitting Bull and the Hunkpapas, and by the Minneconjous. Spotted Tail, disappointed but still reluctant to inflict war upon the Brulé, led those who would follow away to the south to hunt the diminishing buffalo. The rest joined Red Cloud.

The Army completed three forts on the Powder before Red Cloud's forces arrived and prevented further construction. But because of new Army cannons and repeating rifles, the forts could not be taken. The Sioux held them under siege and were able to successfully control the surrounding countryside. White overland travel was disrupted for the next year and a half. Finally, General William Sherman of the War Department journeyed from Washington, D.C. to Laramie to make peace with the Sioux.

Spotted Tail agreed to meet Sherman, but Red Cloud would not. Despite his love of peace, Spotted Tail had no intention of compromising the last Sioux hunting ground. His message was simple—if there were no road along the Powder River and the three forts there were dismantled, then peace could be restored. Sherman stalled. He advised Spotted Tail and other Sioux with him to accept government land and a reservation on the Missouri River some hundreds of miles away. The proud and still free Sioux could hardly believe their ears. The talks broke up and the war continued.

Two months later, Sherman asked for another meeting. Red Cloud again refused to come, claiming that until the three forts were dismantled, there was nothing more to discuss:

> If the Great Father kept white men out of my country, peace would last forever, but if they disturb me, there will be no peace. . . . The Great Spirit raised me in this land, and has raised you in another land. What I have said, I mean. I mean to keep this land.

Sherman returned to Washington, but in 1868 he made a second journey west, this time with direct orders to accede to Sioux demands and abandon the Powder River country. After more than two years of war, the United Sates Army accepted defeat. Red Cloud rode triumphantly into Fort Laramie. There he and the other chiefs signed the Treaty of 1868.

This treaty, which would be disputed for years to come, granted the Sioux ownership of a vast area of land including the entire western half of South Dakota. Negotiated in victory, it guaranteed that no white men would be permitted into the Powder River country or the Black Hills of South Dakota without prior permission from the Sioux. Great hopes were placed in it by the Sioux people. But for the next 20 years, the Laramie Treaty of 1868 would be continually and recklessly ignored by the government of the United States. One hundred and five years later, at Wounded Knee in 1973, the Sioux continued to embrace it. This treaty, fought so hard for by their ancestors, was still seen as the key to their survival as a separate people.

For two years after the signing of the 1868 Treaty, there was relative calm on the Plains. But then the government unilaterally insisted that despite the land the Sioux formally owned, they must instead live on a bleak reservation on the Missouri River. In 1870, Red Cloud and Spotted Tail traveled to Washington to ask President U. S. Grant not to resort to forced eviction. When they arrived, they found that the eviction order had already been drawn up. Red Cloud negotiated forcefully in several tense meetings with Grant and other officials. The old Sioux chief won his second victory against the U.S. government, this time at the bargaining table. Grant agreed to let the Sioux pick a reservation somewhere in western Nebraska, in the rich Platte River Valley.

Before returning home, Red Cloud stopped in New York. He spoke to a large public gathering there in Cooper Union and proceeded to win their enthusiastic support:

> When you first came we were very many and you were few. Now you are many and we are few. You do not know who appears before you to speak. He is a representative of the original American race, and first people of this continent. We are good, and not bad. The reports which you get about us are all on one side. You hear of us only as murderers and thieves. We are not so. . . .
>
> You have children. We, too, have children, and we wish to bring them up well. . . .
>
> All I want is right and justice. I have tried to get from the Great Father what is right and just. I have not altogether succeeded. I want you to help me to get what is right and just. I represent the whole Sioux Nation, and they will be bound by what I say. . . .
>
> I am poor and naked, but I am the Chief of the Nation . We do not want riches, but we want to train our children right. Riches would do us no good. We could not take them with us to the other world. We do not want riches, we want peace and love.

CRAZY HORSE AND SITTING BULL

Red Cloud returned to the Great Plains and worked among the Lakota tribes to promote peace. He involved many influential chiefs in the decision about the exact location of the reservation, including Big Foot of the Minneconjou who had always shunned the white man. But most of the Hunkpapas, including Sitting Bull, refused to have anything to do with reservations. Even some of Red Cloud's own Oglala Tribe avoided the reservation. They followed a young medicine man named Crazy Horse and lived free of Red Cloud's band. Nevertheless, the reservation was duly established. For several years, under the leadership of Red Cloud and Spotted Tail, an uneasy peace prevailed on the Plains.

The next crisis came in 1874. Gold was discovered in the Sacred Mountains of the Sioux, known to the white men as the Black Hills. In violation of the Treaty of 1868, the U.S. Army ordered a reconnaissance of the area. The unit selected for the job was the 7th Cavalry, Gen. Custer in command. Over 1,000 soldiers brazenly rode into the Sacred Mountains. When the "reconnaissance" was over, newspapers announced that the Black Hills were solid gold—"from the grass roots down." This stupid remark insured an invasion of gold-crazy white men. The fortune hunters appeared in droves, illegally entering Sioux lands and walking off with wealth that belonged to the Indians.

The Sioux were enraged at the violation of their Sacred Mountains and talked incessantly of war. Red Cloud advised patience. He dispatched a strong protest to Washington and in response was notified that a commission would be sent to negotiate the "relinquishment" of the Black Hills. The land grab was on once again. But Red Cloud had underestimated the depth of his people's fury. More Oglalas left for the camp of Crazy Horse to prepare for war with the whites. The unusual young medicine man-warrior had never lived on a reservation. "One does not sell the earth upon which the people walk," he said.

Commissioners from Washington arrived in the fall of 1875. Red Cloud and Spotted Tail negotiated stubbornly, but to no avail. The commission's final offer was $400,000 a year for the mineral rights in the Black Hills or $6 million to buy them outright (rather cheap considering that only one of the gold mines there would eventually yield over $500 million). The offer was flatly refused by the Sioux. Long Mandan, one of the chiefs, summed up their position:

> My friends, when I went to Washington I went into your money-house [the U.S. Mint] and I had some young men with me, but none of them took any money out of that house while I was with them. At the same time, when your Great Father's people come into my country, they go into my money-house [the Black Hills] and take money out.

The Secretary of War in Washington announced that the United States would have to "insist" upon possession of the Black Hills. In the early part of 1876, again without consulting the Sioux, the U.S. Army moved a large force into the Powder River country where ten years before Red Cloud had begun his fight to protect the last Sioux hunting ground. The Army was looking for the camps of Crazy Horse and Sitting Bull.

Crazy Horse was only a youth at the time of Red Cloud's successful fight for the Powder River land, but he decided early that war would be the only way to preserve the Oglala way of life. He was a man who drew his energy from contradictions. Despite his bravery as a war leader and his sympathy as a chief, he purposely led a very solitary life. A frequent seeker after the wisdom of visions and mystical experiences, Crazy Horse also made a careful study of the U.S. Army's military tactics. The Oglalas knew him as their most able war chief, and when the country filled up with Bluecoats once again, they flocked to his leadership.

The first confrontation occurred in June 1876. Crazy Horse had fundamentally altered the strategy and tactics of the Sioux warriors, introducing flanking attacks, decoying actions, and a generally more mobile and flexible offense. The first large-scale battlefield test of the new tactics was a rout. The Sioux sent a column of U.S. Army soldiers fleeing back to the protection of a nearby fort.

Crazy Horse joined forces with Sitting Bull. They moved their camps to the banks of the Little Bighorn River to establish a village, confident that the Bluecoats had been taught a lesson and would leave them alone. But only a week later another column of soldiers found their village. The reckless horsemen were their hated enemies, Custer and the 7th Cavalry, but this time they were no match for the Sioux. The famous "last stand" on the Little Bighorn was the worst defeat inflicted upon the Army in all its years of Indian fighting. Custer and over 180 of his men were killed.

When news of the defeat reached Washington, the government went berserk. Unable to apprehend Crazy Horse and Sitting Bull, they attacked the Sioux who had stayed on the reservation away from the fighting. These people were subjected to martial law and declared prisoners of war. Ignoring the Laramie Treaty of 1868, Congress passed a law requiring the people of the Sioux Nation to simply sign over both the Powder River country and the Black Hills. Most refused, but a new treaty commission explained what would happen to them if the tribe did not sign—their rations on the reservation would be cut immediately (the buffalo by this time had disappeared), their guns and horses would be taken by the Army, and all of them would be deported to Oklahoma.

There was no choice. Red Cloud, Spotted Tail, a few other chiefs, and a minority of the tribe were forced to sign. Despite a clause in Article 12 of the Treaty of 1868 which stated that no land guaranteed to the Sioux in the Treaty could be taken away unless an agreement was "executed and signed by at least three-fourths of all the adult male Indians," the government accepted the new "treaty" as a legally binding document.

But there was still Crazy Horse and Sitting Bull. For an entire year, the U.S. Army sent Bluecoats to hunt them. The large Sioux force divided into separate bands. Under constant harassment, they remained on the move and had little time to hunt and supply themselves. Without adequate preparation, the Dakota winter was harsh and difficult. Finally, Sitting Bull and the Hunkpapas had enough and crossed the border into Canada. Crazy Horse and the Oglalas kept fighting.

In April 1877, after a long winter, Red Cloud was asked to find Crazy Horse and offer him and his followers a reservation in the precious Powder River country in exchange for their surrender. The 900 Oglalas in his band were out of food and ammunition. They accepted. Crazy Horse, never defeated in battle, moved into a U.S. Army fort. Four months later there was still no sign of the promised reservation. Crazy Horse left the fort to take his people to the Powder and claim the land that was theirs.

Eight companies of soldiers were sent to arrest him. Late one night, they returned him to the fort where he was given to an Army captain to be jailed until morning. The officer was accompanied by an Indian policeman, a turncoat named Little Big Man who had been one of Crazy

Horse's trusted lieutenants only a year before. The Army captain and Little Big Man led Crazy Horse to a cell containing several chained prisoners. At the sight of it, Crazy Horse instinctively drew back. The two escorts grabbed his arms while an Army private plunged a bayonet into his stomach. Crazy Horse died that night. He was thirty-five years old.

The body was placed on a scaffold and Crazy Horse was mourned by the Oglalas for many weeks. Afterwards, his mother and father kept the remains, his heart and bones. Months later, the Sioux were finally forced to leave the Platte River in Nebraska and accept the barren reservation on the Missouri River in South Dakota. The Army drove them like cattle. A small group, including Crazy Horse's parents, escaped. They walked to Canada to join Sitting Bull. Somewhere along the way, at an undisclosed place near the creek called Wounded Knee, they buried the heart and bones of Crazy Horse.

As a result of the war for the Black Hills, the Teton Sioux lost more land in 1877, not just the reservation lands in Nebraska, but all of the sacred Black Hills and the extreme western part of South Dakota as well. In addition, the government constructed six Indian agencies for the Sioux on what was left of their reservation. At these they would have to trade and around them build the first permanent settlements in their history. The agency for the Oglala Tribe was put in the southwest corner of the reservation, at Pine Ridge. The different Oglala bands, nomads and tipi dwellers all, began to construct their permanent camps along the various creek beds in the area—the Medicine Root, Porcupine, White Clay, and Wounded Knee. Spotted Tail and the Brulé Tribes were settled just east of Pine Ridge, at an agency called the Rosebud.

Meanwhile, Canadian authorities, with some encouragement from Washington, denied Sitting Bull a reservation on their land. Tired, impoverished, with no place to go and no way for his people to support themselves, Sitting Bull finally agreed in 1881 to return to the U.S. and live peacefully on a reservation. That same year an unusual event occurred at Rosebud. Spotted Tail, the old chief of the Brulé Sioux, was shot and killed by one of his own people, a man named Crow Dog. It was never clear whether Crow Dog undertook the killing on his own or was hired to do it by someone else. The Brulé people ordered that the assassin, Crow Dog, and his descendants for all time be barred from ever carrying a gun. Given the time and place, it was no small punishment.

In 1882, the government tried yet another land grab. They wanted to buy part of the Sioux Reservation, which was still a rather large piece of land, and divide the rest into six smaller reservations, one for each of the six agencies they had earlier established. The plan called for one half the Sioux lands to be sold for white settlement. Sitting Bull and Red Cloud organized enough peaceful public opposition to defeat the government's proposal, but the land-grabbing scenario had shown its face once again.

Six years later, the inevitable commission arrived from Washington pushing the same plan. They offered the Sioux fifty cents an acre for the nine million acres they wanted to "buy." The chiefs and elders vigorously objected. The old people knew best that the only way to preserve their way of life was to hold on to their lands. As a result, they were always the most militant opponents of the whites. It would still be the same a hundred years later. The commission returned to Washington empty-handed, and, in the face of a new flood of white migration overflowing out of Minnesota and the eastern half of South Dakota, they recommended that the government again ignore the Treaty of 1868 and simply appropriate the land.

But Washington decided on a different tactic. They renewed their threats to cut food supplies and remove the tribes to Oklahoma. The following year, the threats broke the solid resistance organized by the old chiefs, but only a small minority of the Sioux were convinced to sell. Nonetheless, some signatures were collected on another illegal document to provide at least a semblance of legitimacy. In 1889, the richest lands were taken out of the middle of the Teton Sioux Reservation and "legally" stolen by the government. The rest was divided into six smaller reservations scattered about the states of North and South Dakota. These six bleak outposts have remained until the present day.

The situation was best summed up by a Sioux chief some years before when he told an earlier treaty commission:

> I am glad to see you, you are our friends, but I hear that you have come to move us. Tell your people that since the Great Father promised that we should never be removed we have been moved five times. I think that you had better put the Indians on wheels and you can run them about wherever you wish.

WOUNDED KNEE

The Teton Sioux suffered military defeat and diplomatic treachery. They lost their land and their way of life. It was a fate shared at the same time by the rest of the Indians across the American West. In their despair and confusion, many were swept up by a religious movement in the autumn of 1890. A Paiute named Wovoka claimed to be the Messiah, an Indian incarnation of Christ.

Wovoka taught his followers to do the magical Ghost Dance, prophesying that by the next spring, all white men would be gone. The earth, he claimed, would be covered with new sweet grass and clear running water, the buffalo would return, and all the Indians who had ever lived would be brought back to life. It was a very Christian fantasy, but it swept across the Plains leaving no tribe untouched. The aging Red Cloud said of it:

> There was no hope on earth, and God seemed to have forgotten us. Some said they saw the Son of God; others did not see Him. If He had come, He would do some great things as He had done before. We doubted it because we had seen neither Him nor His works.

> The people did not know; they did not care. They snatched at the hope. They screamed like crazy men to Him for mercy. They caught at the promise they heard He had made.

> The white men were frightened and called for soldiers.

Religious ritual or not, white reservation officials banned the large gatherings of Ghost Dancers. They claimed the size of these groups constituted a threat to the peace. The worshipers, of course, were not in the least bit militant. They would do nothing to alter the present when they believed so fervently in a day of reckoning only six months away.

In any case, U.S. Army troops were brought onto the Oglala's Pine Ridge Reservation. They were there only "to restore order," but their presence was an open provocation, especially when the unit selected for the job turned out to be the hated 7th Cavalry. Sitting Bull had been watching the Ghost Dance phenomenon from afar. The Army, however, decided that he must be behind it and using it to foment trouble. They ordered 43 of their Indian policemen to arrest him. In the course of it, the great leader was killed.

Orders went out to make other arrests, among them Big Foot, the old chief of the Minneconjou Sioux. At the news of Sitting Bull's death, Big Foot began moving his people to Pine Ridge, hoping that Red Cloud would be able to keep the Army from molesting them. There were Ghost Dancers in his band and their ranks had been swollen by many homeless widows taking refuge with them. It was a cold march to Pine Ridge through the December snow. Near Porcupine Creek, they met a troop of soldiers from the 7th Cavalry.

A white flag went up and the cavalry officer in charge ordered the Minneconjou to proceed to an Army camp on the Wounded Knee Creek. Big Foot had contracted pneumonia on the cold march and was spitting blood onto the snow. He agreed to follow. They arrived after dark and were told to set up a camp in a hollow near the creek. The cavalry officer issued them rations and then counted his captives—120 men, 230 women and children.

Later that night, the remainder of the 7th Cavalry rode in. Custer's old outfit was under the command of Colonel James Forsyth. A few of the officers with him had survived the battle of the Little Big Horn fourteen years before. So too had some of the older Minneconjou warriors. When the Sioux awoke on the morning of December 29, 1890, they found that Forsyth had them surrounded with cavalry and had placed four Hotchkiss guns on a nearby hill. The guns looked down on the shallow hollow next to the creek and were positioned to bombard it.

Forsyth told the Minneconjou to surrender all their weapons. They did, stacking their rifles and pistols in the center of the camp. Not satisfied, he ordered that the tipis and young men be searched. Two more rifles were found. In confiscating them, one went off. It was like the crack of doom. The air exploded with gunfire as the cavalrymen began shooting into the camp. Within seconds, dozens of unarmed Indians lay dead. As others began to run for the cover of a dry wash, the big Hotchkiss guns on the hill opened fire and tore them to pieces. Some say 300 people were killed that day; 153 bodies were counted on the site, but most of the wounded crawled away to die in the snow.

Black Elk, a leading Oglala Sioux medicine man, arrived on the scene hours after the massacre. Forty-one years later, he described what he saw:

> I did not know then how much was ended. When I look back now from this high hill of my old age, I can still see the butchered women and children lying heaped and scattered all along the crooked gulch as plain as when I saw them with eyes still young. And I can see that something else died there in the bloody mud, and was buried in the blizzard. A people's dream died there. It was a beautiful dream. . . .
>
> The nation's hoop is broken and scattered. There is no center any longer, and the sacred tree is dead.

Eighteen U.S. cavalrymen received the Congressional Medal of Honor for helping to kill the people's dream that day at Wounded Knee. It was the last massacre in the 400-year war of conquest (1492-1890) successfully fought by the white man against the Indian. Had they known more of the history of this conquest, the American people of 1973 would not have been surprised to find either that the Oglala Sioux had risen once again or that the place of the confrontation was the little village on the Wounded Knee Creek.

3

AIRLIFT
The Plan

Tuesday, April 10, 1973
Boston, Massachusetts

Preparations for the supply flight to Wounded Knee began on April 3. Friends made inquiries about renting an aircraft and raising money. I read as much as possible about the conflict on the Pine Ridge Reservation and the conditions that led up to it. Advice was unanimous: if a careful plan were developed that minimized risk, the project should be carried out. As Americans, as people who worked in opposition to the Viet Nam War, we felt close to the struggle at Wounded Knee and believed that we had a stake in its outcome.

But the flight never took place. On April 5, a formal agreement between the Indians holding Wounded Knee and representatives of the federal government was signed beside a tipi just outside the village. The document called for a disarmament two days later and granted most of the Indian demands. News bulletins describing it came over the radio as I drove home on the evening of the 5th. Later that night, my friend in New York agreed that the flight was no longer necessary, and it was with mixed emotions, including a great deal of relief, that I cancelled it.

During the next few days, my attention shifted away from Wounded Knee. The occupation, however, remained in progress. By Monday, April 9, it was clear that something was wrong. The evening news described differences of opinion regarding the terms of the agreement. Both sides accused the other of bad faith, and no one knew how to resolve the remaining problems. Still, with the flight to Wounded Knee out of the picture, I followed the story—but from the standpoint of a spectator.

On the morning of April 10, another friend in the anti-war movement, Marty, telephoned the Medical Aid for Indochina office asking to see me. I told him to come at noon and we would have lunch together. When I asked what he wanted to discuss, he said he'd rather not tell me over the phone. "What the hell," I thought, "everyone's so nervous about the telephone these days." I should have realized what was up, but for some reason I unthinkingly went back to work.

Marty arrived on time. He wanted to eat where we could talk without being overheard. I led him to a busy restaurant across the street. As soon as we sat down, he said he had just driven in from Wounded Knee. Despite its being the second time I had heard that in a week, I was surprised. Once again I asked what was happening there—without thinking that it had very much to do with me.

"The agreement they signed on April 5 is never going to work," Marty began. "I spoke to someone out there on the phone this morning. The government broke the agreement and people are going ahead with the occupation."

"Wait a minute," I interrupted, "you mean you can just pick up a telephone and dial Wounded Knee? Aren't the lines down?"

"Yes, but there's a legal defense office in Rapid City that's been set up by a support group. It's 100 miles from Wounded Knee, but that's where everyone goes who wants to help. The backpackers are organized there. It's sort of the off-reservation base camp."

"Okay, I understand. What happened with the agreement?"

"It's fairly simple," Marty answered. "The deal was that Russell Means and two of the Oglala chiefs would leave Wounded Knee and fly to Washington for meetings with White House officials. When the meetings got started, Russell would call back to South Dakota and tell the people in Wounded Knee to surrender their arms.

"When Russell got to Washington, they refused to see him at the White House. First they stalled around for two days not saying anything. Then one of Nixon's lawyers, Garment, announced that no meetings would take place until after the Indians surrendered their guns.

"You know, they always exaggerate the importance of leaders. They probably figured that with Russell out of Wounded Knee, they could push the rest of the people around. Well, that's not the way it works out there. The people inside called a meeting to decide what to do.

"Everyone talked about Big Foot and how the 1890 massacre happened when the Indians surrendered their guns. People made speeches about how the ground they were standing on was soaked with their grandparents' blood. So the answer was no—no surrender of guns until talks started in Washington. The government did up a big thing for the press about how it was really the Indians that broke their word, and that was that."

I leaned back in my chair, just beginning to comprehend what Marty was saying. "You mean everything is like it was before? What about food? What do they have to eat?"

Marty explained that food was still a major problem. A little got in on the 5th, the day of the agreement, but by that very night the roadblocks were sealed shut once again. The supporters in the Rapid City legal defense office dispatched more backpackers to hike in with supplies, but their trails were being discovered and the marshals and FBI agents used dogs and trip-flares to stop them. Arrests were common, and the Rapid City legal people had to spend time assisting the backpackers and bailing them out of jail. Marty had been on one of the backpack trips.

"It was tough," he remembered, "and frightening. We started out as soon as it got dark with 40-pound packs on our backs. It was a seven-mile hike before we were even close to Wounded Knee. Every time a flare went off, we had to fall on the ground with those heavy packs.

"There were three of us, me and two women. One of them was an older Oglala woman who was guiding us through. She really knew the country, but once in a while, you know, we'd be walking through a ravine or something and we'd hear a patrol near us, so we had to stop and hide. Once we were down like that for an hour and the marshals were so close we could hear what they were whispering to each other."

"What was it like once you got in?" I asked.

"The food problem is really serious. People are coming from all over the country with carloads of food, but it all piles up in Rapid City because it's so tough to get through. We only stayed inside Wounded Knee for a day. The next night we left and they busted us on the hike out."

"How?"

"We were trapped on the trail. Marshals came at us from two sides waving guns and pushing everyone around. They threw us in the reservation jail for the night. The charge was a five-year rap, a felony—'interfering with federal officers in the lawful performance of their duty.' Can you believe it?"

"Sure I can believe it."

"Anyway," Marty went on, "they dropped charges the next morning. I guess since they didn't catch us with any food or guns, there was no evidence."

Marty talked a while longer about the need for food. I knew what was coming. There was no dodging it any longer.

"I know," he finally said, "that you were asked to fly into Wounded Knee last week. That's why I'm here. They told me to ask you again."

"Yeah, well, I figured. But it's a complicated thing. What are you prepared to do?"

Marty looked a little surprised at my question. "Me? I can raise a few hundred dollars here in Boston, maybe more from some friends in New York. I can put you in touch with trustworthy people in Rapid City. But what else can I do? I can't fly. I'll do whatever you tell me to do."

There was no point in appearing reluctant. I had weighed the pros and cons the previous week. I told Marty that we still had to come up with a plan that minimized the danger of injury or arrest, but if the plan sounded good, I would try to carry it out.

I explained the week-old conversation with my flight instructor friend in Chicago and his advice that I practice flying there in a special aircraft before going into Wounded Knee. I told Marty that flying in to get food stored in Rapid City was not a good idea. It was too close to Wounded Knee and would certainly be under constant surveillance.

A waitress brought our sandwiches and for a few moments we ate and said nothing. Then I began sketching the outlines of a plan. If the people in Rapid City could secretly get 400 pounds of food onto a truck and out of town without being followed, I would rendezvous with them at a quiet country landing strip a hundred miles or so from Wounded Knee. Just before arriving from Chicago, I'd stop and gas up at a nearby airport. Someone familiar with the terrain inside Wounded Knee, who could act as my spotter, could accompany the truck from Rapid City.

We'd meet at the landing strip about an hour before sunset and load the food on board the plane. I'd take off with the spotter and fly directly to Wounded Knee, arriving just as it got dark. The spotter could show me exactly where to land so that circling around beforehand would not be necessary. Afterward, I'd take off when it was completely dark, either leaving the spotter in Wounded Knee or dropping him at some point on my way back to Chicago.

It sounded reasonable, so Marty and I began looking for flaws. Unfortunately, they were easy enough to find. What if the weather changed en route, making it impossible for me to go on? What if something unusual was happening at the landing strip just as I came in, like the local police helicopter practicing takeoffs and landings? What about informers? In a situation like Wounded Knee, the FBI would surely try to infiltrate a few informers into the Indian support group. What if we got to Wounded Knee in the middle of a gun battle? What about the registration numbers painted on the side of the aircraft? They could be traced through the Federal Aviation Agency to the owner of the plane, and from him to me. If I weren't prosecuted, the FAA could revoke my pilot's license. If they did catch me and wanted to charge me with bringing in a planeload of guns and ammunition instead of food, there would be no way I could prove otherwise.

"You know what?" I said, laughing and leaning away from the table. "This plan stinks."

We started designing various back-up systems, like alternate airports and ground-to-air signals with the truck's headlights or a pair of walkie-talkies. But it was soon apparent that we lacked the resources to design a really safe plan. The physical danger could be minimized, but the risk of arrest or loss of my license was difficult to cancel out. I could not count on the same kind of leniency that Marty received; a plane full of food would be much more embarrassing to the government than a couple of back-packers. Much as I didn't want it to, my commitment to the project began to weaken. Marty felt me slipping away, but there was nothing he could do to prevent it. We lapsed into silence once again. Minutes went by; neither of us said anything.

"The best way to get away with something and not be caught is to be the first one to do it," I said, coming back to life. "Then your opposition isn't prepared. Last week I learned that two planes have gone into Wounded Knee so far. The first one landed only a few days into the occupation, unloaded its cargo, and left with no trouble.

"Now, imagine you're the government. You'd be pretty angry, right? You're holding this place under siege and here comes a little airplane; it hops right over your lines and leaves again like you weren't even there. What would you do?"

Without giving Marty a chance to respond, I went on, answering my own question. "What you'd do is make a contingency plan, set up something so you wouldn't be caught unprepared a second time. That seems to be what happened. The second plane came in about three weeks later. When it took off, they had a pursuit helicopter ready to follow it. The plane managed to get away, but only after doing some pretty dangerous flying, in and out of the valleys, and just fifty feet off the ground.

"At this point, which is *now*, the government must be really angry. What are they doing? We don't know, but probably they've set up a better contingency plan, maybe airborne radar or a high-speed helicop-ter like the ones they use in Viet Nam. Or maybe they've made arrange-ments to scramble a jet from the Air Force base near Rapid City. In any case, who's flying in there next to find out? Me! No. What we need to do is figure out something they're not prepared for, something we're the first ones to do so that there just aren't any contingency plans."

It was a pretty good speech, but in reality I didn't have the vaguest idea what it was that we could be the first to do. The expectant look on Marty's face quickly dissolved into disappointment. More time passed as we sat slumped over our coffee, silent and dejected. The problems seemed to be insurmountable.

Suddenly the fog cleared. "Wait a minute," I said, snapping upright in my chair. "I've got it! We don't land! That's what they're not prepared for—parachutes!"

Marty perked up. "Right," he answered, "right. You could be in and out of there before they had time to get the helicopter started. Could they catch you, though, could they chase you down?"

"I doubt it. One minute would be all we'd need to make the drop. If it took them ten minutes to get the chopper in the air, which is moving pretty fast, I'd still be 25 miles away. In hill country and flying low they'd never find me."

"Wow, it's a great idea. But what about rigging the parachutes? You don't know how to do that, too, do you? Why can't you just shove the food out the door without the parachutes?"

"Oh, no," I protested, "that's much too dangerous. If you're a split-second off and you hit someone with a 50-pound bag of flour going 100 miles per hour, they'd be dead for sure. Besides, when the food hit the ground, it would splatter all over the place. We'll just have to find someone who can handle parachutes to ride along with me."

Marty and I were both excited. We started searching for flaws in the new plan just as we had before, but this time with much more optimism. There were problems, some of the same ones in fact, but the new plan was safer, more flexible, and required less dependence on other people. Marty asked me how many parachutes were needed to drop the cargo.

"Well, if I'm carrying full fuel and one other person, I'd be able to haul 400-500 pounds. Two chutes would do it. Of course. . . .there's no real reason. . . .why we couldn't get. . . .a bigger plane."

I was being swept up by an entirely new idea. If we were not going to land, then we did not have to worry about a short runway and using a small airplane. That was the key limitation before. Without it, everything was different. As I pictured the scene in my imagination, the airplane got bigger and bigger and bigger, until I saw a huge craft circling in the sky dropping package after package into Wounded Knee. I was too excited to talk. The possibilities were overwhelming. For a moment, I let my thoughts catch up with me, then explained it all to Marty.

"Listen, listen. We don't have to use a little single-engine plane. Let's get a twin. Let's get a goddamn monster like a DC-3. They used to be airliners, still are in some places. I think you can get 25 or 30 people into one of them. If we got one already stripped down for cargo hauling, we could drop two or three tons of food into Wounded Knee. Yes, tons!"

"Can you fly a plane that big?" Marty asked.

"No. But my friend in Chicago can. He flies them all the time, and he knows other pilots that do, too. Look, we could circle that thing so high over Wounded Knee no one would be able to shoot at us. We could take our time, figure the winds out just right, and sit up there dropping parachutes all day."

Marty's eyes had opened wide at the mention of the word "tons." His excitement swelled. Soon we were both bouncing up and down and smiling like two hysterical schoolboys.

"And you know what?" I grinned. "It's likely to be perfectly legal. We're not sneaking past any roadblocks and we're not interfering with any federal marshals. We're just going to make a regulation parachute drop to friends on the ground who've given us their prior permission. It's beautiful. Even if the government doesn't see it that way, the legal hassles would be worth it for something like this.

"There's a whole other dimension, too. Everybody's been complaining about press coverage. If Wounded Knee isn't in the news a lot, the government's more likely to attack and kill a lot of people, like they did at Attica Prison in New York.

"Well, a DC-3 parachuting two or three tons of food in there is going to be a big story. Especially now. The Pentagon is talking about how they might have to fly an airlift into Cambodia to save the Lon Nol dictatorship. What a great story—while the U.S. Air Force is flying the Phnom Penh Airlift into Cambodia, the Wounded Knee Airlift is in the skies over America.

"The more newsworthy we make the story, the better for the people in Wounded Knee. Right? Well, why don't we take a film crew from one of the TV networks? There's plenty of room in a DC-3, and the TV guys will love it. We could wear masks and get them to not reveal our identities. They'd be willing to do that for a story like this."

"Okay, okay," Marty said, unable to sit still in his chair, "it's fantastic. But can you do it? There isn't a lot of time to pull all this together."

"I know. It'll take a lot of help. Something like this will be really expensive, probably $3,000 to $4,000. I think my friend in Chicago will help us find a plane and a pilot. I'll ask the Medical Aid for Indochina people to help me raise money and contact the press. It's a lot of cash, but I bet there are plenty of people who would help."

"What about a parachute rigger. Can you get one?"

"Marty, I don't have the slightest idea where to look or who to ask, but if we work hard enough, we'll find one. I really want to do this. It could be crucial to the Indians at Wounded Knee. I'm going to drop everything I'm doing and start on it, *now*."

Marty agreed to raise whatever money he could, but both of us knew that it would only be a fraction of what was needed. We paid our check and left the restaurant. He drove away, promising to call me at the office in two hours with a progress report. I started off for my favorite telephone booth to get things rolling in Chicago, obsessed with the idea of delivering the food and determined that, no matter what, the airlift would succeed.

4

Gladys Spotted Bear: The Pine Ridge Reservation

I am tired of fighting. Our chiefs are killed. . . . It is cold and we have no blankets. The little children are freezing to death. My people, some of them have run away to the hills and have no blankets, no food; no one knows where they are—perhaps freezing to death. I want to have time to look for my children and see how many I can find. Maybe I shall find them among the dead. Hear me my chiefs. I am tired; my heart is sick and sad. From where the sun now stands, I will fight no more forever.
—Chief Joseph
Nez Perce, 1877.

Over the opposition of Red Cloud and the other old chiefs of the tribe, the government of the United States finally succeeded in drawing an enduring boundary around the territory of the Oglala Sioux. The final shape of their reservation was determined in 1889, one year before the massacre at Wounded Knee. The land was in arid southwestern South Dakota, just below the sacred Black Hills, on the very western-most edge of the Great Plains. The eroded, often rocky, grasslands have a certain magnificence. In a few places the eye can sweep from horizon to horizon and not see a single, even stunted, pine or cottonwood tree. But the beauty is austere and bold. It is the beauty of the desert, hard to translate into economic gain.

One of the six original Indian agencies where the Sioux were forced to trade was built at a crossroads close to the southern edge of what later became the Oglala reservation. The crossroads settlement was in a flat

57

area next to a long ridge topped by pine trees. The name "Pine Ridge" was applied to this settlement, which later grew into the hub of the federal bureaucracy on the reservation. Soon the entire reservation was also called Pine Ridge.

In Red Cloud's time, jobs on the Pine Ridge Reservation were as scarce as the buffalo. A few of the Oglalas reluctantly went to work for the Bluecoats, as Indian policemen. One of these was Sick Bread. It brought no great honor to him to be so employed. The Sioux called these policemen "metal breasts," a reference to their badges or the brass buttons on their blue jackets or the coldness of their hearts. The Army called them "scouts." Their existence meant that the different Sioux warrior societies no longer rotated the police work necessary to the tribe. The old traditional system successfully avoided just what the whites encouraged—power accumulating in the hands of a single small group.

Sick Bread, the metal breast, had a son named Spotted Bear who came to live on some Reservation land near Wounded Knee. Spotted Bear married, and in 1918 his wife gave birth to a daughter. The girl was given the name Gladys Spotted Bear, as the Sioux now had to conform to the white custom of permanent family surnames. When Gladys was four years old, her mother died. For the next three years, her father raised her by himself. Spotted Bear rode horseback every morning to his job on a farm many miles away. Gladys sat in the saddle in front of him. She spent the day with him on the farm and then was back in the saddle for the long ride home each night.

At the age of seven, Gladys was enrolled in the Holy Rosary Mission School, where she was beaten if she spoke in the native Lakota language she had used her entire life. Nine months out of every year she lived and worked in the Mission School. Like colonial mandarins in an occupied land, the missionaries forced their way of life on the children. This little girl of the Sioux was made into a Roman Catholic, made to speak in English and to pray in Latin.

Those were hard times on the reservation. People lived in tents and tin shacks. Whole families considered themselves fortunate to have a single room to live in, even if it did have leaks in the ceiling and holes in the walls. Some of Gladys' playmates died of curable diseases because there were no doctors to care for them or medicines to treat them. Now and then during the harsh winters, people were caught in a snowstorm and frozen to death out on the Plains. Food was often nonexistent. Some people lived on beans alone, or worse, for months at a time. There were still no jobs on the Pine Ridge Reservation.

But the material hardships were not always the worst of it for children like Gladys. This was a time when the government was making, as a BIA official recently put it, a "conscious effort [to] destroy" Indian heritage and culture. The psychological results of these attacks were as brutal as the physical results of unemployment and hunger.

Beating children in BIA-sponsored schools when they spoke in Indian languages was only one aspect of the attack on their culture. The children were taught that everything Indian was inferior or evil, from the color of their skin to their traditional clothing and long hair to their tribal tendency to act cooperatively rather than competitively. Psychologists once found that Indian school children were performing poorly at blackboard recitation because none wanted to be the first to arrive at the correct answer and thereby make the others in the class look less intelligent. Such "backward" tendencies were rooted out by school officials wherever they appeared. Under the guidance of the BIA, the schools became instruments for the violent destruction of Indian cultural roots. The very process of education was designed to eat away the validity of Indian life in the minds of the school children.

Now and then a tiny number of Indian youngsters were given the opportunity to become doctors or businessmen. But these token few usually left the reservation and never came back. Conditions are too severe there, and it is difficult to satisfy the new tastes and needs that come with privilege and a higher education. Since they so rarely returned, people on the reservation wondered what good that "opportunity" did for all the other children left behind.

In Gladys' time the BIA also launched a frontal assault on Indian religion. Religious ceremonies like the Potlatch (where all or most of one's possessions are given away to other people in the tribe) and the Sun Dance were strictly forbidden. So too were all traditional Indian funerals. Instead of having whites enforce these rulings, the dirty work fell to the Indian policemen, and their unpopularity grew. It was bad enough when they had to bring back runaway children bound hand and foot and return them to the BIA schools. But on the Sioux Reservations, breaking up the Sun Dance was the ultimate sacrilege. It wasn't until the 1950s, after decades of holding it secretly, that this most holy ritual in the Sioux religion was permitted to be celebrated openly. In the meantime, the Fourth of July became the biggest holiday on the reservations. Ridiculous as it was for the Sioux to participate in a celebration of white independence, the BIA reservation superintendents considered it appropriate.

The spiritual leaders and healers known as medicine men were the primary target for religious persecution. They were not only the bearers of Indian religion and the oral transmitters of Indian tradition and ritual, they were also the living embodiments of all that was most essential in the Indian way of life. Orders are on file in the Departments of the Army and the Interior directing the BIA to destroy the influence of the medicine men on the reservations. Again, Indian policemen were employed in this work. They confiscated medicine bundles, smashed sacred pipes, and jailed medicine men for practicing Indian healing. Since many of the metal breasts were recent converts to Catholicism, they performed their job with "missionary" zeal.

These attacks on Indian religion by the government of the United States took place in spite of the Constitution, the Bill of Rights, the Declaration of Independence, and the principle of freedom of religion that presumably was so dear to the Founding Fathers. No other group in America suffered comparable religious oppression. But among the most well-intentioned people, there are still few who even think of these attacks on the medicine men as an issue involving freedom of religion. If religious rituals do not stem from the western Judeo-Christian mythology, it is hard for most Americans to think of them as being *religious*. Unfortunately, that lack of understanding is a sad measure of how profoundly American culture is soaked with racism.

Gladys Spotted Bear was lucky enough to survive childhood. She married, became Gladys Bissonette, and raised a family of her own, four boys and a girl. Eventually she moved off the land near Wounded Knee and into the town of Pine Ridge. She was still living there in 1973, the year of the second historic confrontation at Wounded Knee. Occasionally some kind of job had come Gladys' way, but most of the time she lived on welfare. Things had not changed much on the reservation in the 55 years of her life. Jobs were still hard to find.

In 1973, every six persons out of ten in the work force were unemployed, without even part-time work. One out of every three Oglala families had no one at all working. A few years before, the federal government did offer a subsidy to a fish hook factory if it would locate at Pine Ridge. The offer was accepted. The factory employed 450 Indians at the minimum wage. When the subsidy ran out, instead of continuing on their own, the owners moved the factory to Mexico. It made sense for them to do so; wages were lower in Mexico and their purpose after all was making a profit.

Of all the homes on the Pine Ridge Reservation in 1973, only 9% had electricity. Only one home in twenty had running water. But then when it came to homes, a few people were living in chicken coops and the shells of abandoned automobiles, and occasionally someone still froze to death out on the Plains. Pine Ridge finally got a hospital, but somehow the infant mortality rate remained four times the national average. All this culminated, in 1973, in a life expectancy of 44.5 years.

And still the physical suffering in these harsh and dusty lives is not all that must be endured. Children grow up torn between the assimilated mixed-bloods, who try to make them feel ashamed of their straight black hair and their dark skin, and the traditional full-bloods, who want to

Roadsigns in South Dakota. (*courtesy Mike Abramson.*)

A residential street in Pine Ridge. (courtesy Joanna Brown.)

Indian boys playing in a Pine Ridge backyard.
(courtesy Mike Abramson.)

encourage pride in their own Sioux heritage. The children watch all day long as clumps of jobless men sit forlorn on street corners staring at the nothingness around them. The despair in the eyes of these men is perhaps the first stimulus that moves the children to contemplate what their own futures will be like.

On top of everything else, Oglala Sioux children grow up surrounded by the ghosts and the horror of the 1890 massacre. Wounded Knee is no abstraction for these children, no mere history lesson. In the past, many even learned about it first hand, from the mouths of neighbors who were among the few survivors. In 1973, a single survivor still lived, a woman in her nineties. There was only one answer these few survivors could have given when a young voice asked, "Who shot at you?" "The soldiers of the government." Then, to the inevitable, "But, why?" they might have replied, "Because we were Indians." What child would not shiver then with the thought, "But *I* am still an Indian, and the soldiers are still there, somewhere."

The Bureau of Indian Affairs is supposed to be a social service, a place where Indian people can go for support and help. Instead, the BIA is such a deeply entrenched bureaucracy, its major objective is to protect itself. Material desires, personal ambition, and the alienation inherent in bureaucratic work all reduce the average BIA employee to a point of greater concern for advancing his or her own position than for helping Indians. The situation is made infinitely worse when the stated goals of the Bureau are so obviously divorced from its actual practice.

For example, the Kennedy Special Subcommittee of the Senate on Indian Education reported that in 1953 the BIA started an emergency program to improve the quality of education available to Navajo children. By 1967 supervisory positions in the BIA schools were up 144% and administrative and clerical positions were up 94%. In the same period, teaching positions increased only 20%.

The BIA is charged with licensing and supervising the operation of reservation trading posts, which are the only source of food for most Indians, who do not own cars and cannot shop off the reservations. Again, the idea is to protect Indians who may suffer from corrupt sales practices as a result of language barriers or the absence of any competition. Yet, a Federal Trade Commission report (June 14, 1973) stated what had been clear to Indians for decades—they were being over-charged. On the Navajo Reservation, for example, the report said that trading post prices exceeded the national average by 27%. Traders were charging as much as 60% annual interest on loans made to Indians who had pawned their silver or turquoise jewelry.

Another BIA responsibility is overseeing law enforcement on the reservations. Their abject failure has led to the most barbaric violence being directed at Indians by white as well as BIA Indian police officers. Recently, South Dakota newspapers reported the case of police setting a ferocious dog on six Indians locked in a jail cell. The story on another occasion was that a state policeman fired a tear gas gun into a jail cell packed with Indian men and women. In one county in the state, officers passed keys to the jail around to their friends, police and civilians alike. The recipients who belonged to this "key club" were allowed to enter the cells and rape the female prisoners.

Life in any territory occupied and ruled by foreigners is brutal and demoralizing. Many of the teenagers and older people on Indian reservations turn to the white man's poison, alcohol, in a vain attempt to grapple with their hopelessness. Alcoholism can only be described as an unyielding and permanent epidemic. The cure, jobs and opportunity, remains unavailable. Too often it seems that an Indian must choose between only two alternatives in life: either give up any hope of ever achieving economic and material security or keep hoping and be disappointed. Alcoholism is an all too ready sop for the disillusionment or the disappointment.

The profound frustration that comes from a denial of equality is exemplified in the life of Ira Hayes. Like many Indians, Hayes rushed to enlist during World War II. He was a marine, and when his outfit helped take Iwo Jima, Ira Hayes helped five other soldiers raise the American flag on one of its hilltops. Someone took a picture of it that became the most popular photograph of the war. Hayes returned home a hero and the government put him on tour selling war bonds.

Most Indian GIs came back from World War II optimistic after a few years of relative equality with white enlisted men in the Armed Forces. They expected that America would treat them well after the sacrifices they had made overseas. Hayes, as much as any of them, must have looked forward to the opportunity that awaited him. But back on his reservation in Arizona, it was a life of poverty and unemployment once again. Some of the GIs, like Hayes, started drinking to escape their disappointment and their anger. There was always a white-owned liquor store at the edge of the reservation more than willing to encourage them. Ira Hayes died drunk—by drowning in two inches of water at the bottom of an irrigation ditch.

Any reservation, whether it's in Arizona or anywhere else, is occupied territory. The alcoholism brought to it by the whites is just one part of the physical and psychological onslaught directed against its people. And that onslaught takes its toll. The 12,000 Oglala Sioux people on the Pine Ridge Reservation have a suicide rate that is five times the national average. Teenagers are said to be killing themselves at fifteen times the rate of their non-Indian contemporaries across the country. Most people at Pine Ridge have come to see their relationship to white society in terms of oppression. Although the government guns that surround them are rarely fired, many believe that the oppression is no less violent than it was in the days of the 7th Cavalry.

There is no easy way to explain why life on the Pine Ridge Reservation is so brutalizing. The reasons are many and complex, but two are particularly important: the people's relationship to the land and the political system under which they are governed. The land on the reservation comprises 2.5 million acres. Much of this is arid, yet the Sioux know that if it were managed properly the land is capable of producing a great deal more than it does. Some of the land on the east side of the reservation is suitable for cultivation. More of it would be if money were found to develop adequate irrigation. Many acres are used for grazing and these too could support more animals if there were money for development. The Oglala people are unable to improve this territory and sustain themselves adequately upon it because of its bizarre status under federal law as "trust land."

Individual Indians own much of the reservation, but they do not actually possess it. It is held in trust for them by the federal government through the ponderous machinery of the Bureau of Indian Affairs. This relationship was supposedly created for the protection of the Indians. In fact, it has functioned more to their detriment than almost anything else. Instead of preserving the tribal land base and safeguarding Indians against unscrupulous businessmen, the BIA has helped local white ranchers buy, lease, and manipulate Indian land for their own profit.

Generally speaking, if an Indian turns to the BIA for a loan to develop his land, he will be told that the federal government cannot provide development money for land it (the federal government) is holding in "trust." That, they say, would be a conflict of interest. The alternative is a local bank. But the white-owned banks will rarely deal with a reservation Indian, especially those without collateral. The land cannot serve as collateral because the federal government holds it in trust.

When an Indian family is out of work and cash is suddenly needed to pay for medical expenses or emergency home repairs or food, there is usually only one solution—sell or lease whatever land is still owned by the family. With a median income less than $1,500 per year, few Indian families have savings accounts. Thus, Indians don't sell land that belonged to their parents and grandparents because they want to or because they are after profit. They sell because economically they have no choice.

But because of the trust status of the land, it is the BIA that must administer the sale or rental, not the actual Indian owner. Staffed primarily by white bureaucrats on the local level and controlled entirely by white politicians in Washington, the BIA is open to influence by the white power structure. Their bias can be blatant, like giving preference to whites over Indians when lands are up for sale. Or the bias can be more subtle. Indians naturally prefer to sell their land to other Indians of the same tribe. On the rare occasions when Indian purchasers are available, the BIA often takes a few weeks longer to process the sale or arrange for payment than they would if the purchaser were white. When people are in desperate need of cash, even delays of a few weeks can convince them to pick a white buyer and have the sale expedited.

Over the years, whites accumulated a great deal of Pine Ridge Reservation land. The Holy Rosary Catholic Church, for example, which runs the mission school that Gladys Bissonette attended as a child, is the largest single land owner on the reservation. Their holdings take in an amazing 18 square miles. They even bought the hill in Wounded Knee where the 7th Cavalry placed their four Hotchkiss guns during the 1890 massacre. A Catholic Church, of all things, was built on the spot, right next to the ditch where the cavalrymen threw the bodies. The mass grave was duly sanctified, and the bodies of the Sioux victims were suddenly in a Christian cemetery. The hilltop Catholic Church then became the main tourist attraction on the Reservation.

If, instead of having to sell their land outright, an Indian family can afford to lease it, the land trust policy has other outrageous implications. Most of the potential leasees for reservation land are white. They can more easily afford to expand their farming or grazing operations by leasing more land. They want only the best land, the acreage with water on it. If an Indian family leases out some of their land and tries to work the remainder, they gradually are forced out by competition with the very whites they rented to, since those whites have the better land and in most cases additional money to develop it. The leasees, of course, are not always white. There is a very small group of mixed-blood Indians on the reservation who have become an economic elite by manipulating their neighbors in the style of the whites.

Until 1973, the ultimate absurdity occurred when the land to be leased out was cultivable. Under normal circumstances, such land could have been placed in the Federal Soil Bank, which meant that the owner would get money from the government for not planting anything. But if an Indian family applied for an allotment of this kind, the federal government claimed that it could not pay subsidies on land it (the federal government) held in "trust." That, they said, would be a conflict of interest.

However, the same Indian family could have leased the same land to a white farmer. At Pine Ridge, the BIA regularly approved lease contracts to whites for $5 per acre per year. Sometimes they approved as little as $2 per acre. The white farmer then, not being burdened by a "trust" relationship with the federal government, could turn around and put the leased land in the Federal Soil Bank in his own name. At the 1972 rates, the white farmer would have then received $8-$24 per acre per year for *not* planting the land, while the true owners of the land, the Indian family, only got the $5 or so per acre in rent. The year before the Wounded Knee occupation, 1972, 17 white farmers each received $18,000 or more from the federal government in subsidies paid to them for lands rented from Indians on the Pine Ridge Reservation.

Land manipulation is not always so roundabout. The U.S. government, even in modern times, has also resorted to the outright seizure of land on the Pine Ridge Reservation. In 1942, the War Department (later the "Defense" Department) took 500 square miles from the Oglala Sioux to use as a target range for bombers. Indian families were given from eight days to a month to evacuate their homes. They were told that the land would be returned after the war. Payment was offered for the use of it. A man owning 320 acres was given $232. An Indian woman protested when she received only $200 for 400 acres. The War Department told her she was being unpatriotic. The 500 square miles of land were never returned.

Over the years, Pine Ridge lands became concentrated in fewer and fewer hands. Now they are controlled by outside white interests and a handful of Indians who have grown rich at the expense of other Indians. The BIA, whose mission in part is to protect Indians and their land, has succeeded in stripping them of it. The land policy called "trust" has left a large majority of the 12,000 Oglala Sioux owning no land at all. It's like investing money in factories and governments overseas in order to insure higher profits for U.S. corporations, and then calling the whole operation "foreign aid."

The parent of a land policy that steals under the name of trust is a system of government that tyrannizes under the name of democracy. The two go hand in hand at Pine Ridge. In 1924, when Gladys Bissonette was six years old and Christian missionaries were beating the Lakota language out of her playmates' heads, Congress passed the Citizenship Act forcing citizenship on all Indians. Many government officials thought this would correct some of the wrongs in their Indian policy. Others understood that it would lead to more effective control over Indian people. Ten years later, when Gladys was sixteen, the Indian Reorganization Act was passed. This legislation "encouraged" the various tribes to rid themselves of their old form of self-government, the chiefs and headmen, and reorganize in the style of the whites, with elected officials and a constitution. A model constitution was provided, prepackaged, to each of the reservations.

On paper the Indian Reorganization Act did not look bad, especially to those uninformed about Indian affairs, like most Congressmen. The Act called for a reservation to be divided into districts. Each district would elect a representative to sit on a Tribal Council, and the entire tribe would elect a chairman for the Tribal Council who would be the chief executive officer of the reservation. Just to be sure nothing went wrong, the BIA superintendent for the reservation had to approve all regulations passed by the Tribal Council before they were valid. Even in the face of this "student government" arrangement, a few sincere Indian leaders put their faith in the new system.

But for hundreds of years the Sioux people had been governing themselves in another way, and with remarkable success. The Oglala Tribe, for example, was divided into four different bands, each with one or more chiefs. The four bands were made up of 46 kinship groups, each with a headman and a number of elders. Typically, when important decisions were necessary, they were discussed in the smaller kinship groups. The elders in each of these groups then met to assess the views of the members and to try with the headman to hammer out an opinion. Then the headmen met together with the chiefs and each reported on the opinion of his kinship group. Afterward they each returned to their own groups and reported the opinions of all the other kinship groups. Living the way they did, there was almost always time for careful deliberation. Only then, when information had moved up and down in the system, were further meetings called to actually formulate decisions. Once these decisions were made, though, they could still not be forced on any adult male who disagreed. With the critical exception of male domination, the Sioux had achieved a very high level of democracy.

There were times when a chief from a particular band could exert great influence over a whole tribe, like the Oglala, or even the entire Sioux Nation. But this influence was usually limited to a specific range of activities, such as Crazy Horse in warfare or Spotted Tail in treaty negotiations. All of these chiefs, however, were peculiar in that they led only as long as people were willing to follow. In 1857, Father Jean de Smet, who lived with Indians for many years, wrote about the chiefs:

> Their power consists solely in their influence; it is great or little in proportion to the wisdom, benevolence, and courage that they have displayed. The Chief does not exercise his authority by command but by persuasion. He never levies taxes: On the contrary, he is so much in the habit of giving away his own property, as well to aid a needy individual as to further the public good, that he is ordinarily one of the poorest in the village. I know of no government that allows so great personal liberty, and in which there is at the same time so little of anarchy and so much subordination and

> devotion. . . . is it these people whom the civilized nations dare to
> call by the name of "savages"?

The white man's elected Tribal Council was certainly no improvement
over the traditional system. Elections isolated people from each other by
removing the power of the kinship groups. People who were accustomed
to working together in living communities became fragmented into separate individuals. The communities, after first losing their power, soon
began to lose their cohesiveness and energy as well. Active individual
participation in government became a mere ritual performed once every
few years at election time. In between, elected officials could act virtually
without constraint, in the interests of the people or not. The white men
called this system democratic, but it was only a shadow of the deeper
democracy the Sioux had known for centuries.

Between 1935, when this new system went into effect at Pine Ridge,
and 1973, the year of the Wounded Knee confrontation, fewer than half
of the eligible voters bothered to register. Rarely did more than half of
these actually vote in an election. Indeed, the system was called democratic, but by then the Oglala Sioux were very sensitive to the words of the
white men meaning one thing on paper and another in practice. They
called it "speaking with a forked tongue." So it was not cynicism that
caused the Oglala Sioux people to boycott the electoral process. Rather,
it was their understanding that the "democratic" system of government
imposed upon them was just one more attempt to destroy their traditional
way of life and force them into the alienated, materialistic society of the
whites.

Simply stated, the war against the Indians is still going on. Only the
weapons and the types of injury have changed. Except for the victims and
a variety of BIA and government officials, few Americans are aware of
this. But, also, few Americans understand that in many ways the war
against the Indians was typical of other wars to follow. U.S. treatment of
Indians should not be condemned because it was an unfair deviation
from U.S. treatment of other non-white peoples. With few exceptions,
America has dealt with all people of color in essentially similar ways. The
Indians are unique only in that they were the first victims, and the war
against them has gone on the longest. But there are, for example,
remarkably striking parallels between the Indian Wars and the most
recent American war on Indochina. Even fewer Americans appreciate
these similarities or understand their horrifying implications.

Sometimes the resemblances are easy to see. The U.S. military's
dependence on the high technology of death goes back from bombing
"gooks" with napalm and B-52s to slaughtering "redskins" with Spring-
field repeating rifles and Hotchkiss guns. These massive, indiscriminate

weapons, in both cases, were used to fight a war against an entire people rather than a war against an opposing army. Sand Creek and Wounded Knee should not seem unusual in the age of My Lai and the saturation bombing of Hanoi and Haiphong. It is not hard to see that the forced march of the Cherokee Nation from their ancestral lands in Georgia to faraway Oklahoma was no different than the "resettlement" program in Viet Nam, despite how pretty or technical the word "resettlement" may sound. Refugees are still refugees.

The U.S. military used technical words whenever possible to keep the reality of Viet Nam, and its true place in our history, from creeping into the consciousness of our people. The "strategic hamlets" in Viet Nam were the modern equivalent of reservations. Both are pretty names for con-centration camps. When the Pentagon said "free fire zone," they meant kill everything in sight—men, women, children, animals; when they talked about "resource denial," they meant starvation. Success with the buffalo convinced them to try for the rice. And we the American people found it a little less outrageous to think about and accept strategic hamlets and My Lai because all our lives we had heard about reservations and massacres.

War was even waged against sources of food and against the very natural environment with which both these people lived in such close harmony. Between 1870 and 1890, the number of buffalo on the Great Plains dropped from 50,000,000 to 800. Between 1962 and 1970, U.S. forces defoliated an area in Viet Nam equal to the size of Massachusetts. A country that used to be known as "the rice bowl of Asia" soon had to import the stuff from Louisiana. The poisonous herbicides and other chemicals left in the soil of Viet Nam transformed some of its jungles and farmlands into permanent deserts, just as the Bahaman Islands were denuded of vegetation many years before.

Other similiarities are also painfully clear. The policy of "Vietnamiza-tion," of creating and equipping an army of Vietnamese to fight against other Vietnamese, was no different than using Cavalry "scouts" and BIA police to maintain control over other Indians. By "changing the color of the corpses" (the words are those of an American ambassador to Saigon), U.S. combat forces were withdrawn without losing U.S. control. The Vietnamese, like the Indians before them, were divided against each other and had a more difficult time uniting against their real enemy—the U.S. government.

The high price of this divide-and-conquer tactic was accepted as a bargain. So the U.S. Treasury pays 100% of the cost of maintaining the BIA, just as it paid 100% of the cost of maintaining the South Vietnamese Army (including their salaries). U.S. violations of the Paris Peace Accords of 1973 seemed less outrageous than they should have as a result of our people being taught to scoff at 371 other solemn treaties made with the Indian nations of North America.

Ironically, the Paris Peace Accords of 1973 and the Sioux Treaty of 1868 were both forced on the U.S. government against its will. Both came in the wake of a defeat of U.S. military strategy. This explains why the Vietnamese as well as the Sioux insisted on the enforcement of these documents and believed them to be the key to achieving their respective freedom and independence.

None of these many similarities is very pleasant to think about. But perhaps the worst is the war the U.S. has waged against the very cultures and traditions of the Indian and the Indochinese peoples. Into a land of rice farmers and quiet communal villages, respectful of the aged and the careful wisdom that slowly emerges over countless generations, the U.S. brought pornographic movies and used-car salesmen, and tried to encourage the worship of ever-changing fads and fashions. It may be surprising to think that American consumer culture could be used as a weapon to destroy less technologically oriented (but no less advanced) civilizations. Yet, in the case of the Indians and the Vietnamese, the effort was quite deliberate. Here is a statement about Indians from the U.S. Secretary of the Interior in 1851:

> To tame a savage you must tie him down to the soil. You must make him understand the value of property, and the benefits of its separate ownership.

More than one hundred years later in Viet Nam, an American general argued that consumerism could undermine the national identity of the people and reduce their will to resist the U.S. "Get all Vietnamese males on a Honda," he said, "and the war will end."

On the reservations, the U.S. government sponsored the beating of Indian children for speaking in their own language. In South Viet Nam, the U.S. donated textbooks to the schools, but it happened that they were all in English. In North America, missionaries converted some Indians to a foreign religion, Christianity. This helped create splits in the tribes, thus playing into the hands of government and military men looking for ways to divide and conquer. In South Viet Nam, the work of Catholic missionaries during the French colonial period led to a deep division between 10% of the people who converted and the larger Buddhist majority. Later, the U.S. built on this division by using its dollars and "civilian advisors" to prop up a South Vietnamese government, headed by President Nguyen Van Thieu, that was composed almost entirely of Catholics.

Cut off from their land and their cultural roots, and forced into the abysmal poverty of refugee camps or urban ghettos, many Indians and many Vietnamese were led astray. Men often had to choose between starvation and joining the armies of their conquers. Many women could stay alive and feed their children only by becoming prostitutes. From the mining camps of California and the stockade forts on the Great Plains to the brothels of Saigon, native women were violated by invading whites. When the U.S. had 500,000 troops in South Viet Nam, there were 400,000 daughters of rice farmers registered as prostitutes in Saigon.

Even the original standards of female beauty were eroded as part of the general cultural breakdown. The modern equivalent of Indian women curling their hair and "passing" for white could be found in the brisk plastic surgery business in South Viet Nam. Dozens of operations were performed on women each day to alter the Oriental shape of their eyes and noses and to pump silicon into their breasts. It was a major preoccupation of the U.S.-trained Saigon medical profession. Their principal customers were the prostitutes and the stylish wives of the Catholic minority in control of South Viet Nam's business and government, including the First Lady, Mrs. Thieu.

Wars and prostitutes breed large numbers of orphans and abandoned children. In the old Indian tribes, orphans were always reintegrated into the community, not isolated in separate dwellings and kept apart from other children. So too in Vietnamese villages. But when communities were broken up, families scattered, and poverty imposed by a foreign invasion, orphans had to go where white men told them to.

Indian kids went to BIA orphanages or they lived in the open on the fringes of the reservations. Vietnamese kids were stuck with institutions that could not afford food, let alone beds and medicine. Their only other choice was to live off garbage in the streets of Saigon. Of the approximately 500,000 orphans in the Saigon-controlled parts of South Viet Nam, it was estimated that as many as 200,000 picked the latter alternative. Long ago the U.S. government ignored the Indian orphans it had helped to generate. Later they assumed that Vietnamese orphans could also be ignored without significant protest from the American public. They were right.

The importance that is attached to the fate of orphans and school children has to do with the passing of a culture from one generation to the next. Indian children can only be exposed to so much commercial advertising before they begin to think that what someone owns is more important than what they do. The same message, which leads to excessive personal ambition and selfishness, was received by Indochinese children who saw the very worst of western civilization in U.S.-dominated cities like Saigon. There everything from massage parlors to no-money-down television sets got prominently displayed, and the streets were clogged with cheap hustlers, pimps, cops, garbage, beggars, and a small number of very rich businessmen. Impressionable young children, taught over and over again in the schools and out on the streets to be competitive, to try and outdo their friends, soon came to think that their parents and grandparents were fools for clinging to the cooperative attitudes of the village.

A nation can quickly lose touch with its communal and spiritual roots. Despite their enormity, the physical disruptions and injuries produced by a long war sometimes pale in comparison to the damage done by perverting the values of even a single generation.

Finally, the political or cultural colonist in the occupied land must try to provide an escape valve for anger and bitterness. Not everyone can endure the human distortions and mind-breaking experiences that become the daily fare for the people of the conquered nation. An outlet is necessary, one that neutralizes anger and limits effective organized resistance. White America gave the Indians "firewater;" for the Vietnamese it was the gift of heroin.

Recently it was disclosed that South Vietnamese government officials made three visits to several BIA offices in the United States during 1974. Attached to the Saigon government's Directorate General of Land Affairs, these officials received instruction, at public expense, from American "experts" on how to control the montagnard tribal people who inhabit South Viet Nam's central highlands. The lessons of history are not lost on government officials. Neither should they be on the rest of us.

The parallels between government treatment of the Indians and the Indochinese suggest that the spreading of democracy is not the real goal of American foreign or domestic policy. Studying the true history of Native Americans would help all of us understand what the real goals are and answer some of the many questions we have about why our government behaves as it does. Unfortunately, the patterns of behavior are neither new nor unusual. They are understood by many people in a place like the Pine Ridge Reservation, who then boycott tribal elections and the entire political process imposed upon them by the whites. Such people know that the cards are stacked against them before they start.

No tribal chairman at the Pine Ridge Reservation was ever elected by a majority of the eligible voters. Not enough people ever participated in an election for that to happen. But that fact is not as surprising as it seems. Neither was any President of the United States ever elected by a majority of eligible voters, only a majority of those voting. One difference between the two elections is that the minority actually voting at Pine Ridge is usually so much smaller. Other similarities, however, overshadow this difference, especially in recent years.

On the Pine Ridge Reservation a candidate for tribal chairman has a good chance to win if he is willing to make numerous promises in public that he knows he can never keep, if he understands how the various mass media can be used to saturate the community with his name and image, if he is willing to condone some strong-arm tactics here and a little vote-buying there, and if his rich (and therefore white) backers are willing to spend large amounts of money to pay for all of his electioneering. The backers, of course, get repaid many times over with business contracts, favoritism on land sales, and other government influence once the election is won. Most people on the Pine Ridge Reservation believe that this is exactly what happened when Richard Wilson won the 1972 election for tribal chairman.

One person who fell for the promises Wilson made during his campaign in early 1972 was Gladys Spotted Bear Bissonette. Gladys lives with her younger children in a small four-room house on an unpaved street in the town of Pine Ridge. When it rains hard, the chances are only 50-50 that a car will make it through the mud. But Gladys' accommodations are deluxe compared to most other human habitations in town. Pine Ridge is a hodge-podge of slat-board and tar-paper shacks, one-room cabins, and small buildings in varying states of decrepitude. Along with outhouses of all shapes and sizes, junked cars are the most common backyard fixture. There are some homes like Gladys', and even one street with a row of large white frame houses built by the government for the better-paid BIA employees.

Gladys Bissonette, 55 years old, is an energetic, gesturing, talkative person. When she moves, which is often, her physical strength is apparent. She is short, of medium build, and dark-skinned. Dozens of deeply chiseled lines sweep across her face, cutting patterns into her cheeks and brow. Months after the occupation of Wounded Knee, Gladys explained the role that Richard Wilson played in touching off the confrontation.

"When Richard Wilson became chairman," she began, "he had made all kinds of promises. I myself campaigned for him, and I had my son and his hoop dancin' club dance for him on campaign trips. We campaigned for him and we really worked hard for him. 'Course, he helped me, too. He gave me $50 at one time so I could send my boy to a different school in North Dakota."

Once elected in April 1972, Wilson helped Gladys even more. He fired someone to give her a job in the reservation's old peoples' home. But before long Gladys began to notice irregularities in the budget. When she complained about them, she was fired. As her eyes were being opened to Wilson's real purposes, so were those of others who had supported him or remained neutral. People on the reservation claim that Wilson lost no time in appointing his relatives, friends, and supporters (in that order) to salaried positions within the tribal government.

Wilson, 39, was a plumber before becoming a politician. He is a stout man with an overhanging stomach and a very short crew-cut. A mixed-blood, he is ignorant of the tribe's language and has no respect for its chiefs and headmen. Once in office, many Oglala Sioux insist that Wilson carried out a variety of crooked deals and land manipulations, some for his own financial gain and others to repay those who helped elect him.

Perhaps the worst example of this concerned the Oglala Sioux Construction Company. It was started by the previous tribal chairman, employed Indians, and was managed by an Indian. It held the contract for housing construction on the Pine Ridge Reservation, and it was the first time in all the years of reservation life that Indian people had an opportunity to build their own homes. After taking office, Wilson fired all the Indians working for the company and gave the housing contract to a white firm in Rapid City.

Complaints about activity of this kind are growing more common on Indian reservations throughout the country. Ironically, they stem directly from a huge increase in funds appropriated for Indian use during the Johnson Administration. The problem is that tribal governments suddenly are handling millions of dollars in federal funds with nothing controlling them except the already corrupted BIA. There are no conflict-of-interest laws to prevent tribal contracts from being used for personal gain. There are no laws holding elected officials financially accountable to the federal government or their own tribes. Election laws prohibiting vote fraud do not exist. Elected tribal officials can get away with using federal funds to re-elect themselves. There are no laws giving the federal courts jurisdiction over tribal chairmen who abuse their power. This unfortunate state of affairs is typical of the guidance given to the American Indian tribes by the BIA.

The result of the new influx of money under Johnson was the rise of small political "establishments" on the reservations. These corrupt little tyrannies are usually composed of some members of the Tribal Council, the chairman, and his relatives and friends, all of whom act in collusion with white BIA officials, including the superintendent. They all selfishly and systematically exploit the federal funds and the reservation's resources much as a big city political machine operates. This leads to the antagonism and irritation of ordinary people toward tribal government which is made even worse on some reservations, like Pine Ridge, when white-oriented, culturally assimilated, mixed-blood officials, who do not speak the tribe's language, high-hand it over full-bloods.

Gladys Bissonette and others began to speak out against Chairman

Richard Wilson. It was a difficult thing to do since Wilson controlled most of the available employment on the reservation. Not infrequently, his political opponents were fired from their jobs. But many people, especially the older ones, were moved to speak up by the growing spirit and effectiveness of the new militant Indian movement.

Pine Ridge residents had direct contact with the new movement early in 1972, after Raymond Yellow Thunder, an older Oglala man, was publicly tortured in the American Legion Hall in nearby Gordon, Nebraska, and then murdered. His three sisters tried to get the killers brought to justice, but white officials in Gordon would not even acknowledge that it was a case of murder. They refused to allow the three sisters to view their brother's body or examine the autopsy reports. Appeals went unheeded. Finally, with no place else to turn, Yellow Thunder's sisters asked their nephew to contact his friends in the American Indian Movement (AIM).

The AIM organization had been active in the South Dakota-western Nebraska area setting up anti-alcoholism programs and job placement bureaus. Their work attracted a lot of attention among Indians. Occasionally, AIM staged a peaceful but militant protest at a place like the Mt. Rushmore National Monument. That got them some white attention as well. AIM people from the region responded to the call from Pine Ridge. They traveled to the reservation and held a meeting to discuss the Yellow Thunder case. The next day, AIM led a delegation to Gordon.

In the following weeks, this group publicized Yellow Thunder's murder, called community meetings in Gordon to demand an investigation, and protested what they felt was a pattern of neglect by law enforcement officials in cases involving the murder or beating of Indians. Their efforts were successful. Arrests were made, and when the defendants went to trial, AIM returned to focus publicity on the proceedings and try to prevent a whitewash. Several men were found guilty of manslaughter and given mild sentences in the state penitentiary. Nevertheless, the incident won AIM a following on the Pine Ridge Reservation, particularly outside the town of Pine Ridge. The people living in the countryside are more isolated from white culture. They cling to the traditional Sioux leadership, the network of chiefs and headmen that still survives across the reservation. They were glad for even the small victory over the white man's law won in the Yellow Thunder case.

Months later, as dissatisfaction with Wilson increased, many people looked back to their experience in the Yellow Thunder murder and decided to take action. By October 1972, only six months after Wilson assumed office, there were petitions being circulated demanding his formal impeachment. But October was also the month of the Trail of Broken Treaties.

Organized by the American Indian Movement, "Trail" people traveled across the country stopping at reservations and urban Indian ghettos. They worked to educate Indian people about their treaty rights and to organize support for a caravan to Washington, D.C., where the case for enforcing the old treaties would be laid before the appropriate government officials. Several thousand Indians in a four-mile long caravan arrived in Washington just before the Presidential elections of 1972. No responsible spokesperson in the government would meet with them. Previously agreed upon housing arrangements were cancelled by the Interior Department, of which the BIA was a subsidiary bureau. With no place to go, the Trail of Broken Treaties seized the BIA headquarters. After a frustrating week-long occupation and no meaningful action from the Nixon Administration, the building was abandoned. In their anger before leaving, 'Trail" people damaged furniture and fixtures. Also, files and records substantiating their claims of BIA corruption were stolen and released to the press.

Meanwhile, at Pine Ridge, Chairman Wilson denounced the BIA building takeover, despite the fact that many Oglala Sioux had participated. With his power resting on the current structure of tribal government, it was not in the interests of a tribal chairman to support treaty rights. Granting the rights guaranteed in the treaties would mean a return to democratic self-government by the chiefs and headmen.

His opponents claim that Wilson began circulating rumors that AIM-sponsored "Trail" people planned a takeover in Pine Ridge on their way back from Washington. Having once created this false fear, Wilson convinced Pine Ridge BIA officials to find $62,000 in their spartan budget for use in securing and protecting the reservation.

It is said that this $62,000 was used in November 1972 to start Wilson's infamous "goon squad," a private force he deputized, armed, and trained in "riot-control." This group consisted of a few dozen local toughs and unemployed alcoholics. They answered only to Wilson and seemed to be immune from control even by the local BIA police. It is believed that their real purpose was to threaten, intimidate, and beat people who were working for Wilson's impeachment.

But tactics of this sort simply provoked more opposition from the tribe. First, two Tribal Council members were instructed by the voters in their districts to introduce an impeachment resolution at the next session of the Tribal Council. Wilson allegedly bought them off, promising a high-salaried job to one and giving the other an outright bribe. Then, as people in more of the reservation's voting districts began meeting and supporting impeachment (in some cases unanimously), Wilson cancelled Tribal Council meetings so that impeachment resolutions could not be introduced. By early February 1973, 30% of the reservation's eligible voters

signed an impeachment petition, six of the eight districts on the reserva-
tion held meetings that endorsed impeachment, and nine of the sixteen
Tribal Council members signed a petition protesting the actions of
Wilson's administration.

Even earlier, Wilson had panicked. He issued an order prohibiting
Russell Means, an American Indian Movement leader and one of the
organizers of the Trail of Broken Treaties, from setting foot on reservation
ground. This, despite the fact that Means was a native Oglala Sioux and
lived on the reservation in the village of Porcupine, just north of
Wounded Knee. Three days later, Means defiantly accepted an invitation
from the vice-chairman of the Tribal Council and spoke to a Pine Ridge
meeting about the Trail of Broken Treaties. Wilson had Means arrested
and the vice-chairman suspended from office. The tribal chairman then
banned any AIM member from "his" reservation.

But the tactic of blaming "outsiders," of shifting attention away from
the real issues, did not work. With pressure for his impeachment still
building, Wilson got the Tribal Council to ban all gatherings of five or
more persons anywhere on the reservation. The ban was enforced by
both the BIA police and the goon squad.

It wasn't enough. Like the Ghost Dancers before them, the people
bent on impeachment continued to assemble and spread their views.
Once again, an action of the Sioux people, however peaceful and legal it
was, offended and frightened the authorities. Their response was exactly
what it had been in 1890—they brought federal troops back, after 82
years, to Pine Ridge. Instead of the 7th Cavalry, Wilson and Stanley
Lyman, the white superintendent of the reservation, called for federal
marshals. During the second week in February, wearing sky-blue jumpsuits and armed to the teeth, 84 U.S. marshals went on active duty at Pine
Ridge. Supposedly, they were not there as a provocation, but only to
preserve the peace.

Nevertheless, they provoked Gladys Bissonette. "It was on the 11th of
February, 1973," she recalled, "when my son came up to my house and
said, 'Mom, there's busloads and busloads of people being unloaded at
the Billy Mills Hall [the local community center]. Go down and see,' he
said. So I jumped in my car and got up all of my grandchildren and I drove
round and round and I noticed they were all in blue pajama outfits, like.
They were all white, no, a few were colored, and I thought, well, I wonder
what these people are up to?"

She found out soon enough what they were up to, and by the next day,
in the company of her friends, she decided to do something about it. "I
was sittin' at home drinkin' coffee, as usual. It was on the morning of the
12th. Two of my women friends came in and said they wanted me. They
were going to gather as many people as they could and protest against

Dick Wilson. We decided to demonstrate because we wanted to know why those marshals were there!

"So I grabbed my coat and I jumped in the car and away I went. I picked up somebody else and somebody else and then we went round and round and we made posters and signs for our cars sayin' that we didn't want Dick Wilson no more."

With about forty women and four men, the protest group went to the Bureau of Indian Affairs building, the center of the federal bureaucracy on the reservation. There they demanded to see Lyman. Federal regulations stipulated that this man had to approve all Tribal Council resolutions before they became law.

"We marched right into the lobby," Gladys remembered. "I didn't have no idea who was supposed to talk. Then this one fella stands up in the front and he says, 'Where is the superintendent?' And the superintendent come out smiling from the hallway, and he says, 'Here I am. What did you want?' So he said, 'We came in to talk to you. Here is our spokesman, right here.' And he pointed right at me!

"Now, I never thought that it would be me, but I said, 'Well, are you ready to talk to us, Mr. Lyman?' He said, 'Yes,' so we sat down. The mother of the fella that made me spokesman was really angry. She kept hollerin' that her grandfather had been Sittin' Bull!

"While we were in Lyman's office, Pedro Bissonette [Gladys' nephew and one of the men present] called Dick Wilson, and Dick Wilson said, 'I have nothing to say,' he said, 'I don't have anything to talk to you Indians about.' Now, that's our chairman talkin'.

"Well, then this Stanley Lyman, the superintendent of the Pine Ridge Reservation, says that his hands are tied, he cannot go over the tribal chairman's head, and that he has to take orders from the tribal chairman. Now that isn't so. It's the superintendent that's supposed to help the Indians every way he can. We knew he was just turnin' it around right then and there.

"So I told the superintendent, I said, 'If you're not doin' any good here, if the tribal chairman is goin' to run all over you, too,' I said, 'then we don't need no BIA superintendent. So, Mr. Lyman, you might just as well pack your bags and get the hell off our reservation!'

"'Well,' he said, 'Oh, I wish I could, I'd do it right now.' 'No you wouldn't,' I said, 'this pay is too damn good for you,' I said. 'This is the kind of people they pick to guide the Indians—some hayseed like you that don't know nothin'.' Well, we had a big hassle there."

The BIA police came in with riot sticks. They pushed everyone out of Superintendent Lyman's office, while the U.S. marshals blocked off Wilson's quarters. The "hassle," however, was a reflection of more pent up anger and frustration than could be contained. The two legitimate

channels for obtaining redress of grievances on the reservation had both
been tried, and each had led to a brick wall. One was the Justice
Department's Civil Rights Division. Over 150 written complaints against
Wilson and his goon squad had been submitted, but the government had
not responded to a single one. Then Lyman, during the protest in his
office, also decided to do nothing.

The other channel was the legally constituted impeachment process,
but Wilson had illegally thwarted all attempts to hold a hearing. On
February 14, several hundred people massed outside the BIA building to
make sure impeachment got on the agenda of the scheduled Tribal
Council meeting. U.S. marshals were everywhere. Wilson, citing incle-
ment weather, postponed the meeting for another week. But the anger
that Gladys had let loose on Lyman was spreading too quickly. The
demand for Wilson's impeachment could no longer be sidestepped.

The Council convened on February 21. Most of its members felt
obliged to seek Wilson's permission to even begin the impeachment
proceedings. Originally, the chairman had scheduled the meeting behind
closed doors, but the traditional chiefs of the Oglala Sioux managed to
convince him to hold an open session of the Council. Over 500 people
gathered in the auditorium of the Billy Mills Hall to witness the three days
of impeachment hearings. First, Wilson accepted suspension from office
pending the outcome of the hearings, as he was required to do by the
Tribal Constitution. Then Wilson turned around and told the Tribal
Council which of its members should be appointed as referee to preside
over his own impeachment. Gladys had this to say of the referee:

"Well, we found out that he must have been bought off the night
before at Wilson's residence. These ladies live right close to Wilson and
they see everythin' that's goin on, all the drunken parties and whatnot in
his house. So they told us everything. They said that they had seen this
referee inside of Dick Wilson's house all night, and they partied, and he
was bought off that night.

"The next day, when he went up as a referee or a judge, he was just
stupid. He stood up there and Dick Wilson was speaking for him. Wilson
acted as his own judge, his own prosecutor, and his own attorney, all
three. He put the words into that judge's mouth."

It was a kangaroo court of the worst kind. Outrage followed outrage.
Finally, on the third day, the three members of the Tribal Council who
had actually filed the impeachment motion walked out of the proceedings claiming it was impossible to get a fair hearing. The referee, whom
Gladys refers to as "the bought-off judge," noted the departure of the
three plaintiffs and suggested to the remaining Tribal Council members
that the charges against Wilson be dropped. They agreed with him, 14-0.

Meanwhile, in response to the arrival of the U.S. marshals, people on the reservation formed the Oglala Sioux Civil Rights Organization (OSCRO). Its purpose was to consolidate the opposition against Wilson. The activist backbone of the organization consisted of politically inexperienced middle-aged and older women, like Gladys Bissonette. Immediately after Wilson's 14-0 reinstatement on February 23, OSCRO called a meeting at the community hall in Calico, a reservation village north of Pine Ridge. Angry people flocked there from the aborted impeachment hearing, and by eight o'clock that night, 800 people had signed up as members of OSCRO.

"Then," Gladys recalls, "Dick Wilson put it on the radio that there's to be no assemblies, no meetings of no kind. Any three people seen gathered together were to be put under arrest. There will be no powwows, no Indian celebrations of any sort throughout the reservation, according to Dick Wilson's laws. But as Civil Rights Organization members, we went ahead and assembled. We danced every night, and we had to scrape up here and there to feed the people. We all, everybody, helped, and we fed one another."

The "unlawful" assemblies that Gladys referred to were a series of remarkable meetings held over four consecutive nights, beginning on February 23. Hundreds of OSCRO members met in Calico Hall to discuss how to respond to the Tribal Council's impeachment whitewash. People assembled in the late afternoon and were fed by a community kitchen. They held careful deliberations, took time off to sing and dance together in the old Sioux fashion, and then departed by 10:30 p.m., trying to avoid goon-squad violence on the highways. The meetings had a solemn air. There seemed to be an unspoken awareness that any action they decided to take would likely have a profound impact on the tribe and on the lives of the people participating. Everyone was concerned that the old chiefs be consulted on all questions and that the meetings be guided by their wisdom.

Wilson did not try to interfere with these nightly assemblies in Calico Hall. However, informers and BIA police in plain clothes were frequently seen in and around the area. Wilson was more concerned with barricading his own position in Pine Ridge. Sandbag bunkers went up on the BIA building. Rifles and pistols were plentiful in the hands of the police and the goon squad. Incredibly, the federal marshals began patrolling with M-16s, the standard automatic rifle used in Viet Nam. It was a staggering weapons buildup, given that no arms had been observed at Calico Hall, nor were any present. People were frightened. With so many guns around, no one felt safe.

In other parts of South Dakota, the American Indian Movement had been visible and active. Earlier in February, first in Custer and then in Rapid City, AIM organized militant demonstrations to protest unfair treatment of Indians. Some had led to violence. White officials around the state were out to break them. On February 25, after two nights of painstaking deliberation, the Oglala Sioux at the Calico meeting decided to ask AIM to return to the Pine Ridge Reservation and help them. The decision had the unanimous consent of the participating chiefs, medicine men, and headmen.

The Oglala Sioux Civil Rights Organization asked AIM to assist in removing Wilson from office and in altering the Tribal Constitution so that similar men could no longer come to power. They wanted the Oglala Sioux people to govern themselves in the old ways. Given Wilson's hatred for AIM and the number of guns and armed men in Pine Ridge, it was a difficult and a frightening request to make. Gladys Bissonette endorsed it, not realizing at the time that in two days it would catapult her into a position of leadership in the first large-scale armed confrontation between Indians and the United States government in the 20th century.

5

AIRLIFT
The Crew

Tuesday, April 10, 1973
Boston, Massachusetts

The idea of flying to Wounded Knee in an aircraft as large as a DC-3 was intoxicating. I walked away from my lunch meeting with Marty captivated, clearheaded, and anxious to begin. The plan we developed was ambitious, perhaps even a little grandiose. But I was sure we could deliver those thousands of pounds of food to the Indians.

After leaving Marty, I went to a telephone booth and called my flight instructor friend in Chicago, Bob Talbot. He listened to the whole plan: circling the DC-3 high enough to be out of range of rifle fire from the ground, precisely computing the wind direction and speed, dropping parachute after parachute to the people below, and all of it filmed in the air for the evening news. Bob said we had a good chance of pulling it off, and he agreed to locate a DC-3 that I could rent for a fews days. He wasn't sure about flying the big plane himself, but he did promise to help us find someone who would.

The only hitch was money. The round trip between Chicago and Wounded Knee was almost 2,000 miles, and renting a DC-3 to fly that distance cost $2,500. But we had no choice. Bob was known in Chicago and only there could he rent a DC-3 without a flight crew to go with it. The crew would add more expense—to say nothing of their likely unwilling-ness to fly such a mission. I told Bob that if he could find an available ship, he should reserve it.

But neither of us knew a single parachute rigger who might be interested in helping, or even where to begin looking for one. Before hanging up, we agreed that Bob would check with the FAA on the legality of the flight. We were probably in a gray area between clear lawfulness and a clear violation. If the flight was definitely illegal, we'd go ahead anyway, but with more caution.

I turned from the telephone booth and started back toward my office. There were several problems to solve, and for each one I had to find people to help me, people with special skills and experience. Bob Talbot was handling the search for a DC-3 and a pilot. I had to find someone to locate a parachute rigger and to contact a TV newsfilm crew, but neither was worth doing unless a large amount of money could be raised very quickly. Top priority was to finance the airlift, and my friends at Medical Aid for Indochina were the perfect ones to turn to for that kind of assistance.

Inside the office, I gathered the five people I had worked with for the past year and quickly explained the airlift plan. Everyone was flabbergasted by the enormity of the project, but they all encouraged me to take time off and do it. We had already discussed the pros and cons of getting involved in Wounded Knee. This was the week before, after the first request for a food flight but prior to the broken April 5 agreement between the Indians and the government.

"All of a sudden this whole thing's been dumped in my lap," I said to them. "I really want to do it, but it's got to happen fast. Besides everything else, I have to raise at least $4,000 by tomorrow night. I need your help with the money."

It was a logical proposal. We were an experienced and successful fund-raising team. Medical Aid for Indochina got started in late 1971. For a year we raised money to purchase medical equipment for the revolutionary forces in Viet Nam, Laos, and Cambodia. We wanted to alleviate suffering in Indochina and also provide the American people and the anti-war movement with a new way of opposing U.S. military operations in Asia. We wrote and distributed literature encouraging people to get involved. We stimulated street-corner and door-to-door collections, benefit concerts, fund-raising parties, public lectures and slide shows, and so forth. During 1972, affiliated groups were started in several cities, and we raised over $40,000 from people all over the country.

Then, in the last days of December 1972, two months after their pre-election promise that "peace is at hand," Nixon and Kissinger unleashed the most destructive aerial bombardment since the days of Hiroshima and Nagasaki. The Christmas saturation bombing of the cities of Hanoi and Haiphong killed large numbers of civilians and levelled innumerable buildings. One was Hanoi's Bach Mai Hospital, the largest medical facility in all of Viet Nam. Containing over 1,000 beds, advanced research laboratories, and sections of the Hanoi University Medical School, the hospital was wiped out in three separate B-52 attacks. Medical Aid for Indochina responded by launching a campaign to raise money in America to rebuild Bach Mai.

In a very short time, public outrage at the Nixon/Kissinger bombing produced widespread support for the Bach Mai Fund. We were able to place full-page ads in major newspapers, long articles were written about our work, endorsements came in from political figures, church leaders, prison inmates, prominent physicians, and even the relatives of POWs being held by the North Vietnamese. The Medical Aid for Indochina office was quickly transformed from a handful of people into a headquarters staff of thirteen workers and several volunteers. Anti-war activists around the country set up a network of full-time offices in ten cities and part-time projects in dozens of others. Four months after the bombing, at the time of the airlift to Wounded Knee, over half a million dollars for Bach Mai had come into the Boston office.

So it was with some justification that I sought the help of people at Medical Aid for Indochina. I asked two of them to spend the rest of the afternoon working on money for the airlift—Karl to call all the well-to-do people we knew in Boston and Larry Levin to telephone several activist friends in New York and ask them to call reliable anti-war supporters in their area.

Karl asked how secretive he should be about what we intended to do with the money. I told him to call only people we could trust, to tell them we were flying food to Wounded Knee, but not to divulge our plan to use parachutes.

"If too many people find out about this, you're going to get caught," he argued.

"We're bringing food to hungry people, not running guns," I answered. "If we get caught, there's not much they can charge us with. They'd be going out on a limb to say feeding people from the air is a crime. If they do, we'll beat them in court. Right now the most important thing is to get the food there fast. We've just got to be a little cautious so they don't get wind of it beforehand and try to stop us."

"Except for one thing," Karl objected. "Just suppose they accuse you of bringing guns and ammunition. All they have to do is find one defendant willing to testify to that in court. They could offer to drop charges against him in exchange for his saying that. Then they'd get you, which I'm sure they'd enjoy doing anyway. You know where that'd leave me? I'd be baking steel files into chocolate cakes for the next twenty years!"

Everybody laughed. "You're right," I grinned, "but that's just another reason to bring a TV crew or a few reporters. If it comes to a trial, they can testify that the cargo was only food."

We were ready to proceed. Karl, Larry, and I scheduled a four o'clock meeting to review our progress. As the group got up to go, I asked in a halfhearted way if anyone knew a politically committed parachute rigger. It seemed absurd to put the question to people with no connection to flying. I expected them to laugh, but instead Lois turned to Tim and reminded him that years before he had known a skydiver in college in North Dakota. Tim looked at her skeptically, but when Lois insisted, he realized that she was right. He had not seen the skydiver in four or five years, but Tim offered to try and track him down by phone.

The plan began to gel. Karl, Larry, and Tim left the office, heading for various neighborhood telephone booths. I reached for the yellow pages and started phoning Boston-area parachute jumping schools. On the third call, I connected with someone talkative and asked him every dumb question I could think of about the use of cargo chutes. My obliging informant explained how much weight could be suspended under different size parachute canopies, how fast in feet per second they would each descend, how big an inventory skydiving shops usually kept on hand, and other such details.

Next, I called an acquaintance at CBS News in New York. We had once worked together on a Viet Nam news story. I made sure that he would be in town for a few days and mentioned that I might drop in to see him. Then Marty, who had delivered the food flight request at lunch just two hours before, called the office with a report on his own fund-raising activities. Wealthy people he knew were ready to contribute $500 the next morning. He had spoken to a good friend in New York who was also an acquaintance of mine. She, too, was interested in making a contribution if I could meet with her first and explain our plans.

At four o'clock we gathered again for a meeting. Karl had promises for another $500 from a group of well-to-do Boston young people who regularly supported left political work. He was optimistic about raising more money that night and the following day. Larry told us that anti-war activists in New York were anxious to help and were confident they could successfully raise funds for the airlift. Work was beginning immediately. Tim reported last. He learned that the parachute jumper was living in Albuquerque, New Mexico. No one answered at the telephone listed under his name, but Tim would call him back later that evening.

I felt ready to move. We already had a good beginning with the fund raising. Valuable time would be lost if the other preparations were delayed until all the money was in hand. I proposed a three-stage plan. Stage one was to do more fund raising and firm up the TV news contacts in New York. The second stage was in Chicago: rent the DC-3 and gather

Gladys Bissonette, left. *(courtesy Melinda Rorick.)*

Dennis Banks. *(courtesy Chicago Sun-Times.)*

parachutes, food, and other necessary materials. Stage three would be to actually pack everything and take off for Wounded Knee. I wanted to leave immediately for New York to begin working on stage one. With $1,000 already promised, the expense was quite justified.

I asked Larry to come with me to help with the work and to criticize my planning. Speed was crucial and I didn't want to rush into stupid mistakes that another person might easily detect. Larry knew New York and could coordinate the fund-raising efforts there. If things went well, I'd go on to Chicago and start stage two of my plan while Larry remained in New York and finished the funding and press work. Meanwhile, Karl could continue gathering money in Boston since he knew that area best. When he and Larry had wired enough money to Chicago, I would launch stage three. If we failed to raise the necessary money, we could stop the plan at whatever stage it had reached and return all the unspent contributions.

The meeting ended cheerfully. Everyone wished us luck and assured us that we were doing the right thing. As we left the office, Larry stopped me and said that when the time came, if there was any job he could possibly perform on the Wounded Knee flight itself, he badly wanted to go along. Neither of us had any idea then how fateful a request that was to become.

Before driving home I stopped at a friend's house and asked her to write a letter that we could put in the food parcels parachuted into Wounded Knee. I wanted her to express our reasons for helping the Indians and our support for what they were trying to do. When it was needed, I would call her from Chicago and take the statement over the telephone.

As the seven o'clock shuttle flight lifted off the runway in Boston, Larry Levin and I sat in the back drawing up two lists of people to contact after we landed, one for money, the other for press coverage. Larry had experience in both fields and knew New York City well. He had, in his twenty-five years, lived in several cities on both sides of the Atlantic. Like many young people, his personal development had mirrored the unusual political events bursting around him in the late 1960s.

Larry was of medium height and build, blond and already balding. His sharp features and gentle manner combined into a picture of nervous intelligence. He was born into a working-class neighborhood on Chicago's West Side. While he was still in elementary school, his parents, a saleslady and a steel worker, moved to San Bernardino. Larry grew up in California where his political life began early. At fifteen, despite his background, he had his first confrontation with ghetto poverty, doing door-to-door voter registration work in black and Chicano neighborhoods for the Democratic Party. By the time he graduated from high school he was the state-wide vice president of the Young Democrats, one of the youngest people ever to hold the office. His dedicated work in the successful campaign of a liberal local Congressman was rewarded with a nomination to the U.S. Air Force Academy. But Larry declined a free military education to work his way through school at American University in Washington, D.C.

Larry was attracted to the intense political life surrounding the seat of government. Older friends from the Democratic Party organization in California treated him as something of a protegé and arranged a job interview in the office of the newly elected Senator from New York, Robert Kennedy. It was the fall of 1965. Hired to work only a few hours a day, Larry spent more and more of his time doing odd jobs in Kennedy's office, ignoring the overcrowded, impersonal university. He believed in the commitment of the Johnson Administration, and of Senator Kennedy in particular, to combat poverty and racism, and he was swept along by the excitement of the Great Society programs. He didn't study and he didn't save any money.

The following year the liberal California Congressman asked for help on his fall campaign and Larry agreed to move back to San Bernardino. The election was lost, and after a quiet semester in a state college, Larry returned to Washington in the summer of 1967. He re-enrolled in American University and got his old job back in Senator Kennedy's office.

But Washington had changed. The Democratic Party was being torn apart by the war in Viet Nam, and Robert Kennedy was increasingly projected as Johnson's main protagonist within the Party. In October 1967, tens of thousands of anti-war demonstrators marched on the Pentagon. Larry wandered through the crowds, a lonely observer, not feeling a part of what was taking place. For him, the arena of politics was not in the streets but in the offices of government. Still, the Pentagon March had a tremendous impact on Larry, and indeed, on all of official Washington. The young staffers in Kennedy's office urged the Senator to come out publicly against the war. They, and Larry with them, assumed such an announcement would have far more impact toward ending the fighting than militant protest.

Kennedy did condemn the war, and several months later decided to actually oppose Johnson's renomination in the upcoming Democratic primaries. Larry did extensive work on the presidential campaign, researching issues and organizing college students. He was deeply committed to Robert Kennedy as an individual and to the notion that a new President could fundamentally alter and improve the nation. In the spring of 1968, Martin Luther King was assassinated. Two months later, Kennedy was shot in California. It was the end of an era. For Larry, it was a staggering personal blow. His work for social change had been focused on Kennedy, and with the man who represented the solution gone, Larry became demoralized and began to think of political work as futile and meaningless.

Too depressed to take his final exams, Larry left American University and spent six weeks driving back to California with a friend. They went through the South very slowly, picking up jobs for a day or two on oil rigs and at construction sites. It was Larry's first opportunity since high school to meet again and talk with a cross section of the working people of America.

Six months later, Larry slowly came out of his isolation in order to work in the campaign of a young Congressman named John Tunney who planned to run for the U.S. Senate. Contrary to Larry's expectations, Tunney eventually refused to support the United Farm Workers of California who were on strike against the state's grape growers. Larry feared that the decision was based on the advice of media experts who essentially recommended that Tunney run on his good looks and steer clear of a strong stand on any issue. Confronted with what was called a "necessary" political compromise, Larry was shocked and disappointed once again. Disillusioned with political work, he quit the campaign and was soon preparing to quit the nation.

In December 1969, with no plans and no ambition, Larry packed a bag and left for Europe to live on his savings of $1,000. After traveling for a short time, he settled down in a London rooming house. It was tough going, but he was soon supporting himself in a modest way as a writer. Toward the end of 1970, after a year abroad, a small magazine asked him to go to Belfast, Northern Ireland, to do a story on the armed attacks against British rule.

Larry went in cold, walking into a corner grocery store in the Catholic ghetto in Belfast and asking strangers to help him meet people and find a place to stay. The ghetto reminded him of similar places he had seen in America. Larry was introduced to members of the Irish movement who passed him along from one group to another. Interviews were arranged with people who organized non-violent civil rights demonstrations and with others who were part of the underground Provisional Wing of the Irish Republican Army. Larry spent day after day with them, captivated by their intense commitment and their loyalty to each other and their cause.

He lived with the IRA for two weeks, going to their meetings and learning to sing their songs. Then, he was permitted to observe them on a combat mission. Having passed through stages of political idealism, disappointment, and eventually despair, Larry came in contact for the first time with armed political struggle. He was surprised at the existence of a well- developed underground movement in a white, urban, English-speaking country. But even more surprising were the fighters who accepted the necessity to use violence in pursuit of their freedom, yet seemed unusually sensitive and gentle in their human relations.

Larry's cynicism had come from his dependence on charismatic leaders and his alienation from mass movements of ordinary people trying to change their lives. He had never experienced the profound friendship and cooperation he felt surrounded by among the Irish. In spite of the need to use violent methods, Larry saw the fight against British rule as a life-giving force. The people of the Irish movement believed in the possibility of a better future. There was no hopelessness among them and no belief in the magic of individual leaders. They understood that their fate rested squarely in their own collective hands. Larry was captured by these new thoughts and ideals. With a reawakened sense of purpose, he made up his mind to go back to the United States. He filed his story in London, but returned to Belfast for three more weeks to tape a series of radio interviews with members of the IRA. Larry left Ireland when IRA intelligence informed him that the British Army knew of his activities and had put a price on his head.

Safely back in California in the spring of 1971, Larry sought out the radical left and the political movements that he had never participated in and knew very little about. An old friend from Washington introduced him to several people she knew in Los Angeles who were active in the anti-war movement. They wanted to learn more about the resistance in Ireland. Larry soon began learning a lot more himself, about Viet Nam. His new friends recommended material for him to read, including works on political theory, the Vietnamese revolution, the women's movement, and American Indian history.

Larry got more and more involved in the activities of his anti-war friends. He joined a small educational project that designed posters and wrote pamphlets about the war in Viet Nam. From the American anti-war movement, he began to learn about the humanity and dedication of the Vietnamese revolutionaries, and to think about similarities between them and his friends among the IRA.

As the 1972 presidential campaign got underway, members of Larry's small educational group in Los Angeles became apprehensive about the possibility of George McGovern's backsliding on the issue of Viet Nam. They wanted the war to remain a major focus during the election period so that Nixon could not hide the devastating intensity of his bombing in Indochina. With that in mind, the group worked for months creating a national organization called the Indochina Peace Campaign. Well-known anti-war spokespeople agreed to go on extensive lecture tours. Large amounts of money were raised to distribute slide shows and films and to print hundreds of thousands of leaflets. Larry moved to New York in the fall of 1972 to coordinate Indochina Peace Campaign activities on the east coast. By then, the anti-war movement and the struggle for political justice had become the focus of his life. After a long preparation, he stepped into the organized political left in America.

Following Nixon's landslide victory, Larry spent a month on a journalistic assignment back in Northern Ireland. Shortly before he returned in January 1973, Kissinger had urged the American bombing of Hanoi which resulted in the destruction of the Bach Mai Hospital. Larry decided to move to Boston and accept an invitation to join the staff in the national office of Medical Aid for Indochina.

It was three months later, after working closely together on the project to rebuild Bach Mai, that Larry and I were flying into New York to raise money for the airlift to Wounded Knee.

We didn't get into Manhattan until nine at night. After dinner we went to the apartment of Larry's friends, a couple who had been active years before in Robert Kennedy's campaign. They helped us prepare yet another list of people in various New York circles who might donate money to the airlift.

Just before going to sleep, we called Tim in Boston. He had gotten through to the skydiver in Albuquerque. Miraculously, the man had all the skills we needed—over 600 jumps and plenty of rigging experience to boot. He wanted to help, but had once known a Chippewa Indian in North Dakota who would be even better for the job. If he couldn't locate the Chippewa, he asked for some time to think about whether or not to join the airlift himself.

At that point, only twelve hours had passed since Marty and I first discussed the Wounded Knee flight over lunch.

Wednesday, April 11, 1973
New York, New York

Larry and I ate an early breakfast in Greenwich Village with Marty's wealthy friend. She was active in the women's movement and I had met her several times before at anti-war events. We explained our plans. Glad to learn that someone was ready to supply Wounded Knee, she offered us $1,300. At exactly 9:00 a.m. she and Larry left for her bank to withdraw the cash. Afterwards, they went together to the office of a New York anti-war organization. Two people who worked there had offered to help with calls, and before long the four of them were telephoning all the people on our various lists and asking for airlift contributions.

Meanwhile, I went back uptown to see the producer I knew at CBS News. It was too early. I walked around the corner to a liquor store and called Bob Talbot in Chicago. He was trying to reach an acquaintance of his in Michigan, named Jake, who had a DC-3 for rent. Explaining that our financial situation had improved and that we even had a good lead on a parachute rigger, I told Bob to commit us to renting Jake's aircraft and arrange to take possession within forty-eight hours. It was still a little awesome for me, renting a plane as big as a DC-3, when what I was used to were little single-engine, four-passenger models.

My producer friend arrived at the television studio. Despite his previous openness to Viet Nam and anti-war news stories, Wounded Knee left him cold. He was suspicious about the motivations of the leaders and somewhat outraged by their use of weapons. There were more practical difficulties as well. The news correspondent most interested in the story was marooned with a film crew in Beirut, Lebanon. All flights out were grounded because of intense fighting between Israeli and Palestinian forces. But before refusing to cover our story, my producer friend sought the opinion of some of his network colleagues. They agreed—CBS was not going to send one of its camera crews to Wounded Knee strapped inside a left-wing DC-3. After giving me the name of somebody at ABC who might be interested, they sent me on my way.

Outside, I called Larry at the anti-war office and asked that he meet me for a quick assessment of our progress. When he arrived, I learned that the fund raising was going very well. People were pledging specific amounts of money over the telephone and Larry planned to go around collecting them that night and the following morning. Anti-war activists had come in from all over town to give Larry more names of people to call for contributions.

Nevertheless, the setback at CBS punctured my optimism. We still had to buy two tons of food and enough parachutes to float it all down into Wounded Knee. We did not yet have firm commitments for either an aircraft, a pilot, or a parachute rigger. Too much could still go wrong. We decided that I should make the first contact at ABC News and then take the next plane west to Chicago. Larry would complete arrangements with the media and wire me whatever money he collected. Then he would return to Boston. I left for ABC not expecting to see him again until after the airlift was over.

My reception at ABC was quite different than what I had experienced at their competitors. CBS had been scooping them for over a month on the Wounded Knee story. I told them that I was in contact with people intending to parachute food to the Indians. When I added that they might be convinced to take a camera crew along if their identities were protected, the newsmen jumped at the chance. Other people were called in immediately and they too were enthusiastic. Clearance from the network's operations executives was necessary before making final arrangements, so I asked them to contact Larry later in the day. Once again, things were looking up. I started downtown to catch the airport bus.

Chicago was my home town. I had grown up, gone to school, and later taught at a university there. Many of my old friends were still around, and I planned to ask some of them for help. One, a graying professional gambler ten years my senior, picked me up at O'Hare Airport when I arrived from New York. During a very prosperous period several years before, he had generously supported civil rights and later anti-war activities. On the long drive down to the South Side, I explained what had brought me to town. By coincidence, my friend had a brother-in-law who owned a supermarket. He offered to visit the grocer that night and learn how to purchase a large quantity of food in Chicago's vast wholesale markets without attracting unnecessary attention. We separated after a happy dinner in an old hangout.

From the restaurant, I walked to a telephone booth with pen and notebook at the ready. Boston was first on my list. Marty had the $500 promised the day before. He offered to pay his own way to Chicago to bring me the money and lend a hand with whatever else there was to do. We arranged for him to be on an early flight the next morning. Karl was still at the Medical Aid for Indochina office but had not yet reached all the people in the Boston area he was after. A woman from the staff was helping him, and even though they already had promises for a few hundred dollars, they wanted the rest of that night and the following morning to find other contributors.

Next I called Bob Talbot to check on the DC-3. He had spoken to Jake, the man in Michigan. Jake's plane was in the shop for maintenance. If the work was done on time, we could have it. If not, Jake knew about another DC-3 in Michigan that we might be able to rent. I told Bob that I'd see him early the next morning. If the money was available, we'd wire Jake a deposit.

The critical information was then with Larry. I reached him still at work in New York. The results were wonderful. He had promises for $1,000 beyond the $1,300 we got that morning. Individual donations ranged from twenty dollars to several hundred. They came from people who had quietly supported anti-war activities for a long time—lawyers, physicians, professors, journalists, the children of wealthy families, people in the arts, movie stars, and so forth. All were told something about what was going on, but none was given any names, dates, or staging locations regarding the airlift. We were over the top, past our first major obstacle. With total monies promised already in excess of $3,500, we were almost certain to be able to finance the airlift.

Larry planned to scurry around like a tax collector the next day picking up all of the promised cash. And beyond the money, there was other good news from ABC-TV. Their operations chief approved a camera crew and a correspondent to accompany our flight. Network lawyers were being consulted overnight, and they expected to be ready to make final arrangements with me in the morning.

It was time for stage two of our plan. I called Tim in Boston to check on his skydiving friend in Albuquerque. The Albuquerque man had not been able to locate the Chippewa Indian parachute jumper from North Dakota. Furthermore, he and his wife had questions about his participating directly in the airlift, since as a white person, they were not certain he should take sides in what looked like a conflict between two groups of Indians. He wanted more information about Wounded Knee. I told Tim to call him back and ask him to fly up to Chicago from Albuquerque the next morning at our expense in order to discuss it. Ten minutes later we had his agreement to make the trip.

Finally leaving the phone booth, I walked a few blocks to the apartment of another old friend, Chet. He loaned me his car so I could drive to Midway, the nearby South Side airport, and wire an airline ticket to Albuquerque. By the time I got back, it was close to ten o'clock. Two hours later I was asleep on a mattress on Chet's living room floor.

Thursday, April 12, 1973
Chicago, Illinois

Chet and I woke up before 7:00 a.m. I had recruited his assistance the night before. Once, during a time of financial difficulty, Chet and the woman he lived with agreed to spend six months managing a small grocery store in St. Louis owned by his father. The work was tiresome and boring. The only part of it that Chet genuinely enjoyed was the daily visit to the wholesale market to buy stock for the store. It was an ironic twist, putting him in charge of actually purchasing thousands of pounds of food for the airlift, but he was happy to do it. He never imagined that the commercial skill he acquired in St. Louis would someday be put to use in such a worthwhile way. We laughed over a quick breakfast and rushed off to meet with Bob Talbot before his 9:00 a.m. class.

Talbot taught aviation technology at a small junior college on the Southwest Side of Chicago. To supplement his income, he did flight instruction and charter work after hours and on weekends. We had met three years before when I was also teaching in Chicago. I had gone to Midway Airport one day shopping around for a flight instructor to help me upgrade my pilot's license from private to commercial status. Someone told me about Bob and we started flying together. Soon we became occasional friends, despite wide differences in our interests and life styles.

Talbot had given himself completely to flying. He lived with his four children and a new wife in a small house directly across the street from

Midway. In his mid-thirties, he stood a trim, muscular six-foot-two. His height contributed to an energetic, often overbearing and larger-than-life quality about him that people found difficult to accept. I liked him and the very thorough and spirited way he did things. Flying airplanes was his passion. After his family, it was that and teaching that he loved best in life.

But flying had not always been Bob's career. Before being a pilot, he had been a cop. He studied criminology in college and after graduating was made the chief of police in a small North Carolina town. The police force there consisted of "six full-time officers, six part-time, three dispatchers, a jailer, and a clerk." Bob lasted only as long as it took him to spot the mayor embezzling public funds. Naive and honest as he was, Bob dragged the mayor before a grand jury, lost the case, and was fired. It was then that he took to the air, and in all the years since, he had given up political activity in favor of taking care of his own family.

Like many civilian pilots, Bob started as a crop duster and slowly worked his way up to midnight mail runs. Eventually, he got to fly charters and cargo during the day and soon was hired to captain on a very small commuter airline. But the company floundered and Bob got interested in flight instruction. He pursued his craft with a voracious appetite. He learned to fly everything from Piper Cubs to four-engine transports, then branched out into seaplanes, helicopters, and gliders. He finally came to rest as a college instructor with a stable income and a job that was uniquely suited to his interests.

But Bob had a rebellious side, as well, a soldier of fortune side that would not die off beneath the mantle of his new respectability. That was why he found the airlift to Wounded Knee so appealing, not because of a political commitment to the Indian struggle. To Bob, Indians were "a good cause," but hardly people he would go very far out of his way to help.

At 8:15 a.m. Chet and I walked into the office marked, "Mr. Talbot." Bob had a class 45 minutes later, so we didn't waste any time.

"Yesterday, when you talked to Jake," I asked, "did you tell him why we wanted his DC-3?"

"No," Bob answered, "not yet. We'll have to tell him everything before we take his plane, but yesterday I just said we'd be parachuting stuff out of it. He didn't give a damn what the hell it was, as long as it was legal."

"Well, is it? What did the FAA have to say."

"There's nothing in the regulations to prevent anybody from dropping supplies out of an airplane. They just need permission from the people who own the ground. Of course, if the airspace they fly through is restricted, that's another story. But so far, there are no restrictions over Wounded Knee. So as far as the FAA is concerned, it's legal. I don't know what the marshals or the FBI are going to say though."

"All right," I smiled, rubbing my hands together, "let's call Jake and sew up that DC-3. We got a parachute jumper coming in from Albuquerque at noon. Larry's got a solid $2,300 in New York, probably more. Marty's coming in a couple of hours with another $500 and Karl's going to get more today in Boston."

Bob reached for the phone and dialed the Michigan number. He told Jake exactly what we planned to do and said that if there were no objections, we were ready to come to Michigan immediately, give him a deposit, and take the DC-3. Jake wanted to talk to his lawyer before agreeing. He also had to check with the mechanic to make sure that the aircraft was ready to leave the shop. Jake promised to get back to us within the hour and Bob went off to teach his class.

When Jake called back he had bad news. The lawyer approved the rental, believing that at worst our flight was a borderline case. The problem was the maintenance shop. The mechanic estimated three more days of work before the DC-3 was airworthy. That meant that Jake's plane was out. Before hanging up, he offered to contact the owner of another DC-3 he thought might be available.

Bob returned from class and we discussed the flight to Wounded Knee—navigation, charts, balanced loading, ideal altitude and airspeed for the drop. Finally, Jake called again. The other DC-3 owner would not rent us his aircraft to go to Wounded Knee. He was afraid that we would be arrested and that the government would impound his plane.

The blow was severe, but it was pointless to waste another minute thinking about Jake or his contact. Bob got back on the telephone and called all the other DC-3 owners he knew. There were three. The first two had already committed their aircraft for flights in the next few days. The third refused to rent his plane unless his own company pilot flew it. When we told him where we planned to go, and for what purpose, he said, "Forget it," and hung up. It was over. Ten minutes after Jake's call, we had to face the inevitable—there just wasn't going to be any DC-3.

Looking at Bob, I asked, "What's the next largest twin-engine cargo plane we can get, a Beech 18?"

"Yep."

"What'll it haul?"

"Oh, you can figure about 2,000 pounds of cargo at 60 or 70 cents a mile."

"Half the payload of a DC-3 at half the cost. Hell, its a lot better than nothing. Let's get one."

Bob spent the next hour on the telephone while Chet and I paced up and down his small office. Beech 18s were more common than DC-3s, but many of the owners Bob called were out. Others had planes in the shop for maintenance work. One, in Milwaukee, did have an available craft, but when Bob told him where we were going, the owner made an impassioned speech about his loyalty to President Nixon and said no. By that time, we were all very exasperated.

"Look," Bob finally said, "why don't you put the whole thing off for three or four days? Then you can get Jake's DC-3, or one of these Beech 18s."

"No, damn it. The people in Wounded Knee needed this food three days ago, not three days from now. How do I know if Jake's plane is going to be ready in three days? That's just what the mechanic is saying right now. Somewhere there's got to be an airplane we can get. We're leaving tomorrow and that's all there is to it."

"Well, what if there is no airplane? What's going to happen if I sit here all day on this goddamn telephone and I don't turn up anything?"

I didn't know how to answer him. The airlift, which had become such a tangible reality, suddenly started slipping through my fingers. I did a few more turns around the office as Bob and Chet sat waiting. Then, in a flash, I had it.

"Listen, you guys," I exclaimed, slapping my hand down on a tabletop, "whatever we can bring to Wounded Knee in one big plane, we can bring in a half-a-dozen little ones!"

It was a genuine solution. I painted an elaborate word-picture—a squadron of single-engine aircraft flying in formation through the skies of South Dakota making a coordinated, simultaneous parachute drop over Wounded Knee. But Bob immediately understood that it was, in fact, a very sensible picture. The little planes were numerous, easy to rent and easy to fly. Each could carry several hundred pounds of cargo. The main problem with the idea was in recruiting enough pilots.

Chet and I left for the airport to pick up the people flying into Chicago to meet us. Bob kept trying to get a Beech 18. The big twin was still easier to deal with than a flock of small planes. Also, it was the only way there would be enough room to take along a TV camera crew. If Bob could not find a Beech 18 by dinnertime, we would change our plans and round up pilots and small planes that night. In any case, we still planned to be airborne and on our way west by the next day.

Marty was waiting for us at the United ticket counter at Midway Airport. He gave me the $500 he had just brought from Boston. But the Albuquerque skydiver was arriving soon at Chicago's other airport, O'Hare, twenty miles across town, so we hurried north. When the Albuquerque jet landed, we were waiting for it. None of us knew what the jumper looked like, only his name, Jim Stewart. But as the long line of passengers filed off the plane, our man was unmistakable. He was in his late twenties, sunburned, slender, about six feet tall, wearing faded blue jeans and a blue ski jacket. He had longish blond hair and a closely cropped blond beard. Strapped over one shoulder there was a bright red bag that looked like a parachute pack. I walked up to him and said, "Jim?" He replied, "Bill?" and immediately we were deep in conversation. Not until several minutes later did I realize that James Stewart's western drawl and the way he looked and walked, all reminded me of the movie actor of the same name.

The four of us made our way to a table in the crowded airport coffee shop. I briefed Marty and Jim on the problems we encountered locating a big aircraft and suggested that we temporarily limit our planning to the delivery of 2,000 pounds of food. Jim asked more about the situation at Wounded Knee. Marty, who had been there only a few days before, began a long explanation of the occupation as a conflict between Indian people and the federal government, not as a struggle between two equally legitimate Indian factions on the Pine Ridge Reservation.

With Marty talking to Jim, and Chet eagerly listening, I slid into the nearest telephone booth. It was 1:00 p.m. in New York and I found Larry back at the office he had been using. He was recuperating after a mad chase around the New York metropolitan area. At 8:00 a.m. he hailed a taxi on Manhattan's West Side. When the driver stopped, Larry asked if he was free the entire morning. For four hours, Larry went in and out of apartment buildings, homes, and offices. Each time he emerged, the increasingly astonished driver saw Larry stuffing another envelope into his pocket. When it was over, Larry was clutching $2,650 in cash promised the day before by airlift contributors. I congratulated him for the remarkable performance.

But Larry had bad news as well. ABC-TV network lawyers would not permit one of their news teams to fly with us. It probably would make no difference because of our own inability to get a DC-3, or perhaps even a Beech 18. We had to fall back on the printed media. Larry, anticipating this, was already at work calling various newspaper reporters. There were several at liberal papers like the New York *Times* or the Washington *Post* whose coverage of past anti-war events had been sympathetic and fair. Hopefully, one or more would want to go on the airlift, even if it meant flying in small, single-engine planes. But the fast-breaking Watergate story and Nixon's stepped-up bombing of Cambodia were occupying everyone's attention and making reporters difficult to find.

I asked Larry to fly to Chicago instead of going home to Boston. Everything was still too uncertain, and I wanted his help with whatever improvising I had to do that evening and the next morning. A pacifist friend of ours was arranging for Larry to see a New York woman who was considering giving $2,000 to the airlift. After he spoke with her and successfully arranged for a reporter or two to accompany us to Wounded Knee, he would meet me in Chicago.

Next, I called Karl and the woman he was working with at the Medical Aid for Indochina office. They had collected another $2,000 in Boston. But it was to be used only in an emergency. I promised to return it first out of any surplus and asked them to wire it immediately to the Western Union office in Chicago. Finally, I called my friend the gambler and got a concise report, via his brother-in-law the grocer, on where to purchase large quantities of food cheaply and inconspicuously.

Meanwhile, back in the airport coffee shop, Marty persuaded Jim to work as the parachute rigger on the airlift. It didn't take much convincing; Jim had come quite inclined to do it. I rented two station wagons, and the four of us split up. Marty and Chet, armed with the information I had just received, went off in one wagon to buy a ton of food. Jim and I prepared to go purchase parachutes. From my quick telephone survey earlier in Boston, I had learned that a typical parachute shop normally carried a good supply of cargo chutes. But Chicago was not Boston, and when Jim and I began calling stores in the general vicinity we quickly discovered that we had another crisis. None of the usual shops had any full-canopy parachutes for sale. Skydiving parachutes, with big holes and slits for directional control, were plentiful, but difficult to use for cargo.

We finally found an advertisement for an army surplus outlet that sold secondhand parachutes, and we drove right over. It was an enormous delapidated warehouse. The unshaven owner, an older man whose stomach bubbled out from under a dirty T-shirt and rolled down in front of his pants, led us around in semidarkness past huge stacks of nondescript junk. Each item was replicated thousands of times—helmets piled from floor to ceiling, barrels and barrels of belt buckles, boots as far as the eye could see. Finally, in the back, we came to a mountain of jumbled cloth and string. The old proprietor took another chew on an unlit cigar stub and nodded with a smile at his stock of parachutes. Jim and I grabbed a few off the bottom and pulled them free.

One by one, we discovered perfect canopies, but every one had its lines cut halfway down. In an indignant voice, the gruff old man told us that the only customers for used parachutes were hippie campers who made gigantic circular tents out of the colorful nylon canopies. In the best tradition of his trade, the owner was cutting off the "unnecessary" lines and selling them separately as used rope. Jim and I walked out disappointed and groaning, but laughing to ourselves at the same time. The proprietor shouted after us, asking how we were "fixed for mosquito netting." "Fine," I called back, "but we could use a gross of bulletproof vests!"

After more searching we found a parachute shop that had two full-canopy chutes for sale. We needed ten. Jim started a long discussion with the salesman about techniques of dropping cargo—the proper use of fasteners, opening shock on the lines, the design of cargo webbing, and so forth. Feeling useless, I gave Jim money for a cab and told him to meet me later at the downtown Western Union office where I had to pick up money being wired from Boston.

Before driving off, I stopped at a corner tavern and climbed into another telephone booth. Bob Talbot had still not been able to nail down a Beech 18. Larry Levin, when I reached him, was frantic. He had been on the phone all afternoon chasing after reporters in New York and Washington.

"Now listen, we're really in trouble," he told me, the tension in his voice all too evident. "The *Times* correspondent in Washington is very interested, but he says he's too busy with this Watergate thing to leave town. The *Post* has a guy who's spent a month at Wounded Knee. He wants to go with you, but his editor says no because he just got back a few days ago."

"What about the *Times* man in Chicago?" I interrupted. "He writes pretty good stuff."

"Yes, right, I know. Well, he's on the road driving back from Detroit. We'll get him tonight. There are a few others to call tonight, too. Meantime, I've only got one good lead. I sort of ran out of names, and then I remembered that young guy at the Boston *Globe*, the one who's been writing those stories on Viet Nam that always include the latest bomb tonnage figures. You know who I mean, Tom Oliphant."

"Right," I answered. "His stories are good. No one else has been printing any of that stuff."

"Well, I made some calls to Boston to check up on him. He's got a good reputation. People think he's trustworthy. Then, I called him and he said he wants to come. He works out of the *Globe*'s Washington bureau and he's got to check with his editors in Boston first. He's scheduled to call me back in an hour or so."

"Okay, I'll be at Talbot's in an hour and a half. Bye."

I left the tavern and drove downtown, suddenly realizing that it was after 3:00 p.m. and the banks were closed. If Western Union didn't have $2,000 in cash to give me, they would write a check that I couldn't cash until 9:00 a.m. the next morning. Sure enough, when I reached the front of the line in the aging telegraph office, the man in the cage stamped out a check, apologizing because he lacked sufficient funds to honor Karl's wire from Boston with cash.

It was another setback. We were probably going to need the money that night to put a deposit down on an aircraft. Disappointed, there was nothing I could do but wait for the check. I glanced up at the long line in front of the next window. Most of the people in it were rather poor. But toward the rear stood two black men dressed in the ruffled shirts and colorful high-fashioned dress suits that were the style among ghetto coke dealers and well-to-do pimps. One clutched a wad of twenties too thick for his pocket. I slid off to the side and waited until it was their turn at bat.

"Say, brother, ah wanna wire this $3,000 to ma' man in Kansas City."

The solution was obvious. Reclaiming the front of my own line, I indicated the transaction taking place at the next window and asked the teller to cash my check. He saw the logic of the request, reached into the adjacent cash drawer just after his colleague deposited the large stack of twenties, and counted me out a hundred of them. There were several other customers in the small room, and the irony of this peculiar transaction escaped no one. The depositor of the money was especially affected. His eyes darted suspiciously back and forth between me and his money, which was now mine, as we all tried to get a grip on the laws of credit that had allowed such a strange thing to happen.

Finally, the tension broke and he flashed me a wide grin. "Ah sure do hope you gonna enjoy alla ma money, there."

I stopped counting and looked up with a smile. "Not just me, my friend, a whole lot of people are going to enjoy your money."

Jim's cab arrived fifteen minutes later. I was waiting outside, having just drawn up a record of the airlift's income and expenditures up to that moment. We loaded the two parachutes and a lot of cargo webbing into the station wagon and drove south to Bob Talbot's house. Somewhat later, Chet and Marty arrived in the other station wagon which was sagging under the weight of the food they had just purchased. With the help of Bob's two teen-age sons, we carried it all in and stacked it in a corner of his basement.

Exhausted, we got a round of cold drinks, and under the direction of Bob's wife, Cindy, we all prepared dinner for ourselves. With four guests added to their six-member family, it was a loud and crowded meal. Everyone admired the balanced diet that Chet and Marty had selected for the airlift. There were huge sacks of flour and beans, 50-pound bags of onions, carrots, and other vegetables, boxes of butter and cheese, crates of fruit, 155 pounds of ham, and much more. Chet had insisted on getting a bag of peanuts that was almost as big as a person.

Having a literal ton of food piled in the basement beneath us gave the airlift a new reality. Eating dinner on top of all of it while Indian people were starving at Wounded Knee reminded us of the urgency of our mission. Serious problems remained. Bob had completely struck out in his attempts to get a Beech 18. We had no choice except to revise our plans and go in with a fleet of single-engine planes. After discussing it, the new alternative did not seem bad at all. Marty was skeptical, but the rest of us guessed that if a small armada flew up in formation, we might get even more press coverage than with a big plane—and besides, we would still be delivering the same amount of food.

But we had to find airplanes and pilots that very night. One way or another, we were determined to take off early the next morning. Bob recommended the largest single-engine planes, six-passenger rather than four-passenger models. Taking all but two seats out, there would be room for 700-800 pounds of cargo in each one. I was qualified to pilot such aircraft, even though I had never flown anything quite so heavy. Unexpectedly, Jim Stewart, the parachute rigger, told us that he could fly too, and had a private pilot's license. So with me and Jim as definite pilots and Bob qualified but still undecided about participating, we had 2½ birds in our fledgling air force.

Bob agreed to arrange for the rental of several planes and to inquire among his pilot friends if any would fly with us. Meanwhile, our big problem was parachutes. We had bought only two that afternoon. Jim came with another, thinking he would wear it while standing next to the open door of an airborne DC-3. Bob owned one which he immediately donated. That gave us four. We needed ten to make a minimum drop of 2000 pounds. Jim said that his wife could probably round up a few more from skydiving friends in Albuquerque and airfreight them up to Chicago. Luckily, there was a midnight flight from New Mexico that arrived at Midway at 5:00 a.m. Jim telephoned to make the necessary arrangements and Bob added parachutes to the long list of things he had to make calls for later that evening.

At the same time, Larry called from New York. He was at LaGuardia, about to board a jet for Chicago. Tom Oliphant, the Boston *Globe* reporter, was at Washington National Airport also about to board a Chicago flight. The two of them planned to meet at O'Hare. Larry had seen the wealthy anti-war movement backer late that afternoon. She gave him $2,000. So, thanks to Larry, we had press and we had money. I asked him how he felt about the airlift becoming a fleet of small planes instead of one big one. He thought it would be harder to organize and carry out, but agreed that the morale and publicity impact might be greater.

While I was on the telephone, Marty and Chet returned with twenty-five heavy-duty army duffel bags and several hundred feet of thick nylon rope. Bob's two older boys had shown them where to shop. As we started packing the mountain of food in the basement into the duffel bags, Bob took over the telephone. In a short time he was able to make preliminary arrangements for us to rent at least three single-engine, six-passenger aircraft, the number we would need to haul the 2,000 pounds of food we already had. Somewhat later, Bob announced that two pilot friends of his who occasionally accepted "unusual" flying assignments were on their way over and were willing to talk to us about "a job."

Packing the food was slow and difficult. Fifty-pound sacks of grain or vegetables are not easy to work with or stuff tightly into other containers. Bob took a break from his telephoning and sat down with Jim to talk about cargo nets. The salesman in the parachute shop had convinced Jim that duffel bags were good to use but were not strong enough to attach directly to the parachutes. When the big canopies first filled with air, the opening shock would be severe enough to burst even the thick duffel bag cloth. With pens, papers, and rulers spread out before them, Jim and Bob designed a cargo net made of crisscrossed lengths of tough cloth webbing or rope sewn together into cylindrical shapes and sized to hold two or three duffel bags each, about a 200-pound package. With the nets gathered at the top, a metal D-ring could be used to attach them directly to the parachute lines.

Bob dug into a storage bin and came out with an old relic of a sewing machine. He and Jim figured out the different lengths of webbing and rope needed to make the cargo nets. Then, with the sewing machine whirling, Bob started to work on the first of at least ten nets. Jim turned to designing parachute deployment bags. These fragile cloth packs would contain the folded parachutes and be torn open at the critical moment by a ripcord attached to the airplane.

Once he had the bag size and design worked out on paper, Jim calculated the number of yards of lightweight cotton cloth needed to make ten deployment bags. Marty went to purchase the cloth with one of Bob's boys before the neighborhood stores closed for the night. The rest of us continued cutting, sewing, packing, tying, and stuffing. There was more work to do than we realized. But we still expected to finish late that night, be on our way west in the morning, and make the drop at the very next sunset or sunrise.

At 8:30 p.m., Bob's two pilot friends arrived. They were professionals trained several years before by Bob himself and more recently his colleagues and friends. They were both in their late twenties, medium height, slender, and neatly dressed. One was white, the other black. Neither knew anything about the airlift. Bob took me and the two of them up to his living room, closed the door, and introduced us. With a slight nod, he indicated that I was to take it from there.

I asked the two pilots if they were aware of what was going on at Wounded Knee. They said they were. Then I asked each how he felt about what the Indians were trying to accomplish. Both were sympathetic. Next I asked if they supported the use of arms in such a situation. We were playing a cat-and-mouse game. I wanted to draw them out as much as possible, and they, not knowing who I was, wanted to stay cool and hold back as much as possible. It took a little time and a certain amount of cageyness, but after a while I grew more confident in their sincerity. Also, it was soon clear that they were not the sort of people easily shocked by a suggestion that they involve themselves in a project of questionable legality.

Cautiously I explained that some people I knew in another city were planning an airlift to Wounded Knee and were looking for pilots. Their faces relaxed into smiles of interest and favorable nods. I felt more sure of them and revealed the truth, describing the packing work taking place under them in Bob's basement. We talked about the situation on the reservation. They asked a lot of questions about the Indians and about our own operational plans. They were interested in money, but in the end, I said I had nothing to offer them except an opportunity to do good work. Both leaned back in comfortable overstuffed chairs, eyes glancing thoughtfully at each other and over to Bob. I sensed they wanted me out of there and told them to talk it over by themselves while I resumed work in the basement.

Twenty minutes later they came downstairs with Bob. The white pilot wished us luck, but declined to help. He had a charter flight scheduled in two days and didn't want to risk missing it and losing his job. The black pilot, Billy Wright, wanted to talk more. We went upstairs together and got a couple of beers. It didn't take very long. We liked each other immediately. Billy was smart and game and he seemed to be the kind of person who could think fast on the run. His flying credentials were superb. Besides coming with a high recommendation from Bob, he was a fully qualified single- and multi-engine pilot, airline transport and instrument rated, with several thousand hours in the air. If Bob decided not to come, Billy would make a perfect flight leader.

After a short conversation, Billy slapped his knee, told me with a laugh that he would really enjoy helping the Indians, and said that I should count him in. He was busy later that night and had to leave. Also, the next day there was an early appointment with a flight student that he could not break. When he finished at 9:30 a.m., he agreed to come back to Bob's house and be ready to go. Counting Jim and me, we had three committed pilots. With money on the way from New York, we were past the second major obstacle in our overall plan.

After another half hour of packing and sewing in the basement, Larry walked in with the reporter from the Boston *Globe*, Tom Oliphant. I introduced them to everybody. Larry was happy to see food already purchased and being packed. He quietly handed me close to $5,000 in cash and then pitched in to help Jim and the others sew cargo nets together. Oliphant was a slim six-footer in his late twenties. His shoulder-length brown hair was longer than one might have expected on the head of a Washington correspondent for one of the nation's major news-papers. His clothing was equally unusual. Beneath a business suit, dress shirt, and tie, I found myself staring at a pair of threadbare gym shoes. I took him aside for a private talk.

It began somewhat formally. I told him that many of us in Boston appreciated his informative stories on the continuing war in Viet Nam and Cambodia. He said that he had followed our work at Medical Aid for Indochina with equal regard. Both of us were anxious to establish as soon as possible the terms of our agreement, in order to avoid misunderstand-ings. Oliphant asked what besides our names I did not want him to mention in his articles on the airlift. I said all locations, including Chicago and any other cities we might pass through on the way to or from Wounded Knee, as well as the organizational affiliations of any of the participants, such as Medical Aid for Indochina. He assured me that those conditions were agreeable and that he would abide by them. I took him at his word. His reputation was good and his career as a journalist depended in part on having access to stories like the airlift. If he broke his word, he would quickly lose that access.

Oliphant hesitantly inquired about our cargo. Were we bringing any guns or ammunition? He apologized for having to ask again since Larry had already told him no. I said that we were not, but that we didn't want him to take our word for it. We expected him to inspect each duffel bag packed that night. I made no secret of the fact that we intended to use his testimony as an insurance policy if we were arrested and charged with gunrunning.

It was close to ten o'clock. Larry walked across the street to one of the hangars and used a telephone there to try and recruit more reporters for the trip. Oliphant went along, volunteering to contact some of his friends. Back at the house, Bob was still on and off his own telephone trying to find more pilots and parachutes. Jim, overseeing the rigging work in the basement, was beginning to get nervous about the time. Only one cargo net was complete. If more people didn't help with the sewing, Jim warned that we would be up all night, and then some.

The doorbell rang, and a moment later Bob came downstairs followed by a wild-eyed character with foot-long curly black hair standing up on end all around his head—and a bushy black beard to match. Short, thin, and bursting with energy, he was in his late twenties and he looked like an electrified hippy. Given who Bob was, I was surprised to hear him introduce the newcomer as a friend. His name was Strobe. He was a Viet Nam vet and he had two parachutes slung over his shoulder. Jim sprang to his feet and checked the chutes. They were perfect. Within minutes Strobe was hard at work with the rest of us putting the complicated cargo nets together.

When Larry and Oliphant got back from their calls, they had two more reporters who wanted to fly with the airlift: one from the New York *Times*, the other from the Chicago *Sun-Times*. Meetings were arranged for early the next morning. Next I went out and called the woman in Boston who had written our letter to the Indians—the letter we would pack into the food parcels and later release to the press. I scribbled down the draft she read to me and returned to Bob's house to type it up. By that time, there were seven of us working in the small basement, in addition to Bob's family. The place was taking on the air of a crowded makeshift assembly plant, with people, equipment, and food scattered chaotically around the room. When Jim complained again about the late hour and the enormous amount of work still left to do, Bob got up and walked out mumbling something about getting more help.

Bob returned fifteen minutes later with three women: a mother and her two grown daughters. They were neighbors. For an uncomfortable moment, they stood silently in the doorway staring at us. Bob announced that they had volunteered to help with the sewing. I was furious with him. We were in Chicago's Southwest Side, a white, working-class neighborhood famous for its Nixon supporters and its blind prejudice against anybody darker than a good suntan. At eleven o'clock at night, Bob had waltzed into the home of people he only knew casually, told them all about the airlift, and asked them to help with something we were not even sure was legal.

As the three volunteers stood there, I realized that the basement was full of an assortment of characters closely fitting the stereotypes women like them were taught to shun. Of the seven of us, not counting Bob and his family, three were bearded and all had hair considerably longer than what was proper on the Southwest Side. Besides, the way some of us were dressed must have seemed downright bizarre in the context of that neighborhood. I didn't know what was going to happen, but I did know that Bob had acted on his own and had flagrantly broken security.

But Bob had a better sense of his neighbors than I did. The three women hesitated only a moment and then cheerfully waded into our frightful-looking assembly, stepping over and around the confused tangle of duffel bags, cargo nets, parachutes, 50-pound sacks of onions and other outsized containers of food. Friendly, warm, talking to each of us as though we were all red-blooded American examples of the boy next door, they gathered around the ancient sewing machine at the table where Jim was working. The mother told us that she had two modern sewing machines at home. And besides her two daughters who each wanted to help, her own mother was also waiting back at the house to find out what she could do.

It was agreed that the neighbors would take on the job of sewing together the parachute deployment bags. Jim gave them the large roll of bright orange cloth that Marty had purchased earlier. He explained how to construct the bags so that the ripcords could easily tear them open. The three women assured us that they could handle the job, and if need be, they promised to stay up all night to finish it. They took the orange cloth and left Bob's basement on a wave of good will and friendly laughter. The cynics among us stared after them, speechless. Three generations of working class women from a redneck neighborhood in Chicago were about to go to work at 11:00 p.m. to help a bunch of radicals and hippies help another bunch of redskins who were locked in a shoot-out with official United States cops and FBI agents!

"Talbot," I growled, turning on him as soon as they were out the door, "how the hell did that happen? Who are those people?"

"They're just neighbors," he explained, not hearing the astonishment and indignation in my voice.

"But how'd you know they'd be willing to help? What are they, the neighborhood revolutionaries? What did you say to them?"

"Jesus, I don't know what their political beliefs are. They're just a decent family that lives down the block. You know, Mr. and Mrs. Average American. They've got six kids. He drives a fuel oil truck and has a second job at night. I just went over there, told them what we were doing, and said we needed people who could mend straight and who could keep the whole thing to themselves because there might be other people who would be against it.

"She said, well, sure they wanted to help, they knew about Wounded Knee from the news, and what worthier cause was there than the Indians anyway? So, I said, fine, and brought her back, and her daughters said they wanted to come, too."

I wanted to criticize him, but I couldn't bring myself to do it. I looked over at Larry and shrugged, feeling that somehow Bob had done a wonderful thing. In any case, the incident left us optimistic and happy. We returned to work cheerfully struggling with the lines and the tangle of cargo nets. We all had a firm sense that we were going to make it, that the airlift was going to succeed.

As the hours passed, we talked about how our little formation flight would look as it came in over Wounded Knee and how good the Indians below would feel when they saw such dramatic support. We also gleefully imagined the disappointment of the marshals and FBI agents when the food came floating in past their blockade. Someone thought the parachutes might even force them to give up the very tactic of starving the Indians out. If so, that would be the airlift's biggest contribution.

Midnight came and went. There was no longer any question that it would take the entire night, and more, to finish making the cargo nets and rigging the load. Chet said goodbye and went home to sleep. He had an early appointment the next morning. The rest of us—Bob, Marty, Jim, Larry, Oliphant, Strobe, and I—settled in for a long night. We each kept busy at a specific task, and in the midst of the jumbled lines and piles of food bags, some kind of order prevailed. Occasionally, the neighbor women walked happily into the chaos to check with Jim on a detail in constructing the parachute packs. The basement overflowed with community spirit.

At one point, working next to Jim and already feeling like he was an old friend, I realized that beyond his expertise as a skydiver, I knew nothing about him.

"What do you do in Albuquerque when you're not jumping out of airplanes?" I asked, still struggling with the cargo net I was putting together.

"Well," he answered, in his western drawl, "up until last week I was teachin' fifth grade."

"A teacher!" I was quite surprised. Sitting there in blue jeans with his suntanned cheeks rising out of a closely cropped blond beard, Jim looked more like a person who worked outdoors, even though it was clear from his conversation that he was well educated. "How did you get to be a teacher?"

"Oh, I guess it goes back to 1968, when I got out of the Air Force. I went to Rochester, New York, to be with Peggy, and we got married. But after a bit, we both wanted to get out of there. When the summer of 1970 came, we packed up all our stuff and took off for a two-month camping tour around the Rocky Mountains. Our plan was to look for teaching jobs as we traveled.

"But that summer there was no longer a shortage of teachers. Suddenly you needed a teaching certificate instead of just a college degree in order to get a job. Well, we heard about this experimental program for training teachers back home at the University of North Dakota. It didn't look like the usual "School of Education" bullshit, so we moved to Grand Forks and we both enrolled for a year.

"It was a good program. Peggy and I spent all our time working, trying to find out about education, figuring out how to work with kids, observing different classrooms and teachers. For a while, we watched a classroom on the Cannon Ball Indian Reservation. That was probably my first real contact with Indian problems. There were a lot of Indians in our program, too, Chippewas and Sioux who were going to teach on the reservation.

"At the end of that year we tried to find jobs in places that we wanted to live, like around the Rocky Mountains. But toward the end of the summer, we still hadn't found even one job. We were getting ready to go rent a little cabin in Montana and I was going to see how many deer I could shoot for the winter."

Jim was laughing heartily, but it wasn't hard to imagine this young James Stewart striding into the Montana hills to do just that.

"Well, anyway," he continued, "this guy from Albuquerque called up one day and said, 'I'd like to offer you a job.' I said, 'You would? I'll take it!' So, we left right away and that's where we've been ever since, over a year and a half."

"But, wait a minute," I insisted, "you said before that you stopped teaching a week ago. What happened? This is only April."

"I know. I got into a hassle with the principal. The Indian and Chicano kids in the school were getting a raw deal and I let people know about it. One thing led to another, and the principal said he was not going to renew my contract next year. I could have fought it, and I think I could have kept my job, but I didn't. I was so fed up with the school at the time that I just told him to go to hell and left right then."

"What're you going to do now?"

"Well," Jim answered, putting down the webbing he was sewing together, "I got to start making some money soon. Peggy is going to have a baby this coming summer. I've kinda had this idea for a long time to start a summer camping trip service for kids. You know, take them up into the high mountains for a week or so at a time and teach them survival skills and stuff like that. Damn, I'd love to do that. I'm going to try to put ads in some of the eastern newspapers. Maybe I can get a few customers and build the thing up over the years."

"You said you were in the Air Force. Is that where you learned to parachute jump?"

"No. There's no application for jumping in the Air Force. It's only an emergency procedure. I started jumping before then, back in 1965. A couple of buddies of mine started. I just thought it was a challenge, so I did it, too. I guess I really got into it. I've been doing it ever since."

Jim was being a little modest. He had jumped over 600 times and had worked as an instructor and knew a good deal about parachute rigging. He was a frequent competitor in skydiving contests and was considered quite good. Eventually, I would hear him talk lovingly about diving out of an airplane onto the top of a cloud and staying in free fall until he popped through the bottom.

"What was it like in the Air Force? You must have gone through a lot of changes between there and here."

"Most of the changes," Jim answered, "actually took place *in* the Air Force, not after it. I was at the University of North Dakota in 1965 when they held their first teach-in on the Viet Nam war. Me and some other guys organized a pro-U.S. rally and went over to harass the anti-war people. Your friend Tim at Medical Aid for Indochina was one of them.

"I was in the ROTC then, and in 1968 I joined the Air Force as a 2nd Lieutenant and started pilot training, you know, to fly fighter planes or bombers. I guess what changed me as much as anything were some of the guys I met in pilot training. Most of the instructors had been to Viet Nam and they talked a lot about killing people and strafing.

"There was one instructor there who was a Medal of Honor winner. He was very religious, a real fundamentalist type. But he was very proud of what he had done to win the medal. He talked about it all the time, you know, how he had bombed a radar site in North Viet Nam, strafing and killing, seeing people running around and shooting them down.

"I asked him, 'Well, what did you think while you were doing that? How did you feel about it?' He said, 'Well, it was my job.' The way he talked about it, that kind of detachment, really frightened me. I'll tell you, the Air Force doesn't build up that racist 'gook' or 'slopehead' stuff the way the Army and Marines do. They're just sending you over there to do your job. You're a professional.

"You know, you're supposed to be very detached from the real meaning of the whole thing. It's not really a person down there, it's just a target. Well, no amount of Air Force training was going to convince me that a living person is anything but just that—a living person. So, I was in trouble then. I knew they were training me to go to Viet Nam to fly combat missions, and I knew that I didn't want to go. I couldn't decide what to do when I got my orders to Viet Nam, whether I was going to refuse them or what."

I glanced over at Jim. "But if you refused," I interrupted, "wouldn't that have meant a court-martial and a jail sentence?"

"Oh, yeah, for sure. But I just didn't want to go kill anybody. What was going on in Viet Nam wasn't worth my risking my life. And it sure wasn't worth my going over there to kill a bunch of farmers and country people caught in the middle of all that bullshit. I mean, the whole thing was totally wrong. Ho Chi Minh probably had a good claim to be the legitimate head of state, and it was just so obvious all along that the dictators in South Viet Nam were really puppets of the U.S.

"Anyway, refusing orders was a decision I never had to make. One day me and another student pilot went off the base to some civilian town down there in Oklahoma. The whole thing had become too much to take, and we got ourselves really drunk.

"Somehow, the two of us wound up getting into a fight in a pizza parlor and really tearing the place apart. I don't know how that happened. I had never done anything like that before. I guess it was partly the military. I mean, you spend every day going to classes in how to kill people, so eventually violence seems like the normal way of doing things.

"Well, they kicked us out of pilot training and all my worries were over. We were put in limbo, you know, restricted to quarters. I sat like that for four months. Then they discharged me for being unfit to be an officer.

Can you imagine that shit? If you go and blow apart a couple of hundred people in their homes with high explosives and flaming gasoline, they give you a medal. But don't dare break a couple of chairs in a pizza parlor or the brass will think you're a barbarian!"

"What happened after your discharge? Is that when you went out to Rochester?"

"Yep. Peggy was working at the university there. We got married and I found myself a job as a management trainee. In a bank! I don't know how I did it, but I lasted eight months at that job. Then, I guess it was in November 1969, they had the first big national moratorium against the war. I told my boss at the bank that I was going to take the day off, you know, that it was part of a one-day strike to end the war. Well, it totally freaked him out. He just couldn't believe it. It was beyond his comprehension.

"I went around that day and I met a lot of people who were doing anti-war work in the community. Peggy introduced me to the anti-war types at the university, but they kind of turned me off. So I got involved with these community folks and started going to meetings all the time. You know, meetings that went on all night—What are we going to do? How are we going to organize this demonstration? What are we going to write in that leaflet? On and on.

"For a while I worked on a newspaper, the Rochester Journal. It wasn't exactly an underground paper because it was written for community people, not students or hippies. But it was anti-war and it was part of the political movement in Rochester. Then I administered the Rochester Free School for a few months. We tried to make it into an information center and meeting place for people, as well as a school.

"We did okay for a time. But then Peggy started getting tired of her job and I was becoming very frustrated with what I was doing. Partly it was the people I was working with, but partly it was just that political work gets really frustrating after a while—all those meetings and hassles. So, that's when we left Rochester and wound up in that teacher training program in North Dakota, in the summer of 1970."

When Jim finished, I looked up nodding sympathetically. It was good to hear that along with the many differences between us, there were similarities as well. I was glad that he was relaxed enough to be so open in telling his story. Exhausted, we all worked on through the night in Bob's crowded basement, talking to each other and becoming friends. Despite our efforts, though, the rigging work seemed endless. Hour after hour went by and still we didn't finish.

6

Dennis Banks:
The American Indian
Movement

"Then Long Hair [General Custer] came. . . . They say we massacred him, but he would have massacred us had we not defended ourselves and fought to the death. Our first impulse was to escape with our squaws and papooses, but we were so hemmed in that we had to fight."

—Tashunka Witco (Crazy Horse)
Medicine Man and Chief,
Oglala Sioux, 1877.

Dennis Banks is not what white officials and bureaucrats would call a "good Indian." In fact, Banks is an ex-con. In 1964, he served a year in the Minnesota State Penitentiary. The charge was burglary. Shortly after his release, he was re-arrested for forgery and he did another six months. Then, after a second release, he was charged with a parole violation and sentenced to one more year in the maximum security prison at Stillwater. By that time, Banks had graduated into the category of "habitual criminal."

But Dennis Banks never went back to prison. Instead, in 1968, he helped start the American Indian Movement, AIM. As one of its leaders, he played a central role five years later in the seizure and occupation of Wounded Knee. When the confrontation ended in May 1973, the government tried to put him behind bars once again. The U.S. Department of Justice secured an eleven-count federal indictment against Banks that

110

included charges of possessing illegal weapons, conspiracy to commit arson, and deadly assault on federal officers. The eleven felonies carried jail sentences totaling 180 years. After a nine-month trial in 1974, a federal judge dismissed the charges against Banks, ruling that FBI agents had violated innumerable laws during their investigations and were guilty of sufficient "misconduct" to preclude a fair trial.

During the occupation of Wounded Knee, the press projected Banks and a handful of others as the real "instigators" of the confrontation. Another one of these "instigators," Russell Means, was catapulted overnight into a position of national visibility by the media. Although Russell Means could hardly be described as someone liked or respected by the press, he was, nevertheless, occasionally portrayed as "reasonable," in contrast to the more militant Banks.

Eventually, the media stereotyped Banks as the head of a small faction of violent fanatics within the larger group occupying Wounded Knee. This portrayal was drawn more sharply when Banks alone among the Indian leadership refused to sign the ill-fated April 5 agreement, arguing that it was unworkable and that it constituted an abject surrender of Oglala Sioux objectives.

Several months after the Wounded Knee confrontation, while still under the shadow of the federal felony indictment, Dennis Banks relaxed long enough to describe the various forces that had brought him to the little village in South Dakota. He wore a plain sport shirt and western-style pants. Long, black braids hung down on either side of his head, tied at the end with strips of rawhide and bright green cloth. He was clearly proud of his Indian blood; dark-skinned, thin-lipped, he looked his age, 41, but was lean and sturdy.

The story Banks told went back to June 9, 1972, the day a great flood struck Rapid City, South Dakota. He and other AIM representatives arrived there the next day bringing flood relief supplies to the sizeable Indian community. Fearing that Indians would be ignored in the larger relief effort, they helped start a coalition of Indian people to coordinate various relief projects. Substantial amounts of money were due to come into the area from the U.S. Department of Housing and Urban Development (HUD). AIM warned that if Indians were not represented on the agencies that received these funds, relief would not reach the Indian families in need of it.

Eventually, Banks moved on, relying on Rapid City AIM members to continue the coordinating effort. Three months later, in September 1972, he was hard at work with other AIM people in Denver, planning the Trail of Broken Treaties. In the months before the presidential election, "Trail" caravans traveled to 33 reservations educating Indians about their rights under the 371 treaties signed by the U.S. government and the various native tribes of North America. AIM encouraged Indian people to come with them, en masse, to Washington in order to force a discussion of these treaty rights with the appropriate government officials.

"When we organized the Trail of Broken Treaties," Banks explained, "it was our intent to go to Washington in order to set up a week-long series of meetings with various government agencies. The occupation of the BIA building came as a result of the government people refusing to talk to us for three straight days. We were not only ignored for those three days, but we had no place to sleep.

"HUD was supposed to provide us with tents for 400 people. But the chief of the Bureau of Land Management, which at that time was over the BIA, told all the government agencies not to give us any kind of assistance. We didn't know that, of course, until we got to Washington with all those people. So we didn't know we were going to occupy the building until it actually happened."

After the highly publicized BIA building occupation, which included major property damage and the "theft" of files and Indian art, the Trail of Broken Treaties left Washington, bitter and disappointed. In order to explain the results of their Washington journey to the Indians who had remained behind, they traveled back in three caravans to the thirty-three reservations they had previously visited.

"Coming back," Dennis explained, "we went to the Pine Ridge Reservation. Russell [Means] lived there and he organized some meetings there. It was at that point that Dick Wilson, the tribal chairman, issued his now infamous order that he would not allow AIM, AIM sympathizers, or AIM members onto the Pine Ridge Reservation. I was there on Thanksgiving Day, and I was arrested."

After the "Trail" caravans dispersed, Banks and his wife moved to Salt Lake City. There, in his capacity as National Field Director of the American Indian Movement, he helped establish an alcoholism program with the AIM state coordinator for Utah. Working on skid row, they tried to rehabilitate and find suitable employment for Indian alcoholics.

When asked why Salt Lake City, Banks replied, "It was a good place because of the Mormons. They've exploited Indians throughout their religious history. You know, it's in Mormon doctrine that Indians were the chosen people, but they never chose them to be anything but housemaids and shoeshine boys."

In the middle of December, Banks' work was interrupted. "I received a call from one of our national field representatives, Ron Petite, who had established an alcoholism and employment program in Rapid City. He said that several of the big firms were refusing to hire the Indian applicants that he sent down because, of course, they were alcoholics. Further investigation by Ron revealed that a lot of these large firms in Rapid City

were receiving a substantial amount of HUD-related flood relief funds
and using them to rebuild their businesses.

"We knew that the monies HUD was sending to Rapid City carried
stipulations about minority representation in employment. Ron asked me
if I could help expose the noncompliance of the guilty firms. So I made a
quick trip to Rapid City and we prepared a written complaint against the
City Council. We submitted the complaint to the Regional Director of
HUD in Denver around the 2nd or 3rd of January 1973."

Dennis interrupted his story, pausing to light a corncob pipe. For a
moment he seemed distracted, fingering the rawhide on one of his braids.
Then he continued, more slowly and with sorrow in his voice.

"On the 24th of January someone called from Rapid City informing
me that a man by the name of Wesley Bad Heart Bull was stabbed to
death at Buffalo Gap, South Dakota, outside of a bar. He was stabbed to
death by a white man named Darald Schmitz. No arrests were made in
the first few days, and they wanted me to come back and see if I could
help bring some kind of attention to that. That call came from Ron Petite
who was asked by Sarah Bad Heart Bull, who was Wesley's mother, if
AIM could help her out.

"So I flew back to Rapid City and organized some community meetings about what had to be done at Buffalo Gap. In the meantime, an
arrest was made on Darald Schmitz. He was charged with manslaughter,
second degree. We felt, based upon the information that we had received, not only from people who witnessed the crime, but from the
arresting officers as well, that Darald Schmitz had gotten into a fight with
Wesley Bad Heart Bull on Friday night and was beaten, and that he came
back on Saturday night looking for Wesley with a knife. . .and when he
found him, he stabbed him.

"It was based upon that that we felt that *first*-degree murder charges
should be placed against Schmitz. We made calls to the sheriff of that
county and to the governor's office. The calls frustrated a lot of us
because they fell into the same pattern that has been established in
western Nebraska, South Dakota, North Dakota, Minnesota, Wyoming,
Montana, the whole area.

"Indians have been murdered by white people," Dennis continued,
his sad voice becoming increasingly bitter, "and very little effort is ex-
pended to charge those persons, those persons who commit the crimes
against Indians. Very little effort is put out to bring them to justice, to bring
them into the courts and charge them with what should be the maximum
for their crimes. Throughout the past years we found that where whites
have killed Indians, they have been exonerated by the judicial system in
South Dakota, Nebraska, and these other states.

"That was the case with Yellow Thunder in 1972. He was beaten to death in Gordon, Nebraska. He was stripped naked and he was thrown onto a dance hall floor and he was made to dance. Then they beat him to death with tire irons and stuffed him inside of a trunk. They charged the people that did that with manslaughter, too. It was this kind of damn pattern that had been going on for years that led us to the decision to make a stand with the Bad Heart Bull killing.

"On the 3rd, 4th, and 5th of February, we had a three-day Indian civil rights conference in Rapid City that we had planned back in January. It was at that conference that a lot of feelings were expressed by Indian people about the rip-offs of money from HUD that the big business firms in Rapid City were getting, and about the totally insensitive judicial system in South Dakota and Nebraska.

"We invited government officials to that conference from HUD, the Justice Department, the BIA, and the OEO [Office of Economic Opportunity]. There were civil rights monitors there from as far away as Kansas City and Denver. But they didn't take any of our complaints very seriously. At that Rapid City conference, we set February 6th, the day after it was over, as a time to go to Custer, South Dakota, the county seat for Buffalo Gap, and protest the judicial handling of the Bad Heart Bull case.

"When we gathered in Rapid City for the ride to Custer on February 6th, there were four or five hundred people, so we decided to go to Custer in two caravans. We called ahead to the Community Relations Service people from the Justice Department and asked them to set up some meetings with the mayor and with the county attorney in Custer, and also with the sheriff.

"We wanted to get some kind of community board established between Indians and non-Indians so that these kinds of things would not happen any more, so that there would be a concentrated effort to reduce the ill feelings between the Indian and non-Indian communities.

"When these large caravans finally got to Custer, we were greeted by them telling us that we were late, that we were supposed to be there at 9:00 a.m. The county attorney refused to allow any of us into the courthouse. Eventually, he did say that he was willing to talk, but only to four of us. I was among the four that went inside.

"We asked him if the rest of the people we came with could come into a hearing room which could easily have held 100 people. He refused to allow any more people to come in. It was while the four of us were inside the courthouse meeting with him that a fight started on the front steps between members of the caravan and police officers. And, of course, all hell broke loose after that."

The hell breaking loose that Dennis referred to began as a face-off between approximately 200 Indians from the caravans and half-a-dozen of the 50 state policemen hastily called in to do riot duty that day in Custer. The police, armed, helmeted, and brandishing 3-foot long wooden clubs, formed a line blocking the courthouse door. Several steps below them, insisting on their right to enter the building, were the Indians. Harsh words were exchanged and two or three baseball bats appeared among the crowd. Suddenly it turned into a melee.

There were other protesting Indians and other state police scattered about downtown Custer. The fighting spread quickly. Before it was over, two sheriff's cars were damaged, eight of the 50 state policemen were injured, and three fires were set. One destroyed the one-room Chamber of Commerce office while another caused smoke damage to the courthouse.

A dragnet went into effect. Indian people were indiscriminately arrested in Custer and surrounding towns. Since the time of Crazy Horse and Sitting Bull, white lawmen have had the habit of attacking or arresting innocent Indians whenever they were unable to kill or capture the guilty ones, as though all Indians were equivalent regardless of their behavior. Community sweeps and dragnet arrests have long been the source of great bitterness.

In Custer, one of the sheriff's officers said, "We're patrolling the streets right now to see what we've got left in the way of Indians." The patrols arrested 34 persons, presumably on more substantial grounds than suspicion of being an Indian. Arraignments were held the next day. Custer bristled with outraged white citizens, many of them armed.

All of the Indians arrested were charged with felonies, like riot and arson. Many of the townspeople believed that AIM had planned the fighting in advance, sending their four representatives to meet with the county attorney as a decoy while hundreds of their followers fired the town. Russell Means claimed that the accusation was absurd. "I would not bring old women and children to a place where I plan violence," he said.

Some of Custer's leading citizens, on the other hand, made no secret of *their* plans for violence. As the arrested Indians were marched to their arraignment, one prominent businessman observed, "This [town] is an armed garrison, but we have to be ready. They [the Indians] say they aren't coming back now, but you can't trust them. If they try anything now, we aren't going to be arraigning people here—we're going to be burying them."

Another respected Custer proprietor had this to say: "The people in town are pretty worked up. They are not going to stand for any more of the nonsense that took place yesterday. I had my employees armed all last night and they're armed today. I've instructed them to shoot first and ask questions later if life or property are threatened. If trouble arises again and the officers do not do some shooting, the townspeople will."

The mayor's response to a situation where local businessmen were in command of private armies left something to be desired, at least from a constitutional point of view. "It looks like the people will have to take up arms if we're ever faced with a situation like we had Tuesday," he said, admitting that this would inevitably mean "there is going to be bloodshed."

Indian people in Custer resentfully wondered what response the mayor would make if the tables were turned, and if *they* rather than influential *white* citizens took up arms to protect themselves from what they believed to be a threat to their safety.

Dennis Banks was as angry as anyone that day. At his arraignment, he pointed to the irony in the case of Sarah Bad Heart Bull, who was in the prisoner's dock with him. If convicted of the charge of rioting in the protest of her son Wesley's murder, she could receive a sentence of up to twenty years in the state penitentiary. At the same time, Schmitz, the man charged with the murder itself, could only receive a maximum of ten years for second-degree manslaughter.[1]

Dennis' account of the Custer incident ended. AIM did not return to demonstrate in Custer again, as the focus of their conflict shifted abruptly, first to Rapid City and then three weeks later, on February 27, to Wounded Knee. But before resuming his story, Dennis explained how he personally came to be an Indian political activist, what his life had been like before the American Indian Movement, and why had he decided to devote himself to the struggle for Indian rights.

Dennis Banks is a member of the Chippewa Tribe. He was born on the Leech Lake Reservation in northern Minnesota. After remarking that he was 41 years old, he laughed and said, "Average life span for an American Indian is 44.5 years. That means I have 3.5 years left, and that's ironic because the government wants 180 years from me for Wounded Knee, and for that Custer incident they want another 103 years, plus a life sentence.

"Since I lived on a reservation," Dennis continued, "I was forced into the Bureau of Indian Affairs boarding school system. With or without your parents' consent, on a reservation, the BIA can take you away to an Indian school. In 1940, I was bused to the Pipestone Indian School which is about 400 miles from the reservation I was born on. I went to school there for nine years, and then I was bused to North Dakota to another Indian school, and then bused from that school to another school in

---

[1]Sarah Bad Heart Bull was convicted and sentenced to five years in prison for her role in the Custer demonstration. She served time in a South Dakota penitentiary and was released in 1975 following widespread national protest. Schmitz was acquitted of manslaughter charges.

South Dakota. I got home to Leech Lake eleven years later.

"Back on the reservation, I went to public school for about six months. Then I worked for a while, and in 1953, I began military service in the U.S. Air Force. I was overseas for three-and-a-half years in Tokyo and Osaka, Japan, and in Korea. I got back in 1958 and bummed around in Minnesota for a while, mostly in Minneapolis.

"I didn't want to go back to the reservation because there was no employment there. I didn't want to get there and starve and become another statistic in alcoholism and die that kind of death. So, beginning in 1959, I did some community work in Minneapolis, you know, setting up Little Leagues and different kinds of social programs. I did that for four years, but the programs weren't doing that much good and I just couldn't get anyplace. Then, finally in 1963, I just ended up on skid row, drinking.

"I got busted in 1964 for burglary and went to prison for a year. Then I got out and went back on a forgery rap and did another six months. I got out after that one, and about a year later, in 1967, they sent me up for another year on a parole violation. That was in a maximum security prison and I did nine months in solitary confinement."

Dennis said it almost casually, but nine months in solitary confinement required some explanation. He leaned back in his chair, closed his eyes for a moment, and then slowly resumed.

"Well, I guess basically it was because I didn't want to spend all of my time making twine and license plates for the State of Minnesota. I was really fed up with being in prison and, surprisingly, I kind of felt that I had failed as a citizen of the United States. I know that must sound strange, but I really thought that my current troubles resulted from my not acting like a responsible citizen.

"I decided at that point that I should be doing good instead of being in prison. I also decided to think the whole thing out inside of solitary, so I just refused to be part of prison society and they locked me up in a cell by myself.

"But it was in there in 1967 and 1968, during the nine months in solitary, that I began to read quite a bit about civil rights. I read intensively on treaties between the U.S. government and the Indian nations. I made comparisons between the treaty rights that Indians were deprived of by the government and the civil rights that black people were deprived of by the same government.

"Then, I began to realize that it was not a question of me being a good United States citizen. It was a question of this government being responsible to me, and not seeing to it that I had an opportunity to lead a decent life, or to own a piece of land, or to find a good job, like they had promised my ancestors in all these treaties. They broke all of those promises. They stole everything from them and wrecked their way of life—which was a good way. It was the government not fulfilling its responsibilities to me as an American Indian that was the greatest reason for me being in prison in the first place.

"It was in solitary there in late '67 and early '68 that I started following the whole anti-war movement, all the marches going on, and the SDS [Students for a Democratic Society] people being busted everywhere. I realized how we didn't belong in Viet Nam and how this goddamn government was running over people there just like they had in Korea and just like they had 100 years ago to the Indians in America.

"It had a tremendous impact on me, what was going on outside of prison that year. Sitting in that jail cell I began to understand there was a hell of a goddamn movement going on that I wasn't part of, the anti-war movement, the Black Panther movement, the civil rights movement, the SDS.

"I began to see that the greatest war was going to go on right here in the United States; and I began to realize that there was a hell of a situation in this country—all these different kinds of people trying so hard to straighten this country out.

"It was inside the jug there that I thought there has to be an Indian movement, too. Otherwise, it'll pass us by again. And realizing then what was really going on, I made a commitment that there would be an Indian movement."

Dennis paused again to relight his corncob pipe. When he resumed, the anger and excitement had left his voice, but the strength of his feeling was quite evident.

"When I got out of prison, I called George Mitchell who I had been in school with and who I had done community work with in Minneapolis in the early '60s. I figured that between him and me we could put together a meeting, or a series of meetings, that would start to get the whole Indian community in Minneapolis moving behind a new effort to fight the government, a new effort to begin making some of the changes that we needed.

"So George and I organized for three months there in the summer of 1968. When we were done, we called together a mass meeting in Minneapolis that 250 people attended. They were from twenty different Indian organizations.

"We decided to lay it on the table at that meeting. 'Here it is,' we said, 'for 200 years they've been killing off our people, and now, what the hell are we going to do about it? People are fighting battles in the streets of Chicago'—by then the '68 convention demonstrations had just happened—'they're fighting in Chicago to stop the Viet Nam War and bring about changes in the party system; they're fighting in the streets of Alabama to correct the situation for the blacks; the SDS movement is trying to change the whole goddamn structure of the universities; the anti-war movement is fighting to bring the U.S. military under control. People are fighting and what the hell are we going to do? Are we going to sit here in this Minneapolis community and not do a goddamn thing? Are we going to go on for another 200 years, or even for another five years, the way we are, without doing anything for our Indian people?'

"There was one guy at the meeting who spoke out a lot and kind of led the exchange, the dialogue. He talked about many things that he saw as wrong and he spoke with a lot of feeling. Eventually, I asked that the chairman of all the twenty Indian organizations that were there come up and sit on the stage.

"Then I said, 'Now, here's the people and here's the chairmen. Let's get a new organized effort going, a new coalition that will fight for Indian treaty rights and better conditions and opportunities for our people. Let's elect someone from out there to head it up, some new blood for the thing, not any of these chairmen up here or myself. And let's have all of these twenty chairmen make a commitment to support whoever we elect.'

"This one guy kept speaking all night. He had a good delivery and spoke very strongly, so they elected him to be the first chairman of the coalition. His name was Clyde Bellecourt, and that's how the first American Indian Movement meeting happened.

"George Mitchell eventually dropped out, but Clyde and I pushed this new AIM organization. Mostly it was Clyde in the beginning because I was working for Honeywell, of all corporations. I was a recruiter for them, I recruited Indians to go to work for Honeywell making residential electrical heating equipment.

"Well, at that time, anti-war people in Minneapolis were putting together the Honeywell Project to protest them making fragmentation bombs and other of these barbaric weapons. I started supporting what they were doing. The war in Viet Nam was illegal and immoral, and the anti-personnel bombs that Honeywell was making were one of the greatest sins of all.

"You know, on the one hand Honeywell is producing residential electrical heating equipment for use in people's homes, and on the other hand they're destroying homes and people in Viet Nam. I just felt that I couldn't be part of that anymore, even though none of the 430 Indians I recruited for Honeywell were ever put to work in the defense plants.

"But Honeywell had been in financial support of a new Indian movement, so I just asked for a leave of absence to go to work for AIM and they gave it to me. Our ideas collided when I took a public stand that I could no longer recruit for the Honeywell Corporation, and they released me.

"At the same time, Clyde Bellecourt was working for Northern States Power Company, the biggest rip-off of Indian people's treaties in the

Wisconsin and Minnesota area. Northern States Power has nine dams on Indian reservations in direct violation of treaties. Clyde couldn't become part of that either, and he and I realized that in speaking for what we believed in, we would also have to take a stand on things that affected our own personal lives, like the companies we worked for. Clyde was eventually released, as I was.

"Organizations and companies like that are willing to give you the help you need as long as you don't step on their toes. But once you turn around and start criticizing them and biting the hand that feeds you, well, they're not going to give you any more. That's exactly what happened to us; they decided not to feed us anymore. But it's going to be the other way around some day, you know, because it's really us that's feeding them, and pretty soon we're going to cut off their food, too.

"When we first got started on AIM, Clyde worked on pulling things together in Minneapolis and it became my responsibility to organize chapters of the American Indian Movement across the country. At one point, I got an invitation to come to Cleveland and speak there and I, in turn, invited the Cleveland Indian Center to send people to the first AIM pow-wow that was held in Minneapolis.

"It was our first wild rice festival, in 1968, and this one guy came from Cleveland. He was the executive director of the Indian Center there and he had some very strong feelings about Indian issues and the kinds of things Indians should be doing. He spoke with the same kind of enthusiasm that Clyde spoke with at that first AIM meeting. He spoke very well at that first AIM pow-wow, and he still speaks good to this day —Russell Means. He started the second chapter, the one we opened in Cleveland.

"About a month after that first pow-wow, we went to a conference on Indian alcoholism in Denver. There was another guy we met there who spoke very well on ways that Indian people should deal with the problem of alcoholism. That was Herb Polis and he organized the third AIM chapter, in Milwaukee. In a little while, Clyde's brother, Vernon Bellecourt, helped start a chapter in Denver.

"Pretty soon the American Indian Movement just started going all over—North Dakota, Oklahoma, everywhere. Four years later, just before Wounded Knee, we had about forty chapters across the country. Since Wounded Knee, we've got close to eighty chapters."

Dennis talked about the number of people in America whose lives, like his, were profoundly affected by the political turmoil and activism in the 1960s, even though many never participated directly. Like sparks starting a prairie fire, single events in that period led different people to new understandings. It was a gradual process, but steady, and it continues today. Much of its impact was not visible for years. The process proved beyond any doubt that Americans are capable of profound change, not merely of moving from the Republican to the Democratic Party, but of changing utterly both the style and the purpose of their lives, as Dennis Banks had.

Indian people, no less than other Americans, were influenced by the political upheavals and the activist climate of the sixties. The first demonstration of Indian militancy to receive national attention occurred at Frank's Landing on the Puyallup River just south of Seattle, Washington. In 1966, members of the Puyallup and Nisqually Tribes began a series of annual fish-ins there, claiming that the Washington State conservation authorities were violating treaty agreements by restricting Indian fishing in the river. Once each year the impoverished Indians caught the running fish and were arrested. While these fish-ins, and the eighteen-month occupation of Alcatraz Island in 1970-1971, attracted the attention of the news media, Indians across the country mounted dozens of smaller actions that received little if any news coverage. But they were after change, not coverage. Despite their efforts, little meaningful change occurred. More and more Indian people, young and old, became hostile to bureaucratic avenues of change and turned to militant activism, believing that they would have to be more forceful to be more successful.

Dennis resumed his story of the events that led up to the occupation of Wounded Knee, starting with the aftermath of the violence in Custer on February 6. Racial tension throughout western South Dakota was driven to the boiling point by the Custer incident. In Rapid City, the area's major population center, hostility was already building as a result of Indian protests over the misuse of flood relief funds. On the night of February 6, AIM called a meeting in Rapid City to evaluate what had happened earlier that day in Custer.

"It was at that meeting," Dennis recalled, "that we were first approached by a couple of representatives from the Pine Ridge Reservation. They told us how they were pushing for an impeachment of Richard Wilson, the tribal chairman, and they wanted to know if they could get AIM support. Up to that time, AIM had a firm policy never to get involved in the internal problems of a tribe when there were differences between rival groups within the same tribe.

"So we said that all we would do is write letters to Congressmen and Senators and remind the Pine Ridge tribal chairman of his responsibilities to the people, and stuff like that. Back in November, I had been arrested just for setting foot on the Pine Ridge Reservation, after the Trail of Broken Treaties. I just stayed away from there after that; I didn't feel like going back to Pine Ridge. My wife, Kamook, incidentally, is from Pine Ridge. Anyway, we offered those people that kind of assistance."

But Pine Ridge was not the main topic at the February 6 meeting in

Rapid City. There was trouble enough on the scene, and tension continued to mount. On the night of February 9, it exploded. An Indian walked into a white bar in downtown Rapid City. There was an exchange of ugly remarks and the Indian was struck on the head from behind with a beer bottle. When the police arrived, they arrested the Indian. Shortly after, a group of 60-70 Indians assembled in the area and proceeded to tear apart four other white bars, breaking windows and bottles and smashing furniture.

Dennis described these four bars as places "where Indians were often abused and mistreated." The police then went on a rampage of their own. Within fifteen minutes, they indiscriminately arrested 40 Indians. A crowd of about 150 gathered outside the jail to protest the random arrests. After some dancing and the beating of a drum, the crowd retired at the urging of Dennis Banks and Russell Means to attend a meeting in the Mother Butler Community Center.

The next two nights, February 10 and 11, fights broke out between Indians and the Rapid City police. On the 10th, in another attempt to reduce tension, Banks asked all Indians to keep a voluntary 9:30 p.m. curfew. He also asked officials to close all city bars at that time. The officials refused, but several Rapid City bars closed voluntarily, despite at least one threat by white customers that if the bar they were in closed down, it would be reopened by force. After three nights of violence, 200 Indians were under arrest.

Regular evening meetings then began in the Mother Butler Center in Rapid City. Organized with the help of AIM, these gatherings drew as many as 200-300 Indian people. At the meeting on the night of February 15, Russell Means brought news from Pine Ridge that Tribal Chairman Richard Wilson had postponed his own impeachment hearing for another week. Means, a resident of Pine Ridge, had been going back and forth between there and Rapid City keeping AIM people in town informed about events on the reservation.

The next day, February 16, in response to an earlier invitation, Dennis Banks gave a speech at a session of the State Senate in South Dakota. Dressed in a bright red shirt and wearing a headband, Dennis told the legislators, "I come here today to make a state-wide appeal, and to pledge to the citizens of South Dakota what we hope will become a move to further ease the tension." He described "meaningful" talks held earlier with authorities but warned that if a settlement was not reached, serious trouble would result. He said that the disturbances in Custer and Rapid City, though unfortunate, were necessary to bring about significant change. Ironically, one person observed, Banks was very probably the first native American ever to address the State Senate.

"The weekend of February 17th and 18th," Dennis said, continuing his narrative, "we had an AIM pow-wow in Rapid City. It was there that a guy by the name of Pedro Bissonette from Pine Ridge came to us and made a plea to the American Indian Movement to come and give them some assistance down on the Oglala Sioux reservation. He explained to us that Wilson's impeachment had been postponed and postponed and postponed and that there were a lot of people there who were desperately waiting for the American Indian Movement to come down and help.

"Everyone at that pow-wow voted unanimously not only to commit the kinds of support that we had already given them, but now to begin moving away from our old policy in a direction that might mean direct intervention on behalf of the Oglala Sioux attempting to impeach Wilson. It was decided that all the Oglalas from the American Indian Movement would go down there and help out the people on the reservation."

After the pow-wow, on the night of February 18, another mass meeting was held in the Mother Butler Center to elect the Indian representatives for a city-wide Civil Rights Working Committee, a coalition of Indians, whites, and clergymen trying to reduce Indian-white tension in Rapid City. AIM members reported that similar coalitions had been useful in other cities. They also argued that such a committee was an effective means of transferring Indian leadership and initiative from AIM to local community people. The next day, February 19, the Rapid City white and Indian committee met. They decided to place certain requests before the City Council, one request being that Rapid City's churches all ring their bells at noon on the 21st as a sign that Indian frustrations were coming to an end.

The City Council met on February 20 under heavy police guard. It denied the requests of the Civil Rights Working Committee. Not stopping there, it passed a resolution condemning the American Indian Movement. A motion to reconsider the condemnation led to a bitter debate that was interrupted by Indians taking the floor to state their views. At one point, AIM people walked out after Dennis Banks observed that the church bells of the city were supposed to ring the following noon as a sign of a new day for Indian people. "The bells of peace will not ring tomorrow," he said. "We'll see you in the streets." Later, after yet another reconsideration, the offensive resolution was overruled and dropped.

The next day, February 21, AIM formally passed the leadership of the Indian rights struggle to the new Civil Rights Working Committee. That night, at a pow-wow of appreciation in Rapid City, the Committee officially expressed its gratitude to AIM for "effective work in sensitizing the Indian and white citizens of Rapid City to the problems of racial prejudice that exist here."

"On the 22nd of February," Dennis said, with a sudden note of seriousness in his voice, "a couple of Indian guys were beaten in downtown Rapid City and things got very bad there. The police were all riding around with shotguns in their cars. There were rednecks and vigilantes openly carrying guns in downtown Rapid City. They were openly carrying guns as far away as Kadoka and all the other towns surrounding Pine Ridge, and over in Nebraska, near the reservation.

"Based upon this open carrying of weapons by white people, based upon the beatings of Indians, the killings of Indians, based upon the increased police surveillance, the hostilities that the Rapid City Police Department showed against us, we called a major meeting there on the night of February 23rd.

"I asked at that meeting that all Indian people in South Dakota arm themselves and prepare for open attacks by white vigilantes. I asked that they prepare to defend themselves in back alleys, on the streets, on the lonely roads, wherever there was a possibility that they might meet death. I asked them to prepare themselves physically and mentally to resist that kind of oppression.

"It was at that meeting in Rapid City that we received another request from the Oglala Sioux. Pedro Bissonette again came and explained to us that the impeachment hearing was finally held but it had ended in failure. He said there was a lot of frustration, and a lot of anxiety, and a lot of hope down there that AIM would now do something to bring the story of what was happening at Pine Ridge to the attention of those officials who could do something to correct it.

"At the final hour of the impeachment, Wilson elected to preside over his own hearing. He ruled the three councilmen out of order who had signed the original complaint against him, charging him with misconduct, charging him with theft, charging him with nepotism, charging him with carrying out policies and procedures contrary to the constitution of the Oglala Sioux. So AIM reaffirmed its earlier decision to support Wilson's impeachment.

"The next day, on the 24th, I received a call from an Indian family on the Cheyenne River Reservation. I went up there to Eagle Butte to respond to their request that AIM get involved in some of the problems they were facing on that reservation. While I was up on the Cheyenne River, there was a series of nightly meetings going on at the Calico community center on the Pine Ridge Reservation.

"On the night of February 26th, at the Calico meeting, the Oglala Sioux chiefs joined the Oglala Sioux Civil Rights Organization and asked for physical support from the American Indian Movement. There were five of the traditional chiefs and a medicine man there—there was Chief Red Cloud, Chief Iron Cloud, Chief Fools Crow, Chief Bad Cob, and Chief Kills Enemy. The medicine man was Pete Catches. They all asked for direct intervention by AIM.

"The people and the chiefs were scared because there were so many Bluecoats on the reservation. There were ninety federal marshals there and they had set up bunkers on top of the BIA building in Pine Ridge and they were patrolling the streets and pushing people around, even the older Indian people. On top of all that, Wilson had hired these goons to protect him.

"Russell [Means] attended that meeting and it was taped. I later heard Pete Catches on the tape. He spoke at length from a medicine man's point of view. He said that there was a time to fight and there was a time to die. And he said that it's not how you die that counts, it's what you've accomplished in your lifetime. 'If we all die today,' he said, 'we'll all die as dogs because we've let one man, Wilson, dictate to us.'

"He wanted AIM to help the Oglala Sioux because for them it was a time to fight now. He said that as long as he's been a medicine man he's never asked people to fight, and he was an old man, in his 70s. 'But today,' he said, 'I'm asking AIM, I'm asking those young Indians to come down and help us fight.'

"So Russell responded that AIM would make a decision, and that he would get word to me up on the Cheyenne River to come down and be part of that answer. I didn't know what was going on at Pine Ridge then. But somebody took that tape and left Calico that same night, on the 26th, and started driving it up to the Cheyenne River Reservation.

"About noon the next day, I was talking to a family up there and these guys came running up and they said they wanted me to hear something. I listened to the whole meeting; it was about two hours long. I heard the chiefs requesting my presence down on Pine Ridge and Russell wanted me to come down there. And so I immediately packed all of my stuff and left for Pine Ridge. A lot of people up on the Cheyenne River came down with me, about nine cars of them.

"We got to Pine Ridge on the evening of the 27th. People were eating at the community center in Calico. I met all the chiefs there and they asked again if we could help them. All those old chiefs were the most respected men in the tribe. Looking at them was like looking back at our own Indian past, and they were asking us to help them. Right then and there. It really made me feel that AIM would have to make its stand there, with those people. Then Pedro [Bissonette] got up and spoke very strongly and with a lot of feeling."

"Finally, these two women, Helen Moves Camp and Gladys Bissonette [Pedro's aunt], got up. Gladys spoke for about twenty minutes in Lakota, the language of the Sioux. Then she turned around to us and she spoke to us in English. She started crying, and she said to us that we had to realize that for many years the Oglala Sioux had lost their way to fight. 'For many years,' she said, 'we have not fought any kind of war, we have not fought any kind of battle, and we have forgotten how to fight.' Then she asked if we would help them.

"Then Helen Moves Camp got up and she spoke along the same lines, and she started to cry during her talk to me. She came right up to me, crying, and she was begging for help. She said that if it's the last thing we do, we should fight for Indian people, and fight there.

"So I knew then that AIM would have to make its stand there, on the Pine Ridge Reservation. But none of us knew how, none of us knew what we could do. And none of us, of course, could give them an answer because what could we say at that point? The people just stared at us. Finally, they demanded an answer.

"Russell [Means] and I and Clyde [Bellecourt] and Carter [Camp] got together and talked it over. We made the decision that of all the things that AIM had been working for, that this would have to be it. There would be no more American Indian Movement if we left without helping those people . . . and there would be no more Indian fight if we left.

"I had the pleasure of delivering the answer to the Oglala chiefs that AIM would stay and give all the necessary protection and all the necessary help in bringing their situation to the attention of the United States government. But, at that point, we still didn't know what course of action we were going to take.

"By then there were hundreds and hundreds of people who were gathering outside of the Calico Hall. We were down in the basement with the Oglala chiefs, four Tribal Council members, and the leaders of the Oglala Sioux Civil Rights Organization. Eventually we had to go outside and give AIM's answer to all the people that were waiting. There must have been about 1,000 of them.

"We asked everybody to come inside the Calico Hall, but there were too many people. So we decided to take the meeting to Porcupine, which is about thirty miles from Calico. They have a bigger community center there. It holds 400-500 people and there's an outdoor P.A. system.

"We decided it was best to go over to Porcupine in a caravan, so we lined up all the cars, all sixty or seventy of them. We started off to Porcupine with all the chiefs, all the medicine men, all the women, men, kids, babies, a lot of people in pickups—fifteen, twenty people jumping on pickups, people squeezing inside of cars, jumping on top of cars to ride over, people singing, people happy. Some were crying that they knew finally they were going to do something, but at that point nobody knew what. On the road between Calico and Porcupine the caravan had to go through two communities; one of them was Pine Ridge and the other was Wounded Knee."

Dennis' voice slowed to a crawl. Reclining in his chair, almost whispering, he seemed to be visualizing the events he was describing and trying, perhaps, to experience them again as he spoke.

"We went through Pine Ridge and all of the horns in the caravan were blowing. You could see the federal marshals out there, radioing to each other, running and jumping into their positions. They had their guns drawn and rifles pointed at us. They were on top of the buildings there and moving all around in patrol cars. They even had jeeps moving around there.

"We went right through Pine Ridge without stopping, all the cars in that big caravan. It shocked the marshals to see us drive through. They thought we were going to take over something in Pine Ridge and they didn't know what to do when we just drove in one end and out the other. But our people were angry seeing how the Bluecoats had taken over the town.

"Half an hour later we came to Wounded Knee, and at Wounded Knee there is a mass grave site where victims of the old massacre are buried. I was in the lead car with one of the chiefs, Chief Fools Crow, and we decided that we would stop and pray at the grave site before we went on to Porcupine. Everybody stopped and pulled up into the parking area there, and they all got out and we gathered around that grave site.

"Pete Catches, the medicine man, and Chief Fools Crow, and Crow Dog, the medicine man for AIM, began to pray. Crow Dog said that many years ago there were Indians just like us who came to this spot. They were going to turn themselves in. They were going in the other direction. They were going toward Pine Ridge to be chained and to be arrested and to be put on reservations.

"And Crow Dog said, 'Here we come going the other way. It's just like those Indian soldiers in Big Foot's band who were going to Pine Ridge, and now they're coming back,' he said. 'We're those soldiers, we're those Indian people, we're them, we're back,' he said, 'and we can't go any further. Wounded Knee is a place where we can't go any further.'

"We all knew when he got done talking that we really couldn't go any further, that we would have to do or die at Wounded Knee. After he got done talking it just seemed like everybody knew that this was it. Everything pointed to one course of action—retake Wounded Knee, seize it, hold it, and let the chips fall. And that's the way it happened, that's just how it happened.

"The medicine men brought wisdom to us. They gave us the spiritual direction we needed. They showed us that after all the years of misery Indians have lived through, all the broken treaties, all the Indians that were ripped off, all the Indians dying needless deaths, all the Indians killed in Oklahoma, New Mexico, all the Indians that have died in South

Dakota, Montana, that this finally would be a place to die with them, and that this would be a place to make a last desperate attempt to bring about change. The spirits in Wounded Knee would have to teach us, the warriors and the people who died before in Wounded Knee would have to show us what to do.

"And those medicine men were right, we couldn't go any further. There was no going to Porcupine, there was no writing letters to the government and sending them demands any more. That's exactly what the medicine men said to us—'when you put your words on paper, then they step on them.' So the direction that we received was good. And that was February 27."

7

AIRLIFT
Blind Departure

Friday, April 13, 1973
Chicago, Illinois

At 5:00 a.m. we were still working in Bob Talbot's basement. Only five of the ten cargo nets we needed were complete. Bob and his two teen-age sons had gone to sleep around 3:00 a.m. The neighborhood women had finished sewing their ten parachute deployment bags at 4:00 a.m. We thanked them profusely for helping us, but they wouldn't hear of it. At 5:00 a.m. Larry, Marty, Jim, Strobe, Tom, and I were all still going.

It was a good time for a break. I got out the statement that my friend in Boston had written to go with the food parcels and read it out loud for criticisms. Marty was the only one to suggest serious alterations, but no one else agreed with him. Larry offered a compromise, but Marty held back. The disagreement was too much for Jim, who had already told me about his dislike for long political arguments.

"Let's quit screwing around and sew these nets," Jim shouted. "We're not here to write political statements. We're here to deliver this food to people."

It was the first tense moment we had with each other. We were too far behind schedule and too exhausted to stay relaxed. With a lot more rigging and check-out flights still left to do, we realized that if we flew at all that day, it was not going to be until the afternoon, and no one was going to get any sleep beforehand. Larry went into the kitchen to revise the food message. Strobe left for the Midway freight terminal to pick up the

129

parachutes from Albuquerque. The rest of us, disappointed, went back to work.

An hour later Strobe, whom none of us could quite figure out, burst into the basement with five big, beautiful cargo chutes. Four came from Albuquerque. Strobe woke up a friend to get the fifth. The bushy-headed Strobe was just learning to skydive, and he knew a few people around Chicago who owned parachutes. With the new additions, we had our ten full-canopy parachutes, one for each of the cargo nets we were so laboriously manufacturing. It was the last obstacle in our plan. We had money, pilots, press coverage, and parachutes. Having decided to use single-engine aircraft, renting planes would be relatively easy.

The ten parachutes were different sizes. Jim computed the weight each could handle while I figured out how many pounds of cargo we could carry in three six-passenger aircraft. The pay load totaled 2,100 pounds, allowing for a pilot and a cargo handler in each plane. We weighed everything piece by piece on Bob's bathroom scale. There was room for 150 more pounds and Marty volunteered to go make the purchases. We took another break to draw up a shopping list. Sitting around in the early morning light, we decided on more meat, lard, baking powder, cheese, prunes, halizone water purification tablets (because we had heard that the government was periodically cutting off the water supply and forcing the people in Wounded Knee to use contaminated water), and tampax (because maybe nobody had thought of it).

By 10:00 a.m. the end of the rigging work was in sight. Marty was back with the extra supplies. Billy Wright, the pilot who had agreed to join us the night before, showed up, but saw that we were not ready and went back to work, promising to return later. Meanwhile, Larry typed up the revised message to the Indians and a complete list of all of the food. He went off to xerox enough copies for each of the twenty-two duffel bags. Bob spent most of the early morning on the telephone, looking for more pilots and finishing arrangements for renting the aircraft. Jim kept sewing cargo nets.

"I've got three Cherokee Six's lined up for you," Bob said. "You can pick them up anytime this afternoon and they're clear for at least forty-eight hours. I couldn't find any other pilots, though."

No more pilots and only three airplanes—that meant that Bob wasn't going to fly with us. I was very disappointed. I trusted his flying skill and especially his judgment in emergencies.

"That means you're not coming, huh?"

"No," he answered, "I can't. It's really been tearing me apart. This is one of the best things I've ever been asked to fly. Cindy said she'd stick with me, too. She said if I went to jail or got in trouble or lost my job, she'd back me up as long as I thought I was doing the right thing.

"But I started thinking, you know, about how the last couple of years have been pretty good for me. I bought this house. If I keep my nose clean, I'll get tenure at the college next fall. So my family is well taken care of and I don't want to jeopardize that."

I didn't want to argue with his decision, but I didn't endorse it either, and I didn't feel like politely telling him he was right. It was too complicated a discussion to have at that point, so I simply said, "Okay," and walked downstairs into the basement.

Larry was back and busy stuffing xerox copies into the duffel bags. He handed me a card with the name and phone number of a New York lawyer written on it. The lawyer was frequently involved in "political" cases and had told Larry that he was willing to be on call in case we needed any legal assistance. Larry had written out a similar card for everyone present.

The rigging work was nearly done. Marty, exhausted like the rest of us from the long night's work, decided to go back to Boston. He did not want to fly with the airlift, either. He told us that he was nervous about flying and that, if he were cramped up in a small plane on a long flight, his nervousness might keep him from functioning well. He wished us luck and I thanked him for all his help.

Meanwhile, two more people arrived in Bob's basement, adding to the crowd. One was an aviation student of his from the college, the other his secretary. They calmly announced that they were there to help with the rigging. Bob had done it again. Like the previous night, when he brought home three neighbors to help with the sewing, Bob had taken it upon himself to invite the two young people, violating what the rest of us considered minimum security precautions. The airlift, which began as a semisecret operation, was fast becoming a community social project. We were not so concerned about arrest but about the government's blocking us from making the food drop. Nevertheless, it was impossible to argue with Bob's good intentions, especially when he told us that yet another student was on the way over to help. At that point, we were beyond effective secrecy. Our best defense was simply to get our planes into the air as quickly as possible, disappear into the western sky, and not emerge again until we came out of the dawn over Wounded Knee.

At noon we assessed our progress. We had three aircraft. We had three pilots: the professional, Billy Wright; the skydiver, Jim Stewart; and me. Twenty-two duffel bags of food were packed and inside the ten completed cargo nets, two or three at a time. All that remained was for Jim to supervise the folding of the parachute canopies into the bright orange deployment bags.

We were ready to fly with what we had. Delivering the food on hand was better than delaying the flight any longer in hopes of finding more pilots and increasing the size of the load. Three food-bearing airplanes was something less than a fleet but one hell of a lot more than they had inside Wounded Knee.

It was time for our check-rides. Neither Jim nor I had ever flown an airplane quite as big and heavy as those we were about to use for the airlift. We were both licensed to fly any single-engine land aircraft. But going from a lightweight to a heavyweight airplane is not the same as switching from a Volkswagen to a Cadillac. We were accustomed to four-seat aircraft with 145-horsepower engines. The six-seat, 300-horsepower Piper Cherokee Six airplanes we were soon to fly had different takeoff, landing, and in-flight characteristics. They were also equipped with far more complex radio navigation gear. Customarily, a pilot takes a few hours of flight instruction in an unfamiliar aircraft before flying it as pilot-in-command. But Bob, who was a licensed flight instructor, was ready to give Jim and me a quick one-hour course and run us through a few emergency and off-field procedures that are usually of little concern on such check-rides.

Walking out the door, we met Larry and Tom Oliphant on their way back from taking Marty to the airport. They had some bad news. They had checked on the other reporters who wanted to go with us: the Chicago *Sun-Times* columnist was up all night with the flu and felt too sick to make the trip, and the New York *Times* correspondent had been reassigned to a Watergate story. I slapped Tom on the back and jokingly congratulated him for getting an "exclusive" on the Wounded Knee airlift. He asked to come on the check-ride with us. Larry went down to the basement to help Strobe supervise the first stages of the parachute packing.

As we were about to cross the street to the airport, a car pulled up in front of Bob's house. It was his other student, coming to help with the rigging. We stood on the street talking to him for a while about the flight to Wounded Knee. With twenty hours in the air as a student flyer, he was the closest thing to an extra pilot we had seen all day. Bob liked him a great deal and he seemed to us to be an honest and decent person. We invited him to join the airlift as a co-pilot. He said he would help with the rigging, think it over, and let us know when we returned from the check-ride.

At the airport, we climbed into the cabin of one of the Cherokees. Bob and I took the pilot and co-pilot seats up front while Jim and Tom strapped in directly behind us. The cabin was tiny, only two seats wide and three rows long. It was not nearly high enough to stand up in. Besides the cabin door over the right wing, the plane had another door at the back of the fuselage on the left side. It was through this opening that we planned to unload the cargo. We would take the door completely off its

Prior to departure from Chicago's Midway Airport, the duffel bags inside their cargo netting are sorted on the ramp and readied for loading. (courtesy Richard Bresden.)

Final flight briefing, without maps, just before take-off from Midway Airport. From l. to r., Bob Talbot, Billy Wright, John Adelman, Strobe, the author and Larry Levin. *(courtesy Richard Bresden.)*

hinges just prior to the actual drop. With the rear seats already removed, the cargo nets could be tumbled out the rear of the cabin through the open doorway.

Bob flew the takeoff from Midway while I handled radio communications with the control tower. We climbed to 3,000 feet and headed south, clear of the high-density traffic area around Chicago. Five minutes later Bob took his hands off the control wheel and nodded for me to take over with the duplicate set of co-pilot controls. He talked me through normal climbing and gliding turns, crosswind S-turns above a country road, and figure eights around two farm silos a quarter-mile apart. Next I did steep circular turns, leaning the airplane so far to the side it began to feel like we were going to flop over on our backs. It was only the beginning of what pilots refer to as "a rigorous check-ride."

We flew for another half hour, practicing blind flight on instruments, slow flight, and eventually "stalls." An aerodynamic stall, as opposed to an engine failure, occurs when the aircraft slows to the point where air does not pass over the wings fast enough to provide enought lift to keep the plane up. As soon as the stall speed is reached (63 mph in the Cherokee Six), the airplane suddenly falls out of the sky. It drops several hundred feet, and as the nose points toward the ground, the ship starts to move through the air faster than the stall speed. The newly created lift from the wings is then sufficient to make the aircraft flyable once again. The whole procedure takes less than a minute. We did it six or seven times. At one point, I glanced behind me to check on Tom. He had almost no idea what was happening and was pale and white with fright.

But the worst was yet to come. Some thirty miles south of Chicago, Bob pointed toward a grass landing strip. I swung the plane around into a normal approach pattern, but botched the landing so badly that Bob had to take the controls at the last minute. I was used to the shallow sink characteristics of a smaller plane. We kept going around the grass strip until I successfully completed four or five landings. They got gradually better, but were never very precise.

Suddenly, about 1,000 feet up and a mile or so from the landing strip, the engine sputtered out and the propeller jerked to a halt in front of me. Bob had taken the key out of the ignition! I knew he would do something like that during the flight. It was a simulated emergency but actually stopping the engine, rather than letting it run at idling speed, was a lot more realistic than the usual way power failures are practiced. I had to make a full-stop landing on the grass without restarting the engine. I nosed the aircraft over into an 80-mph glide and banked to the left, heading directly for the approach end of the landing area. On the way down, I turned around and reassured Tom that nothing was really wrong. As we glided past the end of the grass strip, I rolled the Cherokee into a steep-banked spiral descent. We lost the right amount of altitude and came out of the spiral lined up reasonably well with the runway. The plane settled safely, but the touchdown was not as smooth as it should have been.

We rolled to a stop. Jim and I changed seats. The whole check-ride process was repeated, this time with Jim at the controls in the co-pilot's seat. Tom, sitting in the rear next to me, was turning green. With an encouraging smile, I showed him where to find the airsickness bags, but he never quite needed them. Jim's piloting held my attention. I wanted to see if my own clumsiness at the controls was a normal reaction to the unfamiliar heaviness of the aircraft. After a while, it was clear that Jim was doing noticeably better than I had.

On the flight back to Midway, Bob showed us how to operate the advanced navigational equipment and radio gear aboard the aircraft. We used it to simulate a bad weather radar approach on our landing. After crawling out of the plane, Tom, ashen-faced and frightened, pulled me aside and quietly asked if the maneuvers on the check-ride were as terrifying as anything he was likely to encounter on the flight to Wounded Knee. I assured him that the trip west would not call for anything nearly that rough. We agreed that it had been smart for him to fly with us on the check-ride. Being familiar with the worst of it would help make normal flying less upsetting. Little did we know then what was actually in store for us.

Once the plane was tied down, Jim wanted to get back to Bob's basement and take care of the last of the parachute packing. He took Tom with him as Bob and I walked toward a nearby hangar to place a deposit on one of the airplanes. The poor landings on the check-ride stuck in my mind.

"Look, Bob, I don't think I'm capable of flying that Cherokee. I mean, I can fly it all right, but I shouldn't be in charge of one of the planes. I should be flying co-pilot, not pilot-in-command."

Bob turned to me, his voice calm and self-assured. "You were worked to your limit up there. You're exhausted from staying up all night. When you get out to South Dakota, you'll be flying in very adverse conditions. I made it tough on you because I wanted you to know your limits and the limits of the aircraft. You did okay for someone who's never flown a heavy single before."

"You're sure?"

"I'm sure."

"Well, I'm not. It would be a mistake for me to do it."

"That's bullshit."

"It's not bullshit. I don't want to be responsible for the lives of people on board. I didn't feel in command behind that control wheel. I didn't feel like it was my ship, like I could tell it what to do."

"You're overplaying it," Bob countered. "You've got 1,000 miles of practice between here and Wounded Knee. You'll be fine before you're half way there. Take my word for it."

"I can't take your word for it. It's got to be my decision and I'm deciding no. We have to find another pilot or you've got to go."

"Oh, shit."

We walked into the office of the flight service that rented the Cherokee. Bob knew the owner, so before I handed him the deposit, Bob explained where we were going and why. The owner, in typical Chicago fashion, threw up his hands and said he preferred to know nothing except when we would be back and how we would pay. The unresolved argument about Bob's flying to Wounded Knee hung in the air between us. But Bob was determined not to go. He asked the flight service owner if there were any pilots around who might be interested in the airlift. The man directed us to the other side of the huge hangar where we were to look for a part-time flight instructor who was not only young, but had once participated in a civil rights march. Normally that wouldn't be a very convincing recommendation. But given our desperation and the narrow-minded world of private aviation, it wasn't bad either.

We found the flight instructor, introduced ourselves by first names only, and asked his opinion of the Wounded Knee confrontation. He indicated sympathy with the Indians, so we explained our plans and asked if he would consider leaving with us in two hours. It was preposterous. Yet, remarkably, the instructor said he was interested. First, he wanted to check on the legality of the airlift, then he would give us an answer. We didn't tell him where or how to contact us. Instead, we agreed to meet back in the hangar exactly an hour and a half later. It wasn't much of a precaution, but caution had long before been thrown to the wind.

We walked across the street to Bob's backyard. The entire parachute packing operation had spilled outside the house. Before he could fold the chutes into the deployment bags, Jim had to stretch out and check each of the numerous lines that led down from the canopies themselves to the loads attached below. Here and there a few lines were cut and had to be retied. One billowing white parachute was spread across the backyard. Two people held the huge piece of nylon down as the wind rippled through it. Out on the sidewalk next to the yard, Strobe supervised work on another wind-tossed parachute canopy. It was bright red. As Bob and I walked up, Larry stopped me on the street, half crying and half laughing.

"Do you see what's going on here," he sputtered, hardly able to contain his indignation. "People walking down the street have to step over parachutes just to get by this house. Parachutes! Do you think they're going to forget that at our trial? I mean, when was the last time you were walking down a street and you had to step over a goddamn parachute?

"I've been keeping this whole thing secret. I didn't even leave our phone number with those reporters I called. You know—'We'll call you, don't call us.' Now, these guys are hanging red parachutes out on the sidewalk. Red, no less!"

We picked our way through the tangle of chutes and lines and people helping. Despite the seriousness of the situation, Larry made us laugh. Nothing could be done. Perhaps actually becoming a full-fledged community social project had its advantages. We looked the opposite of suspicious working out in the open in broad daylight. Anyway, we had no choice, and the audacity might provide us with some short-term protection.

"Hey, Larry," I yelled, "why don't you call some of those reporters to come down and cover this scene. Think of the headlines: CHICAGO NEIGHBORHOOD ARRESTED FOR SUPPLYING WOUNDED KNEE—TWO-BLOCK AREA GOES OVER TO REBELS."

I left Larry laughing and went into the house. I wanted to get more information from Bob about the student pilot we had invited to join the airlift just before the check-ride. Over a cup of coffee at the kitchen table, Bob told me that the student had just decided to accept our invitation.

"Fine, but just exactly who is he?" I asked, recalling his lack of knowledge about Wounded Knee.

"His name's John Adelman. I see him every day at school. I think he's twenty or twenty-one. He's a regular junior college student where I teach, but in the afternoons and evenings he works an eight-hour shift on a forklift truck at the Sears, Roebuck warehouse.

"He's been taking flying lessons on weekends for a while, but he doesn't have the money to really get into it. He's just a nice guy. He doesn't have a pot to piss in, but he'll give you the shirt off his back. I don't think he cares much about the Indians, but I told him to go, that it was a good chance to get some free flight time as a co-pilot.

"I explained the whole deal to him and he muddled it around for a while. Then he said, 'What the hell, you can't go through life just working at Sears. If you're going to get in trouble, you might as well get in trouble for doing something good.' It's not like John to talk that way. He's usually pretty conservative. So he's going. But remember, he's got no real commitment to what you're doing. He's only in it to get some free time in the air."

It was three o'clock in the afternoon and yet another hour went by before all the parachutes were properly packed. The five of us who had stayed up all night were sleepy and tense. We were anxious to be gone, to finally start on the trip that we had been preparing for so long. Billy Wright, the pilot who had signed on the night before, arrived at the house. He and Bob and I went to the airport to get the three Cherokees. We took four seats out of each airplane. Then we kept our appointment with the flight instructor we had promised to meet an hour and a half earlier. He was willing to go, but at the same time he was either suspicious of us or completely lacking in enthusiasm.

We climbed into the three airplanes and taxied, single-file, out of the hangar and over to the most deserted section of the airport. Our friends were waiting for us. Strobe had borrowed a yellow truck, and the people at Bob's house had loaded all the cargo and parachutes into it. Then they piled into our rented station wagons and all three vehicles pulled onto a taxiway at the far corner of the airport. It was a frenzied scene. There were 15 people trying to quickly transfer the food from the truck to the three planes. The duffel bags were already inside the cargo nets, two or three at a time, and each full net had been weighed and labeled at Bob's house. But there were snags. The loads had to be divided equally between the airplanes. The transfer operation had not been planned carefully and was unnecessarily slow and confused.

Besides his secretary, his other student, and three of his four kids, who were all helping transfer the load, Bob had invited a photographer friend to take pictures. The man was trustworthy and was willing to make his photos available to Tom Oliphant's newspaper or any other news media. Furthermore, we were to inspect the photos first and if any had airplane numbers or faces we did not want published, the negatives would be turned over to Bob. While everyone in the crowd worked on the cargo, the photographer shot off a roll of film.

The newly recruited flight instructor, who had reluctantly joined us just minutes before, took one look at the picture-taking and stopped in his tracks. "What's going on here?" he asked, his voice breaking with anger. "I thought this was a mercy flight, not some kind of publicity stunt."

It is often hard to understand that creating favorable publicity and political support for people is sometimes just as merciful as bringing them food. Realizing how delicate the situation was, I moved quickly to offer the young flight instructor a patient and sympathetic explanation. But Bob, standing tall and indignant next to one of the airplanes, immediately started shouting at him.

"Look, buddy, everybody here is in this because they want to be. We didn't have to be talked into it and now we don't have room for any wishy-washy horseshit. You're either in it or you're out of it. If you're in it, you do things the way we've all agreed to do them."

"Well, I'm out of it!" the instructor snapped back, zipping up his flight jacket and walking off.

"What? Bob, how could you do that?" It was all I could say before rushing after the instructor to apologize. I had only one thought—we needed him to fly the third plane and somehow I had to get him back. But Bob shouted after me to let the instructor go. He would fly the third plane himself. The offer stopped me cold. It was just what I wanted to hear. I walked back, letting the anger slowly drain out of me. But Bob still had one more surprise in his bag of tricks. He took my arm and led me off away from the others.

"Look, that guy didn't belong here," he began. "You have a long way to fly before you get to Wounded Knee. Who knows what's going to happen between here and there. You've got to have a solid group, a unified group. If you get into a tight spot and you have to depend on each other, an oddball like that could destroy everything."

"Maybe so, but that's not the point," I protested angrily. "It's your damn individualism. Every time you work with a group, you go off on your own and do something like that without talking to anyone first. Why didn't you ask me before getting rid of that guy?"

"Simple. Because I was right and you just wouldn't have listened to me." Bob was chuckling to himself. His arrogantly comic reply broke the tension.

"All right, damn it," I laughed, "you probably were right. Now let's get back to those birds and get out of here."

"Oh, I'm not going," Bob calmly announced, "but I'll go back and help you load."

"You bastard. You just told me you'd fly the other plane."

"I know. I lied. I can't go. I'd love to fly with you, but it's too risky for me. I want tenure and I teach aviation. Even if I just got a minor violation from the FAA for this, the college would use it as an excuse to deny tenure. I'm sorry; I've got more at stake than the rest of you.

"Anyway, I know that you can fly that plane, even if you don't. You've been working for thirty-six hours without any sleep. The last few days have been a real strain. You flew that Cherokee better than you thought you did. Take my word for it. Really. I know a lot more about it than you do."

He was right. Besides, he had worn down my resistance while building up my confidence at the same time. We walked back along the deserted taxiway, past row after row of parked aircraft. A light breeze was blowing under a cloudless sky that swept out all around us. The loading was complete. Everyone agreed that as long as I felt good about flying the third ship, it was all right with them. The time had come to decide who would be on the flight crew. We crowded around the wingtip of one of the planes and made our decision.

Each aircraft needed a pilot and a cargo-handler, someone to kick the food out over Wounded Knee. If possible, the cargo-handler could double as co-pilot, but a co-pilot was not necessary. Billy Wright, the only professional among us, had the least need for a co-pilot. He was assigned to fly the lead plane with Strobe as cargo-kicker. Strobe had no flying experience, but he knew something about parachutes. Jim Stewart, the sky diver, would fly the second airplane with John Adelman, the student pilot, as his co-pilot and cargo-kicker. I took the third ship with Larry Levin handling cargo. Larry had done a little co-piloting with me previously when the two of us had gone flying together. Tom Oliphant was assigned to ride with Billy Wright or me. Jim Stewart's plane was too heavy to carry a third person.

Larry and Strobe were very happy. Unlike the others, they were not sure until the very last minute whether they would fly with the airlift or not. Both had told me beforehand that they wanted to go. Especially Larry, who had mentioned it repeatedly, every day, since we first developed our plans back in Boston.

With the crew selected, we said goodbye to the others and moved toward our planes. Larry stopped me as I was climbing up on the wing.

"Look at the sun," he said, pointing at the round red ball a few degrees above the horizon. "It's five o'clock. It'll be dark soon. No one's slept. Why are we going now? Are you sure we shouldn't wait 'til morning?"

"Absolutely sure," I replied. "There is very little holding this group together right now. People have just met each other. They don't know a lot about Wounded Knee. If we hang around much longer, some of them might have second thoughts about going.

"I want to get the thing started. I want to move everybody out of Chicago so it's easier to go forward to Wounded Knee than it is to turn around and give up. Anyway, every third person in this neighborhood knows what we're doing. If we don't leave soon, we may not be able to."

"What about those bad weather reports you and Billy were talking about before?"

"The weather's beautiful half way to South Dakota. Then it gets lousy in the Omaha-Council Bluffs area. But if we wait for it to clear there, it'll probably turn bad here. I say we go now, fly as far as we can, wait there for an improvement, and then go on. It's clear that we'll never make the drop by dawn tomorrow. So we do it at sunset, or we wait for dawn on Sunday. Let's get as far as we can now and worry about the rest when we're closer to Wounded Knee."

Just then Billy Wright came running over from his plane to ours. "Say, man, you got any maps with you?"

"Oh, no," I groaned. "I forgot to go buy them this afternoon. Are there any old ones lying around in your plane?"

"Nope, none. There's an out-of-date one in Jim's plane and that's all we got. I know we ain't gonna be able to buy any more here at Midway, not at this time of day."

"Well, we've got to do something," I insisted. "Can we follow a highway? Interstate 80 goes direct to Omaha from here."

Billy's answer was quick and firm. "Oh no, man. I ain't going up with no charts in a three-plane formation when two of you guys been up all night. Flying with no charts means you don't know the radio frequencies, you don't know where the airports are if you get into trouble. Come on, you know all that. You don't just pull off to the side of the airway if something goes wrong up there. The FAA district office at Aurora airport has charts we can buy. It's forty miles west. I'll go that far without them."

When it came to flight decisions, Billy was boss. We gathered together and spread our one map out on the concrete ramp. Billy knew the area by heart and could easily find Aurora without a chart. I could find the airport by following the highways, which I knew well from growing up in Chicago, but I studied the chart for a few minutes to refresh my memory. We agreed that Jim should take the one outdated map. He did not know the area at all, but John, his co-pilot, had flown over it several times and was confident he could find Aurora. It was a bad way to start—no sleep, no charts, almost no daylight left. But we all felt the same urge to fly, to be gone from Chicago. We separated with shouts of "See you in Aurora."

I slid behind the control wheel, adjusted the seat, and strapped myself in. Larry was beside me. Tom was riding in the back of Billy's plane, sitting on top of the cargo where the rear seats had been. The cockpit dashboard was still unfamiliar, so I used a printed check list to get the engine started: wheel brakes locked—carburetor heat off—propeller pitch control full forward—fuel on proper tank—fuel mixture control full rich—throttle cracked open—electric fuel pump on—engine primed—master switch on—magnetos on. The big engine cranked over smoothly. While it warmed up, I tuned the aircraft radio to the ground control frequency, picked up the hand mike, and read my aircraft registration number (5753R) off the dashboard plaque.

"Midway ground, this is Cherokee five-seven-five-three-romeo. We are ready to taxi from the west ramp. Over."

"Cherokee five-three-romeo, Midway ground. Cleared to taxi to runway two-two-right via the north ramp. Wind, two-four-zero degrees at eight knots. Altimeter, three-zero-one-niner. Over."

"Five-three-romeo, roger."

We swung out of the parking place onto the taxiway and lined up behind Billy and Jim. It took us several minutes to get to the apron of the active runway. Big as we were for single-engine planes, we looked like three little insects parked next to the jet airliners waiting beside us for their rush-hour takeoffs. I went through another check list for takeoff: flight controls checked and free—flaps set one notch down—trim tab set—propeller speed set to maximum—fuel mixture rich—carb heat off—fuel tank selector set—fuel pump on—engine oil pressure and temperature gauges checked—doors latched—altimeter set—directional gyro set. When we were number one in line for the runway, I switched the radio from the ground control frequency up to the tower. We had to wait for a jet to land. Then they gave us our outbound clearance.

I pushed the throttle all the way in and the Cherokee began to roll down the long runway. It wanted to climb at 75 mph, but I held it on the ground until the airspeed indicator hit 85 mph. We were loaded, and I wanted the added lift and greater control that came with more speed. The runway dropped away and seconds later we were over the houses next to the airport. At 500 feet, I pulled back a little on the throttle and adjusted the propeller speed for cruise-climb. The visibility was unusually good. As we continued up, the city spread out all around us. The network of expressways stood out sharply against the checkerboard streets. I pointed the aircraft northwest, toward the Eisenhower Expressway. West of Chicago it became U.S. Highway 30 and passed by the Aurora airport.

For the first time in my life, I was flying from one place to another without an aeronautical chart, the "roadmap" of the air. I felt ill-equipped and uneasy. Aurora was not going to be difficult to find. There were familiar landmarks around and an expressway to follow. But if something went wrong and an emergency landing became necessary, without a chart there would be no way to find the nearest airport. Even a simple mistake like following the wrong expressway would be hard to detect and once made even harder to correct.

A pilot's dependence on a chart is far greater than a motorist's on a road map. As Billy said, if something goes wrong, there is no way to pull over and stop. That's when the difficult work begins, the safe descent. The chart not only tells the pilot where he is and where he has to go, but also what to expect when he gets there—the runway direction, the control tower frequency, and a host of other essential items. Such information is no less important if *nothing* goes wrong. The pilot still has to make a safe descent.

When we reached 2,000 feet, I pushed the nose down to level the plane, then adjusted the engine controls for cruising speed. The urban sprawl of metropolitan Chicago gradually fell away behind us. Fifteen minutes later, I could see the small city of Aurora dead ahead. I knew the airport was ten miles farther west, but it was difficult to find against the

background of Midwestern farms. Again, I felt the need for an aeronautical chart, but I soon had the airport in sight and made radio contact as I
prepared to enter the traffic pattern. It was a small airfield. We were well
out of the city. There was nothing but flat farmland all around us. I slowed
down the plane, dropped the flaps, and descended to a fairly smooth
landing.

There was a parking spot in the tie-down area next to Billy's plane,
which had already landed. Larry and I got out, walked into the terminal
building, and found Billy, Strobe, and Tom in the pilot's lounge. Jim and
John had taken off ahead of us, but had not yet arrived. Billy reminded us
that neither of them could navigate very well—Jim didn't know the area
and John was too inexperienced. But Billy wasn't concerned. He was
troubled by something more important. There were no charts for sale in
the Aurora airport. Their stock had just been cleaned out.

Aurora was barely beyond the Chicago suburbs. We sat down to figure
things out. In effect, we were back where we started from, and the same
reasoning still applied.

I looked around at the four others and said cautiously, "We are going
on, aren't we?"

Slowly, reluctantly, they each nodded their agreement. Then, Billy
sprang to his feet. "All right, goddamn it, let's do it! The weatherman says
it's perfect all the way to Omaha, and that's halfway to Wounded Knee.
We'll fly in a tight formation and keep an eye on each other. We can set
the radios for air-to-air communications and be talking back and forth the
whole trip.

"I've flown the route hundreds of times," Billy continued. "I'll copy the
radio frequencies we need off the wall chart over there. There's even an
airport I know in Council Bluffs, across the river from Omaha. The control
tower will be shut down by the time we arrive, so we can land without
going through traffic control. It's just a bitch that it's gonna be dark so
soon."

Billy went to the wall map to get the radio navigation frequencies
between Aurora and Council Bluffs, 400 miles to the west. I walked
around asking people in the terminal for any old charts of the Chicago to
Omaha route. All I got was a slightly outdated map of the northern Illinois
segment. Meanwhile, John and Jim had not arrived. Strobe called Bob
Talbot's house to see if they had gotten lost and returned to Midway. Bob
hadn't heard anything; we began to worry. Forty long minutes after my
own landing there was still no sign of them. All of us were at the window
checking the numbers of each plane that landed. Another call was made
to Bob, but there was still no word.

Finally, just as it was getting dark, we saw them touch down. A few
minutes later, they strolled into the pilot's lounge comically trying to
pretend that nothing had happened. But their act quickly dissolved under

our questioning, and they admitted getting lost. We explained the lack of maps and our decision to go ahead anyway. When the scene quieted down, I pulled Jim to the side and asked him to account for the long delay.

"Once we took off from Midway," he began, "I headed northwest and said, 'John, where's this Aurora?' He says, 'Oh, it's off in this direction somewhere.' Well, it was soon apparent to me that John didn't know where the hell Aurora was. We were lost. I decided to use the radio, dug out that outdated chart I had, and dialed in the Naperville omni.

"You know, it's been a while since I've done any flying. Well, god-damn it, I started flying backwards on that radial without realizing it. I was flying *away* from the station when I thought I was flying toward it. I knew something was wrong because pretty soon the terrain didn't look like the chart said it should."

Jim was making fun of his own clumsiness. He went on with the story laughing between sentences. "So, I'm going through all of this shit trying to figure out what's wrong. Finally, I decided to forget about the radio and do a little old-fashioned navigation. I dropped down to a hundred feet and read the name of a town off the side of a water tower.

"The place was called DeKalb and it was way past Aurora. That's when I turned around. It was really funny, you know. Poor old John figured I was going to kill us before we got to Aurora. He was so shaky about my flying that he started trying to override me with the co-pilot's controls, and him being just a 20-hour student pilot.

"He was sitting there, shaking his head and grabbing at the controls, probably thinking, 'Wow, what did I get myself into?' I sort of slapped him away from the wheel and told him, 'Now look, John, I don't know shit about radio procedures and navigation, but I can fly the airplane. You take care of this other stuff and I'll do the flying.'

"I'll tell you," Jim continued, still chuckling to himself, "that whole thing was a good little incident. We established, John and myself did, that I had enough ability to keep us alive. That is, once I discovered that I was flying backwards on the radial. I think we're going to be all right now, as a team I mean. We sort of know each other. We broke the ice."

When Jim and I rejoined the others, they were huddled over an instrument chart that a local pilot had just given Billy. The chart was used only for blind flying. It was plain white paper with no terrain features or landmarks, only the radio beacons and airways necessary for instrument flight. The chart was up to date and covered the entire distance between Chicago and Council Bluffs. At night it was all we needed, at least for one of the planes. We were ready to fly. This time we planned to stay together. We walked to the tie-down area and climbed aboard our aircraft.

Billy took off first, followed by Jim and then me. The two of them circled a few miles from Aurora until I caught up. Then the three of us turned west toward the only portion of sky still faintly blue. We gradually formed ourselves into a very wide triangular, or "V," formation. Billy flew point, out in front, while Jim and I stayed a half mile behind and off to either side. We climbed slowly to 4,500 feet and leveled off. I was dead tired, but the job ahead of me was fairly simple. Billy was doing most of the work. Once an aircraft is cruising at the proper altitude, much of the cockpit time is spent on navigation. Since I was only following the lights of the lead plane, I didn't have to worry about navigating. Besides keeping the aircraft in straight and level flight and occasionally checking the engine gauges, all I had to do was stay a half mile behind the rotating red light on the tail of Billy's plane and a half mile to the right of the rotating red light on Jim's tail. I settled back for the three-hour trip to Council Bluffs.

Soon it was completely dark. I could see nothing of the other two aircraft except their rotating red beacons. Night flight is often eerie, but doing it after 36 hours without sleep was positively disorienting. Inside the dark cabin, Larry's face was bathed in a faint red glow from the dashboard instrument illumination. Outside, the inky blackness was all around us, not just above and off to the sides, but beneath us as well. We were very isolated. The twinkling farmhouse lights were the only sign of earthbound life, though occainally we seemed to float slowly past a large cluster of lights from a town or city far below. The airplane bored on through the night. At times, I was very relaxed, as though I were simply sitting in a comfortable chair reading dials and moving levers. Then, abruptly, I realized that the chair hung a mile above the earth mysteriously suspended in the dark and moonless sky.

I began to lose the lights of the other two planes. They were easy to see at first, but soon were hard to distinguish from other lights we were flying over. It was important to keep a half-mile separation between the airplanes. Closer than that at night was not safe; farther apart made it too easy to lose track of each other. If we did get separated, even with radios, three planes flying at night in slightly different directions with no maps would never find each other again. Since Billy had the only chart that went all the way to Council Bluffs, Jim and I might have a difficult time just finding an airport to land at in the dark.

It was very difficult to judge the distance between my plane and the other two with only their rotating red taillights to guide me. First I got too close. Then I drifted too far away. I couldn't stay awake, and my judgment of distance got a lot worse as I became more and more drowsy. I needed something to do to keep me awake so I called Billy on the air-to-air radio frequency.

"Four-one-juliet, this is five-three-romeo. What is the city off to our right at two o'clock? Over."

"Five-three-romeo, four-one-juliet. I make it Rock Falls." I called over and over again as the light-cluster cities slid by—Clinton, Davenport, Iowa City. But my eyes kept closing and I had to slap my face to stay awake. It was hypnotic staring into the black void around us at two special little specks of light in what was often a sea of lights. I dozed off, woke up with a start, and dozed off again. I asked Larry to massage the back of my neck to keep me awake. I sang, I made small talk on the radio, anything to avoid falling asleep.

Two hours from Aurora, in my exhaustion, I got angry. I didn't know what I was doing in that cockpit, why I had let Bob talk me into flying the plane. Finally, I told Larry that I just couldn't follow the rotating red light on Billy's tail any longer. He had to do it. I leaned my head against the window and luxuriated in the closing of my eyes. Larry watched the beacons on the other two aircraft and woke me every time he thought a slight course correction was necessary.

Meanwhile, conditions were a lot better in the other airplanes. Billy had not stayed up all night helping with the cargo rigging. He was wide awake in the lead aircraft. Jim, in the third plane, had turned the controls over to John and was napping. John was only a student pilot but knew enough to follow Billy and keep his ship flying on a straight line. Larry did not have the same level of skill, so I had to force myself to stay more or less awake.

Through it all I remained outraged at myself for flying at night without a map. At 120 miles from Council Bluffs, I began a period of intense clock watching. Forty-five minutes to go. The hands of the dashboard clock glowed red in the dark cabin. Each five-minute advance seemed like a great victory. Forty minutes to go. Thirty-five. Thirty. Twenty-five. The magic position, where I knew the hands of the clock would be when we arrived in Council Bluffs, was all that mattered in the entire world. At last, with ten minutes left to fly, the lights of the Council Bluffs-Omaha metropolitan area appeared in the distance ahead.

Billy picked his way through the dazzling glitter, leading our little triangle of airplanes toward a single point, a green and white rotating beacon that marked the Council Bluffs airport. We descended, slowed the airplanes, and lowered our flaps. As expected, the control tower was closed for the night. We flew over the field to get a good look at the runway and then circled back to land. One at a time, each plane broke from the formation and went down. Ours was last. I lined up the Cherokee for final approach and very slowly the rectangle of runway lights floated up out of the surrounding darkness. A minute later the wheels screeched on the concrete and we were down.

We taxied to the dark and deserted parking area, tied down the wings and tails, and locked up the aircraft. There was a telephone booth outside one of the hangars, and in a short time a cab pulled up in response to our call. We drove to a motel, staggered into the dining room, and ordered dinner. Besides our lack of sleep the previous night, most of us had been too busy to eat anything all day.

The meal was loud and boisterous. We were giddy with relief and renewed confidence. We were halfway to Wounded Knee. Billy, neither tired nor hungry, ordered only dessert—a strawberry sundae and beer. The combination seemed ridiculously funny to the rest of us. So one by one we went back around the table topping off our own dinners with orders of strawberry sundae and beer, laughing more uproariously as each new convert joined the parade.

Later, Billy called the local weather service and got an optimistic forecast. The heavy snow west of us was predicted to pass through the Council Bluffs area that night, leaving high clouds and good visibility all the way to South Dakota the next morning. We planned our drop over Wounded Knee for sunset the following day. An early takeoff would enable us to fly past South Dakota and into Wyoming, so we could approach Wounded Knee from the west rather than the east. If our approach were spotted on government radar screens, we wanted to help the FBI jump to the wrong conclusion and assume that we planned an escape back west after the parachute drop. While they focused their search in Wyoming and beyond, we would be en route back east to Chicago. If the good weather held, it would be a simple matter to return to Midway Airport late that same night.

There was still a little work left to do in the aircraft. The parachutes had to be attached to the duffel bags, and the ripcords had to be fixed to the parachute packs. If we took off early, all that could be done at a leisurely pace while we waited at some quiet country airport in Wyoming. Then just before sunset, we would make the 45-minute flight back east to Wounded Knee, drop the food, and continue east at low altitude below the radar coverage. It sounded quick and clean and very satisfying, but in a fashion that was fast becoming typical, its simplicity would vanish like a morning haze.

8

The Seizure
of Wounded Knee

*"Our land is more valuable than your money. It will last forever.
It will not even perish by the flames of fire. As long as the sun
shines and the waters flow, this land will be here to give life to
men and animals. We cannot sell the lives of men and animals;
therefore we cannot sell this land. It was put here for us by the
Great Spirit and we cannot sell it because it does not belong to
us. You can count your money and burn it within the nod of a
buffalo's head, but only the Great Spirit can count the grains of
sand and the blades of grass of these plains. As a present to you,
we will give you anything we have that you can take with you;
but the land, never."*

—Northern Blackfeet chief

The Oglala Sioux chiefs and headmen were removed from formal
authority over their tribe by the Indian Reorganization Act of 1934. They
were replaced by a "constitutional" tribal government, presided over by
officials like Dick Wilson who were elected once every two years.
Nevertheless, the chiefs and other "traditional" leaders retain considerable influence on the reservation. Despite U.S. government attempts to
undermine them, they survive as a parallel, if officially unrecognized,
force. On their shoulders is the mantle of history. They are the main link
to the last proud years in which the Sioux were a whole people.

The traditional leadership is especially influential outside the town of
Pine Ridge, among people living in the countryside on family land or in
one of the small settlements scattered about the reservation. Their set-

147

tlements, like Porcupine, Manderson, Kyle, Calico, Wounded Knee, and others, date back only two or three generations. Before that the Sioux were nomads. With no modern conveniences, these people are isolated from white civilization and more directly in touch with the traditions of their own past. The chiefs, medicine men, and headmen are the grandsons of the last generation of Plains warriors. Regardless of their lack of "legal" power or status, people constantly look to them for advice, whether on questions of great or little consequence.

Gladys Bissonette, as one of the organizers of the Oglala Sioux Civil Rights Organization (OSCRO), spent many hours in discussion with the tribe's traditional leadership during the days before the seizure of Wounded Knee. OSCRO sought the guidance of the old chiefs. Indeed, one of the organization's long-range goals was to dispose of the constitutional tribal government and replace it with a government under the traditional leaders. But in the short run, OSCRO was working to get rid of Dick Wilson. When the impeachment hearings failed on February 23, and OSCRO began holding nightly meetings in the Calico Community Hall, everyone understood that to succeed the struggle against Wilson would have to be seriously escalated. Among other things, people at the meeting discussed whether or not to ask the American Indian Movement to come back to the reservation and help them. Given Wilson's intense hatred for AIM, it was a grim decision. The chiefs, who were not directly a part of OSCRO, were consulted.

"We tried to stick as close as we could to the laws of the 1868 Treaty," Gladys remarked, remembering those consultations. "You know, we never violated that treaty. The government's broke it all kinds of times, dozens of times, but as far as we're concerned, that treaty is still the law 'cause we never agreed that it wouldn't be.

"So on the 25th of February, we asked all the chiefs to make a decision for us about AIM. They told us it was up to us. They were along with us because they could see the dirty, crooked, corrupted work that Dick Wilson was bringing on. They could see how he was trying to starve the people off the land and how he was leasing Indian land dirt-cheap to white ranchers and all the time living high and mighty himself."

The hundreds of people participating in OSCRO's nightly meetings at Calico voted overwhelmingly to request help from AIM. But two days later, on February 27, there was still no plan for using the help they were likely to get. An OSCRO leadership meeting was called for the afternoon to discuss the question.

"Somebody spoke up," Gladys recalled, "and said, 'Well, why don't we go right in and take over the BIA office in Pine Ridge with the chiefs?' Now, there was always informers hanging around. So those informers rushed back and made their report to Wilson. But we knew they were doing that."

All during the afternoon of the 27th, people talked in small groups about what action they should take. No large meetings were held. Various rumors made the rounds. Wounded Knee was only one of the undercurrents, as different people contemplated different actions and tactics in different locations. No one knew what was going to happen, but no one would contradict the most public of the rumors—namely, that under the leadership of the chiefs, OSCRO planned to storm the BIA building in Pine Ridge and occupy it the way AIM had occupied the BIA building in Washington four months before.

As evening approached, Gladys and another person from OSCRO drove out to see Red Cloud, one of the old chiefs. They knew that another mass meeting was scheduled at Calico that night. An action decision could not be put off any longer. They wanted to find out where Red Cloud stood.

"The old man spoke straight," Gladys said. "He told me, 'Whatever the people decide, if it's for the good of the Indians, my vote is in there and it'll be yes.' "

This Red Cloud was the great-grandson of the original Red Cloud, the 19th century chief who led the Sioux to victory over the U.S. Army in the two-year war for the valley of the Powder River. It was that victory that resulted in the Sioux Treaty of 1868. Later, Red Cloud negotiated successfully with President Grant in Washington and shepherded his people through the first difficult years on what became the Pine Ridge Reservation. In the end, Red Cloud suffered through the theft of the sacred Black Hills and saw, in his old age, the bloody snow at Wounded Knee. It was he who said of the white men, "They made us many promises, more than I can remember. But they never kept but one—they promised to take our land, and they took it."

To the people on the Pine Ridge Reservation, Red Cloud represented the living history of their tribe, a history that had unfolded on the very land upon which they stood. Few among them were not moved by the fact that the old man they called Chief Red Cloud was the great-grandson of the first Chief Red Cloud, and the grandson of another Chief Red Cloud, and the son of another.

"When we came back from Chief Red Cloud's place," Gladys said, continuing her description of events on February 27, "it wasn't dark yet. It was between the sun going down and dark; it was still light out. We had to go through Pine Ridge to get back to Calico from where Chief Red Cloud lived; and when we went through Pine Ridge, we saw that BIA building there, the top of it was so full of machine guns you would've thought there was a whole army comin' in."

Once back in Calico, Gladys and the OSCRO leadership met with Dennis Banks and three other AIM leaders. It was then that AIM finally decided to take action with the Oglala Sioux Civil Rights Organization.

After the decision, there was some whispered talk about various tactical alternatives, including a sit-in or demonstration at Wounded Knee. But even as the huge caravan of cars and pickup trucks left the Calico Community Hall, for the announced purpose of shifting the site of the meeting to Porcupine, still no one was willing to deny the possibility that they were going to take over the BIA building in Pine Ridge. It was a thoughtful trick. The heavily armed U.S. marshals and BIA police stood scratching their heads in confusion as the long line of vehicles drove into and pulled away from Pine Ridge without a single car so much as stopping for gas.

OSCRO leaders had helped government officers get entangled in their own erroneous assumptions. Police typically assume that informers deliver reliable information. They have few other sources. They also assume that the range of tactics that can be used against them is limited and that once a successful tactic is found, like the Washington BIA building takeover, it will be tried again and again. The police officers in Pine Ridge stumbled over both of these assumptions, plus one more. They assumed that power lay exclusively in the bureaucratic center of the reservation, Pine Ridge, rather than in the symbolic and spiritual center, Wounded Knee. Thus, all federal forces had been concentrated in Pine Ridge. Wounded Knee, among other places, was left "unprotected."

Gladys described those first moments in Wounded Knee. "When we got there, my power-steering apparatus went out on me and I really had to struggle with that jalopy. It took ten acres to turn around in my car. So I parked in a position where I wouldn't have to do any turning to go right on out. Then I looked around, and oh, there was a lot of people. You didn't know who you were going to run into. It was just a mad scramble there."

The Indians' first act was to occupy the Sacred Heart Catholic Church. It was the small, isolated, white-steepled structure that sat on a low hill overlooking the village. Next to the church was the long trench turned into a Christian grave that contained 153 bodies of people killed by the 7th Cavalry in the 1890 Wounded Knee massacre.

"So I called my kids," Gladys continued, "two of my boys were with me, and pretty soon someone come and said, 'File on up to the church.' Well, we went up to the Catholic Church and they shooed us right straight down into the basement. There was quite a few of us, my sister and I and our kids, and her daughter and her grandchildren, and a lot of others. We filled up the basement, and that's where we stayed all night."

Upstairs some of the church pews were pushed to the side. Young Indian men and women danced to the beat of a drum. Later that evening the white pastor of the church recuperated from the ordeal in the living room of the white trading post owner. The priest complained about the

The Sacred Heart Catholic Church in Wounded Knee on the hilltop used by the 7th U.S. Cavalry to mount their Hotchkiss guns during the massacre of 1890. Behind the church is a small pillar marking the mass grave of the victims. (*courtesy Joanna Brown.*)

Federal roadblock outside Wounded Knee. Two armored personnel carriers (APC's) are visible on either side of the cluster of automo-

Indians mistreating a "sacred place." An Oglala woman, one of Gladys' friends and the wife of a medicine man, heard his complaints and replied that it was the church that had mistreated a sacred place of the Indians.

"Those people who died here, the ones they threw in the trench on top of each other, they weren't Catholic people," she said. "They were never baptized. They followed the Original Ways, the Sacred Pipe Ceremonies. They were doing a ghost dance, a spirit dance.

"We believe that our body is just a robe which our spirit wears, and that when our body is buried, our spirit remains. White people say, 'father, son, and holy ghost,' but they say they can't understand Indian people believing in spirits.

"Maybe somebody figured this place would make a lot of money because everyone would come to see that grave. So they built a Catholic Church almost on top of them, and put a cross over the trench. Then some more people come along and said let's put up a trading post and a museum and make some money from the tourists who will come here. They are all making money off our dead people."

As some of the Indians moved into the Sacred Heart Church, others spread out across the dark countryside to set up blockades on the four roads leading into Wounded Knee. At first, the roadblocks consisted of picketing that began as a nonviolent demonstration.

"The purpose of the roadblock," according to Dennis Banks, "was just to stop the commercial traffic. We made an immediate decision in the beginning not to stop any Indian families, whatever their business was. Our roadblocks had a bunch of people and a couple of cars turned in across the road. Mostly, we just stopped cars and then let them go on without any kind of confrontation. We were all unarmed at that point."

The people at the roadblocks and inside the church were only a handful compared to the hundreds left milling about the area. No doubt it was a plan in the minds of some and just random action for the others, but these hundreds began to occupy the remaining buildings in Wounded Knee. Included was the white-owned trading post. Only one story high, it was nevertheless the largest structure in the village. All of the food and other supplies in it quickly disappeared. Some was taken to the basement of the Sacred Heart Church. The rest was confiscated by members of the 40 or so Indian families who were permanent residents of Wounded Knee. For decades, this trading post had been the only food and general supply store in the settlement. All of the people who lived there had been indebted to it at one time or another.

The trading post was also stripped of its small firearms inventory —perhaps a dozen rifles and shotguns, some handguns, and a quantity of ammunition.

"The first shots fired," Dennis continued, "were immediately after we had secured the town. We had an exchange of gunfire in the first few hours there with the BIA police. It wasn't an exchange really, they were just firing a few shots at us. In the meantime, we had some guns that we found in the trading post. So when they started shooting at us, in about the third hour, some of our people started shooting back.

"Of course, there were two miles in between all of this shooting. It wasn't effective. No one was hurt. You couldn't possibly hurt anyone at that range. But it was effective to the point that the BIA police and Wilson's goons knew that we wouldn't permit them to come into Wounded Knee—that we would shoot back if they fired on us."

"About that time, we realized that roadblocks were being set up on the other side of our roadblocks. I was up at the church the first three or four hours trying to organize what had to be done, then and in the morning. There was a lot of talk about exactly how far to carry the thing. What we were sure of was that we wanted the kind of occupation that allowed Oglalas in and out but denied commercial traffic the right to come in and out.

"We wanted to emphasize that there was a definite occupation going on and that we would not give it up until the Oglala chiefs and headmen had an opportunity to express their concerns about what had been taking place on their reservation. By morning the chiefs got together and issued a statement."

This statement contained three demands which remained the basic Indian negotiating position during the entire period of occupation. The demands pointed to the most fundamental grievances of the Indian people who seized Wounded Knee. First, they wanted Dick Wilson removed from office and new elections held either to replace him or, preferably, to totally alter the tribal government by replacing the existing constitution with another that recognized the authority of the tribe's own chiefs and headmen. Second, they wanted an immediate dismissal of the two ranking BIA officials on the Pine Ridge Reservation and a full investigation by the U.S. Senate of corruption in the national operation of the BIA. Third, they wanted the Senate Foreign Relations Committee to hold hearings on 371 treaties negotiated between the United States and various Indian nations, few of which had been honored by the U.S. All things considered, these were hardly unreasonable demands.

But early on the morning on the 28th, as the Oglala Sioux people issued these demands through their chiefs and headmen, the situation at Wounded Knee rapidly degenerated. The 84 U.S. marshals on anticipatory riot duty in Pine Ridge were moved into position around Wounded Knee. Seventeen Indians were then arrested attempting to leave the area when they ran into the newly imposed federal roadblocks. Each was charged with three felonies—burglary, larceny, and conspiracy. FBI agents arrived on the reservation. Then ranchers with pistols in their belts and rifles in the rear windows of their pickup trucks started roaming the area between the roadblocks. They were observed talking to U.S. marshals on citizen band radios. When newly arriving reporters asked what they were doing, one rancher replied, "Just rabbit hunting." Before the battle had even been declared, let alone begun, law enforcement officials were in the grip of one overriding preoccupation —reinforcements.

Gladys recalled that first long night in the church basement. "We heard a few gunshots outside. One man came down and said that they had gotten a police radio and they heard the BIA police callin' for help from the Nebraska State Police, and the Nebraska State Police told them they were too busy and that they didn't have anything to do with anything that was going on on the reservation. They ignored the Pine Ridge police."

Throughout that uncertain first night, law enforcement officials made no attempt to speak with the people in Wounded Knee. Instead of negotiations, they relied on containment, arrest, and the calling in of more guns. One FBI spokesman revealed his lack of concern about the shooting incident during the night when he told a reporter, "We just wanted to let them know we were there."

Most observers agree that if federal officials had negotiated at the beginning, they could have easily avoided a battlefield confrontation and the bloodshed that followed.

"When we first went in there," Gladys remembers, "I didn't expect it to turn out the way it did. You see, I've heard of these demonstrations, but I had never been in one—in my life. 'Course, these mild marches we put on at the superintendent's office, well, they never amounted to anything.

"I never once thought that we'd be arrested, because I thought that we were protesting the BIA and that we had our rights, civil rights and treaty rights. Now I know that we can't stand on our civil rights, but we can still stand on our treaty rights. I never once give it a thought that we would be there more than two, three days. I got the surprise of my life, staying there as long as we did."

In the first critical hours, police officers refused to exercise the same degree of restraint common in strikes and university building takeovers. They were presented with a rather ordinary scenario—a set of demands; a blockade of some sort; minor, primarily symbolic, destruction of property. Hardly a university in the nation is unfamiliar with such events, to say nothing of numerous factories, draft boards, lunch counters, and so on. Even firearms have occasionally been present, for example, in the hands of Black Panther Party members on the steps of the California State Legislature in 1967 or in the administration building of Cornell

University in 1969. But lawmen around Wounded Knee started shooting (from two miles away!), making their intentions, if not clear, at least open to question. Inevitably, some Indians inside the settlement made the logical and all too obvious assumption that even their protest was going to be treated with special harshness by the white government.

Then, during the afternoon of the first day, two tank-like olive drab armored personnel carriers came lumbering up to the government road-blocks. Over 100 additional FBI agents arrived. Government weapons were distributed, including automatic rifles. U.S. marshals already on the scene in their sky-blue jumpsuits acquired flak-jackets and helmets and started carrying riot guns. Finally, the FBI agent-in-charge agreed to a cease-fire and met with AIM and Oglala representatives. The Indians, outnumbered, heavily out-gunned, and anxious to avoid further shoot-ing, were surprised when the FBI man impatiently announced that he was not interested in their demands. He had come prepared only to negotiate the conditions of their arrest. The Indians turned on their heels and walked back into Wounded Knee. They considered, for the first time, that law enforcement officials, either intentionally or because of their poor application of police tactics, were shaping the situation in a fashion that would make armed confrontation inevitable.

This conclusion made more sense when the angry people inside Wounded Knee saw the kind of information government spokesmen released to the press. It was an AIM takeover, the government said, organized and carried out by non-reservation Indians. Despite publicity surrounding the three demands made by the Oglala chiefs, the govern-ment disclaimed any knowledge of why the occupation had occurred. As a result of these distortions, when news of Wounded Knee first appeared in the newspapers and on radio and television, it looked like a few dozen young, male Indians had vandalized a store, stolen an entire arsenal of guns, gotten themselves into a desperate shoot-out with police, and then tried to avoid the consequences of their criminal acts by appealing to the public's guilty conscience about Indians. When the people actually inside Wounded Knee saw the press coverage on their own radio and television sets, they quickly realized that the picture being drawn would make it that much easier for government forces to come in shooting.

The government very quickly barred all newspeople from Wounded Knee. Thus, official statements became the only source of news. Stopped at roadblocks that looked more and more military, some veteran report-ers grew more and more skeptical. Among themselves they compared the situation to Saigon news conferences where government officials would present their interpretation of events and then forbid reporters to accompany combat missions in order to check for themselves. The more enterprising of these skeptics made arrangements in the town of Pine

Ridge to be taken clandestinely into Wounded Knee by Indians sympathetic to the occupation. Guided overland around the government blockades, a few TV cameramen and reporters hiked into the settlement through several miles of back canyons, dry creek beds, and foot trails. It is commonly believed that the early presence of these newspeople effectively prevented law enforcement agents from launching a full-scale armed assault.

Before long, people in Wounded Knee understood that the government's first exaggerated responses were not going to soften. Members of AIM, the only ones present with experience in even remotely similar situations, were looked to for leadership and coordination. Numbering only a dozen or two, they began to direct, but not control, what was done. They saw that preparations had to be made for more than a two- or three-day sit-in and suggested that buildings in Wounded Knee be taken over and assigned community functions. Some of the small cabins and church buildings were converted into kitchens, while others became dining areas, storehouses, sleeping quarters, child-care centers, defense headquarters, and a medical clinic. People who lived in these houses were asked, but not forced, to share their space. Most, but not all, complied.

Cars were scattered about the streets. It was a crowded, hectic, sometimes jubilant scene. Campfires burned against the cold March wind. Drum beats and Indian chants could be heard. People began to decorate their jackets and hair with strips of colored cloth and paint. Ironically, there was an Indian-ness in the air that is rarely felt on American Indian reservations.

Dennis Banks and Russell Means were given responsibility for overall coordination. During the night of the 27th and the early hours of the 28th, their primary task was to keep everyone in communication with everyone else. In the uncertain atmosphere, they tried to prevent gunfights from breaking out, except where necessary to defend people who were under fire. By the afternoon of the 28th, it was clear to them that Wounded Knee was not only going to be an occupation from their point of view, but also a siege under force of arms from the point of view of the government.

"We tried to keep all the people informed about what the government was doing," Dennis said. "But there was a lot of confusion that first day. There was a series of meetings—meetings after meetings. People were assigned to guard duty, people were assigned to kitchen duty.

"Even though there were no gunshots on either side that first day, only those few the night before, we realized at that point that arms were going to be involved. We didn't know who might be out there shooting at us: FBI, marshals, BIA police, Dick Wilson's goon squad, or just some racist white ranchers.

"We weren't going to let people come up there and take shots at us just because they had some badge or other to hide behind. So, some of our people were assigned to bypass the government roadblocks at night and bring more guns and ammunition into Wounded Knee.

"That first day the traditional chiefs and headmen took a public stand that what we had done was the only course of action that was left available, and that they would continue to support the occupation. We gathered all the people inside the perimeter and explained to them that the time had arrived, not only for Oglalas, but for Indians all across the country, that we were embarking on a very important mission, a dangerous mission, and that it could result in people dying at Wounded Knee.

"There must have been three to four hundred people there, young and old people, children, babies. They were the ones that remained out of the thousand or so that came to Wounded Knee the night before. They said that they were staying until all of the demands of the Oglala Sioux were met.

"That's how I remember that first day, that kind of commitment that came from all the people that were there: that we can't leave Wounded Knee now, our time has arrived, it's here and this is it."

The most damaging news to emerge from the little reservation village in the first 24 hours of the occupation was that eleven white persons were being held as hostages: the priest and members of three small families, interrelated by marriage, who owned the trading post and the small tourist museum. Several of these people were 70 years of age or older. Together, the eleven made up the entire white population of Wounded Knee. Government spokesmen accused AIM of holding them prisoner at gunpoint and threatening to kill them if the settlement was invaded. To the few who would listen, AIM representatives admitted that the eleven whites were inside Wounded Knee but denied categorically that they were being held as hostages.

Preoccupation with the status of the "hostages" became paramount in the minds of the press, and, consequently, the public. So much so in fact that on the morning of the second day of the occupation, March 1, both South Dakota Senators flew into Pine Ridge in a U.S. Army helicopter. They denied that they had come to negotiate Indian demands. Instead, Senators George McGovern and James Abourezk stated that they were there to try to secure the release of the "hostages." FBI men advised them against actually going into Wounded Knee, claiming that their safety could not be guaranteed. As a result, the two Senators spent part of the day talking to reservation residents and officials in the town of Pine Ridge. By evening, though, they were satisfied that the FBI's advise could be safely ignored. The two Senators traveled to Wounded Knee and spoke in person with the so-called hostages.

Coming out four hours later, McGovern told reporters that he had offered to take the "hostages" with him, but "they didn't want to go." He said they were free to leave whenever they wished, or to move around inside Wounded Knee with Indian escorts. "They don't want to leave because they consider that to be their home," McGovern said.

Abourezk was able to give reporters an accurate description of the three Oglala demands and the conditions that had brought about the occupation. He also deplored the fact that law enforcement officials had not set up a direct line of communication, by telephone or otherwise, with the leaders inside Wounded Knee, arguing that it created a dangerous situation in which "rumors replace fact."

By the third day of the occupation, March 2, the few reporters who had managed to slip past the government roadblocks filed equally surprising stories about the "hostages." They were described as being more frightened of the marshals and FBI agents than they were of the Indians. One of the "hostages" told reporters, "AIM has not held us hostages so much as the military that is surrounding us. AIM would have let us leave at any time, but we don't want to leave our homes here."

Of course, none of the whites was happy about the occupation or the confiscations and property destruction. It was a major disruption in their lives. But they recognized that fate had thrown them into a life or death situation and they had sense enough to opt for life over property. "The fact is that we as a group of 'hostages' decided to stay to save AIM *and* our own property. Had we not, those troops would have come down here and killed all of these people. The real hostages here are the AIM people."

Dennis Banks, remembering the first days of the occupation, had this to say regarding the false issue of hostages.

"It was my responsibility in the first two or three days to inform all of the people in the community about what was going on. That meant the Indian community that lived there too, not just the white community. We explained to them our position, the chiefs' position, and what we were going to do, so that they would understand what had happened.

"There were eleven non-Indian people there who were members of the family that owned the trading post and grocery store. We told them that the occupation was going on, and we did not know how long it was going to go on, and that they were free to go if they wanted to go.

"They said they didn't want to, that that was their property and they weren't going to leave. So, we told them that we were going to have to put guards around there because we wanted to give them protection from the occupation and we didn't want them getting hurt or going out and getting into any misunderstandings or heated arguments with people from the occupation. They said, okay, but they weren't going to leave.

"Then, the next day after the occupation first happened, word got out that there were eleven hostages. To this day I still don't know how or why that got started. It was never our intention to hold anybody hostage. We certainly would not gain anything from holding anybody as a prisoner or a hostage."

On March 1, Ralph Erickson, a special assistant to U.S. Attorney General Richard Kleindienst, flew out from Washington to take charge of all federal forces around Wounded Knee. The next afternoon, on the third day of the occupation, he held a press conference 20 miles away in Pine Ridge. The atmosphere in town was remarkably military. Marshals and FBI agents, including those off duty, moved around wearing combat fatigues and carrying sidearms and Viet Nam-era M-16 rifles.

Even the press conference bore the stamp of a Pentagon briefing. Erickson expressed his outrage that during the previous night officers of the United States government had come under fire from the Oglalas. Journalists pointed out that the tank-like armored personnel carriers, in which the officers were riding, were hardly endangered by the hunting rifles fired by the Indians. Furthermore, they said, the big APCs drove within a few hundred yards of Wounded Knee, thus violating a cease-fire agreement made the previous day in which the government promised to keep them five miles back. Erickson categorically denied that the APCs had been closer than five miles to Wounded Knee. He had nothing to say when several reporters informed him that they had seen the vehicles' telltale tracks only a few hundred yards from the Sacred Heart Church.

Erickson kept insisting that it was too dangerous for newspeople to go into Wounded Knee, that the Oglalas were firing indiscriminately. Under sharp questioning, he admitted that staff members of the Justice Department's own Community Relations Service had driven unescorted into Wounded Knee. A few of the journalists also pointed out that they had hiked into Wounded Knee over the back trails and were welcomed by the armed but cordial Indians. Once inside Wounded Knee, they said they were free to roam where they pleased. One reporter contrasted this with the treatment they received at the government bunkers. "Hell, we're not worried about the Indians," he said. "It's *our* side that I'm afraid of."

The most alarming episode at the press conference was the government's treatment of the hostage issue. Disregarding the claims of two U.S. Senators, numerous press personnel, and the so-called hostages themselves, Erickson continued to maintain that the eleven were being held in Wounded Knee against their will. He threatened to charge the Indians with kidnapping. Several reporters present wondered if the government wasn't continuing to project the eleven as hostages in order to justify their own enormous military escalation. Such tactics were regularly used in Viet Nam. Later that same afternoon, five of the so-called hostages left Wounded Knee to buy groceries in Pine Ridge. When their shopping was completed, they went back. Yet, for almost a week afterward, government spokesmen through the mass media continued to perpetuate the myth of "hostages."

Finally, when asked about negotiations, Erickson told the press conference that it was impossible to negotiate with the Indians since he did not know what their demands were. If that were true, he was probably the only person in Pine Ridge who didn't. The Oglalas had published their demands two days before. The news had penetrated at least as far as Little Rock, Arkansas, where Senator William Fulbright had indicated a willingness to comply with the third demand, that his Senate Foreign Relations Committee investigate the 371 broken treaties. One of the journalists at the news conference handed Erickson a copy of his newspaper, published the day before, which contained a full description of the three Oglala demands. Erickson responded that he was "not prepared to negotiate on the basis of a newspaper article."

On March 3, a new force entered the complicated Wounded Knee situation. Another government press conference was held in Pine Ridge, presided over by Justice Department spokesman Horace Webb. After answering questions, he announced that Dick Wilson, the Pine Ridge tribal chairman, was in the next room and wished to speak to the press. As Wilson came in, Webb went out.

Wilson told reporters that hundreds of "my people" were determined to attack Wounded Knee and that he could no longer be responsible for holding them back. In fact, he stated, "I will join them with my gun." When asked about the size of his forces, Wilson replied, "Eight or nine hundred—guns!" Reporters pressed him about the possible danger such an armed attack would present to the members of his tribe who were permanent residents of Wounded Knee. Many had chosen to remain inside the area controlled by the occupation. The tribal chairman said that these people had been given their chance to leave and didn't take it. "If they get killed," he said, "that's the way the ball bounces."

Once again, Wilson insisted that aside from the permanent residents, there were really only ten or fifteen Oglala Sioux with the occupation. The rest, he claimed, were outsiders from the American Indian Movement, "vagrants and goons who will not work." Wilson also complained about the federal authorities. For the past two weeks he had been trying to cooperate with them, but was told only to keep quiet. Apparently, at some point well before the occupation of Wounded Knee, a few FBI agents had quietly assumed control of the reservation and without any real authority to do so ordered both tribal and BIA officials to be silent.

When Wilson finished, he left the room, just as Justice Department spokesman Webb returned. Reporters asked Webb what the government would do if Wilson carried out his threat to invade Wounded Knee. Webb told them that he was out of the room when Wilson's statements were made and therefore he could not in good conscience comment on them.

Wilson's new threats of violence further polarized the Indian population in the town of Pine Ridge. People were forced to take sides, and their choice had very real consequences. For example, those supporting the occupation were frequently subjected to bullying shakedowns and weapons searches by BIA police. At the same time, Wilson's supporters were well armed and unmolested. "I've got three guns right out there in that convertible," one Wilson man informed a reporter. Occupation supporters were at a terrifying disadvantage having to move about unarmed in a town where they could be preyed upon at any moment by gun-toting rivals. Many of them were severely beaten, in spite of the massive presence of federal law enforcement agents.

In the midst of this tension and lawlessness, some journalists in Pine Ridge got an occasionally clear look at the quality of life on an Indian reservation. Once, a few were approached on the street by a tearful woman whose uncle had just died. She was trying to notify her relatives of the death, but the BIA police station and the BIA agency office, as well as the U.S. Public Health Service Hospital, all refused her permission to use their telephones. One of the white reporters took her back to the Public Health Service Hospital and asked for the telephone on her behalf. It was offered graciously. Press people had been using the phone all day.

On March 4, Wilson's 800-900 guns failed to appear at Wounded Knee. Toward evening he issued a statement from the American Legion Hall in Pine Ridge postponing the invasion for another day. It was to be the first of many postponements. For while Wilson's men were responsible for a great deal of shooting and sniping around the edges of Wounded Knee, they never constituted a force large enough to attack it. In fact, throughout the occupation, Wilson never fully controlled more than the two dozen or so men whom he had employed all along in his private "goon squad."

Thus, events during the first five days of the occupation convinced people in Wounded Knee that the government was determined to provoke an armed conflict. Federal officials rigidly and persistently gave distorted information to the press. Wilson was being led around on a government leash, like a snarling dog. Massive buildups of military hardware and personnel were well underway. More armored personnel carriers arrived and soon could be seen in any direction, as could scores of uniformed men carrying M-16s. Photo reconnaissance planes flew over the settlement. Air Force Phantom jets occasionally buzzed as low as

200 feet off the church steeple. Truckloads of weapons were delivered, along with flak-jackets and searchlights. There were machine guns, high-powered rifles, night-vision infrared Starscopes. After dark, huge flares lit the countryside, and then gently floated down to start grass fires. Almost every night, sometimes more than once, the armored vehicles pushed forward to provoke serious exchanges of gunfire with the Indians in Wounded Knee.

People learn from their own history. When the Sioux saw the military buildup taking place around them, they understood it as a declaration of war by the government of the United States. Under the leadership of AIM, they began making their preparations. Viet Nam combat veterans supervised Indian security operations with a grim determination. Indian work crews constructed bunkers at the four roadblocks, each with out-lying foxholes. The bunkers were topped with sandbags made from cardboard boxes, plastic garbage bags, and pillowcases. The walls of several of the small buildings were fortified against bullets. One house, selected as the "command post," was surrounded by mud-filled wooden walls 16 inches thick. Rear-area trenches were connected to the bunkers by narrow escape slits. In several places, gasoline and cloth wicks were used to turn cases of empty soda pop bottles into stacks of small Molotov cocktails.

Meanwhile, a warriors' society was created under the leadership of Carter Camp and Stan Holder, AIM coordinators from Oklahoma. Its members stood guard duty, reconnoited federal positions, used their own two-way radios to monitor government and police communications, maintained a supply of weapons, and defended the settlement against attack and against snipers. Guided by medicine men, the warriors' soci-ety practiced many of the rituals their ancestors had performed during previous military encounters with the United States. Traditionally ex-cluded from these societies and from open combat, several young women insisted on their right to bear arms and were accepted.

Much of the military responsibility (scheduling around-the-clock guard duty, keeping abreast of the many sources of intelligence information, designing the physical defense of Wounded Knee, etc.) fell on the shoulders of Stan Holder. Holder, a Wichita, was 25 and a veteran of two tours of combat duty in Viet Nam. He was a decorated hero and knew a great deal about counter-insurgency warfare. But like many young men who went to Indochina to kill for Uncle Sam, Holder came back a changed person looking for a new way. With an unusually even temper and an uncanny ability to stay calm in a crisis, he went to work as an organizer for the American Indian Movement.

Holder was roughly ten years younger than the rest of the AIM leader-ship, but at Wounded Knee he was entrusted with the position of chief security officer. He forged a small army out of dozens of volunteers, training, drilling, instructing, and learning from them. But the little army was a warriors' society and not at all like the military units any of the veterans remembered.

"In this warrior society," Holder explained during the occupation, "there's no discipline except self-discipline. I don't raise my voice at the men I supposedly command because I don't command them. We haven't had any trouble at all with this, because people realize the need for this, they realize that once there is a breakdown in this trust we have, there will be no Oglala Nation. So it's an army, but it's an army born purely out of love for the Indian race and not hate for the white race.

"It's a 180-degree change from the U.S. military. The men here—they don't gripe, they don't say, 'It's cold out,' or anything like that. They realize that there's a need to defend their women and children here, and a need to defend the sacred land that we're living on, and they do it. They keep their respect for nature. They don't go around wanting to defoliate, as the United States did in Viet Nam. They don't go around wanting to indiscriminately kill people, because they realize that the loss of a life, whether a white, black, red, or yellow, is still the loss of a life, and it's a loss to nature, it's upsetting the balance.

"The American fighting forces and the American Justice Department are so dehumanized that they can't even bring the personal aspect into their wars. They just want to wage wars on a mass scale and keep identity out of it. We're trying to regain what we had in the past, being human beings and being involved in society. We're going to accept some forms of technology to defend ourselves until such time as we don't have to defend ourselves at all."

From a military point of view, Wounded Knee was barely defensible. It sat in a shallow valley surrounded on all sides by low ridges or gently sloping hills. It was upon these slightly elevated positions that the marshals and FBI agents mounted their guns, just as the 7th Cavalry had in 1890. But Holder was an expert, and he planned his defenses with great care and precision. His skill was recognized by both sides in the conflict. Rumor has it that when the occupation ended, Holder was even offered a job as a United States marshal—provided he could clear up the 180 years worth of felony charges they levelled against him at the same time.

Military help came from outside Wounded Knee as well. Dennis Banks, recalling those first few days, said, "When we finally realized that guns were definitely going to be involved, that we were going to have to defend ourselves against attack, we decided that there would be a call to arms across the country. It was a call to arms to Indian people everywhere, and even without announcing it people began to come to Wounded Knee. They knew what it meant and they just began to come in through the hills. Indians from Oklahoma, New Mexico, California, all over the west, even from Canada. Some of them were armed and some of them weren't, but they came there to be part of the occupation, to help protect it."

Security was only one concern as people began the work of transforming Wounded Knee into a living community. Another was the creation of a cultural life that reflected the Sioux heritage. AIM people encouraged this. They normally thought of themselves as a spiritual movement. The theft of Indian culture, they argued, robbed the Indians of their self-awareness as a people and hence their ability to fight with the all-important advantage of unity. From the very first days in Wounded Knee, much time and energy were devoted to the celebration of Sioux rituals and ceremonies. Large pieces of red, yellow, black, and green cloth were hung from the church steeple, representing the four directions of the universe and the four winds. The old dances were performed, not at the behest of paying white tourists but for the benefit of the participants. Some of the younger people, born and raised in big city Indian ghettos, were moved to tears as they felt the joy and understood the ritual significance of these dances for the first time in their lives.

More mundane concerns were also important, like sharing food and housing. Gladys Bissonette, who once managed the reservation's old people's home, had skills that were put to good use.

"I performed the duty," she explained, "of seeing that food was being prepared. I was something like an overseer of one group of cooks. I was the head cook, in other words, and I had to put people on duty in shifts. Several other women had positions like mine. We had Wounded Knee divided into different areas and in each one there was someone like me that supervised the cooking.

"Of course, I was on the negotiating team, too. I met with those government men, and that took a lot of time. But I had to make sure, especially, that our security men got their meals. They were on shifts twenty-four hours around, so I had to see to it that we had food, that there were cooks there for twenty-four hours around. Some of those cooks worked all day and some of them all night."

Life in Wounded Knee was a strange mixture of wild west melodrama and deadly seriousness, of war whoops and people genuinely preparing to die. At night, the cold but resolute loneliness of the warriors in the bunkers contrasted with the intense community life of free Indian people singing around campfires and crowding into common rooms. At odd moments during the day, disciplined work unexpectedly gave way to some high-spirited amusement. Privacy disappeared. People talked and listened to each other with a new warmth and attention.

And the whole world was watching. Wounded Knee was the biggest news story in the country. The mass media, both here and abroad, devoted extraordinary amounts of space to it. The few skeptical journalists who made the dangerous hike into Wounded Knee filed exciting and unusual stories, behind "enemy lines" in America. Unfortunately, most of this material did not survive being squeezed under headlines or into 60-second slots on the evening news.

But editorial cutting was not the worst problem. Sadly, the majority of the press outside Wounded Knee lived up to government expectations that they would be lazy, gullible, and easily impressed. This majority was run through a series of official government press conferences, complete with slides and wall maps. They were handed stacks of elegantly printed press releases. When they wrote their stories based only on official information, it was no surprise to find them describing the government not as a contending party in the conflict but in the role of a neutral and unbiased referee keeping two warring factions of Indians from killing each other.

The government got more help from right-wing columnists and editorial writers, who also lived up to expectations by raving about shadowy communists pulling strings in the background. They called AIM Indians everything from "red storm-troopers" to "rifle-waving hoodlum kidnappers," and they were quick to recommend an early showdown. One actually went so far as to say that if the government stormed into Wounded Knee with their guns blazing, "the vast majority of Americans would cheer the cavalry!"

But it was the liberal metropolitan newspapers and TV networks that were the biggest disappointment. At times their coverage was accurate. More often it was determined by correspondents and editors who had no experience on the scene. They described the occupation as an event designed in advance by AIM to attract national attention to itself. These commentators, as they had so often done with demonstrations in the past, allowed their personal displeasure with the Indians' tactics to be a substitute for any thoughtful consideration of the real issues at stake. The Oglala Sioux people, who initiated everything that happened at Wounded Knee, were pictured on opposite sides of the roadblocks, equally divided between the "AIM faction" and the "Wilson faction."

The liberal media projected an event that smacked of "outside agitators" bent from the first on provoking an armed confrontation. The shallow level of their analysis played well into the hands of the government, anxious to avoid being displayed as the major antagonist in a struggle against Indians at Wounded Knee. All the usual clichés were dutifully trotted out. Many news reporters simply took it for granted that federal officials were there to "help the Indians." Benevolent marshals and FBI agents were pictured "exercising restraint" in the face of severe provocation. More often than not, the media referred to Dick Wilson as "the duly constituted authority" or the "democratically elected chairman," phrases which were technically correct but which hardly conveyed the truth of the situation.

Perhaps the low point in confusion came when media commentators decided that they themselves had become part of the story. A few accused AIM of staging the entire occupation for the benefit of the press. These commentators argued that they were being manipulated by sophisticated AIM public relations experts into providing free national publicity for the organization. With a profound lack of sensitivity, they saw some sinister design in AIM's "choice" of Wounded Knee, a place of such dramatic historical significance, for their protest. Under normal circumstances, these same correspondents would have been sympathetic to the plight of the reservation Oglalas. But that sympathy was easily swept aside by their irrational fear of manipulation. At times they were actually on the verge of holding AIM responsible for Wounded Knee's *historical* significance, as though it were the fault of the Vietnamese that My Lai is notorious.

One day, early in the occupation, a picture from Wounded Knee appeared on the front page of nearly every newspaper in the country. It showed a single Indian holding up an AK-47 automatic rifle. Headlines screamed the news that there were communist submachine guns in Wounded Knee. The AK-47 is the standard infantry weapon in communist nations around the world, including Viet Nam. Thousands were brought home, illegally, by returning American GIs. For many it was more than the usual captured enemy souvenir. Their own standard rifle, the M-16, had an embarrassing habit of jamming when it was most needed—in the heat of battle. Pentagon officials, for reasons known only to them, refused to cancel their M-16 contract with Colt Industries and continued to send the defective rifle to GIs in the field. As a result, many took up captured AK-47s to use as their personal weapons.

Regardless of appearances, however, there was only one AK-47 in Wounded Knee. The government, allowing appearances to stand uncorrected, decried the presence of a machine gun "capable of wiping out a whole group before they can react." Government officials, and the press with them, neglected to mention that the AK-47 was an operational equivalent of the M-16, of which there were hundreds on the government side of the roadblocks. Later, most reporters failed to point out that the rest of the Indian arsenal in Wounded Knee was exclusively twenty-twos, thirty-aught-sixes, and other assorted hunting rifles, not to mention a small selection of pistols, knives, and Indian lances. In no event were they a match for armored vehicles, helicopters, gas grenade launchers, searchlights, tracer bullets, or other government military equipment. And no one realized it more profoundly than the people inside Wounded Knee.

The Oglala Sioux had few illusions about the government's "restraint." They understood that each addition to the federal weapons stockpile increased the likelihood that the weapons would be used. The massacre at Attica Prison only a year and a half before was in the forefront of their minds. There, too, armed insurgents made demands and were surrounded by government law enforcement officers. If the liberal Rockefeller could refuse to negotiate, if the liberal Rockefeller could order an armed assault that resulted in 43 senseless deaths, surely the reactionary Nixon could do likewise.

Those who seized Wounded Knee knew full well that their meagre armaments would be hardly better than toys if the government decided to attack. But in their defensive arsenal there was another weapon, perhaps more powerful than any of the government's guns—America's guilt and the resulting attention their actions drew in the mass media and in the moral imagination of the public. The Oglala Sioux understood the power of Wounded Knee as a symbol of the country's shame. They realized that a second massacre in the little South Dakota village perhaps might be more than even America's tarnished history could endure. The Sioux made no secret of their willingness to take tactical advantage of these circumstances. Precious few weapons were still left to them. In the first days of the occupation, Russell Means sent this message to the United States during an interview with the press.

"Either negotiate with us for meaningful results, positive results, or you're going to have to kill us, and here at Wounded Knee is where it's going to have to happen."

The U.S. Justice Department in Washington and the federal law enforcement officials on the scene in South Dakota responded just as the U.S. War Department and the 7th Cavalry had a century before. They began by mounting a vastly superior armed force. They placed a low value on the patience and mutual respect necessary to understand their adversaries. They lied, distorted information, and consistently appealed to the worst instincts in the people around them. By their lack of charity, by their ineptness, and by their primary reliance on violence, a reliance first nurtured in the old Indian Wars themselves and most recently reinforced in Viet Nam, the federal government made death and injury a virtual inevitability at Wounded Knee.

9

AIRLIFT
Machine Guns in the Snow

Saturday, April 14, 1973
Council Bluffs, Iowa

Waking up early in the morning after our mapless night flight from
Chicago, a single glance out the motel windows told us that our plans
were wrecked. The sky was a dull white. Heavy snow fell on the other
side of the glass. Discouraged, we assembled in the restaurant downstairs
for breakfast. Billy called the weather people and came back to the table
with the obvious bad news.

"This shit is all over the place, man," he reported. "We're under a
frontal system right now. It's just moving in here. When it passes, there's a
big low pressure area to the west that'll come in right behind it. We got a
chance of getting a little farther west this afternoon, but there's no way
we're going to make it to Wounded Knee."

We were disappointed, but bad weather always passes and we had the
entire weekend in front of us. After a big breakfast, John stopped me in
the motel lobby and complained about Strobe. It seemed that Strobe,
who had been up the entire previous night rigging cargo and parachutes,
stayed awake most of another night. John claimed that a good part of it
was spent in a monolog about how the sun and the moon were destined
to collide, and therefore the study of astrology was the key to the future. It
was too absurd to deal with, so I naively dismissed it as a mere misunderstanding.

167

We split up in two rented cars. Billy and I took one across the river into Omaha. We went to the city's major airport, Eppley Field, to purchase the aeronautical charts that we had failed to get the previous day. Jim, John, Strobe, Larry, and Tom took the other car back to the suburban Council Bluffs airport where we had left our planes the night before. They went to work on the cargo. There was still some weight balancing to do, and the static-line ripcords were not yet rigged. If nothing else, the bad weather gave us a chance to finish the chores left undone because of our hasty departure from Chicago.

When Billy and I saw all the charts for sale in the FAA office at Eppley Field and remembered the anxiety of having to do without them the night before, we bought everything we could get our hands on. That particular office had maps covering a twelve-state area on all sides of South Dakota. We purchased three of each. By that time the heavy snowfall had stopped, but overcast clouds were still too close to the ground for us to take off. We decided to visit the meteorological station at the airport, hoping that if we scanned their teletype machines and radar screens ourselves, we might find our own little path through the foul weather.

We were right. After hanging around the weather station for close to an hour, we could see the gradual development of a break in the weather. A narrow path of clear air was about to open up between the backside of the cold front that was just passing through and the leading edge of the low pressure area that was trailing behind it. It would be like flying down a valley between two mountains of unstable air. That wasn't so bad. The problem was that the valley led northwest, straight from the Council Bluffs-Omaha area to the eastern part of South Dakota. Then it stopped. If we were not going to be able to make it all the way to Wounded Knee at the west end of South Dakota, the last place we wanted to pass the time waiting for the next break in the weather was in the same state. Three plane-loads of parachute cargo would attract attention anywhere, but accompanied by seven scruffy looking young men just 200 miles from Wounded Knee, attention would spell suspicion. Besides, if we did follow the weather valley up to eastern South Dakota, it would be much harder to use Wyoming as a staging area and confuse the FBI by coming in from the west.

Billy and I discussed the alternatives as we drove back to Council Bluffs. Despite the danger of flying into South Dakota, where the Indians in Wounded Knee had little if any support and were a constant public preoccupation, we agreed that we had no choice. Getting closer to our destination was more important than avoiding the risk we might run by spending a day in some small South Dakota town.

Back at the Council Bluffs airport, we found our five friends nervous and uncomfortable. The onboard rigging work was only half done.

Earlier, several National Guard pilots had shown up in uniform. A few of our people thought that the Guard officers were police closing in for an arrest. The incident was past, but it had provoked a noticeable increase in collective paranoia. Our friends thought that every other person in the airport was watching them suspiciously, and by then their behavior seemed to warrant it. When Billy and I told them about the channel of clear air up to eastern South Dakota, they were only too happy to risk going there as long as they could get out of Council Bluffs.

But leaving was not as easy as we had thought. When we walked through the snow to taxi the three big Cherokees over to the gas pumps, Billy's plane would not start. He decided that the battery was dead, and he proceeded to convince a mechanic to drive his car onto the aircraft ramp and boost the plane's battery with jumper cables. It worked. As the last plane was being gassed up, Billy decided that the weather had improved just enough to allow us to take off. We huddled around a map in the pilot's lounge and worked out the course we would follow.

FAA regulations specify that when the weather is worse than certain minimal conditions, aircraft must be flown solely by reference to dashboard instruments. This is the case when the bottom of a solid layer of clouds (the "ceiling") is less than 1,000 feet above the ground, or the visibility is less than three miles. If either condition prevails, pilots must be in constant communication with and under the direction of air traffic controllers at ground radar stations. This is instrument rather than visual flight. It requires a special license, and among us only Billy had the necessary credentials. When both the ceiling and the visibility are greater than 1,000 feet and three miles, respectively, aircraft can be flown visually, by looking out the window. Under these conditions, pilots are not answerable to ground controllers except when they are in the immediate vicinity of a major airport. Collisions are avoided on a see-and-be-seen basis only. Because Jim and I were not licensed to fly on instruments, the airlift would always be grounded by low clouds and poor visibility.

Outside the Council Bluffs pilot's lounge, as we plotted our course, low clouds covered the sky. The ceiling fluctuated between 800 and 1,500 feet. Visibility was only just improving after the snowstorm and was not more than three miles. Conditions were right on the borderline, but the weather bureau reported improvements farther down our valley of good weather toward the northwest. We decided to go despite these marginal conditions but to fly the safest possible course. An Interstate divided highway, number 29, came out of Omaha, heading northwest in just the direction we wanted to fly. By following the highway at low altitude, instead of using a straight-line compass or radio beacon course, we would reduce our navigational work to near zero. If the weather suddenly closed in and we could not see to go on, the highway would double as an emergency runway. With traffic divided and no telephone poles, a small aircraft in trouble could land at 70 mph by settling down between automobiles going approximately the same speed.

We planned to follow Interstate 29 as far as we could, until we ran into the cul-de-sac of bad weather where the cold front joined the low pressure area. We hoped to fly about 350 miles to Miller, a tiny cross-roads town in east central South Dakota. The aeronautical chart indicated a single 2,800-foot landing strip there. Miller was 200 miles from Wounded Knee and on the map it looked like as quiet and safe a place as we could find.

We taxied the three planes to the active runway. The tower cleared us, and one at a time we rolled down the concrete and took off. There was hardly any room to climb under the low ceiling. We immediately formed into a half-mile-long single file and went scurrying over the farms at 500 feet looking for Interstate 29. We were starting from a point about 20 miles away with no visible landmarks to guide us over the monotonously consistent midwestern countryside. Using the compasses, we pointed the aircraft northwest and waited for the divided highway to appear.

The first few minutes of the flight were quite difficult. The visibility did not allow us to see more than two or three miles in any direction. The air was very turbulent and we hit several violent bumps. All the while we had to keep a sharp watch for stray clouds hanging down lower than the rest of the ceiling. Flying into one and completely losing visibility at such a low altitude is about as safe as driving on a mountain road blindfolded.

Ten minutes later, Interstate 29 came out of the haze in front of us. We were low enough to read the green and white road signs. Billy, flying the lead plane, led us into a course that paralleled the highway. The twin ribbons of asphalt were off to our right and stretched out to the horizon as far as we could see, like gigantic pointers showing us the way. Off to the left side of our path, also roughly parallel to the Interstate, was the wide and majestic Missouri River. It meandered along in an endless series of S-turns, dividing the states of Iowa and Nebraska. We kept our planes between the river and the highway, like horses racing between the rails. The view was breathtaking.

The weather gradually improved as the towns, highways, and railroad tracks marked on the map slowly slid under our wings. Larry sat in the co-pilot's seat on my right. The reporter, Tom, rode with us that day. He was squeezed in back on top of the cargo, his long legs twisted around one of the duffel bags. Strong tail winds pushed us along. Half an hour out of Council Bluffs, we banked into a wide sweep around the Sioux City, Iowa, airport, avoiding the commercial jet traffic taking off and landing there. By then the cloud cover above us had gone from overcast to broken to scattered, and most of the sky was a deep clear blue. The turbulence had passed and the visibility was unrestricted in bright sunshine. We were in the valley of good weather that had been predicted, but in the far distance on either side we could see the towering storm clouds.

The flight was magnificent. Landscape was visible for dozens of miles all around us. I gave Larry the controls and stared out the window at the rivers and roads and towns that sat on top of the checkerboard farmland. Soon the Missouri River and Interstate 29 forked apart. The river turned west and the highway swung north. We stayed with the highway as it became an unswervingly straight line cutting across more than 100 miles of flat midwestern cornfields. We were.2,000 feet up at that point and could see quite a distance in front of us. Billy contacted us on the radio. He wanted to practice flying in tight formation, a skill we had to learn before making the parachute drop over Wounded Knee. I took the flight controls back from Larry and started inching closer to the other two planes.

Back in Council Bluffs, Billy, Jim, and I had decided to use a half-V formation for the drop. It would look like one side of a "V," with each of us behind and off to the right of the aircraft in front. Jim and I had no experience flying formation, and this was the safest one we could figure out. From the rear position, I was able to look out the left side window of the aircraft and see Jim's plane on an angle in front of me. Beyond it, but on the same line, I could see Billy's. I didn't have to look across the inside of my cabin to see either of the other airplanes. In an emergency, each of the two forward aircraft could turn left and leave the formation suddenly without danger of colliding with a trailing plane. Also, the parachutes would be coming out on the left side of the planes. The half-V formation, staggered back toward the right, prevented chutes from floating back into other aircraft.

The formation work was far more delicate than I had expected. Our planes were strung out over a quarter of a mile. Gradually closing in on Jim's plane in the number two spot in front of me, I noticed that extremely minor adjustments in the speed or flight path of my aircraft made large differences in the relative position of our two planes. At the same time, Jim was having similar difficulties lining up with Billy's airplane in front of him. Normally an aircraft flying through the empty sky goes up or down 20 or 30 feet without the pilot even noticing. There is no outside point of reference and the instruments are not always able to register such small changes. But with another airplane flying close by, minor deviations are glaringly obvious, and much more work is necessary in the cockpit in order to fly straight and level.

For a while we looked like three drunken birds, staggering closer to each other and then suddenly veering off. But gradually we got the hang of it, and the wobbling and lurching disappeared. After a half hour of practice 2,000 feet above the farms, we mastered the formation and were able to hold the airplanes about 100 yards apart. By then it was genuinely fun. We gave each other encouragement and friendly criticism over the radio. We practiced peeling off and re-entering the formation. Finally, we tried improving on our 100-yard separation, gingerly bringing the planes closer and closer together.

In Council Bluffs we had decided that 40 yards was the ideal separation for the drop over Wounded Knee. Up in the air that afternoon, 40 yards seemed damn close. We moved in on each other very cautiously. It took a lot more practice, but eventually we squeezed ourselves to a point 40 yards apart. It was a happy moment. We made jokes over the radio and waved to each other through the windows. I had never been nearly that close to an airplane in flight before. It was a startling perspective. I felt wonderful. The sun was shining and we could see for 50 miles in any direction. We flew along in tight formation for some minutes, taking pleasure in the graceful lines of the neighboring airplanes. Below us the sun highlighted the rectangular symmetry of the farmland as it stretched out to the horizon on all sides.

Sioux Falls, South Dakota, went by, and before long so did half the rest of the state. We were planning to leave Interstate 29 at Brookings, South Dakota, turning left there onto a westbound rather than northbound course. Brookings was in the extreme eastern part of the state. Miller, the little airstrip we were trying to get to before the weather caved in, was 120 miles west of Brookings, about one-third the way across South Dakota. Wounded Knee sat at the other end of the state.

We were so engrossed in our formation flying that we went right past Brookings, continuing north along the Interstate highway. Each of us noticed it at about the same time, but Billy was first on the radio. He said he had just taken a fix and that we were five minutes north of where we should have turned west. Sitting next to me, Larry laughed at how three licensed pilots flying in crystal clear air couldn't find the proper place to make a simple left turn.

One at a time, we peeled out of the formation, turning around 180 degrees back to Brookings. Billy went first, announcing the start of his turn over the radio. Looking past Jim's plane, I could see Billy's wings swiftly and gracefully come up 45 degrees to the horizon as he banked into the turn. For a moment he seemed to float slowly toward the left. As the turn brought him around in the opposite direction of flight, his plane shot past us. An instant later, Jim rolled to the left and followed him around. I waited for that moment of apparent acceleration as Jim's airplane went by us, then banked into my own turn. We felt like dancers in the sky.

Back over Brookings, Billy found the highway that led west to Miller. Beneath us the countryside underwent a subtle but distinct change. It was still checkerboard farmland, but as we continued west it became noticeably drier and a little more barren. There were fewer towns and more scattered farmhouses. The elevation of the land was getting higher as the Mississippi Valley gradually gave way to the Great Plains.

Twenty miles west of Brookings, we flew over an enormous flock of wild geese. There must have been a thousand of them. They were far below us, only a hundred or so feet above the ground while we were 2,000 feet up. Our paths were perpendicular to each other. We were heading west and the geese were flying north back to Canada after the winter. It was an unusual sight. I radioed their position to the other two planes. Happily, nobody said anything about a wild goose chase.

As we continued toward what we hoped would be a safe hideaway in Miller, South Dakota, the weather gradually deteriorated. Clouds appeared above us, blocking the sun. Out to the sides, other clouds looking gray and heavy dropped down very close to the ground. In front, puffy cumulus were building up into very tall towers. We were flying into a meteorological dead end. It was the predicted confluence of the cold front and the low pressure area. The forecasters said it wouldn't happen until past Miller, but it was no great shock to us when it began to look like another of our plans was not going to materialize.

Within minutes there was a billowing gray mountain of a thunderhead directly in front of us. Its tops rose to at least 20,000 feet, but the bottom was obscured by lower clouds. Jim radioed that he wanted to turn around immediately and fly back to Brookings, 50 miles to our rear. Billy overruled him. The thunderstorm might be another 75 miles ahead, he argued. We could always turn back once we got right up to it. Meanwhile, we had a chance to make Miller. If that wasn't possible, there was another airport only 30 miles ahead at a place called Huron. Earlier we had vetoed going to Huron because there was an FAA office and weather station at the airport there. We were afraid of inquisitive officials and possibly embarrassing questions. But looking up at the awesome thunderstorm, we held a makeshift meeting over the radio and decided that if we had to, it was better to land at Huron than backtrack all the way to Brookings and be farther from Wounded Knee.

Billy radioed "Huron Weather" for their latest report while Jim and I listened on the same frequency. Radar screens were picking up a line of severe thunderstorms that were already halfway between Huron and Miller. Billy asked about gaps in the line, but there was no way through. Miller was out. The thunderstorms were moving east toward Huron and were expected to arrive within minutes. We were still ten miles away from Huron.

One by one, with Billy leading the way, we pushed our throttles wide open for maximum speed and nosed our planes over to begin losing altitude. We were in a close race with the storms. If we beat them to Huron, we would have to swoop in for an immediate landing. If we lost, there would be no choice but to turn around and fly back to Brookings. The town and the airport were visible in front of us. Just beyond, a solid wall of dark gray cloud rained on the land below. We were going to make it. Overflying the town on the way into the traffic pattern, I saw a single large motel and knew that in a short time we would all be safely inside.

The landings went well. I was getting much better at it. Jim took charge of tying down the three airplanes while Billy and I paid a visit to the FAA office. The seven of us looked like the last people in the world to be flying around in three $45,000 airplanes. Billy and I were taking the offensive, heading into the office to give everyone there some good answers before they had a chance to think up any difficult questions. The two FAA officials inside welcomed us and offered hot coffee. We struck up a conversation, gradually letting them discover that we were rich rock musicians and hippies from New York off on a big-time camping trip into the southern Rockies. Parachuting our gear in and everything, we were.

As we stood there talking, a local dentist arrived. He, too, had just beaten the storms in, and on behalf of all our friends we accepted his offer of a ride to Huron's only motel. Meanwhile, Strobe, the "hippiest" of us all, left the airport to do some errand of his own. Several people were tiring of Strobe, up two nights in a row and still jabbering away. We decided that he would find us at the motel and left with the dentist.

Next to the motel there was a single-story roadside liquor store with a flat roof. On top of it was a bizarre plaster sculpture of a bird, fully two stories in height and brightly painted. The gigantic creature was perched on a sign proclaiming the little town of Huron to be the "world's capital" for shooting whatever the bird was, pheasant or duck or prairie grouse. Also next to the motel, behind the liquor store, was a bowling alley and next to it the "world capital's" only large restaurant.

We spent the remainder of the afternoon in our three motel rooms, hiding from the big bird and from what we expected would be the overly inquisitive eyes of every other person in town. However, as we avoided attracting any attention, Strobe, of the foot-long beard, was parading all over town. Eventually, he showed up at the motel having thoughtfully purchased a few razors and toothbrushes. Thinking that it would be a fast round trip, most of us had left Chicago without them.

At 7:00 p.m. we walked to the restaurant. It was packed with Huron's Saturday night crowd. As the seven of us walked in, I realized with a shudder that we were going to be the main attraction of the evening. Compared to everyone else, there was too little flash in our clothing and too much hair on our heads. Worst of all, with Billy along, we were integrated.

As every eye turned to examine us, we decided to reduce our impact by sitting at two separate tables. Once settled in, I gave some thought to our own morale. With more thousands of dollars in my pocket than the airlift was ever going to need, seven steak and lobster dinners with a few bottles of champagne seemed a cheap enough price for lifting our spirits and breaking the tension. Of course that didn't make us any less conspicuous. Quite the contrary, but we tried to savor our meals as quietly as possible.

After dinner we gathered in Billy's motel room. He and Strobe got into a loud argument in the bathroom. I went in to see what was wrong, and when Billy saw me coming he threw up his hands in despair. Strobe, who was serving as his cargo-kicker, planned to shoot film during the parachute drop. He had brought along a little 8 mm movie camera. Billy told him that filming was impossible since he would have to use both hands to get the cargo nets out of the airplane.

But the excitable Strobe had grown very attached to the idea of filming the chutes floating down into Wounded Knee. He refused to give up. Billy had just stopped him from telephoning a local doctor to ask that his camera be sewn on to his hand so he could shoot film and move cargo at the same time. I asked Billy to leave the bathroom, then had a very calm but very firm discussion with Strobe. We agreed that he would not call a doctor and that if anyone did sew his camera into his hand, an idea that bordered on the unthinkable, it would be me.

At 10:00 p.m. we found a car to rent and the seven of us drove to the Huron airport through light rain showers. Under cover of darkness, we planned to finish the rigging work left undone that morning in Council Bluffs. The airport hangar was conveniently closed for the night, but the FAA weather bureau was a 24-hour operation and had a window facing directly onto the ramp where our aircraft were parked. Billy and I were elected to go in and decoy the night-shift weatherman while everyone else went to work on the planes.

It was easy enough to distract the one man on duty. We asked for a detailed forecast and insisted on carefully checking the satellite pictures and radar screens ourselves. In the process, however, hopes for a dawn food drop were shattered. The weather could not possibly improve in time. Another plan had to be scuttled. At one point, while the weatherman looked directly at me, Billy pointed to something on the bulletin board from behind his back.

Several minutes later we had reshuffled our positions so that I could look at the bulletin board while Billy held the weatherman's eye. On it was an FAA teletype notification that the area for a five-nautical-mile radius around Wounded Knee, South Dakota, stretching from the ground to 9,000 feet above sea level, was declared a restricted zone effective two days earlier, on April 12. Permission to fly into this area had

to be obtained from the U.S. Department of Justice, upon whose request
the restriction was being instituted. I nodded to Billy that I had seen the
notice and rejoined him just as the conversation turned to camping and
fishing.

The talkative weatherman invited us into a side room for coffee. Since
the little office lacked any windows facing the area where our friends were
working, we happily accepted. When the weatherman heard that we
were headed for the southern Rockies, he first told us that he had a son
living in that area and then mentioned how many airplanes were used
there to smuggle marijuana across the border from Mexico. Billy and I
looked at each other struggling to contain our laughter. The weatherman
thought we were dope runners! What a lucky break! With that in his
mind, he would never consider the possibility that we were actually en
route to Wounded Knee. And there was no reason for him to notify police
as long as we were going south. For the next fifteen minutes we decried,
somewhat less vehemently than the weatherman, the horrible effects
marijuana had on the nation's youth.

But our decoying conversation took an ugly turn. The weatherman
asked what we thought of "those goddamn Indians down on the reservation." He said they had a lot of nerve complaining about the government when "most of them live off the government" anyway. It was
impossible to change the subject. We had to sit listening to how Indian
women purposely had a lot of children "to get bigger welfare checks"
and how Indian men "would rather get drunk than hold down a decent
job." He asked what more they wanted from whites since white people
like himself paid the high taxes that supported them. Coming from a big
city in the East, it all sounded painfully familiar to me. Finally Larry came
in to get a drink of water. It was the signal that work outside was finished
and we could leave.

On the way out to the car, Billy started laughing. "You know what?" he
said, slapping me on the back. "That dude would've been saying all of
that shit about 'niggers' if I wasn't sittin' there beside him."

"That's right," I answered, "but wouldn't you like to see his face when
he picks up the paper in a day or two and reads about the airlift to
Wounded Knee. He'll be kicking himself remembering who he was
talking to tonight."

Back at the motel Billy opened a bottle of fifteen-year-old bourbon,
and we started passing it around. The cargo was all set to be dropped, but
we were under another front that was going stationary on top of us. It was
virtually certain that we could not fly visually the next morning, Sunday.
We would probably still be grounded at sunset. Sunrise Monday began to
look like the earliest possible drop time.

But Billy had a regular job back in Chicago. He had promised his boss that he would be there on Monday to fly a special charter. There were too many unemployed pilots hanging around Midway Airport to expect any consideration from his employer if he didn't show up on schedule. I was suddenly worried that some of the others might also have conflicts that would undermine their determination to carry out the airlift. Apprehensively, I asked Billy what he was going to do about his job, wishing we did not have to discuss it in front of everybody else. But Billy's answer was not what I expected.

"Look, man, the job is gone. I might as well do what I'm doing now and do it right. When you commit yourself to something, you're supposed to do it. Even if you decide somewhere in the middle that you don't like it, you got to do it 'cause you said you were going to do it. Like, I want to relax about time, man. I don't care any more when we do this, what day it is. Let's just take our time, relax, and do it right. This is a job that I want to see done. This is the kind of thing people would've done a few years ago for those blacks down South."

I looked up surprised. It was not the kind of thing Billy usually said. The idea that we all indefinitely postpone our other responsibilities until the airlift was accomplished made an impact on everyone. We went around the room, one by one, agreeing "to relax about time." Jim had walked off his job the week before. John said that he would telephone his parents to call in sick for him at Sears. Strobe promised to get friends to do likewise for him. Tom, who sat watching it all, was doing his job by being there.

We still had to deal with the teletype FAA notice declaring Wounded Knee a restricted air zone. But that took only a minute. No one cared much what the U.S. government decided to call the air over the Pine Ridge Reservation. We were going in anyway. Again Billy reinforced our decision. He pulled a copy of the Federal Air Regulations out of his flight case and read us the section on restricted air space. It stated in no uncertain terms that the FAA had to give 45 days notice prior to the declaration of a new restricted zone. Billy insisted that it didn't take a lawyer to figure out that the restricted zone over Wounded Knee was illegal and that the Justice Department had simply seized the airspace from the FAA.

With the decision-making behind us, there was time to relax. The seven of us were crowded into one small motel room, and it was past midnight. Billy's bourbon loosened our tongues and for the first time it felt like we were all there as friends, not people who had just met to do a fast job and disappear. But most of us *had* just met. We each talked some about ourselves as the others listened with interest. I learned a lot about the people in that room that night, but the story of Billy's life stood out with the most clarity.

He had grown up in Chicago's black South Side ghetto where kids don't survive intact without a lot of street savvy. Billy survived, but like his other friends who managed to finish high school, graduation left him with nothing very interesting to do. As it did with most of them, the U.S. military sponge soaked up Billy's life. He was 19, and it was 1965. Six months later he was in Viet Nam. They made him a "combat engineer," the public relations term for an army construction worker. Sitting in our motel room in Huron, South Dakota, Billy kept us laughing with stories about life as an American GI in Da Nang, South Viet Nam in 1966 and 1967. But the stories were more about battles between GIs and their own officers than about the war between Americans and Vietnamese.

Once Billy and his buddies were ordered to build a needlessly deluxe latrine building for the exclusive use of officers. They constructed a beauty, but the first night it was open for use, they blew it up with army dynamite. Another time one of the more arrogant officers warned experienced men not to leave a huge construction crane parked too long on soft ground. After dark they deliberately drove the crane out to a swamp and by morning it had sunk into uselessness.

One afternoon a shiny new chaplain, fresh from the States and dressed in sharply pressed trousers and shirt, came prancing across the wet ground Billy and some men were working on. One of the men hid behind a bulldozer and shot off an M-16 so that another could yell for everyone to hit the dirt. The chaplain went down, his neatly pressed uniform another casualty of the mud.

The most awesome story concerned unloading a huge bulldozer from the deck of a Navy ship onto a nearby pier. A friend of Billy's was in charge of directing the crane operator with hand signals. The friend waited until the bulldozer was clear of the side of the ship but not yet over the pier. Then he turned around, smiled at Billy, and gave the unknowing crane operator the signal to release the 'dozer. Billy said it was the biggest splash he had ever seen.

Some people in the motel room were surprised that mutiny and sabotage were so commonplace in Viet Nam. Billy was surprised that the Army had managed to keep it all out of the newspapers. But some of Billy's stories were not so funny. One day at Da Nang an old Vietnamese woman dressed in rags wandered into the enlisted men's compound where Billy and his fellow construction workers lived. It was a bad mistake. Vietnamese people of all ages carried bombs into areas frequented by Americans. One of the GIs grabbed her, flung her down, and started questioning her in English. She didn't understand him and remained silent. The GI became exasperated and began to shout. Finally, instead of simply searching the barely clothed woman and sending her on her way, the enraged GI started kicking her. Billy intervened on her behalf, physically, and was later rewarded with a courts-martial.

Asked why some men in Viet Nam had retained their humanity while others had not, Billy guessed that it was related to how bad conditions were where they had grown up. Ghetto kids like himself, he insisted, were better able to escape the brutalization of Army life because they had learned to resist brutalization in the ghetto. In the Army as well as in the inner city, the price of retaining one's humanity was to rebel "against the way things were." But Billy admitted that in the early part of the war most GIs did not understand why they were in Viet Nam. They rarely sought the causes of the war, and with no overall analysis their opposition remained sporadic and disorganized. Billy, who was one such man, went to Viet Nam tricked by patriotic propaganda into risking his life for an America that had largely ignored him. He returned a different man, but not a social revolutionary. Instead of wanting to change the society that had sent him to Viet Nam, he was bent only on changing the conditions of his own life.

Back in Chicago, Billy took up flying. But he was black and could not get a job with the airlines. Instead, he supported himself as a charter pilot and private flight instructor. At 23 he got married. Later he bought a small home and fathered a little girl. Piloting was a profession and with it Billy "rose" into the middle class. But he still lived on the South Side, and the life of the street was never very far behind. Billy was 28 years old when he told his story that night in South Dakota. He was profoundly skeptical of the United States, of the war it continued to wage long after he left Viet Nam in 1967, and of its many false commitments to black equality. Still, on a day-to-day basis, it would be fair to say that cars, clothes, and good times meant more to Billy than politics.

As the bourbon kept making the rounds after Billy finished talking, I claimed that it was really the war that had brought all of us together.

Jim objected. "I don't understand what Viet Nam has to do with any of this. We're trying to help the Indians, aren't we? The American Indians?"

"We are," I answered. "But you wouldn't be sitting here in South Dakota if it wasn't for Viet Nam. Neither would I."

"How do you figure that?"

"Because the war in Viet Nam changed our lives. It taught us all those deep dark secrets about the U.S. government."

"Like what?" Jim pressed on.

"Like the secret that the war was absolutely evil and the government knew it all along. Or the secret that the most selfish men in the country controlled what the government did. Or that most politicians considered the American people their enemies and kept things secret from them, like the Pentagon Papers. Or the secret that our economic system was so fundamentally wrong it actually needed colonial-type relationships with places like Viet Nam.

"Suddenly a lot of people could see that the United States was not governed of, by, and for the people, and that perhaps it never had been. It was the big 200-year-old secret, but the Indians could have told you about it anytime. People started building political movements to change things—not just the anti-war movement, but dozens of others too. A whole generation got used to getting up and doing something about what they didn't like."

"Well, I suppose that's all true," Jim conceded in his mountain drawl, "but I ain't here as part of any political movement. I'm helping those Indians because morally it's the right goddamn thing to do."

Larry put down his glass and turned toward Jim. "You think morality and politics are always that easy to separate?" he asked. "Night before last, when we were sewing cargo nets in Chicago, you told us you were ready to refuse direct orders because you didn't want to bomb people in Viet Nam. That was a moral decision. But while you were making it, so were thousands of other guys. That was a political movement. Eventually it was strong enough to undermine the whole U.S. war effort.

"You told us the other night that you helped organize a pro-war rally in 1965. You've done a lot of changing over the years. We all have. People don't usually change that much all by themselves. You'd have had a much harder time with your own moral decision about the war if you didn't know all those other guys were making their decisions at the same time. Maybe it never would have occurred to you that anything was wrong with the U.S. involvement in Viet Nam. It hardly occurred to anyone during the Korean War."

"Wait a minute," Billy said, "all that may be true for Jim, man, but you guys can't say that it's like that for most people."

"Why not?" I argued. "You just got done telling us that in 1965 you stood in line to go risk your neck for Uncle Sam. Now you can't wait to kick his ass in South Dakota. What changed you? Viet Nam, right?"

"Yeah, I guess that's right."

"Well, look at this whole group," I continued. "You and Strobe are both Viet Nam veterans. Larry and I are both full-time anti-war activists. Jim was almost a Viet Nam fighter pilot. Tom spends most of his time writing about Viet Nam. John's the only exception and he's almost ten years younger than the rest of us.

"And it's more than the war that brought us together. It's the fact that there was an anti-war movement. Tom would be just another Harvard journalist if there wasn't an audience for material exposing government lies in Viet Nam. I'd still be a university professor if the movement hadn't given me a way to fight the Army's making weapons out of my research and drafting students right out of my classes. Jim might be an Air Force officer now if anti-war people hadn't provoked him to ask the right questions at the right time. And Strobe, the all-American Viet Vet back from the war, burned up, freaked out, whatever the hell you are, Strobe. You'd probably be in some snake-pit government VA hospital if there wasn't a whole movement of Viet Vets who helped each other face the truth about what you guys did in Viet Nam.

"A lot of people forget that the anti-war movement was the largest radical movement in the history of America. In some way, either directly or indirectly, it was a turning point in the lives of millions of people, just like World War II was a turning point in the lives of people a generation ago."

Billy and Jim both nodded their heads in hesitant agreement. Jim spoke. "I guess that the things you're saying sound pretty true. It's just that from one day to the next, it never seems like you're making much progress when you do that kind of movement work."

"You're right," Larry answered, "but progress is still being made. It just can't be seen on a day-to-day basis. You've got to look at things over a longer period of time. Then the changes are clear. Glaring, in fact."

"We're part of those changes right now," I added. "Maybe we're just bringing food to Wounded Knee, who knows. But maybe we're doing something more, adding a little bit to an atmosphere in this country that tells people they don't have to sit by and do nothing when things like Wounded Knee come up. We don't know what'll develop out of Wounded Knee. There were no guarantees when we started those tiny little anti-war demonstrations in 1965."

"Hold on a second. What about me?" It was John, coming to life after sitting quietly through the discussion. "I'm only twenty-one. I never been on a peace march or a demonstration. Never been in the Army. I don't know shit about Viet Nam. I don't think I'm even that concerned about the Indians. I just want some free flyin' time, man; I'm just after the hours."

"No, John, it's not that simple," Larry said. "You wouldn't have dreamed of doing something like this a few years ago. Now you don't think anything of taking a stand against the government, even breaking the law if you have to. The atmosphere's changed, even at the Sears warehouse where you work. You got here because you knew someone, Bob Talbot, who knew someone, Bill, who worked with the anti-war movement. That would not have been true a while back."

"Hey, John," I asked, "if this was 1963 and you got offered some free flying time to airlift food to black civil rights workers in Mississippi, would you go?"

"No way, man. Not in a million years!"

"A million, huh? It's only been ten."

Sunday, April 15, 1973
Huron, South Dakota

I woke up at 7:00 a.m. to the sound of Jim's knocking on our door. As the only country boy among us, he had been assigned to permanent wake-up duty. Larry let him in and I stayed in bed. Without saying a word, Jim walked over to the window and pulled back the curtains. Our room looked out on the dull whiteness of a parking lot covered with snow. More of it was falling out of the dark gray sky.

"You guys might as well stay in the sack. The ceiling out there is just scraping the top of the motel."

We stayed. At 11:30 a.m. I opened my eyes a second time to find Larry shaking me awake.

"You better get up," he said in an alarmed voice. "Everybody's in Jim's room having a big argument about whether to go on to Wounded Knee or give up. It really looks bad."

I sat up in bed, instantly alert. Larry explained what was going on as I hastily threw on my clothes.

"We were upstairs in Jim's room watching television a couple of hours ago. Everyone's been awake for a while except you. A local interview show came on with a priest who was talking about Wounded Knee. So we listened. He had been inside with one of those mediating groups from the National Council of Churches. He talked about how courageous the people in Wounded Knee are because they're in there facing so many guns. Well, to make a long story short, he claimed that Wilson's goon squad had fifty-caliber machine guns! Not the feds now, but the goon squad."

"Fifty-caliber machine guns?!"

"That's right. People got very upset, especially Jim. He called the TV station right away and they told him that the show was taped a week ago. So he got the phone number of this priest's church. It's in some other little town around here somewhere. Well, Jim called the church, but the priest couldn't come to the phone because he was delivering a sermon. Do you believe it? It's Sunday morning and he was actually delivering a sermon.

"Anyway, Jim left a message for the priest to call back and a little while later he did. Jim was talking and Strobe was standing right next to him trying to get him to ask certain questions. It was hard for Jim to talk because, you know, he didn't want to give the priest his name or tell him why we were so interested. So Strobe started really freaking out; Jim told him to stop, and Strobe disappeared.

"The next thing we knew Strobe had talked the desk clerk in the motel office into hooking a phone in the other room into the conversation Jim was having with the priest. Jim got furious and made up some excuse for hanging up on the priest. Then he started yelling at Strobe and when I left, everyone was hollering at each other about fifty-caliber machine guns."

As we walked into the noisy room, it became suddenly silent. Everyone looked self-conscious. When I asked what had happened, they all spoke at once. I held up my hands and asked them to start over again, one at a time, beginning with Jim.

"Look, I just think we need information." He was calm, but forceful. "We're going in there absolutely cold. We need to make some contact with the Indians and find out what's happening there. It's one thing to be shot at with twenty-two's and thirty-thirty's, but it's a whole other thing if they got machine guns. It's not that hard to hit a slow moving airplane with a machine gun. Anyway, I was about to get some information from that priest when this yo-yo cut in on the line."

He indicated Strobe who was sitting defiantly cross-legged on the bed. I asked Strobe why he had done it.

"I wanted to hear what the guy had to say," he replied angrily. "Like, I wanted to hear his words with my own ears, you know, so they could register on me. I didn't want to have to stand there and talk to him through Jim. I mean, we're all the same, right? I wanted to rap to the cat, too. I ain't afraid of fifty-caliber machine guns. I been around 'em plenty, you know, in Nam. I remember. I just wanted to find out what I was getting into. That's all right, ain't it?"

I look at him, finding it easy to be sympathetic. "Sure, Strobe, it's all right. Let's forget the phone call. What does everybody else think about the machine guns? How about you, John?" I was going around the room and John sat next to Strobe.

"Well, I really do want to deliver that food. I guess we put a lot of time and effort into this. But I think Jim's right. We ought to get more information before we go in there. I wouldn't have come if I knew they were going to be shooting at us with machine guns."

"You're right, John, none of us would' have, at least not like this. Larry?"

"I don't believe it about the machine guns. The FBI has them, but they're not going to shoot down civilian airplanes with machine guns. They're more disciplined than that. Look, it's one thing for the government to let the goon squad take potshots at people with hunting rifles, but they can't sit by and let vigilantes use high-caliber machine guns. Anyway, if they did, it'd be all over the papers, and we haven't seen anything. I think what we got is a panicky priest on television for the first time in his life just trying to be a little dramatic."

"Billy? How about you?"

"Listen, that priest don't fly airplanes, man. What he's got to say don't mean shit to me."

"Tom? Your press card won't stop a bullet. You want a say in this too?"

"Whatever you guys decide, I'll go along with. I suppose I would feel safer knowing about the machine guns, but I haven't felt safe since we left Chicago, so what the hell."

"All right," I said, "some people want information, others don't care one way or the other. With this snow falling, we've got nothing else to do today. Let's go get ourselves some information."

"Where?"

"Rapid City, at the Wounded Knee legal defense office where they're doing all the support work. We can go there and find someone who's been backpacking food in and out at night. They'll know who's going to be shooting at us, and with what. Maybe we can get some detailed maps of the area drawn, too."

"Wait a minute. How are you going to do that," Larry asked, pointing at the snow falling on the other side of the window. "There's a blizzard out there and Rapid City is 250 miles away."

"Billy has an instrument license," I answered. "A few of us can go in one plane and get on top of that snow. If we leave now, we'll have a couple hours in Rapid City and be able to get back here by late tonight."

"Why don't you just call them?"

"Oh, come on, John," Jim snapped at him impatiently. "If anybody's phone is tapped in this whole goddamn country, it'll be theirs."

"Not only that," I added, "We have to be careful who in Rapid City knows about us. It's one thing to be sloppy about security in Chicago, but it's different here. I haven't told anyone with the Indians when we're coming. They don't even know that there's more than one plane or that it's going to be a parachute drop instead of a landing. We've got to figure on informers. Until this machine gun thing came up there was no reason for anybody to know anything. They need food, we're bringing it, that's all."

It was agreed. One plane with three people would go to Rapid City. Billy had to be one since he was the instrument pilot. I was another because I knew who to contact at the legal defense office. Jim was the third since it seemed sensible to send the three pilots. John drove us to the airport in our rented car.

"That bird that Jim's flying has more instruments than the others," Billy said, looking up from the charts he was checking in the back seat. "We'll take it, but first we got to move some of that food out. We'll be climbing up through a lot of snow, and if that plane starts to pick up ice, man, I want it to be as light as possible."

Jim turned back from the front seat. "OK. When we get out to the airport, we'll go into our old routine. You and Bill keep the weatherman busy—shouldn't be too hard with all this snow—and me and John here will move the loads around when he ain't looking."

It wasn't hard at all. Billy told the FAA weatherman we were off to visit a cousin of his at the Air Force base in Rapid City while the other non-instrument pilots were grounded by the snow. After filing our flight plan, the weatherman was nice enough to explain the intricate workings of the radar screen, while Jim and John were doing their own intricate work outside his window.

The runways and ramps at the Huron airport were already plowed, so it was no problem taxiing out for takeoff. The ceiling was only 400 feet; visibility was down to a mile-and-a-half in blowing snow. We got the complex instrument clearances over the radio and Billy pushed in the throttle. The Cherokee rolled down the runway, picked up speed, and leaned back to climb. For a moment after lift-off we could see the flat, square farmland all around us, then nothing. The inside of the snow cloud was a formless gray void. It wasn't possible to tell which way was up and very dangerous to try. The instruments on the dashboard were all that mattered, our only lifeline back to the planet. Without them we would not know we were even moving, and vertigo would be quick and inevitable.

Jim was flying the plane from the co-pilot's seat under Billy's watchful eye. We had decided that Billy would work on instrument flight instruction with Jim on the way into Rapid City and with me on the way back. The first few minutes in the clouds were noneventful. Then ice began to build up on the wings and on the radio antennas. It was not enough to worry about, so Billy continued to point out various readings on the instrument panel that indicated a course, speed, or rate of climb correction necessary in Jim's flying. All that time, though, Billy's attention never strayed very far from the ice on the wings. Occasionally on the ground, there was an element of bravado in the way Billy talked about flying. But once in a cockpit, he planned every move with precision and took his work quite seriously.

After ten minutes, the ice was still building and had become a definite concern. We had not finished our climb, but were almost at our assigned cruising altitude of 6,000 feet. We discussed radioing a request for a higher flight level. Just as we were about to do so, we broke out of the clouds into deep blue sky and bright sunshine. We were on top. The thick clouds that were so dark and sinister on the inside became the picture of innocence on the outside. Puffy, pure white, billowing cloud shapes stretched as far as we could see in any direction. Above there was only blue. With direct sunlight and less moisture in the air, we knew the wing ice would gradually disappear.

We flew along the upper edge of the clouds. The tops formed a slightly billowing but nearly flat plain just below 6,000 feet. It was a breath-takingly beautiful sight that too few people have the good fortune to experience. The flat cloud tops, extending to the horizon on all sides, seemed to form a new layer over the world, a floating white ocean that looked every bit as solid as any stretch of land or sea. We skimmed along close enough to the top of it to feel the rare sensation of speed in flight as we shot by little puffs and bulges at 155 miles per hour.

Billy took the controls back from Jim. He wanted to play. Suddenly, like a soaring bird, we were going up and down with the contours of the cloud tops, diving into the shallow hollows and climbing up to get over the little hills. Billy flew the airplane only 20 or 30 feet above the thick white mist. The solid clouds created the illusion that in fact we were zooming along close to the ground, but we had the added exhilaration of knowing that if we struck anything, it wouldn't matter at all.

Billy started flying around the little hills instead of over them. Each time he made a noise like a siren, banking the plane over on its side and screeching around the next obstacle, trying as hard as he could to avoid crashing into its white nothingness. Then the strangest sensation of all—purposely flying into the misty outcroppings and overhangs that began to resemble terrestrial slopes and cliffs. In the bright sunshine, the clouds looked as solid as snow-covered mountaintops. Billy pointed the airplane toward one of them and we sat transfixed as the heavy white cumulus rushed up to the window at unbelievable speed. It was hard not to duck as the plane went hurtling into it. A split second later, the gray turned back to blue and white as we popped out into the sunshine.

We continued west toward Rapid City gradually escaping from the stationary front dropping all the snow around Huron. Soon there were breaks in the clouds and no snow on the ground underneath. An hour after lift-off, the overcast below had completely evaporated and we flew on through a cloudless sky. But the terrain had undergone a remarkable change in the short distance from Huron. It was barely cultivated and almost treeless. Instead of the flat checkerboard of farms and long straight roads, we were over little rocky hills heavily scarred by erosion and bearing few signs of human habitation. The roads curved in every direction, yet there were no real mountains. The land looked flat from a distance, but up close the unevenness was clearly visible. Areas level enough for a safe emergency landing were hard to find.

Billy looked out the window for several minutes, shaking his head. Finally, he said, "You see that tiny little town down there? That looks to be about the size of Wounded Knee, at least from what this map shows here. We been passing a few little towns about that size, and goddamn, I can't tell 'em apart. There are no railroads or big highways to use as landmarks. The roads are twisted up and they go into the towns from all kinds of different directions."

For the next ten minutes we watched the ground, trying to practice identifying towns with whatever landmarks were available.

"Listen here, man, we got a problem." Billy's head kept going from the window to the chart resting on his lap. "I'm flying the lead plane, right? That puts me in charge of navigation. I say it ain't going to be easy finding that place. I mean, we're going to find it, but coming in there when it's barely light out, we better be damn sure we don't drop that food on the wrong town."

The farther west we flew, the more barren the land became. The outlying little towns were even harder to identify. Forty miles from Rapid City, we looked down on the Badlands, only five miles to our left. Fifty miles beyond that lifeless wasteland, due south of our position, lay Wounded Knee. After flying over so many miles of rich Midwestern countryside, the stark emptiness of western South Dakota was shocking.

On our approach into Rapid City Regional Airport, we were sequenced behind a Frontier Airlines jet. The delay gave us a chance to look around. Like Denver, Rapid City had been built on the border between the Great Plains and the western mountains. The houses on its eastern side touched the dry barren country we had just flown over. On that end of town, we could see the Indian shacks and cabins covering acre after acre of dusty sand and clay. On the other side, the thickly forested slopes of the Black Hills rose out of the western edge of the city. There in the green distance, we could see the affluent suburbs and the mansions of the rich, spreading themselves over the Sacred Mountains of the Sioux Nation.

Jim brought the Cherokee Six in to a smooth landing. We taxied past the main terminal building and parked at the office of one of the local flying services. We were expecting to see government planes and helicopters all over the airport: Rapid City was the closest major city to Wounded Knee. But everything appeared quite normal. With only one aircraft, we didn't worry about attracting attention to ourselves. We registered our landing and strolled over to the passenger terminal. There, too, we saw nothing to indicate that the Rapid City Airport was being used as a staging area for U.S. government operations at Wounded Knee.

Since we had to assume that the telephones in the Wounded Knee legal office were tapped, our plan was simply to walk in and tend to our business in person. Outside the airline terminal we climbed into the back seat of a cab. I gave the driver an address two blocks away from the office we actually wanted.

She turned around with an ear-to-ear grin on her face, and said, "Far out! That's only a few blocks from my garage. You guys are my very last fare. Not just for today, but forever. I'm quitting this damn job in about a half hour. Me and my boyfriend saved enough to get a little place up in the mountains, and we're going!" She drove like a madwoman and never stopped talking about how happy she was. It was a good omen, and I wanted to return the favor. As we pulled up to get out, she had the three of us still laughing, and I couldn't keep from giving her a ten dollar tip out of the airlift's money.

We were on a residential street in a lower middle class neighborhood, lined on both sides with small one-story ranch-style homes. There were modest lawns and driveways between each house. I was surprised to see that the support group was operating out of a home instead of an office, but I quickly realized that security was much easier to handle if one had control of an entire building rather than just a single room inside it. As we walked the two blocks to the address I had been given in Boston, my eyes scanned windows and parked cars for the FBI surveillance I knew must be around. This was the main off-reservation center for assisting people in Wounded Knee. The volunteer lawyers were there with a whole array of other people who were raising money, recruiting help, putting out news bulletins, buying food and other necessary supplies. Billy, Jim, and I were a little nervous, not knowing exactly what to expect.

"Listen you guys," Jim urged, "let's not waltz into this place like we're the movement air force on a hotshot mission. There are probably agents all over. We're not going to be able to tell who's who right off the bat."

"Or ever," I added. "Remember Marty, the guy from Boston who helped buy the food back in Chicago? He gave me the name of a woman who works here. We talk to her and no one else, okay? Marty said she's a legal worker from some Washington law firm. Came out here four weeks ago to do volunteer work for a few days and she hasn't been home since. Her name's Rita."

The address we were after was a house with a side door that faced across a narrow driveway to the side door of another house. The defense committee seemed to control them both. At least people were going back and forth. Someone acting like a guard was at the door of one house and was obviously concerned about who went in and out. We turned toward the other door and opened it into a kitchen. A roomful of Indian faces gave the three of us, two whites and a black, a thorough visual examination.

"Hi. We're looking for a woman named Rita. She around?"

"She's not here right now," a young man answered. He was wearing a colorful beaded headband and he came over to where we were standing. "What's it about? Can I help you?"

"We wanted to talk to Rita, you know. She's the person we were told to see."

"Well, that's cool," he replied, "she'll be back soon. She's just next door in a meeting with the heavies."

In the adjacent house, some well-known leaders of the black civil rights movement were consulting with some increasingly well-known leaders of the American Indian Movement. No one knew how long we would have to wait, but everyone seemed at ease about mysterious characters coming in at odd hours and being closemouthed about what they wanted. Still, it was uncomfortable standing around with nothing to do in a roomful of busy people. We decided to wait outside.

Eventually, a young woman emerged from the next house and had a whispered conference with the guard, who nodded in our direction. She walked toward the three of us, holding out her hand. We introduced ourselves, first names only. Rita was friendly and obviously a lot more at ease than we were. She asked what was happening.

"Well, we need your help," I answered. "We want some particular information about what's going on at Wounded Knee. But before we ask you for it, we want to be sure about who you are and we want you to be sure about who we are."

I told her that we had a mutual friend in Boston named Marty and suggested that we go to a telephone booth and call him. He could talk to both of us and verify our identities for each other. Rita agreed and led us to a car. Once we were inside, she asked if we were pilots. Marty had been asked by their people to contact me, and she had correctly put two and two together. It was a good sign, but I just smiled, not quite ready to say yes.

Marty was away for the weekend and unreachable. In the process of trying to track him down, Rita and I discovered several other mutual friends from around the anti-war movement. It soon made no sense at all to be suspicious of her. I pulled Billy and Jim off to the side and asked their agreement to drop the security precautions. I suggested we go along with Rita's natural assumption that we had come in one aircraft and planned to land it inside the Wounded Knee defense perimeter. The information we needed was the same either way, and the fewer people who knew what was really happening, the better. Let the truth be a welcome surprise.

I told Rita we were the pilots she was expecting and we had come with our own food and our own plane. A smile flashed across her face. The food situation in Wounded Knee was desperate, she told us, and we had arrived in the nick of time. I asked if we could meet with people who had recently been inside. We wanted to know what arms were being used and we wanted accurate maps of the surrounding terrain. Rita nodded and led us right back to the car. The perfect people were available at the houses we had just left. They had come out of Wounded Knee that very morning.

Driving back to the house, we asked Rita to bring the people out to the front lawn. There was no reason for others to overhear us. A few minutes after our arrival, three young men walked toward us in the dark with Rita at their side. Two were Indians and the third was white. All had shoulder-length hair and headbands, and all were dressed in levis or buckskin jackets.

"Hey, are you guys the flyers? That's really great, man."

"What kind of plane do you have?"

"Wow, those people inside are going to love you. They been practically starving for days now."

They all talked at once, shaking our hands and asking our names. Whatever tension we came with quickly disappeared in the spirited welcome. It had been a long trip from Chicago, but instantly we knew we had done the right thing. They told us how government lines around Wounded Knee had tightened considerably in the past few weeks. Police dogs and trip flares were in use and the newer tactics were taking their toll. More and more backpackers were getting arrested going in or coming out. The need for food was so great that people who had been inside all along and who knew the country best were going out to try and return with supplies. Our three new friends had already done this twice.

As we expected, the story about fifty-caliber machine guns was entirely false. The marshals and FBI agents were using them, but none of the white vigilantes or anyone in the goon squad had ever been seen with heavy weapons. On two separate occasions much earlier in the occupation, planes smaller than ours had flown into Wounded Knee. Each landed on the main road and discharged a few hundred pounds of supplies. Neither was shot at by federal agents, but the second plane did have to outrun an FBI helicopter. Billy, Jim, and I received the news with knowing smiles. Our plan was perfect. By making a parachute drop rather than a landing, we would be gone before the FBI had time to get its helicopter airborne. At worst, we would have to face a few sleepy potshots from the goon squad.

We asked the three men from Wounded Knee to draw us a map of the town showing all the landmarks that would be visible from the air and the exact location of the defense perimeter. We didn't tell them about our parachutes, but we had to find out where the bunkers and gun emplacements were so we could tell which terrain was safe to drop supplies over. One of the Indians said he could draw such a map. We walked back to the house and followed him into a bedroom. He sensed that we were reluctant to talk in front of the other people there and asked them to leave. I closed the door and turned up the volume on a radio to keep our conversation from being overheard.

Our Indian friend carefully drew a detailed map on a pad of yellow paper. While he was working, one of the others told us that there was a person in the next room who had accompanied the pilot of the second aircraft to land in Wounded Knee. "Yes," we answered, we certainly did want to talk to him.

They brought in a young white man in his mid-twenties. He wore a headband and a levi jacket with the words "Wounded Knee" written in red embroidery thread across one of the pockets. His name was Oliver. In Viet Nam, he had worked on medical evacuations and had spent most of his time crewing on a helicopter. A few days after the Wounded Knee occupation began, Oliver showed up and volunteered his services. He had been inside for weeks, working alternately as a medic and a warrior. He was familiar with the terrain, but more importantly for us, he had flown in once before and knew how to recognize landmarks from the air—something not as simple as most people imagine. Oliver was just what we needed. He was too good to be true.

Jim asked him to please wait outside for a minute. Billy and I knew what was on Jim's mind—invite Oliver along as a spotter for the drop. It would solve our navigation problems and that was a big advantage. But there were risks as well. Despite our distinct impression that the people around us were competent and careful, we were not prepared to endanger the airlift or ourselves on the basis of our casual impressions. We simply didn't know Oliver and would have no control over who he talked to or what he said after the airlift. But we wanted him along, and we could at least control what he said before the airlift. In reality, there was no reason to suspect him of anything, but we couldn't be too careful. If he did turn out to be an informer, we at least wanted the situation set up so that the drop itself could not be stopped.

We asked Oliver back into the little bedroom, and with the radio still blaring invited him to fly with us. We told him we were very concerned about security and had to insist upon certain conditions. He had to leave with us immediately: no phone calls, no last minute goodbyes to anyone, just right into Rita's car and out to the airport. He let out a happy hoot and agreed, saying that his bag was in the next house and that he would get it and be back in ten seconds. He was. We went over the map that had just been drawn for us, made sure we understood it all, and thanked everyone who had helped us. The three men from Wounded Knee came over one at a time to wish us luck. They shook hands warmly, looking at us with eyes full of strength and pride.

As we walked to the car, we agreed in whispers not to brief Oliver until our plane was airborne and headed back to Huron. But driving out to the airport, Oliver won us over. He kept saying how glad he was to be coming along. We heard one remarkable story after another about life in Wounded Knee, all of which he told with tremendous enthusiasm. We were glad he was there and that he was willing to go off with us so suddenly, not knowing his destination or who we were, but only that we had come with some plan for helping the people in Wounded Knee.

We got to the Rapid City airport at 9:30 p.m. It was already deserted. Rita asked if we wanted word sent into Wounded Knee about when we would arrive or about any special preparations like signal fires. We said no, thanked her very sincerely for all her help, and waved goodbye. Billy and Jim went off in the dark to do a preflight check on the airplane while I stood on the ramp in the cold night air talking to Oliver.

"Three nights ago in Wounded Knee," he said, "we had a pow-wow. Everyone from the warriors' society was there and all the medicine men. It was real amazing, man, people dancing around a fire, chanting, drums beating. Wow! The medicine men told us that a plane was coming with food and that they wanted to pray, you know, to ask the Great Spirit to protect it on its way. We're really in trouble for food in there. Rice is all that's left and there ain't much of that.

"The medicine men got out their holiest objects, man, pipes and medicine bags, stuff that had been handed down from the grandfathers a hundred years ago. Then they went around the fire and one by one each warrior thought about the airplane and tried to help it along, you know, in their heads. Then we sacrificed flesh and we knew you guys would make it."

The words hung in the air like a neon sign going on and off. I had an idea what they meant, but I wanted to be sure.

"Sacrifice flesh," I said, "What does that mean, sacrifice flesh?"

"Each of the warriors takes a knife and cuts off a little piece of himself, you know, as a sign. The medicine men say that flesh is the only thing that anyone really has to give."

His answer was more than ironic. It revealed the profound difference between Sioux culture and white materialism. I was repulsed at the thought of cutting off little pieces of my body. Yet, I also felt my spirits lifted by the fact that other people had done it. I took it as a sign of their need and of their confidence in what we were doing. It made me feel buoyant and more confident myself. I didn't believe in the ritual, but in some strange way it had done what it was supposed to do, even for me.

We climbed into the airplane. I took the co-pilot's seat. Oliver and Jim got in back and sat on the floor. It was my turn to practice instrument flying under Billy's instruction. We strapped in, got our clearances from the tower, and a few minutes later, despite the cloudless night sky, I was nosing the ship off the runway looking only at the instrument panel. Outside there were stars all around, but I was too busy to see.

In the back of the plane, Jim began a detailed description of our plans for Oliver. He did not say where we had been or who we were, only where we were going and how. Oliver learned that we were on our way to Huron and that several hours after we got back, we would depart for

Wounded Knee in three aircraft, arriving there at dawn to make a parachute drop of 2,100 pounds of food. Until we left Huron, he would stay with the rest of us in a motel. His job was to guide us in over the last 10 or 15 miles and then verify when we were inside the Wounded Knee defense perimeter. Afterward, he would be dropped off a few hundred miles away and given air fare back to Rapid City.

Oliver was delighted. He had not expected the cargo to be so large or the mission to be so well organized. The idea of using parachutes especially pleased him. Crouched in the back of the plane, he excitedly told Jim that when we were done with this drop, we should all get together and do it again, over and over if necessary. Then he said that he knew where we could get a load of M-16s to fly to Wounded Knee. It was the last moment we trusted him.

My eyes met Billy's in the faint red glow from the instrument panel. One quick glance told each of us that we had heard correctly. There was nothing more to say. Less than an hour after meeting us, Oliver not only revealed the location of a cache of illegal automatic weapons, he also suggested that we conspire to transport them across state lines to Wounded Knee. Oliver was either naive and stupid or a government agent. Either way, he was no bargain.

Entrapment was a common FBI tactic. Provocateurs suggested illegal acts to people, like raids on draft boards, sometimes even offering essential information or equipment, like burglary tools. Then they worked with the same people, all the while planning to show up at their trial to testify for the prosecution. Other provocateurs regularly attended meetings and demonstrations in order to shout the loudest for violence. The idea was to provoke an incident that would give the police an excuse to attack. They were old tricks, but they still held a certain attraction for FBI agents.[1]

---

[1]In the fall of 1974, a year and a half after the occupation, one provocateur surfaced in federal proceedings against AIM members charged with conspiring to purchase illegal weapons. During the occupation, Lon Smith of Phoenix not only volunteered to purchase arms and fly them to Wounded Knee (he was a pilot), but also to contribute $4,600 in "Communist Party" funds to help pay for the operation. All along he was in daily and often hourly contact with the FBI.

Only two months later, another FBI informer had his cover blown in Iowa. Doug Durham of Des Moines, also a pilot, had joined the Wounded Knee occupation and become an active member of AIM. Later he rose to be the organization's chief security officer. In early 1975 Durham admitted publicly that he had been in the employ of the FBI all along and was receiving more than $1,000 per month from them.

A month later, yet a third pilot was exposed as an FBI informer. Gi Schafer of New Orleans spent time in Wounded Knee during the occupation and then, in its final days, offered to carry out a parachute drop of supplies. (It was two weeks after the mission described in this book.) "Bad weather" delayed Schafer's flight until the occupation was over. Schafer's employment by the FBI, along with that of his wife, Jill, went back beyond the summer of 1972 when both helped organize demonstrations at the Democratic and Republican conventions in Miami.

It is after repeated experiences like these that my friends and I have come to see the FBI as a kind of secret police whose mission is, in part, to subvert political freedoms cherished by the American people since 1776.

Oliver was going on and on in the dark behind us about guns and clips and ammo. For a while Billy and I tried to hear him over the noise of the engine. Gradually it got boring and we gave up. Jim's tone of voice and words had shifted immediately to vague and noncommittal replies. There was no other way to handle it. We had to tell Oliver as little as possible and get rid of him at the first opportunity that would not anger him and jeopardize our mission even more. It was too bad, I thought, because Oliver was probably just naive and stupid. I went back to practicing my instrument flying, confident that in spite of our not having said a single word to each other, Billy and Jim understood the situation exactly as I did. We were beginning to feel like old friends.

The flight was easy. There wasn't enough fuel left to make it all the way back to Huron, so shortly after 11:00 p.m. we landed in Pierre, the state capital. Like the Rapid City airport, Pierre was quiet, relaxed, and nearly deserted. While Billy saw to the gas, I called the motel in Huron, asked that the car meet us at the airport, and warned everyone to guard what they said in front of Oliver.

An hour later, we touched down in Huron. The front had dispersed and the weather was clear. Billy and I had to decoy the night-shift weatherman all over again as Jim reloaded the plane we had been flying. By 1:30 a.m., the eight of us, including Oliver, were all crowded into my motel room. Our three planes sat at the Huron airport, ready to go. We planned to be airborne by 3:00 a.m. in order to arrive at Wounded Knee by sunup at 5:00 a.m. With only an hour to spare, we gathered on the floor around the maps and reviewed every detail of our plans. Oliver spoke first about the fifty-caliber machine guns. Despite our skepticism of him, everyone was obviously comforted by Oliver's very detailed and professional description of the armaments in use at Wounded Knee and by his firm assurances that no machine guns would be used against us.

10

The Siege
of Wounded Knee

"Among us we have no prisons, we have no pompous parade of courts; we have no written laws, and yet judges are as highly revered among us as they are among you, and their decisions are as highly regarded.

Property, to say the least, is well-guarded, and crimes are as impartially punished. We have among us no splendid villains above the control of our laws. Daring wickedness is never suffered to triumph over helpless innocence. The estates of widows and orphans are never devoured by enterprising sharpers. In a word we have no robbery under color of the law.

—Chief Thayandangea
Mohawk, 1807.

The Oglala Sioux people and the American Indian Movement held Wounded Knee continuously from February 27 to May 8, 1973. Looked at in any number of ways, for these 71 days the historic settlement was neither a part of the United States nor under the jurisdiction of U.S. law. For the first time since the Civil War, local people living within an organized area of the country carried out what was in effect a successful, temporary secession from the Union.

U.S. domestic power has been temporarily held at bay in other confrontations, such as ghetto rebellions or prison uprisings. From a federal perspective, some areas of the country have been partially ungovernable for brief periods, as in Alabama and Mississippi during the civil rights struggles of the early 1960s. Abandoned federal land has been seized and held for over a year. Alcatraz Island was only one of several such actions, many of which were also carried out by militant Indians. But never in this century has a living American community, with its neighbors and its far-flung friends, belligerently walled itself off from the United States of America and remained free for a period of time to live under a totally different system of ideas and laws.

Despite occasionally overblown claims to the contrary, this achievement was not the result of holding the United States back by force of arms. The security measures deployed for the protection of Wounded Knee were undeniably more efficient than combatants on either side anticipated. But the real force that protected the insurgent community was hardly that of its paltry weapons. Rather, their power came from the audacity they displayed in shouldering those weapons, not from their actual firepower. For it was by the audacious act of taking up arms that the Wounded Knee community found the means to place millions of Americans in a significant moral dilemma. The Indians understood that history was their best ally and that the American people could still be moved by a clearcut issue of political morality, moved not to change the channel on their TV sets but to listen and respond sympathetically to a desperate cry for fairness and respect. The force protecting Wounded Knee came not only from the guns of the few people inside, but also from the power lying dormant in the unorganized and unexpressed opinions of so many people around the country.

The Indians at Wounded Knee were willing to bet their lives, first that the people of America could be moved out of their usual lethargy, and second, that once moved they had the political power to limit the actions of a hostile federal government. They wagered correctly, just as the anti-war movement did when it made exactly the same prediction with respect to Viet Nam.

Nevertheless, Wounded Knee was unique. Even though the physical strength of its tiny army was not its most powerful weapon, the fact remained that it had an army which was in a virtual state of war with the United States for well over two months. If the defiant seizure and control of a piece of America's real estate was remarkable, the spectacle of internal warfare was extraordinary. The unprecedented gun battles that took place at Wounded Knee attracted a disproportionate, but all things considered perhaps not an undeserved, amount of attention.

These gun battles were referred to on both sides as "fire fights," fights in which each side took fire from the other. It was another legacy, this one linguistic, of the Viet Nam war. At first the fire fights occurred only infrequently. They were usually over in less than an hour and seldom involved more than several dozen rounds of ammunition (a round is a single bullet fired from a single gun). Such gunplay can hardly be thought of as limited, but before long it grew far more serious. As the weeks went by, the fire fights increased in duration and intensity, until some were lasting for an entire day or night with upwards of 10,000 bullets streaming into Wounded Knee.

It was never a game and rarely just a symbolic protest; it was a fight for life. And two Indians lost theirs. One was shot from behind at long range. The other had the back of his head blown off when a government bullet came through a wall next to where he slept. At least 15 others inside Wounded Knee were shot and injured. On the government side, one FBI agent was wounded in the wrist and one U.S. marshal was paralyzed from the waist down when a bullet penetrated his spine.

Aside from a few dozen Army combat veterans, the people of Wounded Knee were as unfamiliar with this kind of warfare as any other townspeople in America. Gladys Bissonette was in the settlement for the entire 71 days of the occupation. She remembered her terror and confusion as she described one of the early gun battles.

"The first really big fire fight that we had," she began, "I was in that white building where we had our kitchen. Everybody had eaten supper and the last ones were just coming in and they just sat down to eat. I had a little foam rubber mattress in that kitchen so I made my bed and I was lying in it. I was so tired because I had been up since two o'clock that morning and this was ten o'clock at night.

"I had my head on a pillow on the floor and all of a sudden I could hear something just go 'boom,' and I said, 'Do you know that that sounded just like dynamite?' But everybody was talking and they didn't hear it. So I said, 'Listen, there is something going on.' Then somebody runs in and says, 'Douse the lights, douse the lights.' So they doused the lights in there and oh boy, you should have heard that fire fight. It just come on strong, full blast.

"Somebody ordered us to go into the middle room because them bullets would have to come through two walls before they got to you from either side. So we all crawled. I was crawling and some of these boys were loading up their guns inside of that place. Just as this kid got through loading his gun and lifting it up, I crawled under the barrel of the gun and that gun went off.

"I thought he blew the top of my head off! He just got it up in time, and I went under it, and the gun went off and the slug went right through the roof. Well, somebody was pushing and pulling me along on the floor there so I didn't even have to crawl any myself. Somebody pushed me or drug me or something. It seemed like I was in a mess tangled up with all those other people, like I was in a washing machine or something.

"Pretty soon I got to that middle room and somebody hauled me up and my ears were still ringing. It scared me so bad," Gladys said, shaking her head and remembering the moment. "I mean, it just shocked me at first, and then afterwards I thought, 'Well, how close that was,' because if I had just crawled a little bit farther toward the front of that gun while he was lifting it, and it had gone off then, well, I would have just been blown to pieces because I would have been right at the tip of that gun.

"By the time we got settled, here come a security man and he told us all to get out and head for the trading post. I thought, 'Well my god, head for the trading post? There's one group of federal marshals sitting up at that end of the street, and one group of them at this end of the street, and if we run up that street, that's just right under a heavy cross-fire.' And I thought, 'I'll be darned if I'll run up that street!'

"So I grabbed my little boy and somebody grabbed me by the arm, some security boy, and they ran with me and I said, 'I'm heading for the creek. I ain't running up that road.' So we headed for the creek and just as I ran down the dry bank somebody hollered, 'Gladys, hit the ground, hit the ground,' and my little boy hit the ground and yelled 'Mom,' and he jerked me and I fell down and a bullet just whizzed past me. The bullets were hitting the trees and everything so we layed there for a while. Then it let up and we went down into that gully."

Gladys, sounding younger than her 55 years, gestured more and more energetically as she continued her story. "There's a log house that's across from that gully and I said, 'Well, let's go there,' and they said, 'No, we're headin' for that Catholic church. We're going into that basement.' This security kid says, 'Go straight up the hill here,' and I said, 'Not on a bet! That's a long stretch from this log house to the top of the hill where that church is.' I said, 'Are you kidding? Let's go down along this dry creek and we'll get right opposite the Catholic Church.'

"We had our sweat lodge and our Indian tipi there right below that church. 'There's a dry canyon that goes right up to that tipi,' I said. 'Even if we just get inside that tipi, we'll be safe.' They said, 'Aw, bullets will go right through that tipi,' and I said, 'Oh no,' I said, 'so far I have never seen any, I have never seen a bullet penetrate that tipi.' I said, 'That is a sacred tipi, that just don't happen.' And people didn't believe me, them girls and boys that were running with me.

"So just about that time, we had been running back along that dry creek and we come up right behind the trading post and we started up toward the tipi. Like I said, there was a dry gulch that goes right up to the highway, so just as we landed up there and we lay down to rest, well, everybody started hollering, 'Ceasefire, ceasefire.' "

Gladys leaned back, looking finished. Then, with a hearty laugh, she added, "That kinda made me sick after all the running I did!"

Fragile negotiations were established despite these early fire fights. But by the end of the first week of the occupation, on March 6, negotiations broke down completely and the Justice Department issued a two-day

U.S. Marshal cleaning an M-16 rifle inside a federal bunker on the outskirts of Wounded Knee. Other rifles, mostly M-16s, lie about ready to be fired. (*courtesy Wide World Photos.*)

Dick Wilson, far right, and some of the men known as the "goon squad" control traffic at the Tribal Council roadblock on the Big

ultimatum to the people in Wounded Knee. The government had decided to ignore Indian demands. They insisted that conditions of arrest were the only topic for discussion.

Inside Wounded Knee there were two-way radios used to communicate with federal personnel in the arrangement of ceasefires and other events of mutual concern. Unknown to the government, these radios were modified by Indian and white communications specialists to allow the occupying forces to eavesdrop on other federal transmissions. Late one night, after several hours of Indian drumming and singing in Wounded Knee, the marshals were overheard conversing about Indian warriors planning a suicide attack at dawn. The marshals called their music a "death-dance" song. The officers in the government bunkers acted as though the Indian people in Wounded Knee were the stereotypes that so many Hollywood movies had created for their ancestors.

With the same lunatic reasoning that led American officers to burn down Vietnamese villages "in order to save them," federal law enforcement officers believed that since the AIM leadership in Wounded Knee was crazy, it was up to them to assume responsibility for the safety of the women and children—despite the fact that it was these same officers who did the actual shooting that jeopardized everyone in the first place. On March 6, when the U.S. Attorney General's representative demanded that people in Wounded Knee surrender before darkness fell on March 8, he also called upon them to send out all the women and children. Dennis Banks rejected the request, telling the press that women would not be sent out, but would decide for themselves what they wished to do. "The women who came in with us said they would lay down their lives for this cause. If they decide to stay, that's up to them," he stated to reporters.

That night a large meeting was held in Wounded Knee to answer the ultimatum. It flatly rejected the government's deadline. Banks made a long speech in which he predicted that living conditions would get a lot worse.

"What is most important," he said, "is that we are not doing this for ourselves, but for our children and our nation. We all know we are in a war, and we're beginning to feel the first pangs of war—pangs of hunger and pangs of cold. We know they're going to try and starve us out or freeze us out. But this is our kind of war. We've been fighting hunger and cold all our lives."

Others believed that when the March 8 ultimatum expired, the government would come in shooting. But their determination to resist did not waver. Instead, more people from the reservation and beyond came over the hills into Wounded Knee during the night of the 6th, dodging government searchlights and flares. The next night, the 7th, over 40 others, most of them armed, slipped through government lines and joined the resistors.

During the day of the deadline, the 8th, medicine men inside the settlement daubed red war paint on people's faces. Acceptance of the paint meant that a person was accepting the possibility of death. Less than an hour before the expiration at sunset, the Justice Department in Washington backed down and announced that federal forces would not storm Wounded Knee that night. Other Nixon Administration officials tried to answer public criticism of their hardline policy by insisting that there had never been an ultimatum in the first place. That night a 14-year-old boy guided 39 more Indians through the gullies into Wounded Knee.

The standoff on March 8 brought a subtle but important change in the relative power of the groups contending at Wounded Knee. The Indians, having successfully withstood the physical threat of the ultimatum, forced the government to contradict its previous policy of ignoring Sioux demands and negotiating only on the basis of the conditions of surrender. With widespread publicity focusing so much attention on Wounded Knee, decisions had to be made at a level even higher than U.S. Attorney General Kleindienst's office. Thus, the White House, assuming control without admitting it to the public, decided to allow substantive negotiations to begin before all the opposition negotiators were safely behind bars.

This shift in policy was forced on the Nixon Administration because Americans across the country publicly supported the occupation. The amount of press coverage was unusually high, stimulating, as well as being stimulated by, the intense public interest. The list of media representatives on permanent assignment in Pine Ridge included over a dozen TV crews, journalists from all wire services, most large newspapers and magazines, the underground press, and a selection of reporters from as far away as France, Sweden, Italy, and Japan.

For the most part, early support for the Indians in Wounded Knee came from what the government likes to think of as "the radical fringe." In New York City on March 7, 150 people demonstrated their support at Federal Plaza. The next day, 150 Indians marched in Tucson. Passamoquoddy Indians blocked sections of Route 190 in Maine. Over 50 people occupied the offices of Senator Edward Brooke and the Interior Department in Boston. At Kent State University, 500 students demonstrated, while similiar actions took place at Cleveland State University and Case Western Reserve. Back in New York, protestors marched in front of the United Nations as AIM leaders unsuccessfully appealed to Secretary-General Kurt Waldheim's assistant for a chance to address the General Assembly.

The first impact of such demonstrations is often to prod establishment liberals, who otherwise would be watching from the sidelines, into taking some kind of action. This was the case with Wounded Knee. Senator Edward Kennedy, and many other liberal voices, without going so far as endorsing the occupation, did make strong statements calling for a complete withdrawal of federal forces and heavy weapons. Some major newspapers also issued editorial calls for government disarmament. But like the liberal Chicago *Daily News,* which spoke of "the senseless violence of the radical fringe that calls itself the American Indian Movement," these papers withheld endorsement of the occupation. In striking contrast to their colleagues, the Congressional Black Caucus in the House of Representatives did come out in full support of the Indian stand taken at Wounded Knee.

Even opposition of this sort rarely brings about a direct change in government policy. But it can very effectively limit the maneuvering space within which an administration is able to work. Limitations of this kind are often critically important to the people engaged in direct conflict with the government. As with the anti-war movement, so it was at Wounded Knee. Public opinion prevented the Nixon Administration from using its armored personnel carriers and machine guns to destroy the little Indian settlement, as public opposition to the war had helped prevent the use of nuclear weapons and herbicides to destroy North Viet Nam. Thus the real combatants are given more of a chance to achieve their own victory.

In its frustration at Wounded Knee, the federal government responded just as it had to earlier frustrations in Viet Nam. It relied heavily on advanced military technology and dishonest negotiations. This strategy should have come as no surprise since it had not only been used for years in Viet Nam, but had actually been honed to perfection a century before during the wars between earlier administrations and the Indian nations.

As the government consolidated its two-point post-ultimatum strategy, the military escalation it mounted took the following shape. Over 300 U.S. marshals were deployed around Wounded Knee, including their elite Special Operations Group which had received extensive sniper training. Over 100 FBI agents were assigned to control the roadblocks on two of the four highways leading into Wounded Knee, the roads from Pine Ridge and Manderson. In addition, the FBI was put in charge of interrogating all prisoners and maintaining all covert operations, such as placing informers in various Indian support groups and in the occupation itself. Employees of the Central Intelligence Agency (spies?) operated within the ranks of the U.S. marshals as communications technicians. The U.S. Border Patrol sent in several dozen members, including special non-barking dogs to flush out people infiltrating the area. The dogs were on leave from tracking operations against Mexicans on the California border. The Bureau of Indian Affairs police already on the scene underwent a rapid training and weapons upgrading program. Finally, as they have done on so many occasions in the past, the U.S. Army quietly sent in advisors. High ranking officers of the 82nd Airborne Division were assigned to coordinate tactical planning and logistical support for the FBI agents and marshals in the latter's first paramilitary operation inside the territory of the United States.

It is not known exactly who ordered the raising of this unique federal army. It is known that it was done without the approval of the U.S. Congress and was therefore in violation of the Constitution. The weapons made available to these forces included M-16 automatic rifles, M-79 grenade launchers, thirty- and fifty-caliber machineguns, and a wide selection of illumination equipment and nighttime sensing devices. The U.S. Army, having provided most of this gear, was brazen enough to also deliver 18 armored personnel carriers. Nonetheless, the prospect of khaki-colored helicopter gunships hovering over the plains of South Dakota was too much even for the Army. Instead, three private helicopters were rented and outfitted at the tiny Pine Ridge airport. In addition to this massive firepower, officers in command invited U.S. marshals to bring their personal hunting rifles to the siege of Wounded Knee.

But an escalated offense begets an increased defense, and more Indians, armed and unarmed, continued to make the drive to South Dakota, sometimes over great distances. Puyallups arrived from Washington State. Iroquois came from New York. Metis appeared from across the Canadian border. Penobscots from as far away as Maine joined the struggle in Wounded Knee. It was a great and unusual gathering of the tribes. Non-Indians, too, began coming over the hills to help. Small numbers of militant Chicanos, blacks, Asians, and whites arrived anxious to give more than just lip-service support to an Indian fight they believed was closely related to their own struggles. Although few of the non-Indians remained inside Wounded Knee for very long, many shuttled back and forth with supplies and performed numerous support activities in Pine Ridge and Rapid City.

The number and intensity of the fire fights understandably increased. So did everyone's familiarity with them. Gladys Bissonette described an incident that occurred mid-way through the occupation.

"This one evening," she began, "I asked a friend of mine, she's a pretty heavy-set woman, I asked her to go over to the outhouse with me. We had to go quite a ways. We had to go from this white building where we were staying past the great big brown church, and then a little further to the outhouses. Everybody used the outhouses over there.

"I had finished first and I was standing there waiting for her to finish and I heard something pop. It sounded like a gunshot. But sometimes them boys come out of the brown church and when they slam the door, it sounds just like a gunshot.

"So when we heard that, she said, 'What was that?' I said, 'Oh, it's probably one of the boys coming out of that brown church. When they slam the door, it sounds just like a gunshot.' She said, 'Well, maybe it isn't, let's hurry.' So I said, 'Well, by god, you're the one I'm waiting on.'

"She come out the door behind me, and well, sure enough, they started firing at us from the east and we had to go back out that way. So, we ran round on the west side of the outhouse and on the west side there was snow and mud—ankle deep. But they were firing at us from the east side, and we could hear them bullets pouring down on us.

"So I just ran and said, 'Lay down flat right along this outhouse. We have to lay here because we're protected by this hill on the west if they start shooting from the west. We're protected and we'll be safe here, on the ground.' So we lay down and she said, 'We better start praying.' So I said, 'Yes, you start praying,' I said, 'so nobody gets hurt. I'm not worried about us, we're safe, but there's boys out there.'

"Well, laying there in the snow and mud on our stomachs, that was pretty darn cold, at least on my belly anyway. I looked up and I could see the tracer bullets just zinging past us, but they were still pretty high up, above the outhouse. We must have laid there about 20 minutes.

"Finally, it let up, so I said, 'Let's head for that brown church. Once we get inside there, we won't have to lay in the mud and snow.' So when it let up, her and I started to run and I thought, well, she weighs over 200 pounds, so, I thought, surely I could beat her, I'd be ahead of her. And, oh boy, that was the biggest foot race you ever saw. If it was light out, those people there would have really seen something. She passed me up like nothing flat!"

Gladys, wide-eyed, took off her glasses for a moment and laughed at her own story. "Just as we were both running toward that brown church door," she continued, still chuckling, "there was a couple of security men come by and they said, 'Get in that church. What the heck you doin' out here in a fire fight?' They didn't know that we were forced out there.

"So we no more than open the door and went inside that church, and the barrage of bullets started again. We just hit the floor and lay there. Now this one kid was in there, in the dark—it was pitch black in that church—and there he was, he was playing on the organ.

"Somebody come from the outside and opened the door, one of the security men, and he said, 'Hey kid,' he said, 'get out here and help. What the heck you doin' at that organ when there's a big fire fight goin' on?' Well, this kid stops what he's doin' and just as calm as he could be, he says, 'Oh, I just thought I'd play my last tune!' "

After a while, the gunfights, as well as the humor, were commonplace. Large numbers of children and older people were regularly exposed to fire fights by government forces who, because they were not advancing on Wounded Knee, had nothing whatever to gain by their shooting. Yet, there were remarkably few casualties. The fortifications and security procedures, supervised primarily by Stan Holder of the Wichita Tribe, won well-deserved respect on both sides of the bunkers.

But the gunfights were affected by yet another complicating factor. With surprising speed, federal paramilitary operations developed an increasingly familiar bureaucratic limitation—inter-service rivalry. Stated bluntly, the marshals were under the impression that they had overall control of federal forces, but in practice, the FBI refused to accept their direction. The two organizations had fundamentally different conceptions of the tactics appropriate to the situation. The marshals maintained a tight siege, blocked Indian infiltration routes, and concentrated massive firepower on Wounded Knee in retaliation for gunfire coming from the village. The FBI, on the other hand, used snipers and spies and provoked more frequent gunfights, not in retaliation, but at purposely random intervals. Instead of attacking Wounded Knee directly, both groups tried to undermine Indian morale and determination, the marshals by starving them out and the FBI by terrorizing them.

The FBI was technically in the subordinate position. As a result, they often distorted information given to the marshals in order to keep up their kind of pressure on the Indians. There were at least two well-documented examples of this. On both occasions Wounded Knee took fire from Roadblock #6 (FBI controlled). Government radio transmissions, being secretly monitored by the Indians, revealed that FBI agents there had reported to the marshals' command post that Wounded Knee had fired on them, rather than the reverse. The marshals then radioed Wounded Knee warning them to cease firing or be fired upon. On both occasions gunfights were avoided because security forces inside Wounded Knee managed to convince the government command post that FBI agents were only trying to provoke another fire fight.

Government forces suffered one serious casualty during the 71-day siege—the marshal shot in the spine and paralyzed from the waist down. His injury occurred in a fire fight that began when people inside Wounded Knee shot a steer in plain sight of the government command post. Federal officers opened up with a one-hour barrage. After the marshal was shot, everyone naturally assumed that the offending gun had been fired from inside Wounded Knee. But rumors leaked out that the marshal had been struck by a bullet from a government-issue M-16. Some federal personnel apparently felt that the injured marshal was shot in a cross fire, either by an FBI agent or by a vigilante given an M-16 to use by the FBI. Suspicions understandably mounted when the government refused to release medical data that would have revealed whether or not the bullet came from a government weapon. The question has never been resolved.

The goon squad and the vigilantes complicated the rivalry between the marshals and the FBI. The goon squad, Tribal Chairman Dick Wilson's private band of bodyguards, are not to be confused with the legally constituted BIA Indian police, the old "metal breasts," who were part of the regular coalition of police forces around Wounded Knee. The vigilantes, on the other hand, were armed white ranchers who owned land on or near the reservation. Both extra-legal forces, the goon squad and the vigilantes, maintained their own roadblocks and nighttime patrols in order to cut the flow of supplies into Wounded Knee. Several times a few of them crawled in between Wounded Knee and government bunkers at night. By secretly sniping at both sides, they were able to provoke fire fights between the two sets of bunkers.

"We had a pretty good lookout from our command post at what was happening at the federal bunkers and several times we pinpointed a third force in there that was firing at us," Dennis Banks insisted. "I was positive at one point that we hit one of them, but apparently that was never so.

"But there was a third force that was in between us and the government forces that certainly provoked a lot of gunfire. Of course, most of the time it was hard for us to determine who was the goons and who was the feds."

Against this astounding 71-day backdrop of domestic warfare, negotiations were frequently underway. The various Indian negotiating teams each represented three types of people inside Wounded Knee: American Indian Movement leadership, Oglala Sioux residents of the Pine Ridge Reservation, and medicine men. Dennis Banks, Russell Means, Clyde Bellecourt, and Carter Camp, but most often Banks and Means, negotiated as leaders of AIM. Gladys Bissonette and several others were frequent negotiators on behalf of the Oglala Sioux. The medicine men most often present were Crow Dog and Black Elk. On the government side, a single man was in charge and negotiated as a spokesman for unnamed officials in Washington. Several different men served in this capacity during the course of the occupation.

The basis of the Indian negotiating position was the three demands announced by the Sioux chiefs within hours of the seizure of Wounded

Knee: 1) the removal of Dick Wilson from office and a referendum in which the Oglala Sioux Tribe could decide whether or not to return to a system of self-government based on the traditional chiefs and headmen, 2) Congressional investigation of corruption and malfeasance on the part of the Bureau of Indian Affairs nation-wide and the removal of the top two BIA officials in Pine Ridge, and 3) hearings by the Senate Foreign Relations Committee on the 371 broken treaties between the U.S. government and various Indian nations. Any compromises of the three demands, or any disarmament procedures, required a consultation between Indian negotiators and a mass meeting of all the people occupying Wounded Knee.

On the government side, the consistency that a single responsible individual can provide in a negotiating session was often missing. On the one hand, the government knew a surrender was not possible. On the other, they were unwilling to make any but the most minimal concessions, while still coveting the hopeless surrender. The result was multi-layered confusion.

The most visible layer of confusion was the government's public statements. These alternated unpredictably, often from one day to the next. For example, two weeks into the occupation, the chief U.S. marshal said, "The ultimate objective [of the federal siege] is to bring the leadership of AIM to the negotiating table." This despite Indian requests for talks from the very beginning. Yet, some time after the marshal's statement, the top Justice Department representative on the scene complained, "The United States cannot negotiate with guns at its head."

Beneath the public statements was another confusing layer of personal styles and idiosyncracies. The first government negotiator was the Justice Department's Ralph Erickson. On March 4, a procedure for talks was developed by the Community Relations Service, also of the Justice Department. (The CRS operated independently of other Department functions and officers, carefully preserving their neutrality and trying to keep communications open between the two sides during civil conflicts.) Erickson was to come unarmed to a tipi erected by medicine men halfway between the Oglala fortifications and government bunkers. Oglala and AIM leadership would do likewise. Because they considered the tipi sacred, the Indians felt bound not to commit sacrilege and violate their word. However, when the time came for the meeting, Erickson refused to leave the protection of the federal bunkers. He sent his subordinate, the U.S. Attorney for South Dakota, to the tipi to negotiate for the U.S. Once the latter had safely returned, an embarrassed Erickson made unsolicited statements to the press about AIM leaders being prone to violence.

When Erickson was withdrawn, Harlington Wood, a very different sort of person, was brought in from Washington to be the next Justice

Department negotiator on the scene. He arrived on the morning of March 13 and went immediately to neutral parties in Pine Ridge to request that they arrange a meeting with representatives from Wounded Knee. Suspicious of more government insincerity, the people in Wounded Knee invited Wood to meet with them—inside their own perimeter. Wood ignored FBI opinion that AIM would take him hostage and walked unescorted into Wounded Knee that very afternoon. In an elaborate show of protocol, he was met by Crow Dog, the medicine man, and AIM leaders accompanied by an armed security force. They led him back into Wounded Knee in a procession behind two horses, guns on their hips. The talk with Wood lasted two-and-a-half hours. It was described as open, relatively warm, and highly productive.

Two days later Wood flew back to Washington for consultations "at the highest level" inside the Departments of Justice and the Interior. On March 17, he returned to South Dakota. That afternoon he walked past a federal roadblock and handed a manila envelope to Dennis Banks, saying almost apologetically, "This is the best I could do." The packet contained twelve copies of the government's latest proposals. Then, with a sense of patience and proportion that the government was never to use again, Wood said to Banks, "First of all, I want to thank you for keeping the peace while I was gone. I want you to take your time studying this proposal. If you want to see me again, I'll come back at any time. It will be at your pleasure."

The proposals were read that night to a meeting of over 200 people inside the Wounded Knee trading post. The government was calling for a conference between AIM leaders and Interior Department officials in Sioux Falls, several hundred miles across the state. This would be followed by a laying down of arms in Wounded Knee and the arrest of the leaders. No mention was made of the demands put forth by the Oglala Sioux chiefs. The government proposals were booed by the meeting. Speaker after speaker rose to denounce them. Stan Holder, the Wichita security chief, said, "Many times in the past Indians have been asked to lay down their guns and warriors have been sent to prison while their women and children starve. We can never let that happen. We will never lay down our guns and submit to being caged animals."

Eventually, Harlington Wood was also replaced as top government negotiator. On March 27, Kent Frizzell took over, and the topsy-turvy government position swung back to a hard line. Frizzell, also of the Justice Department, said, "This is senseless. It has got to stop, and it is going to stop one way or the other by negotiations or otherwise . . . The fun and games are over!"

One of the worst but more subterranean layers of confusion concerned the federal government's relationship to local reservation officials. Called in originally to assist the tribal government on the reservation, the Justice Department at one point simply took complete control. This angered both the tribal and the local BIA officials. From then on, their alliance with federal personnel was at best grudging and often even openly hostile.

When Harlington Wood first arrived in Pine Ridge, two weeks into the occupation, he did not ask reservation officials to arrange a meeting for him in Wounded Knee. Instead, he sought help from a National Council of Churches team on the scene to promote a peaceful settlement. The group was under the direction of John Adams, a Methodist minister who set up Wood's first meeting. Later on, Adams and his colleagues also arranged for several short-lived cease-fire agreements. Dick Wilson was angered at being left out of the original negotiations, especially since he had just threatened to "clean out" Wounded Knee with "800 to 900 guns." As a result, he convinced his Tribal Council to pass a resolution barring Adams' team, and then Adams himself, from setting foot on any part of the Pine Ridge Reservation.

Stanley Lyman, the white BIA reservation superintendent in the employ of the Department of the Interior, actually approved the absurd Tribal Council resolution. (Lyman's removal from office was part of one of the three demands put forth by the Oglala chiefs and headmen.) All National Council of Churches personnel were then escorted off the reservation by Indian BIA police. The Justice Department put up only token resistance to the removal of the church personnel by the Tribal Council. Incredibly, they claimed to be unable to stop it. People on the scene wondered if this was another aspect of the complex inter-service rivalry or if Justice Department officials were in fact privately glad to see Adams and his colleagues go.

A similar question came up a week later. On March 25, at U.S. District Court in Rapid City, Judge Andrew Bogue granted a temporary restraining order to lawyers arguing on behalf of the people in Wounded Knee. The judge prohibited federal personnel from engaging in a blockade of food and medicine on the route into the village. His order came as Dennis Banks announced that food stocks inside Wounded Knee were virtually exhausted and violence was bound to result if they were not replenished. Specifically, the temporary restraining order allowed for six carloads of food, medicine, and cooking fuel to enter Wounded Knee each day.

Early the next morning a dozen of Dick Wilson's men, the goon squad, seized the Big Foot Trail, the main road leading from Pine Ridge to Wounded Knee. They halted the first carload of food arriving from Rapid City. Lawyers in the car showed them a copy of the temporary restraining order signed by the judge, but the armed men refused to honor it. They confiscated the food and ordered the car to drive back at gun point. The incident took place only a short distance from where FBI agents and U.S.

marshals were stationed. They looked on but did nothing to interfere, then or during the following weeks of the occupation.

To avoid any further difficulties, Judge Bogue managed to convince himself the next day that there were sufficient supplies inside Wounded Knee after all. He reversed his own order that more food be allowed to enter. Thus encouraged, the goon squad expanded the scope of their activities, trying to block not only food but also reporters and Justice Department Community Relations Service personnel as well.

Again federal law enforcement officers on the scene claimed to be powerless to interfere with reservation decisions, despite their patent illegality and the open secret that the Justice Department was running everything on the reservation anyway. Many assumed that the government actually preferred Wilson and his twenty goons do the dirty work that the federal officials wanted done but were unable to publicly endorse. At the same time, "government spokesmen" in the press tried to create the public impression that federal "peace keeping" forces were all that stood between the Indians in Wounded Knee and hundreds of Tribal Council supporters ready to attack them.

Eventually, another layer of confusion was added to the public's misunderstanding of Wounded Knee by the senior Senator from South Dakota, George McGovern. In the early phase of the occupation, both he and his colleague, Senator James Abourezk, voiced concern about Indian grievances. They took steps within the federal bureaucracy to try to verify claims of BIA corruption, and they made themselves and their staffs available to do whatever could be done to reduce tension. But while Abourezk bravely held out for meaningful negotiations and a nonviolent solution, McGovern gradually turned sour. Some people hoped McGovern would defend Indian rights on principle. Others did not expect him to do so publicly but did assume that the widespread and obvious sympathy for Wounded Knee would at least convince him it was safe to remain neutral. They all forgot that it was 1973 and that McGovern was no longer an outspoken candidate for national office.

Unpopular and cautious after his severe defeat in the 1972 presidential race, McGovern had to face a steeply uphill battle for re-election to the Senate in 1974. In the state of South Dakota, his white constituents were far from neutral on the issue of Wounded Knee. McGovern felt compelled to come out against the occupation. Indians were not surprised at the position taken by the otherwise liberal senator. Liberal whites were. McGovern wrote a public letter to Attorney General Kleindienst calling on the Justice Department to attack and arrest the people occupying Wounded Knee *before* a "bloody confrontation" occurred between them and the "aroused citizens of the Wounded Knee community." The letter accepted many of the myths that the government had created to describe the occupation. Worse, it contained so many law and order clichés that one had to look twice at the signature to be sure it was not Richard Nixon's.

"No matter what the grievances," McGovern argued, casually dismissing the central issue, "we can't have one law for a handful of publicity-seeking militants and another law for the ordinary citizens." Thousands of copies of the letter were printed by McGovern's staff and widely circulated around the state in an attempt to counteract the radical image the senator had acquired in the 1972 presidential campaign. Later, more copies of the letter were reproduced by a radical political organization and widely circulated around the nation—for the same reason.

Beneath the posturing and all the layers of confusion, there was a core of hard reality. The demand that Wilson be removed from office and the Oglala Sioux be given an opportunity to return to traditional self-government by the chiefs was of great significance. If granted it would threaten the entire Bureau of Indian Affairs structure set up on reservations across the country. Interior Department officials admitted privately that if they acceded to this demand it might establish a "dangerous" precedent that could lead to the overthrow of the entire reservation system. As a result, federal negotiators desperately sought a legal means to unload Dick Wilson without endangering the system of government specified in the Pine Ridge tribal constitution. The Oglala Sioux and AIM leadership inside Wounded Knee were well aware of the far-reaching implications of their demand. Overthrow of corrupt BIA control of Indian reservations was precisely what they were after.

More of the hard core of reality materialized on April 1. Up to that date, the Nixon Administration understood that many Americans were in sympathy with the Indians occupying Wounded Knee. This knowledge limited the government's use of certain tactics, for example, taking the village by force. But no one on either side realized just how widespread the sympathy was. On April 1, the government's maneuvering space was even more severely limited. The Harris Poll which was published on that day indicated that of a crosssection of Americans questioned, a startling 93% said they were following the Wounded Knee story in the mass media. Even more remarkable, 51% of those questioned said they supported the ongoing takeover, *even though weapons were in use!* Only 21% were in support of the government and the remaining 28% were undecided. It was a staggering setback for the government, coming in spite of the twisted information published in most of the printed and electronic media. For the first time in recent years, a majority of Americans were actually endorsing a militant demonstration. For the first time in history, a majority of the American people were in support of an armed revolt against the authority of the federal government.

Safely following the lead of the Harris Poll, the influential New York

Times, in its April 1 editorial, condemned federal tactics. They called on the government to "halt immediately its own growing militancy, including the use of armored cars and foolish, provocative suggestions of the possibility of having to storm" Wounded Knee. However, the cautious editors of the *Times* refused to support either side in the struggle, referring to "the irresponsible militants of the American Indian Movement, for whom a second Wounded Knee massacre appears to have a certain romantic appeal." Nevertheless, the government got the message—this time, people were definitely not going to cheer the cavalry.

After a 12-day lull, negotiations began again on March 31. Kent Frizzell, the new top man for the government, announced on the evening of April 1 that a consensus had been reached on at least half the issues at stake. Talks were held inside the sacred tipi with participants sitting cross-legged on the ground. The tipi stood on land referred to as the DMZ, the demilitarized zone between federal and Wounded Knee bunkers. It was yet another linguistic hand-me-down from the Viet Nam War.

Progress in the talks continued. On April 3 the negotiating session was moved inside Wounded Knee. Traveling by helicopter with his aides, Frizzell ventured into the settlement for the first time. Finally on the 5th, a disarmament agreement was signed at an outdoor table in front of the sacred tipi. The news flashed across the American press. Frizzell smoked a peace pipe while Indians in the background chanted ritual prayers to the beat of a drum.

The occasion was indeed a solemn one. Before the signing, Frizzell told the Oglalas, "I pray to my Father in heaven, as you do to your Great Spirit, that the agreement we are about to sign is not full of empty words. . . ." Black Elk, the Oglala medicine man, said shortly afterward, "We smoked the sacred pipe with our white brothers in the past and the treaties were broken. This is real. We are not playing here. Our life is at stake. It concerns our children and children unborn."

For the people of Wounded Knee, the April 5 agreement was signed by Russell Means, Clyde Bellecourt, Carter Camp, and Pedro Bissonette. Notably absent was Dennis Banks. In what appeared to many as an unreasonable position, Banks refused to sign.

"I took part in almost all the negotiations that happened," he said much later. "But at one point I dropped out because I realized that we were falling into a trap there on April 5th. I didn't want to become part of that negotiation, so for a week I dropped out.

"I had nothing to do with the agreement that was signed on April 5. I felt that it was a complete sellout, that we were falling into a trap of surrendering without having gained anything except that we could say we were there for 30 days or 40 days and that was it, you know. Then we would just be arrested."

Within an hour of the signing on April 5, Russell Means submitted to arrest. It was one of the conditions of the agreement. Later that day he was released under $25,000 bond and third-party custody. The next day, Means flew to Washington with Sioux spiritual leader Crow Dog and Oglala Chief Bad Cob. The peace agreement stipulated that the following morning, Saturday the 7th, the three would meet with White House officials, after which there would be a laying down of arms at Wounded Knee. But upon deplaning at Dulles Airport they learned that their scheduled meeting with Leonard Garment, the minority affairs advisor to John Ehrlichman, was being postponed 24 hours to Sunday, April 8.

Then early Saturday morning, Garment said that it would not be possible to meet on a Sunday. Later in the day, he announced that he would not negotiate with the three Sioux leaders at all until people in Wounded Knee surrendered their weapons. Means, with the backing of the Oglalas still in the village, stood firm and insisted that the occupation would end only after meaningful talks with the White House were underway. But everyone in the government, from Garment back to Frizzell in South Dakota, lined up behind the revised interpretation. The Indians occupying Wounded Knee put together another negotiating team, this one led by Carter Camp. They hammered out a new agreement with federal officials on Sunday. It was then taken before a mass meeting of the people in Wounded Knee for their approval. In the ensuing debate, Dennis Banks spoke against the new agreement, advising the assembly to hold on to their weapons until the promised talks actually began. The mass meeting rejected the terms of the new proposals. By Sunday night it was all over. Means claimed in Washington that the United States "had made a farce out of the agreement. They never had any intention of discussing the treaty rights of our people."

On Monday morning, April 9, with the possibility of White House talks behind them, Means, Crow Dog, and Bad Cob went to Congress. By coincidence the House Indian Affairs Subcommittee was holding hearings to investigate the situation at Wounded Knee. Having already scheduled testimony from representatives of the Justice Department and Wilson's Tribal Council, the Subcommittee reluctantly agreed also to hear from the insurgent Oglala Sioux. Means testified, but he was interrupted and attacked in a stinging verbal tirade delivered by Congressman James Haley, a Florida Democrat and chairman of the Subcommittee.

"How do you figure you have a perfect right . . . to go out and break the law?" Haley shouted from behind the Congressional committee table. Making clear his own priorities, he asked, "If you and your bunch of hoodlums go out and destroy property, how are you going to reimburse those people for it?" Congressman Haley finished his remarks by calling the Indian political and spiritual leaders "hoodlums, goons, and gutter rats." The Sioux sat calmly starring at him, virtually ignoring the abuse. The next day, April 10, they left Washington. Simultaneously, Frizzell returned, and a new man, Stanley Pottinger, took over as the top government negotiator at Wounded Knee. At that point, it was clear to everyone that despite the April 5 agreement, the occupation would continue as though nothing had happened.

11

AIRLIFT
Engine Trouble

Monday, April 16, 1973
Huron, South Dakota

Another day without sleep. As soon as Billy, Jim, and I returned to Huron from Rapid City where we had gone to check out rumors about goon-squad machine guns, everyone met in my motel room to review our plans. It was 1:30 a.m. and we intended to depart Huron no later than 3:00 a.m.

Oliver spoke first. He had been in and out of Wounded Knee several times and had worked there both as a medic and as a warrior. In Rapid City we had invited him to join the airlift to be our spotter during the drop, but on the flight back to Huron his loose talk about secret stores of automatic weapons had provoked our suspicion. We had to guard against the remote but conceivable possibility that Oliver was a government provocateur trying to entrap us. There was no other evidence, but given what was at stake, none was really needed. Still, Oliver spoke authoritatively about the weapons in use at Wounded Knee and assured us that goon squad machine guns were only a myth. Despite his limitations, there was no reason not to believe him.

The eight of us surrounded maps spread out on the floor. Our routing to Wounded Knee was more complicated than a straight line. Before making the drop, the rear doors on each aircraft had to be removed. It was the only way we could kick the cargo out while the planes were in flight.

214

The doors had to be taken off on the ground. None of us believed that the Huron weather bureau staff, whose credibility we had already stretched to the limit, would continue giving us the benefit of the doubt if they saw us leave without any doors. So another landing was necessary before our arrival over Wounded Knee.

We picked an isolated little place called Chamberlain, 67 miles south-west of Huron, on the banks of the Missouri River. The aeronautical map indicated the runway lights would be left on all night and no attendants would be on the field before dawn. Unfortunately, there was no radio navigation beacon, but Billy promised to get us there in the dark. We planned to land at Chamberlain by 3:30 a.m., take off the doors, and have all three aircraft flying again by 3:50. Chamberlain was 158 miles on a straight line to Wounded Knee. That was an hour-and-five minute's flying time with eleven minutes left in reserve before the sun came up at 5:06 a.m. It would be a cold flight with no door and the wind blasting by at 155 miles per hour.

After the drop, each plane would dive to tree-top altitude and head directly east. If anyone shot at us, they would have to aim into the rising sun. Once away from the reservation, we would split up, each pilot finding a separate spot for a brief landing to replace his door. Then a quick and hopefully leisurely flight back home to Chicago. Earlier thoughts about hiding for a day or two in some isolated Wyoming or North Dakota town before attempting the return were scrapped.

With the routing worked out, we turned to the drop. Billy had to handle navigation up to the edge of the Pine Ridge Reservation. There, in the predawn light, he would fall back to the number two position in the formation while Jim, the parachute expert, took the lead to command the actual drop. Oliver would ride in the co-pilot's seat next to Jim and guide him over the last few miles of rough terrain into Wounded Knee. Meanwhile, Billy and I would slowly close in on Jim until our aircraft were 40 yards apart. That was the separation we wanted for the drop and that was what we had practiced on Saturday's flight out of Council Bluffs, Iowa.

Somewhere on the way to the reservation, as soon as it was light enough to see, Jim planned to drop his test streamer. It was made of black crepe paper and weighted at one end. As it fell, he could get a reading of the wind direction and speed and then decide how to approach Wounded Knee and exactly where to release the cargo so that it would float down into the center of the village.

As Jim reviewed how the cargo handlers should push the duffel bags out of the plane, something happened that was surprising yet perfectly logical. Tom Oliphant, the Boston *Globe* correspondent, became agitated, as though he had something to say that he wasn't quite sure of. Finally, he started arguing that it was wrong for him to continue tagging along with the airlift as a mere observer. He was bigger and stronger than Larry, and he wanted to be the cargo handler on my plane so Larry could help me fly.

Larry was the first to reply. "Sure," he said, "it makes sense to me."

Looking around the room, I could see the others smiling and nodding their approval. Jim drawled, "Welcome aboard there, reporter," and everyone else voiced something in the way of a positive vote. The change in role made excellent sense. Tom had lived and worked with us around the clock for the previous four days. Gradually, almost imperceptibly, he had become part of the crew. We were all glad to wipe away the label that separated him from the rest of us. Given who he was and what he represented, winning him over made us feel a little better about what we were doing ourselves.

"Before we break up," I said, "let's have Jim run through all the things that can go wrong with the drop."

The room fell silent again as Jim spun out the various possibilities. "Well, one of them chutes might streamer, which would mean a couple of duffel bags splatterin' all over something. Or, a cargo net could bust apart from the shock when the chutes open up. But neither of those things is very likely. I'll tell you what might happen—the cargo kickers might not get all those bags out in time. Then the pilots gotta decide whether to go back for a second pass."

Strobe whistled. "Into the valley of death once again, huh?"

Billy was in no mood for jokes. "Say, man, if I live through the first pass, I sure as hell ain't goin' back for a second."

Still thinking about the possible flaws in our plan, one last frightening image materialized in my mind. "What if one of the ripcords gets tangled up and doesn't break away from the parachute pack?" I asked Jim.

"Forget that," he laughed. "That's a million to one!"

"Well, what if it happens?" I persisted.

"You'd be flying along with 200 pounds of food hanging from your tail," Jim replied.

"Not for long, you wouldn't!" Billy spoke softly, but his words echoed into the room. He explained that a 200-pound weight in the extreme rear would gradually slow the airplane down to its stall speed. But instead of then falling a few hundred feet nose first and regaining sufficient airspeed to fly, the aircraft would fall tail first. "There's no way to recover from that kind of tail-down stall," Billy ominously concluded.

Every head in the room turned toward Jim, the light-hearted atmosphere momentarily broken. Jim looked around and started nodding, very slowly.

"All right," he said, "I'll tape a knife into each plane, up on the bulkhead next to the rear doorway. You can use it if you have to cut away a ripcord."

It was 2:30 a.m. We washed up, packed, and happily left for the airport. A sky full of stars gave us the weather report—no clouds and unrestricted visibility. After all the difficulties we had been through, it was marvelous to finally be on the way. All eight of us marched into the FAA building to hear the weatherman's optimistic forecast. We told him we were leaving early in order to make our destination that same day. He wished us luck, and we left for our planes.

But he didn't wish hard enough. Outside on the ramp, a layer of hard, thin ice covered everything. The snow from the previous day had apparently melted just before sunset. The water then froze in the cold night air. The ice made a glaze that encased all three aircraft, not just the windows, but the whole surface, wings, tail, fuselage, propeller, everything.

We started very gently chipping away with screwdrivers and pocket knives, afraid of denting the airplane's thin aluminum skin. It was slow, tedious work and every square inch of the ice had to go. The job took well over an hour, and before we finished, water had soaked through our gloves and our fingertips were nearly frozen. Shortly before 4:30 a.m., almost an hour-and-a-half late, we held a quick meeting in the moonlight to decide what to do. Billy wanted to go ahead with the drop, but Jim argued for a 24-hour postponement.

"The plan was to go in at dawn and catch those people sleepin'. I say we stick to the plan."

"Ah, what difference does it make if we get there at seven in the morning or at five in the morning?" Billy answered. "The weather's perfect right now. That's the most important thing."

"I'll tell you what the difference is," Jim insisted, "if one more of them goons is awake and ready to shoot at seven o'clock, we should go in at five."

We talked it over for a while. Despite the added risk, Billy's position eventually prevailed. If the weather did get worse, we could be stuck for another two or three days. In Rapid City the day before, it didn't sound like Wounded Knee could wait that long. We climbed up into our cockpits. Tom came with Larry and me. Oliver went with Jim and John. Billy was alone with Strobe.

I turned on the red dashboard lights, ran through the preflight check list, and cranked over the engine. Once it started, I flipped the switch for my wing lights. It was a signal to the other planes that I was ready to taxi. The red and green wing lights on Jim's plane were on, but Billy's plane was still dark. I tried to see down the ramp, unable to understand the delay. Then I remembered Billy's battery, the one that was dead Saturday morning in Council Bluffs. A few frustrating minutes later Billy ran toward us from his plane. The battery was out. His engine wouldn't start.

I killed the lights and shut down my own engine. Jim did the same. Our only chance was to "hand prop" Billy's airplane—turn on the ignition and spin the propeller by hand in hopes that the engine would catch. It was like cranking an old car to get it started, except you had to be careful where you put your head. We climbed back down to the ramp, breathing condensation into the dark night air and stamping our feet against the cold. Billy sat in the dead airplane, his face barely visible in the faint red glow from the dashboard lights. Jim and I spun the propeller several dozen times, but to no avail.

We were stuck. We needed a car and jumper cables to get the plane started. The weatherman had a car, but no jumper cables. Every gas station in town was closed until 8:00 a.m. There was nothing to do but wait for the hangar to open at about the same time.

The sun showed up on schedule a few minutes after five. The sky, as predicted, was blue and cloudless. We kept warm next to the teletype machines in the weather station. At 6:30 a.m., the one-room passenger terminal at the airport came to life in preparation for a 7:10 a.m. commercial airliner. The flight was one of Huron's two regularly scheduled aerial links with the outside world. We took the opportunity to get coffee and eggs in the small diner that had just opened. The old argument about postponing the drop for a day started up again, only then we had to contemplate arriving at Wounded Knee no earlier than 10:00 a.m. Billy still argued for going ahead with it, but this time Jim's position won out. Ten o'clock was too late. We would wait for the next dawn and hope that all the marksmen would be asleep or too drowsy to shoot straight.

One problem had to be dealt with immediately. We had to get out of Huron. The people in the weather bureau had seen enough of us, and we could not create a believable excuse for staying another day when the weather was so good. But where could we safely go?

Billy described the calm and quiet we had encountered the day before at the airport in Rapid City. He suggested we go there and "spend the day right under all those federal noses." It was only 100 miles from Wounded Knee, and we would be in a good position for a sunrise drop the next morning. The four in our crew who had not seen the Rapid City airport the previous day were skeptical about attracting too much attention.

But the rest of us convinced them that, surprisingly enough, the risk appeared minor, more so if our three planes split up and flew in at ten or fifteen minute intervals. For our own protection, we would also have to stay away from the Wounded Knee legal defense office where we had met Oliver and Rita less than 24 hours earlier.

The hangar opened at 8:00 a.m. We got Billy's plane started and invested another half hour of our time in charging his battery. Our three aircraft lifted off Huron just after 9:00. We climbed into the deep blue sky, leveled at 6,500 feet, and set up our engines for economy cruise. It was much higher than we had flown on Saturday when we had to contend with low ceilings at the beginning and end of our flight. The checkerboard farmland below seemed to be made from noticeably smaller blocks. Visibility was unrestricted and the view spectacular. We kept the three aircraft a comfortable distance apart. Larry had the controls and I was watching the land.

Suddenly Billy's anxious voice came over the radio. "Five-three-romeo, five-eight-romeo, this is four-one-juliet. I'm having engine trouble. Undetermined origin. Stand by."

I reached for the hand mike, acknowledged Billy's emergency call, then throttled back to a slower speed. Jim was doing the same. The two of us banked away to either side, leaving Billy plenty of maneuvering space in front of us.

Larry squirmed in his seat next to me, trying to see Billy's plane a half-mile ahead of us. "What's wrong?" he asked. "Do you know what's wrong?"

"No," I answered. "His engine's still running so it can't be too bad."

Just then Billy's voice came back on the radio. "Four-one-juliet here. I'm not sure what's going on, you guys. The alternator's giving me a negative charge and I think the engine is surging once in a while. Maybe it's my imagination, I don't know. Last night I saw a Piper dealer in Pierre. I'm going to head in there and get this bird checked out."

"Roger, Billy, we're right behind you."

I put the hand mike back on its holder just as Larry asked, "Where the hell is Pierre?"

He had the map on his lap. I took it and showed him the Pierre airport, 45 miles ahead of us on a straight line to Rapid City. Pierre was the state capital, and the chart indicated large and modern airport facilities. We tagged along behind Billy, watching for trouble, probably a lot more wary of the whole situation than he was.

"What if he can't make it to Pierre?" Tom asked, leaning over from behind the two front seats.

I looked out the window at the countryside below. It was still flat farmland, and there were plenty of good spots for an emergency landing. "He'll go down in a field," I explained, only half as confident as I must have seemed. "It shouldn't be too bad. With us in the air, we can get help to him fast. It'll mean the end of the airlift, though, or at least part of it."

I picked up the mike and radioed Billy. "Four-one-juliet, this is five-three-romeo. Any change in your status? Over."

"Four-one-juliet. Negative. No change."

Billy's answer made Larry more nervous. "Why aren't you calling in a Mayday?" he asked.

"It's not serious enough. If his engine quits, we will. Meantime, let's not get involved with the FAA."

We flew on until Tom pointed a little to the right of straight ahead and said, "That must be it, way up there. See where that smoke is coming from?"

He was right. I announced the news into the radio. "Four-one-juliet, five-three-romeo has visual contact with Pierre, ten degrees to the right. Over."

"Roger, five-three, I got it."

It took us another ten minutes to reach the field. Jim and I circled single file, watching Billy land, then came in ourselves. It all went very smoothly. We parked the three planes in different locations and met on foot in front of the Piper hangar.

Billy and Jim went inside to get someone to look at the faulty plane. Pierre, just a quiet gas stop late Sunday night, had been transformed into a busy municipal airport in the light of Monday morning. But we soon learned that it was no ordinary Monday morning. The Federal District Court in Pierre was scheduled to begin a hearing at 10:00 a.m. on the question of whether to issue another restraining order preventing federal forces from further blockades of food into Wounded Knee. A complete selection of marshals and FBI agents was on hand to testify against issuing the order. It was a uniquely inappropriate moment for us to come stumbling in.

Cautiously, we divided into two groups to avoid attracting attention. One stayed with the planes, the other walked down the ramp to the passenger terminal. At the last minute before going inside, I realized that Oliver was not only decked out in a beaded headband, but he had the words "Wounded Knee" stitched in red across the pocket of his Levi jacket. We got it off of him just in time. Pushing through the swinging doors, I saw immediately that all our misplaced paranoia in the other airports was going to be justified in Pierre. It was 9:45 a.m., fifteen minutes before the court convened. Every third person in the lobby wore some kind of uniform or could be identified by an obvious bulge under his coat. We would have made ourselves too conspicuous by turning right around and leaving, so we walked into the restaurant and ordered another breakfast.

It went smoothly until Strobe got into an argument with the waiter. The crew-cut young man had looked so disdainfully at the foot-long halo of brown curly hair around Strobe's head and face, it was hard to blame him for getting upset. But the justification didn't matter. I paid the bill, left a big tip, and insisted that everyone leave. Outside the terminal, walking back toward our planes, I gave nonnegotiable orders for the first time on the airlift. We were to split up immediately. I would leave first with Tom for Rapid City. Jim would delay a half hour and follow with John and Oliver. Billy and Strobe would stay behind as long as it took to get their plane repaired. I'd rent motel rooms and a car as soon as I got to Rapid City. Then, as the others arrived, I could pick them up and immediately move them out of the airport. I wanted Larry to stay behind in case there were any legal difficulties. He had more experience than the others.

Three hours later we were reunited in Rapid City. Billy and Jim arrived together, and Tom and I were waiting for them with a car and a prearranged set of motel rooms. There was a six-hour backlog for maintenance work at the Piper hangar in Pierre, so Billy had borrowed some tools, done some tinkering on his own, and concluded that his engine was running well enough to fly. When it turned out to be an easy repair job, Jim decided to wait, and both aircraft made the trip at the same time.

Driving into Rapid City and our hideaway motel, I reminded the others that the Wounded Knee legal defense office did not know we were in town and it would be safer for us if no one disclosed the location of our motel for any reason. It was the government's last chance to stop us, and we wanted to be certain nothing went wrong. No precaution seemed too extreme given how close we were to Wounded Knee.

Oliver balked at having to stay in the motel room all afternoon and all evening when friends of his were right there in Rapid City. Our suspicions increased, but trying to keep him imprisoned all day was probably as dangerous as letting him run loose. If he was not an informer, he would have every reason to be angry. The solution was to drop him off before arriving at the motel so he wouldn't be able to tell anyone where we were staying. We left him on a street corner, promising to pick him up in front of a nearby hamburger stand at precisely 10:30 p.m. At that time he would be taken to our motel where he would have to stay until 3:00 a.m., when we left for Wounded Knee. One of us could check the airport just before the others arrived to see that no one was waiting for us there on Oliver's instructions.

With Oliver out of the car, there was a brief discussion about not showing up at 10:30 at all and leaving him behind. But his help with navigation was still needed, and at that point it was hard to see how his going on the flight could jeopardize us any more than his not going. We took to our rooms and spent the rest of the day making up for sleep lost the previous night.

Early in the evening, Larry and Tom wandered around the Indian ghetto and the honky-tonks and cowboy bars in downtown Rapid City. It was the first time either of them had seen the extremes of Indian poverty, and both were deeply moved. Larry used some of his time to make telephone calls back east. One concerned a system he had set up the day before for the release of press statements about the food shortages in Wounded Knee and about the airlift. It would operate within an hour of the actual parachute drop. The plan was simple. One of our friends in

Boston waited by a telephone at 6:00 each morning. If we did not call by that hour, our friend was to assume that we were still airborne after making the drop. If the drop was aborted, as it had been that morning, we would phone before 6:00 a.m. Earlier Tom had helped Larry prepare a list of the best newspaper and wire service offices to call with details about the airlift. Larry forwarded the list to Boston along with a transcript of the message we had placed inside each of the duffel bags. It was a good way to insure that accurate information reached the press quickly and in a manner that would dramatize the need for food in Wounded Knee.

While Larry and Tom wandered around Rapid City, I slipped away from the others for a half hour and met secretly with Rita a few blocks from the Wounded Knee legal defense office. I needed her help with another little plot. I wanted to create a trail of false clues for the FBI. I knew they would be furious when a ton of food came floating down past their roadblocks into Wounded Knee. In their anger, they would jump at the first good lead that came along. Rita was going to give them one that led in the wrong direction.

I was almost certain that the telephone in the Wounded Knee legal defense office was tapped and being monitored by the government. One hour after the parachutes dropped the next morning, Rita was to place a call on the tapped telephone to the airport in Lusk, Wyoming and ask to speak with one of the three Cherokee pilots who had just landed. The airport operator would tell her that no such planes were there. Rita would say we were due shortly and ask to leave a message for us to call her. The FBI would hear everything.

Lusk was west of Wounded Knee. We were going east. The over-eager FBI agent with his ears between a pair of headphones would make the logical mistake. But I wanted him to be completely sure of himself, so an hour later, at 7:00 a.m., Rita would call the Casper, Wyoming airport, 100 miles west of Lusk, and make the same request. Then at 8:00 a.m., she would place the final call to Riverton, Wyoming, yet another 100 miles in the wrong direction. Frustrated by our uncanny ability to stay one step ahead of them in Wyoming, I assumed that the FBI would continue their search farther west, probably in California, which must have seemed to them to be the source of so many of their current difficulties. While they were sniffing around Berkeley and San Francisco, we would be safely back in Chicago.

Rita was overjoyed at the prospect of tricking the FBI. I gave her the necessary phone numbers and told her that if we were delayed another day, I would telephone her before 6:00 a.m. She kissed me goodbye and I strolled back to the motel.

An hour later, Larry took the rented car to pick up Oliver at the 10:30 p.m. hamburger-house rendezvous. After a brief absence, he walked back into the motel room we were sharing with Tom.

"Where is he?" I asked, anxious to keep tabs on the unreliable Oliver.

"Oh, I tucked him in with Jim. Jim's the lightest sleeper."

"Good. Did you make sure you weren't followed?"

"You're goddamn right I did." Larry was indignant that I found it necessary to ask the question at all. "I went around the block a few times, just to be sure he was alone. When I got him in the car, I raced down that main street the hamburger joint is on for about six blocks. Then I made a fast right turn, went a half a block, stopped the car, turned out the lights, and waited to see if anyone turned the corner behind us. Then I went back the way we came, passed the hamburger place, did a U-turn, went by a third time, and then came here. We weren't followed."

"Okay, okay," I laughed, "I'm exhausted just listening to you. Where'd you learn to do all that, anyway?"

"In Ireland. Where do you think?"

"Hmm, in a war, huh? Look what we're going through just to deliver a few meals to someone."

Billy came in with the latest weather forecast—perfect flying conditions for the remainder of that night and all next morning. The weatherman had given us his blessings once again. We went to sleep, determined that this time we were going to make it.

12
Life in the Occupied Zone

"We did not think of the great open plains, the beautiful rolling hills, and winding streams with tangled growth, as 'wild.' Only to the white man was nature a 'wilderness' and only to him was the land 'infested' with 'wild' animals and 'savage' people. To us it was tame. Earth was bountiful and we were surrounded with the blessings of the Great Mystery. Not until the hairy man from the east came and with brutal frenzy heaped injustices upon us and the families we loved was it 'wild' for us. When the very animals of the forest began fleeing from his approach, then it was that for us the 'Wild West' began."

—Luther Standing Bear, Chief,
Oglala Sioux, 1933

The government's cynical manipulation during the siege of Wounded Knee, and the multilayered public confusion it provoked, stood in stark contrast to the scene inside the village. There, despite clumsiness and frequent mistakes, people tried to recapture a traditional Indian purity and clarity of purpose. Even enemies who came in contact with the Sioux culture which was being revived by the insurgents spoke up for their seriousness, while people farther from the scene insisted it was all theatrics or made tasteless jokes about Indian "mumbo-jumbo." Kent Frizzell, the government negotiator, spoke of one ritual that he witnessed.

"Frankly," he said, "I was very impressed with, for example, the Peace Pipe ceremony at the signing of the negotiated settlement. It was very solemn. It gave the opportunity for expressions of good faith. It seemed very meaningful to me and I couldn't help being taken into its mood. There certainly was nothing cynical about it."

The Sacred Pipe ceremonies were conducted with pipes, medicine bags, and various other accoutrements handed down directly from the medicine men of the 19th century. But these pipe rituals were embedded in a much broader fabric of Sioux religion and culture practiced at Wounded Knee. (Since the Sioux made no functional or philosophical distinction between religion and culture, the two words can be used interchangeably. The idea that one's day-to-day material life, or culture, was separate from one's spiritual existence, or religion, was a distinction the Indians had to "learn" from white men.)

Under the guidance of spiritual leaders, or medicine men, people in Wounded Knee taught each other a host of dances, songs, chants, and drum beats, most of which possessed specific ritual significance. They made and wore traditional clothing decorated with symbols that many learned the meaning of for the first time.

Like the architecture of the Christian cathedrals of Europe, the design of the sacred tipi, the number of logs used, the direction it faced, and so forth were also guided by tradition. Wounded Knee revived the old custom of the sweat lodge, a small hut containing hot stones over which water is poured to produce steam. Medicine men accompanied small groups of people inside the sweat lodge and led them in prayers and cleansing rituals intended to renew their spiritual and physical strength. Sweat lodges had been outlawed on the reservation since the 19th century because the BIA officials thought they were dangerous. Many city-dwelling Indians, born and raised in urban ghettos, came to help the Oglalas at Wounded Knee, having completely lost any knowledge of these practices. For them, participating in the occupation was an experience of profound reawakening. Instead of the shame that many had once felt about their Indianness, there was suddenly a past and a people they were proud to be part of.

Two men were primarily responsible for the cultural renaissance at Wounded Knee, Wallace Black Elk and Leonard Crow Dog, Sioux medicine men. Black Elk is an Oglala Sioux; Crow Dog is a Brulé Sioux. Black Elk grew up on the Pine Ridge Reservation. From early childhood he was guided and rigorously trained by his medicine man grandfather, the original Black Elk. The grandfather was an eyewitness to Custer's defeat at the battle of the Little Big Horn, as well as to the tragic aftermath of the massacre at Wounded Knee. In the 1930s, as an old man, Black Elk told the story of his life and his visions to a white friend who transcribed his words and created the remarkable book, *Black Elk Speaks.* Surrounded by the power and patient wisdom of this old man, and through him in direct contact with the 19th century, Wallace matured and assumed the responsibility of a medicine man in his own right. Like others of his calling, he understood that the simple preservation of Sioux customs and heritage was one of his major tasks.

Leonard Crow Dog was raised on the Rosebud Reservation adjacent to the Pine Ridge Reservation. He, too, had a famous ancestor, but of a very different sort. His great-grandfather, the original Crow Dog, was an assassin. In 1881, for unknown reasons, Crow Dog shot and killed the renowned, peace-loving Brulé chief, Spotted Tail. As punishment, Crow Dog and his descendants for all time were barred from ever using a gun. It does not sound like a very harsh penalty today, but in 1881, with hunting the traditional source of food and war with the whites raging on and off for some 15 years, the sentence was severe indeed.

Leonard grew up in the midst of unspeakable poverty. Church missionaries and BIA authorities forced his parents out of a small reservation town back to the family plot in the countryside because his father belonged to "a sinful Indian religious sect." The "sect" was merely what remained of the original Sioux religion. For centuries Sioux tribes had practiced it on that very land. But with the coming of the whites, several decades before, ageless traditions acquired the new status of "sect." Out on the land, the Crow Dog family was without a source of livelihood. It was grazing land, buffalo country, treeless but not suitable for agriculture. There was no money to purchase animals, so they lived without electricity, good water, heat—and often without food. One of Leonard's brothers froze to death at the age of two. Severe hardship was commonplace, and others in his family died while still children.

Leonard Crow Dog's father refused to allow him to attend white-controlled schools. He wanted his son to follow the path of the medicine men, and he feared that school would so twist the boy's mind that Indian ways would be lost to him. Today Leonard is unable to read. But he is a medicine man, and ironically, for the past several years he has been compiling a dictionary of the Sioux language, Lakota. He believes that the preservation of the Lakota language is essential to the survival of Sioux culture. Crow Dog still lives on the Rosebud Reservation, but travels widely lecturing and teaching. He is spiritual advisor to the American Indian Movement, for whom the preservation of culture is a major objective.

Before Wounded Knee, Crow Dog was with AIM at the 1972 take-over of the BIA Building in Washington. There, he worked as a mediator trying to avoid violence between AIM and the government. As an individual, Crow Dog maintains a persistent nonviolence. He recognizes that there are times when people must fight to defend their freedom, but he personally avoids the use of force. The traditional culture of the Sioux and the shadow of his great-grandfather's crime remain very much alive for him. He has said on a number of occasions, "I am Crow Dog and I may not handle a gun."

More than any others, but with the help of many, Black Elk and Crow Dog passed the old ways on to the people of Wounded Knee. For the first time in almost 100 years, a place existed where the Sioux could practice their religion and be entirely secure from white interference. Their old mythology was experienced anew. It contains a systematic view of the world that many discovered was still useful in the regulation of their own lives. For example, the customs by which their grandparents were able to harmonize themselves so well with the natural world were based on notions of ecological balance painfully absent from 20th century America.

Like the Judeo-Christian tradition, the Sioux mythology included a spiritual Father. In churches He was called God, and in tipis the Great Spirit. But the Sioux also believed in a spiritual Mother, the Earth, more immediate and real than the extra-physical Father. The belief that the Earth was their Mother inclined them to live with nature, not conquer it. They came to see nonhuman forms of life mothered by the Earth as their relatives, including "all the green things that grow, and all the four-leggeds, and all the wings of the air, and all of those that crawl on their bellies in the grass, and all of the finned creatures of the lakes and streams." Relatives are viewed with respect rather than hostility. They can even be a source of instruction.

For instance, the Sioux believed that their "cousin" the cottonwood tree taught them how to regulate their societies during the four seasons of the year. In the autumn, the leaves fall from the tree covering the Mother, Earth, returning to her what she earlier gave to the tree. It is a time to be with one's family, to provide for their protection and nourishment. The winter, when the leaves are gone, is a time to rest and gather strength. It is also a time to tell stories to the young so that they will grow up knowing who they are. In the spring, the tree blossoms. It is a time to go forth into the world and begin new projects. The summer, when the healthy tree is in full bloom, is the peak of existence and the time to enjoy life to its fullest.

Obviously, these are attitudes that lead people to live in harmony with the world as it is, not devote themselves to changing it. In emphasizing their own interdependence with the rest of nature, the Sioux reduced their very human tendencies to feel superior to nonhuman forms of life. Unlike Western civilization, the Sioux Nation did not use the unique powers of reason and language as an indication that the rest of creation had evolved solely for their benefit and use. Thus, they neither manipulated nor exploited nature; and not feeling superior to it, they were free to accept a certain degree of weakness with respect to the natural order, on both a cultural and a psychological level. Accepting the inevitability of this weakness inclined the Sioux to seek direction from the natural world, not try to dictate to it as the white Europeans did.

The world view of the Sioux led to the creation of a society very different from that of the whites. There were no churches because religion was part of ordinary life and was practiced everywhere and at all times. There were no missionaries because each tribe and nation, like each animal species, had its own place in the world, and its peculiar way of doing things was respected. There were no orphanages or old age homes. The thought of children or elders being segregated from their kinship groups was repugnant to the Sioux. There were no prisons. Deviants either changed and adapted their behavior to the group, or they were banished. There were no explorers because there was no word in the Lakota language for "wilderness."

Since religious missionaries, orphanages, old age homes, prisons, and exploration were among the institutions that caused the most trouble in white society, people at Wounded Knee were not quick to dismiss the old Sioux culture as out of date. On the contrary, it seemed to offer them a useful alternative perspective on the chaos of the modern world. This was especially so with respect to white society's most significant departure from Sioux tradition—leaders most frequently come from among the rich, or they quickly become rich as a result of their leadership positions. To the old Sioux, leadership was a personal sacrifice. People were free to stop following a leader at any moment. With an arrangement of such pure democracy, only leaders who genuinely sacrificed their time and wealth for the benefit of the tribe were able to retain their positions. The Sioux believed that when wealth determines who leads, and leadership is a means of increasing personal wealth, there can be no meaningful democracy.

Many people in Wounded Knee understood the wisdom of the old ways for the first time in their lives. Suddenly, the great achievements of the Sioux Nation were clearly visible, not just the shortcomings white culture had focused so much attention on for so long. For some people, the realization was almost startling. And the distance back to those achievements was not very great. Black Elk's grandson was in Wounded Knee. So was the great-grandson of Red Cloud, and the granddaughter of Sitting Bull. But beside the famous ancestors, every Sioux in Wounded Knee had grandparents, or great-grandparents, or at the most great-great-grandparents, who had helped to defeat the Bluecoats in the war for the Powder River country, or had fled from them when the Black Hills were stolen, or had been killed by them at the Wounded Knee Creek. Two to four generations back is not far to look for a lost heritage.

The old chiefs, the headmen, and the elder men and women of the tribe helped the medicine men pass this heritage on to people less familiar

Work underway to fortify the outer walls of a building inside Wounded Knee.

Indian warrior on guard with a shotgun inside one of the Wounded Knee bunkers.

with it. The medicine men did other work as well. They practiced medicine in Wounded Knee. Relying on ritual and a selection of herbs with antibiotic and anesthetic properties, the medicine men worked alongside conventional doctors and medics. The latter, most of whom were volunteers from free neighborhood clinics around the country, had to illegally infiltrate government lines to get into Wounded Knee.

The government made sure they all had plenty of patients. Federal officers brought about a chronic and serious food shortage which led to malnutrition and a generalized susceptibility to contagious ailments such as bronchitis and pneumonia. At one point, they, or the goon squad, cut off the water supply, depriving the people in Wounded Knee of proper sanitation facilities and forcing the use of contaminated water, thus increasing the likelihood of typhoid and other water-borne diseases. Government bullets were also a significant health hazard. Over a dozen were removed from people's bodies by the medicine men alone. Crow Dog successfully extracted a federal slug from someone's midsection. One of the white M.D.s who worked in Wounded Knee, a pediatrician, said, "At first I thought the spiritual things were a lot of hogwash, but I changed my mind." He added that he would "consider it an honor to study with Leonard Crow Dog."

Some people suffered through grave personal and collective tragedy during the occupation of Wounded Knee. Many endured bitter disappointment. But almost everyone who spent more than a few days there came away with a certain pride and a sense of satisfaction. They had created their own community, a community of resistance, and it had sustained them for a longer period and in more ways than any of them had thought possible.

"I think the best thing that happened in Wounded Knee," Dennis Banks recalled with obvious gratification, "was that there was an immediate response from individual members of tribes all across the country. They came to Wounded Knee to help us. At one time there we had 65 various tribes represented . People from 64 different tribes came to help the Oglalas.

"Every night," Dennis continued, "we would have a meeting to explain what was going on with the government, what they were doing, and what we were doing. There was a good feeling amongst those people that came there—no one was a Chippewa, no one was an Oglala, no one was an Osage, no one was this or that. We were all Indian people there, and we were held together by three or four medicine men.

"Every night they held spiritual gatherings where we could learn more about our real culture and history, and where we could try and calm ourselves and gather the strength that we needed to go on. We'd smoke the pipe, and we built a sweat lodge there.

"Crow Dog and Black Elk, in my opinion, were probably the greatest force at Wounded Knee, on the spiritual side. These were two men who I believe did the most to hold us together. That was a good feeling there, to sit down with members of different tribes and smoke the pipe and remind ourselves that we were all brothers and sisters.

"And it wasn't only Indians there. There were a couple of blacks. There were four or five Orientals. There were 15 to 20 Chicanos and 15 to 20 whites. They all joined in the circle with us, they all joined in smoking the pipe with us, joined us in the spiritual meetings we had every night. And they all joined us when we went to the sweat lodge.

"I think that was the greatest thing that happened, in a time of crisis that a lot of people banded together from all the different races of man to help fight the most powerful government in the world—and for us, the most evil."

Life in occupied Wounded Knee could never be described as normal. Yet, a certain regularity emerged as the structure of the community took shape. But despite the tracer bullets, the armored personnel carriers (APCs), and the shooting, this regularity was not a function of the private dwelling units and uneven distribution of wealth found in ordinary American towns. "Downtown" Wounded Knee, where the four roads came together, consisted of about 15 buildings. The old trading post was cleaned out and became the new community meeting and cultural center. The old tourist museum was converted into the new security and defense office. The best house in town became the busy medical clinic.

Two hundred yards east of downtown, up the Denby road, two church buildings and a minister's home were used to house the 75 people in charge of defending that side of the perimeter. Two hundred yards north, up the side of a small hill, the Sacred Heart Catholic Church was turned into housing for people working in that area. Its relatively large basement was used as a community kitchen. So it went around the settlement. The sharing of the buildings made it easier to share everything else: the food, the trouble, the joy, and the work.

Most remarkable, perhaps, was the sharing of the work. There was physical work, like digging bunkers or fortifying the buildings with 16-inch walls made from planks and two-by-fours with a fill-in of dirt. There was clerical work, like mimeographing news bulletins or first aid instruction sheets. There was technical work, like setting up the complex network of radio transmitters and receivers. There was kitchen work, hospital work, hauling work, child care work, everything. And it all got done on a voluntary basis. People did what they felt they were good at and what they thought was necessary and important. In most cases, having freely taken on the job, they performed it with enthusiasm, understanding why they were doing it, and anxious to do it well.

During the 71 days of the occupation, more than a thousand Indian people passed through Wounded Knee, with 300-400 there at any one time. Community services were often disorganized and inefficient. Nevertheless, food was prepared, children were cared for (one was even born), mail was delivered, major political decisions were made democratically, a proper defense was organized, health care, both western and Indian, was provided.

More than that, there was a paradoxical feeling of safety and security. The dangers faced in Wounded Knee were clearer and more tangible than the dangers most Indians face in the course of their normal lives. Yet, in some respects, the anxiety and confusion in a fight against armed men was less than what resulted from more subtle enemies, like racial discrimination, unemployment, and cultural ridicule. At least the attackers could be pinpointed, and a method existed for dealing with them. At times on an Indian reservation people feel like they have so many problems it is not possible to find the cause of any one of them. The desperate, terrifying hopelessness that results was never a part of life at Wounded Knee. When the bullets weren't flying, people were relaxed and happy. For over two months, there was virtually no personal aggression or theft, no problems with alcohol or drugs. A baby was born, a couple was married, and two men were buried in the Indian way. Nearly everyone was armed or within easy reach of a weapon, but there was no fear, and leaders could walk among their people in safety.

All this was accomplished by a very diverse group of Indians. They came from all over the country, some from cities, others from reservations, some for a weekend, and others for as long as it took. There were full-time political activists from AIM and people who had never participated in a political event in their lives. A majority were residents of the Pine Ridge Reservation who had become involved through the struggle to unseat Dick Wilson. Some had their permanent homes in Wounded Knee.

On March 8, with the government's ultimatum scheduled to expire at sundown, the permanent residents of Wounded Knee had to decide whether to evacuate their homes as the government wished or remain behind and side with the occupation. For the most part, these people had not played a part in the anti-Wilson events leading up to the occupation. Yet, only two complete families, plus four mothers and 38 children, departed. Over 150 people stayed and were promptly integrated into the occupying forces.

Three days later, on March 11, Wounded Knee declared its sovereignty from the United States of America, proclaiming itself and the land it controlled to be the Independent Oglala Sioux Nation. The move was an obvious and sensible one to the old chiefs, many of whom had never thought of the situation in any other way. They readily endorsed the declaration of independence. Leaders of AIM saw the move as a method of sharpening the cloudy but central issue of Indian treaty rights.

The declaration was based on the Fort Laramie Treaty of 1868. AIM leaders pointed out that the U.S. and the Sioux Nation signed the treaty as sovereign powers. The sovereignty of the Sioux was not relinquished in the treaty; on the contrary, it was affirmed. In 1868, Chief Red Cloud had defeated the Bluecoats in the Powder River War, and it was the United States that came begging the Sioux for a truce. The 1868 treaty assigned a huge portion of what is now South Dakota to the Sioux Nation, and it guaranteed that no white men would ever set foot in the Black Hills uninvited. The treaty stipulated that revisions would be valid only with the consent of three-quarters of all adult males in the Sioux Nation. Such consent was never subsequently obtained.

Citizens of the Independent Oglala Sioux Nation began to speak of the United States as a foreign country and of their defense perimeter as a border. In mass meetings, they organized Offices of Security, Internal Security, Maintenance, Commissary, and Supply. They passed laws to regulate their community, began a census, and issued visas to those of their comrades who were not Oglalas. Non-Indians promoting their own causes were asked to leave.

When the Justice Department got wind of the Sioux declaration of independence, their response was a predictable over-reaction. An associate deputy U.S. Attorney General announced that the United States was considering bringing charges of conspiracy to commit sedition against those who had proclaimed Wounded Knee a sovereign nation. But the Justice Department quickly backed off when the Indians made it clear they would welcome such charges. Ready to risk conviction, a sedition indictment would give them a perfect forum to argue the legal questions surrounding the all-important issues of tribal sovereignty and treaty rights. When the occupation finally ended and the Department of Justice was able to make its arrests, they carefully avoided indictments with political implications, like sedition, making certain that all charges were straightforward criminal matters, like arson, burglary, illegal possession of weapons, assaulting federal officers, and so forth.

Despite sensational headlines and the news media's tendency to publicize violence, life in Wounded Knee was much more than one continuous gunfight. While not an ordinary citizen of the community, Dennis Banks' description of his more ordinary activities provides a clearer picture of life in the occupied zone.

"A typical day for me," he remembers, "was handing out news bulletins that were coming in from the outside, distributing mail that was being brought in by runners, counseling people with problems, presiding over the daily meetings we had. I must have chaired over a hundred meetings in there.

"I also tried to make sure that people sent out word to their families and friends on the outside just to say what was going on. I wasn't trying to babysit for them, just encourage them to stay in contact. I made a daily list of people who were hurt and I sent word to their families not to worry about them, that they were inside and that they were doing all right.

"A lot of days I spent negotiating with the Justice Department and talking to the Community Relations Service to try and get medicines and supplies through, but when I wasn't doing that, I was doing all this other stuff.

"I tried to be a force that held people together. I gave them the continued encouragement that there were people coming in behind us, there were other organizations across the country that were helping us. It was my job to get that kind of support during the day and keep that support coming in.

"With the leadership of Russell [Means] and Clyde [Bellecourt] and Carter [Camp], we all made a real effort to show the people that it wasn't only Oglalas that were there to protest the government's bungling of Indian affairs and their handling of treaty matters, but that other people came to Wounded Knee as well. We tried to keep the people together in this united effort.

"Russell had a tremendous responsibility as an Oglala to keep the press informed that it was the Oglalas themselves that were leading the fight. My role was to keep the people informed, especially of the kind of support we were getting, not only in America, but before the phone lines were cut we were receiving calls from England, Germany, Japan, France.

"Once we got a telephone call from Viet Nam, from a group of twelve Indians who were over there in the Army. They told us that they realized now that the real war was at home, and that they have no business fighting over on somebody else's property in some foreign country, and that they wished that they were there at Wounded Knee. We began to receive that kind of telephone support from all across the world."

Dennis had two other jobs at Wounded Knee. One was organizing an occasional round-up, "to go out and get cattle that were straying into the Wounded Knee perimeter, into the Independent Oglala Sioux Nation." The other was to do his best to keep people's spirits up, to make them laugh. Once he announced to a nightly meeting, "I just want to tell you that it wasn't a bull you ate last night. That was a horse! One of those urban Indians killed it—didn't know the difference."

The joke underscored the community's very serious concern about food. For the first two weeks of the occupation three meals a day were usually available. After that, supplies dwindled and food became more and more of a problem. Since few supplies were brought into Wounded Knee the night it was occupied, the first major source of food was what was available on the shelves of the trading post. But with federal roadblocks up and several hundred additional people in the tiny settlement, staples in the trading post were quickly exhausted.

At that time, around the end of the first week, help came from the National Council of Churches. In addition to mediating activities and encouraging negotiations, the NCC group on the scene was permitted to bring food into Wounded Knee. Many conservative newspapers complained that this assistance was being inappropriately given to AIM, but actually the food was donated to the equally besieged permanent residents of Wounded Knee who in turn freely shared it with the occupation. American Red Cross officials also came, but the situation was too political for them, and they quickly decided to work in Pine Ridge and stay clear of Wounded Knee.

All this abruptly ended at the beginning of the third week. On consecutive days, the U.S marshals announced a get-tough policy and Dick Wilson pushed his resolution through the Tribal Council ordering the NCC group expelled from the reservation.

On March 11, three days after the unsuccessful government ultimatum, an FBI agent was shot in the wrist. Riding in an unmarked government car, he fired on an Indian van trying to get into Wounded Knee. Indians in the van returned the fire, hitting the FBI agent in the wrist of his shooting arm as he leaned out of the car window to take another shot at them. It was far from the first injury in the battle, or the worst, but it was the first time anyone on the federal side had been hit. The next day, March 12, the outraged chief U.S. marshal, commanding government forces at Wounded Knee, announced that the U.S. would create a "tighter perimeter" and "starve out" the occupation.

"I'm sure as hell planning on changing their life style," he added. "If that means starving, if it means being cold, not being able to read the evening paper, not being able to watch television, it means not being able to make telephone calls, it means not being able to get soap to wash your clothes with." Many Indians said they weren't sure if he was talking about ordinary life on the reservation or if he planned to institute some significant change.

The next day Wilson got his resolution through the Tribal Council and the National Council of Churches personnel were banned from the reservation. The order did not take effect until March 16, when Stanley Lyman, the white reservation superintendent, formally signed it. But after the FBI agent's injury on the 11th, the NCC was prevented from bringing any more food into Wounded Knee. On March 14, Dennis Banks told reporters, "I'd say food will last three days. Each person will have one meal a day. The blizzard and the conditions it's causing make us more determined to fight it out. We're used to this. That's why we think we'll win."

It was at this point that the nightly backpack trains were organized. It was an ambitious project, an underground railway for food and ammunition kept secret from both the government and the goon squad. Supplies were being driven to Rapid City by supporters from all over the country. This material was then taken on back roads to safe drop-off points, usually ten to fifteen miles from Wounded Knee. These safe points were homes and utility buildings in very isolated locations on the reservation. They belonged to people quietly in support of the occupation, of which there were many. The delivery to the drop-off points was often timed to rendezvous with the separate arrival of a group of volunteers ready to carry the supplies the rest of the way to Wounded Knee on their backs.

The low rolling hills in the vicinity of Wounded Knee are crisscrossed by deeply eroded ravines and gullies. Indians from the reservation who knew the area and could follow the land in the moonlight, or find their way by homing in on a distant light, guided the volunteer backpackers through government lines. Each person carried a 40-pound backpack over a distance of ten to fifteen miles, sometimes through snow or rain. When the backpackers passed close to government bunkers and APCs, they often had to walk in their socks over frozen ground or crawl on their stomachs avoiding dog patrols or high intensity lights.

Now and then a backpack train spent too much time evading capture and was unable to complete the long trek before sunrise. There was no alternative but to spend the entire day in a secluded canyon and continue after dark. Occasionally, as a backpack train drew close, Wounded Knee bunkers would fire a few shots at government roadblocks in order to draw massive return fire. While federal attention was diverted in this way, the backpackers could walk through the deep ravines and into Wounded Knee.

On many nights the uncomfortable marshals and FBI agents stayed inside their bunkers and APCs to keep warm. When they did go out on patrol, they frequently built campfires, destroying their night vision. Nevertheless, they made many attempts to ambush the backpackers and eventually had some success. Food trains were captured on the trail and arrested. The charge was usually "interference with federal officers in the lawful performance of their duty," a federal felony punishable by a maximum of five years in prison and $10,000 fine. However, when large groups of backpackers moved with an armed escort, they were able to get through without firing a shot. Government officers, understandably, given their mission, were not prepared to risk their lives unless they had a clear advantage.

These backpack trains kept Wounded Knee alive for over a month. They often required acts of bravery quite uncommon in the lives of the men and women who participated. The courageous volunteers were mostly Indians from the Pine Ridge Reservation, but there were also numerous off-reservation Indians, political activists, college students, pacifists, revolutionaries, and others who spontaneously appeared wanting to help and were asked to carry in supplies. Their appearance no doubt suggested a communist conspiracy to the more naive and paranoid on the political right. But, in fact, no orders had been given. The people who came shared a common understanding of what had to be done, and they came to do it. It was a coordination far more powerful than a mere conspiracy.

With hundreds of armed men, mobile equipment, and sophisticated technology, the government was only barely able to stop the flow of supplies. It required almost a month just to find the main trail being used by the backpackers. There was too much land and too many people willing to help the insurgents for federal officers to successfully isolate Wounded Knee. Government inability to maintain control was evident in other ways as well. The leadership from Wounded Knee was able to move secretly across the entire Pine Ridge Reservation in order to develop support for the occupation. They visited towns many miles away and even called public meetings sometimes attended by hundreds of Indian people.

The insurgents in Wounded Knee functioned much like a guerrilla movement. Widespread support, ranging from direct participation to simply looking the other way at the right moment, was available from a broad cross-section of the reservation's inhabitants. Indeed, if that were not the case, Wounded Knee would have quickly collapsed. But when widespread popular support is present, tremendous odds can be overcome. This profound lesson of the Vietnamese resistance was not lost on the people at Wounded Knee. Many referred to their own overland supply route as the "Ho Chi Minh Trail." Only this time, they said, Washington didn't waste any time trying to win the hearts and minds of the people.

When news first appeared in the press about government attempts to starve the Indians out of Wounded Knee, people across the nation began spontaneously gathering food and medicine to send there. These efforts took place on the reservations and in the big cities. The severe felony charges brought against those arrested during the early days of the backpack trains were intended both as punishment and as a means of discouraging others from helping in the same way. But the intimidation had little effect. As a result, the government escalated the scope of its blockade in an offensive that spread across the entire country.

The anti-Indian offensive was launched by the FBI in Los Angeles. There a group of Indian and white physicians, helped by other concerned citizens, collected food and medicine to be sent to Wounded Knee. Their effort was entirely open, even to the point of being publicized on local television. Three cars containing thirteen Indians and three whites left Los Angeles to bring the collected supplies to representatives of the National Council of Churches in Denver who hoped to forward the goods to Wounded Knee. As they left Los Angeles, the three cars were followed by the FBI, in five. As the parade of vehicles approached Nevada some hours later, the FBI tail grew to more than 50 agents in 29 automobiles.

Immediately after crossing the Nevada border, the supply cars were forced to the side of the road by the armada of FBI vehicles. The 16 people inside were promptly arrested and charged with crossing state lines with the intent to incite or participate in a riot, the infamous Rap Brown Act. One car managed to stop just short of the state line. Its occupants were "escorted" to the other side and then arrested. TV news that night showed the 16 being led off—in chains. But the overkill tactics lost more public support for the government. Even Sammy Davis, Jr. was outraged at their conduct. After being repeatedly photographed during the preceding pre-election months locked in physical embrace with President Nixon, Davis took time off from a very lucrative engagement in nearby Las Vegas to put up some of the money necessary to get the culprits out on bail.

Medicines and food in the three cars were impounded by the FBI. A local grand jury returned federal indictments against 13 of the 16 people arrested. They were all Indians. The Justice Department apparently dropped charges against the remaining three, who were all white. The day after the dramatic arrests on the Nevada state line, an Interior Department spokesman in Pine Ridge, South Dakota, announced that the bust was part of a nationwide sweep. Federal authorities across the country were told to stop all people going to Wounded Knee.

No one explained why an announcement that presumably pertained to law enforcement came from the Department of the Interior rather than the Department of Justice. But the announcement was accurate. In the following weeks a national campaign was directed against people "allegedly" bringing food to Wounded Knee. The FBI made arrests as far away as Oregon, New York, Illinois, and many other places. The charge was the same, crossing state lines with the intent to incite or participate in a riot.

In heated courtroom battles, defense lawyers questioned the validity of these arrests, as well as those of the backpackers on the reservation. They argued that the Rap Brown law was itself unconstitutional. They denied that the government had a right to starve anyone for any reason, with or without due process of law. Starvation, they claimed, was a violation of the right to life, guaranteed next to liberty and the pursuit of happiness. Furthermore, the Justice Department was accused of applying the law in a prejudicial fashion. Earlier, they had encouraged the National Council of Churches to bring food into Wounded Knee, and then later they arrested private citizens for doing the same thing but without a Justice Department invitation.

On March 25, Judge Andrew Bogue issued the temporary restraining order that prevented federal officers from blocking daily shipments of food into Wounded Knee. It was the next day, before the first shipment could be delivered, that goon squad roadblocks took over the food blockade with the tacit approval of nearby marshals and FBI agents. A day later, on March 27, Bogue rescinded his own order, thus alleviating at least one source of conflict between Tribal Chairman Dick Wilson and the federal government. The overall result was no additional food for the besieged Oglalas. Severe rationing was instituted as the backpackers continued to be the only source of supplies.

The food problem in Wounded Knee was aggravated by the inability to stockpile more than a single day's supply. If the backpackers were cut off one night, the next day the people went hungry. The uncertainty was almost as hard to live with as the hunger. Shortages of all kinds became the rule, and three meals a day was only a memory.

Gladys Bissonette supervised one of the kitchens in Wounded Knee when she wasn't occupied as a negotiator. Recalling some of the hungrier times, she said, "Sometimes I stayed up all night and helped folks cook, especially when it got to where there wasn't any food. Then I stayed up and I tried different recipes, which I wished I had taken down.

"Like there was this popcorn seasoning there, a big box of it. It's real orange color and it's got a buttery, salty taste. It's some kind of formula, but I'm telling you, that made the best whipped potatoes we had there. You didn't have to add salt or butter to them, which a lot of times we didn't have. But we did have these instant potatoes and we'd whip them up with that popcorn seasoning.

"We also had powdered milk, this instant milk that they give out for commodities. That was the handiest stuff because there were all kinds of spices in that old cupboard in there and I always managed to make potato soup out of this powdered milk and those instant potatoes. And that came in handy during the real cold nights, when we didn't have anything else to eat. I didn't know what a real potato looked like all that time. Otherwise, during the day, we cooked beans, beans that didn't have anything in them. So we used that same popcorn seasoning in the beans to flavor them a little."

On March 31, the negotiations that led to the abortive April 5 agreement began inside the sacred tipi in the DMZ. The Tribal Council roadblocks were still in place, but Kent Frizzell, government negotiator at that time, spoke as though the Justice Department had some influence over the food blockade after all. Frizzell offered to set up a dining tent near one of the forward federal roadblocks. But he insisted that anyone who came to it would have to submit to search and arrest if there was an outstanding warrant for them. The negotiators from Wounded Knee scornfully admitted that they weren't that hungry.

During the negotiating period, Frizzell refused to allow anything but milk and baby food through the federal roadblocks. Speaking not only of the 75 or so warriors but all 350 men, women, and children inside the Wounded Knee defense perimeter, Frizzell, the highest ranking public official on the scene, said, "To my knowledge, the U.S. government has never given food to the enemy to sustain them." The enemy, indeed!

Another week passed as negotiations dragged on. The backpackers continued to be the only source of food. Then, after the signing of the short-lived agreement on April 5, the roadblocks were open long enough for a few dozen cases of food to be trucked into Wounded Knee. Before more could be delivered, the agreement broke down and the Ho Chi Minh Trail once more became the only available route of supply.

Conditions worsened considerably during the second week in April. Fire fights were down to a minimum, but federal officers relied more and more on isolation and starvation as their primary weapons. Government lines around Wounded Knee tightened. Dogs were brought in. And the backpackers, the real heros of the day, had an increasingly difficult time getting through. Medical teams who had also slipped inside the settlement sent out ominous reports that the first signs of malnutrition had appeared in the children. Certain of the damage was described as possibly "irreversible."

Inadequate diet was not the only health problem. Medical workers reported that contaminated water and poor sanitation had caused an outbreak of diarrhea. With their water cut off from the outside, Wounded Knee was threatened by typhoid fever and hepatitis. By early April, there were over 100 people with influenza or bronchitis. Many others had pneumonia.

Government forces gradually discovered sections of the various trails being used by the backpackers. The number making it through each night began to dwindle. Once federal officers learned parts of a trail, they moved their APCs into position to block it. Then, from inside the tank-like vehicles, the marshals and FBI agents were more than willing to exchange gunfire with the backpackers and their armed escorts. Officers hoped that the shooting would also discourage other people from trying to hike in. It did. So did the misleading talk by government press spokesmen about an imminent negotiated settlement. New backpackers were less willing to risk being shot at when they were under the false impression that the occupation was going to end at any moment.

By mid-April, no more than two or three backpackers got through each night. Sometimes there was none. Food became so scarce people were only able to eat one meal of rice or beans every other day, with a bowl of soup in between. Some were close to giving up. The community's unity and determination began to wither. The government knew this and was counting on making it more painful for them.

13

AIRLIFT
Forty Seconds over Wounded Knee

Tuesday, April 17, 1973
Rapid City, South Dakota

2:30 a.m.—I woke up, instantly alert. At dawn, little more than two hours away, our mission would finally reach its climax over Wounded Knee. The others around me seemed driven by the same sharp anticipation. In only fifteen minutes our car was parked in the dark near the weather bureau at the Rapid City airport. Billy went inside to get the forecast and check the teletype and radar data. Then he looked around the planes to make sure we weren't walking into a trap. When he returned, we still had time before lift off, so he climbed into the car and we drove back downtown for coffee. Weather conditions were ideal and forecast to stay that way. A ten-knot southwesterly wind blew across South Dakota and visibility was unrestricted. The entire area sat under a very high, thin layer of overcast clouds that would figure prominently a few hours later in saving the lives of three of us.

At an all-night Chinese restaurant we filled our three large thermos bottles with hot coffee, a meagre defense against the intense cold we expected while flying with our rear doors off. Strobe acted even more agitated than usual. He talked obsessively about the parachute harness he planned to wear during the drop and how he would tie it to something inside the airplane in case he fell out. Tom, who had been transformed from a nonparticipant reporter into the cargo handler on my plane, planned to use a single safety rope tied around his waist. John, the cargo kicker in Jim's plane, thought they were both crazy.

"I know I'm not going to fall out," he declared, "and if I do, it's not going to do me any good to be dangling from an airplane at the end of a rope!"

Strobe couldn't believe his ears. He offered to sew a harness together for John, a project there was obviously no time to complete. But John's refusal only encouraged Strobe. I walked away from them laughing at Strobe's attachment to the needle and thread. Three nights before he had planned to have a camera sewn into the palm of his hand!

We left the restaurant, parked the car, and reviewed our final plans. We shared a common excitement but also a certain sense of calm and confidence. We were tempered by the troubles of the previous days and were beyond debates and disagreements. The situation was in no way hypothetical now, and we looked to our experts for leadership. Jim laid out the details of the parachute drop.

"The weatherman says the wind is blowing from the southwest at ten," he began. "I think we're close enough to Wounded Knee to forget about dropping the test streamer and just take his word for it. That means our chutes will drift north and east, but not a hell of a lot if we drop them from 500 feet. The chutes will open about 350 feet above the ground. With 200 to 250 pounds on them, they'll descend at 20 feet per second and be down in less than 20 seconds. The total horizontal drift won't be more than a few hundred feet.

"Here's the map the Indians drew for us in Rapid City. If we fly perpendicular to the wind, we'll be over their land for only 25 seconds. That's probably not enough time to get everything out in one pass. We've got to fly a right angle drop pattern to get more time. If we start up here, in the northwest corner of their defense perimeter, we can fly along the west and south borders of their land. The northeasterly drift will carry the cargo on an angle toward the center of the village."

Still pointing to the map of Wounded Knee, Jim asked Billy and me to estimate the time available to tumble out the cargo if we flew the right-angle drop pattern. We both calculated for a moment and came up with the same answer—40 seconds inside the Wounded Knee defense perimeter. It wasn't much of an improvement, but it might be all we needed.

Billy then briefed us on navigation. All three aircraft would lift off Rapid City no later than 4:05 a.m. and rendezvous in the dark just south of town. Picking up the radio beacons that formed the main airway south to Denver, we would fly single file at 2,000 feet with Billy in the lead. As he held a flashlight up to his aeronautical chart, Billy showed us the well-traveled route and insisted that our three-plane formation would not evoke suspicion flying along it.

We were reluctant to take our doors off at the Rapid City airport, so a landing was planned at Hot Springs, 48 miles to the south. It was a little country field with all-night runway lights, and it was sure to be deserted at 4:30 a.m. After the doors were removed, the pilots would take off and fly wide circles around the Hot Springs airport while the cargo handlers positioned the duffel bags in the open doorways for the drop. When Billy had 4:44 on his watch, he would radio the other two planes to break out of the circles and fly east to Wounded Knee. Except for Jim's signal to start tumbling out the bags, that would be our only use of the radio all morning. Wounded Knee was a 22-minute flight from Hot Springs. We would arrive at the besieged village at exactly 5:06 a.m., the moment of dawn.

In the 22 minutes between Hot Springs and Wounded Knee, several things had to happen. First, we would descend to tree-top level to get below radar coverage and avoid being seen from the ground. Second, we had to find the general area of Wounded Knee, 56 miles away over the barren, rocky hills. Third, we had to get the three airplanes into the half-V formation we had practiced on the way west. Fourth, we had to avoid flying over any little towns along the way, particularly Oglala and Manderson, the two closest to Wounded Knee. The noise of our three engines directly overhead would wake almost anyone. Finally, after Billy got us close to Wounded Knee, he had to fall back to the number two position in the formation so Jim could take the lead. They would begin the switch as the lights of Oglala, several miles to the south, passed under our right wing tips. With the switch completed, Jim would lead us three miles south of Manderson, which was only eight miles from Wounded Knee. Marshals and FBI agents were known to be quartered in Manderson, but the distance was safe enough as long as we stayed close to the ground. Even if we were heard in Manderson, flying so low and off to the side, no one would see or be able to shoot at us. The sound of planes they could not see would only confuse them, and before they could react effectively it would be all over.

Oliver, our somewhat suspect spotter, would guide Jim over the last eight miles directly to the northwest corner of the defense perimeter. A few miles away we would shoot up to 500 feet, just as the sun came over the horizon. Jim then had to determine the exact spot for beginning the drop and announce it to the rest of us over the radio. The idea of flying so close together was to insure that we would all reach this spot simultaneously. After the 40-second drop run, each pilot had to decide independently about making a second pass—if one were necessary.

The escape plan was to dive down to low altitude again and fly away toward the east into the sun, then split up into three different directions and return separately to Chicago. Meanwhile, according to the plan I had worked out the night before with Rita, she would be making telephone calls from the legal defense office in Rapid City to trick the FBI into following our trail of false clues westward to Wyoming. Larry's arrangements would have our friend in Boston on the phone giving the story to the press.

Our plans were well laid and we knew it. We sat for a moment in the dark car quietly collecting ourselves, then set off for the airport. It was 3:45 a.m. The atmosphere turned jovial.

"Hey, Billy," John asked, "when we're flying from Hot Springs to Wounded Knee, how low you gonna take us?"

"Low enough to read the beer cans lyin' on the ground!"

The car broke into peals of laughter, except for Tom who was still nervous about flying. He turned to me, his face slowly collapsing, "Is he kidding?"

"Who, him?" I deadpaned. "He never kids."

Over more laughter, Billy told Tom to stop worrying. "Everything's gonna work fine," he said. "We're gonna be long gone before them goons can shake the sleep from their eyes. They ain't gonna have time to lift a rifle and take aim."

"Anyway, if they do," Jim wisecracked, "we won't know about it till we're hit."

"Well, getting hit won't be so bad," Larry joined in, forgetting for a moment that he was driving the car. "They'll get us through the bottom of the plane, in the ass. There are worse places to be shot."

"Oh, Larry, speak for your own ass," John groaned. "I'd like a big piece of sheet metal to sit on."

Tom waited a moment for the laughter to evaporate, then quietly changed our mood. "Forget about the guns, you guys. They're not going to move fast enough to shoot us. Just think about all those hungry people on the ground and how they've been fighting in that little village for so long. Imagine what it'll be like for them to see a ton of food come floating down from the sky." Tom's involvement with the airlift had become complete. It was hard to remember him as the eager reporter who had joined us five days before.

A pregnant silence hung over the car, as though there were something more to say that nobody could quite articulate. Stocking caps were adjusted, more comfortable positions were wiggled into, but still nothing was said. Then Billy managed to capture it.

"You know, we've been through a lot these last few days, a lot more hasslin' than we figured on when we started out. But, well . . . I'm glad we came through all that together, I'm glad we're here. This is probably the most important thing I've ever done."

There was a pause. "Yeah," Jim agreed, "I feel the same way."

It was a comfortable moment and we savored it, confidently smiling at each other and nodding our approval. Minutes later, we arrived at the airport, left the car at the Hertz parking lot, and split up to prepare our aircraft. When everything was ready, we huddled in the dark near Billy's plane, stamping our feet against the cold and slapping each other happily on the back.

"Ain't nothin' gonna stop us now," Billy announced, "except maybe an engine failure." He checked his watch with a flourish. "OK, you guys, here's my thing from the movies. Gentlemen," with as much seriousness as he could muster, "synchronize your watches! The time is now four-oh-one."

Everyone laughed at Billy's parody, but Jim and I quietly set our watches at 4:01.

"OK, let's mount up."

Billy and Strobe climbed onto the wing of their Cherokee and got in. The rest of us waited. We had agreed to leave them and go with only two airplanes if Billy's engine again failed to start. Slowly the battery pushed the propeller around. The engine caught. Billy flashed us a big smile and held his hand to the window in the thumbs-up signal. Jim and I returned the thumbs-up sign and the six of us swung around toward our planes.

The tie-down area had 50 or 60 aircraft parked tightly in four long rows. Larry, Tom, and I wound our way through the darkened maze of wings and tails. When we got to our plane, Tom made a place for himself on top of the duffel bags stacked behind the pilot and co-pilot seats. Larry latched the door. With the master switch flipped on, the dashboard was bathed in a faint red light. I went through the prestart check list, pushed the starter button, and the engine sprang to life. In quick succession I turned on the wing lights, the landing lights, the rotating beacon, and the two radios. Off to our left, I could see Jim's wing lights come on in the next row of airplanes.

Our primary radio was already tuned to the Rapid City tower frequency. I heard Billy call in to request taxi clearance, but instead of the usual response, he was answered by someone in the weather bureau. The voice explained that the control tower was closed between midnight and 6:00 a.m. Weather bureau staff stood by the tower's radio frequency to give weather information and traffic advisories. We hadn't even bothered to check, but it was a good break for us. Not only was the airport terminal area deserted, but no one was in the control tower watching us. The weather bureau building was only one story and well behind the parking area off the field. A sly smile inched across my face. We could remove our rear doors right there in Rapid City and skip the landing in Hot Springs. I had a hunch Billy and Jim were coming to the same conclusion.

With a confident air Billy's voice boomed over the radio speaker, clearing our departure with the man in the weather bureau. "Rapid City Radio, this is Cherokee two-seven-four-one-juliet. We have three Cherokees ready to taxi for a formation flight to Denver. Over."

"Four-one-juliet, taxi to runway three-one, wind is two-four-zero degrees at niner. Rapid City altimeter is three-zero-one-three. No traffic reported in the area. Do you wish to file a flight plan? Over."

There was a moment's hesitation. I wondered how Billy would get out of that one. Then, "Negative on the flight plan. With three of us flying together, we're a lot safer than we'd be even with a flight plan."

Larry and I laughed at Billy's quick wit. Everything was falling neatly into place. I felt like a little kid on a playground slide that led right down to Wounded Knee: our trip was going to be very smooth and our arrival inevitable.

"Roger. Understand no flight plan. Please have the other aircraft in the formation call in their numbers."

Billy had already taxied clear of the tie-down area. Jim radioed in, then I pressed the button on the hand mike. "Rapid City Radio, this is Cherokee five-seven-five-three-romeo starting to taxi. We'll be number three in the formation. Over."

"Roger, five-three-romeo."

I released the parking brake and eased the throttle forward. The big Cherokee began to roll. We inched through the tangle of aircraft in the tie-down area and headed down the taxiway behind the lights of the other two planes. It was more than a mile across the barren airport to the apron of runway 31, plenty of time to enjoy the empty glass bubble atop the control tower.

We reached the runway apron and stopped the single file of airplanes very close together. Ahead, I could see John and Strobe illuminated by the aircraft lights of their planes as they worked to remove their rear doors. Just as I told Larry to take off ours, Billy came running out of the darkness to confirm the unspoken revision in our plans—take the doors off there and circle Hot Springs until 4:44 a.m. without landing. Larry trotted around to the side of the plane. He pulled the entire door out and away from the hull of the ship, twisted it around vertically and pushed it back inside. Tom grabbed it and positioned it in the extreme rear of the cabin. As Larry climbed back into the co-pilot's seat, I looked out at the silhouettes of the other two airplanes and the colored lights on their wingtips and tails. For a moment I felt very much alone out there in the middle of that South Dakota night.

Billy swung onto the runway and began to roll. Jim taxied into position behind him and waited for his lift off while I checked my controls and instruments. Then, as Jim took off, I ran up my engine and taxied the heavily loaded airplane onto runway 31. The lights of Rapid City were directly in front of us. Taking off at 310°, roughly northwest, I had to climb out over the city and the three tall TV towers that rose from a hilltop in the middle of town. That meant gaining altitude quickly and turning to the left in order to rendezvous with the other planes south of town.

As Jim's plane disappeared in the distance, I eased my throttle into the full open position. In the darkness, the runway lights began to slide by on either side of us, at first slow and graceful, then with increasing speed. The takeoff roll took longer than I expected. Rapid City is 3,200 feet above sea level and the propeller had to grab at more of the thinner air for thrust. Finally, the airspeed indicator hit 80 and I pulled back on the control wheel. The nose came up and we were airborne.

It was the first time I had commanded the Cherokee Six on a night-time takeoff. As the long nose came up to climb, I felt a brief rush of fear. Ahead there was suddenly nothing to look at but a black void of empty night sky. The nose was up too high for me to see in front of the plane. Without a clear horizon line, it was disorienting to look at the few lights visible out the side windows. They were points in the void and no indication of which way was up or down. I was not an instrument pilot, but I had to fly entirely by instruments, trusting the needles to tell me that we were climbing high enough and going fast enough and flying straight. According to my calculations we were not going to fly into anything, but I badly wanted to see ahead and be sure. I craved altitude, I hungered for thousands of feet between me and the ground, for the roominess and safety of the empty sky.

Finally, we got to 2,000 feet and I leveled off. The lights of the entire city spread out below. Enough were visible to clearly make out the horizon. From then on, I flew visually, with only an occasional glance at the instruments. The red warning lights on the TV towers were easy to see in the clear night air. I slowly banked into a left turn to look for Billy and Jim south of the city.

With altitude and clear air (and enough sleep and a good map), night flight is an awesome and beautiful experience. The countryside beyond Rapid City was dimly visible in the moonlight. Electric lights sparkled all around us, matched by an enormous number of stars twinkling above. Larry's face stood out in warm silhouette as it picked up the faint red illumination from the instrument panel.

For the first time, I noticed the intense noise in the aircraft. The wind blew by the open rear doorway with the force of a hurricane, 155 miles per hour relative to the aircraft. The engine noise on top of the roar of the wind made it difficult to talk. We were all bundled up with caps and scarves and gloves, but Larry signaled with a mock shiver that he was still cold. I pointed up to the thermometer built into the front windshield. It indicated external air temperature at 22° F.

As the southern edge of Rapid City fell behind us, I scanned the sky ahead for the rotating red beacons on the tails of the other two airplanes. Not seeing them against the background of lights on the ground, I dropped the Cherokee down a few hundred feet so we could look up against the sky. They were several miles in front of us. I pushed in the throttle for more airspeed and a few minutes later was passing both airplanes. Giving them a wide berth in the darkness, I pulled abreast of Billy and rocked my wings several times. The red and green lights on his wingtips went up and down in response. It was a signal that I had caught up and all three planes were together. There was no other way to do it in the dark without a radio. When Billy returned my signal, I slowed down and swung back into the number three position behind Jim.

The air was smooth so I tried to fly the airplane a little crooked, pointing it slightly to the left of the course it was actually moving along. This was to keep the open doorway on the left side of the fuselage shielded as much as possible from the airstream. I also had to concentrate on the mountain peaks off to our right. Our course was southerly along the eastern face of the Black Hills. The peaks were oriented on a north-south line parallel to our course and about 15 miles to the side. Since some of them were higher than we were, and invisible in the darkness, correct navigation was critical.

The faint first light of dawn crept into the eastern sky. For the time being I had little to do. It was Tom's turn. Since we were not landing in Hot Springs, he was able to start moving the cargo back toward the rear doorway. It was not possible to take off with the heavy bags already aft, because their weight shifted the aircraft's center of gravity too far back to climb safely. Only at cruising altitude could they be moved. Tom had to drag the three cargo nets—each weighing 200-250 pounds and containing two or three duffel bags—over all the little bumps and ridges that normally held the four missing passenger seats, making certain that the smaller parachute packs remained on top and that the numerous lines did not get tangled. All this had to be done in the confined space of the small cabin, in semidarkness, working only a few feet from the gaping hole in the fuselage where the rear door had been.

The pale blue in the eastern sky spread somewhat, faintly illuminating the larger objects on the ground. I tried to pinpoint our position on the chart, but there were not enough visible landmarks. We were somewhere south and east of Mt. Rushmore, and with so much bare white rock, it should have been visible in the predawn light. Holding the aeronautical chart in front of Larry and indicating the words "Mt. Rushmore," I pointed vaguely back behind us and over to our right, on his side of the airplane, to suggest that he look for the monument. A minute later Larry tapped my shoulder and pointed to the heads of the four Presidents far in the distance, carved into the Sacred Mountains of the Sioux. The light wasn't sufficient to recognize any of the faces, but the outline of the gigantic sculpture was unmistakable.

Sitting behind the controls, I wondered for a moment if any of the faces on the mountain would smile at us knowing what we were about to do. How ironic, I thought, to be flying past that particular symbol of America. But the scene ahead of us was a familiar one to the four Presidents of Rushmore—heavily armed whites on the offensive against native people defending their last piece of free land. Three of the four had personally killed native Americans: Washington, as he led mercenary colonials in the French and Indian War, fighting for a reward of acreage in the Ohio Valley they hoped to conquer; Lincoln, in two tours of voluntary combat duty during the Black Hawk War in Illinois Territory; and Teddy Roosevelt, leading armed American expansion into Latin America and Asia under the racist banner of "manifest destiny." The fourth, Jefferson, had some admirable principles when it came to white males over the age of twenty-one, but unfortunately he considered the rest of humanity inferior and in need of a strong controlling hand. No, I concluded, the Sioux have to look far beyond the trespassing heads on Mt. Rushmore for help in reclaiming their freedom—and so too do all of us seeking the inspiration to build a new and just America.

We continued flying south as the light of April 17 spread across the sky. On our left, the east had quickly become a light blue. Only in the west, over the mountaintops, could we still see the deep purple of night. The heavy duffel bags full of food were too much for Tom. Larry crawled over the front seats into the rear of the cabin and together they managed to move the cargo closer to the open doorway. For a while there was nothing to do. We sat shivering as the plane hurtled us farther south through the cold South Dakota dawn.

It was like hanging in abeyance 2,000 feet in the air. As we looked to the left, we could see the great brown grassland prairies, the end of the American Midwest; on our right were the pinnacles of the Black Hills and the beginning of the western mountains. In the east, over the prairies, it was a new day, while off to our right the mountains still wore the shroud of the previous night. Behind us was the personal safety of legality, and in front, the unknown response of a legally constituted government acting illegally. From out of the past loomed the 19th-century wars against the Indians, and in less than an hour we would see what the 20th century had brought. It was a strange and unstable point of balance, but there was little time to contemplate it as the rotating green and white beacon of the Hot Springs airport came into view.

Billy banked to the left in front of us making a slight course correction toward the beacon. One at a time, Jim and I followed. There was enough light to see the airport's single runway and the outline of the Angostura Reservoir to the south of it. Visibility, as the weatherman had predicted, was unrestricted by haze or moisture. Above us we could see the layer of high thin overcast that was also forecast. We turned to the right of the airport, then Billy leaned his airplane to the left and began flying a wide circle around the field. Jim peeled off behind him, but hesitated long enough to leave plenty of room between their two aircraft. I followed, setting my plane in a shallow left bank that kept us in a circling pattern about three miles across.

My watch read 4:35—nine minutes to circle until we broke for Wounded Knee. The terrain beneath us was clearly visible. The dry grasslands and low rolling hills were dotted with rock formations and bordered by twisting gullies and dry creek beds, some lined with short, gnarled piñon pine which made them stand out from the air. Aside from the piñon pine and a few pockets of cottonwood, the land was treeless. Ten miles west, where the slopes of the Black Hills rose off the plains, there were rich forests fed by water that flowed down from the mountains. But these forests came to an abrupt halt as they merged into the grasslands east of Hot Springs where the Oglala Sioux had been penned up for almost a century.

While I circled and studied the countryside, Tom began to position the duffel bags in the open rear doorway. Since it was cut into the side of the fuselage about six inches above the floor, he had to lift the front of the bags in the first cargo net over the six-inch lip and then laboriously work them out into the airstream, all the while making sure the small parachute pack remained on top of the net and that its lines did not tangle. As he got the first cargo net in place, with a third of its length protruding out of the airplane, I could feel the increased drag on our left side. It was like sticking a paddle out into the wind, and in such a small airplane the controls were noticeably affected.

Next, Tom had to get the duffel bags in the second cargo net up on top of the first. Once in place, it would be possible to lift the inside ends of the top set of bags and easily topple them out of the aircraft. The parachute pack above would topple separately, be torn open by the ripcord, and release the parachute well away from the airplane. Afterward, by simply reaching down, the whole process could be repeated with the bags in the lower cargo net. In five seconds, two-thirds of our load would be on its way down, leaving 35 seconds to get the third cargo net into the doorway and out of the plane.

But the second set of duffel bags was too heavy and clumsy for Tom to lift up on top of the first. We were purposely circling left around Hot Springs rather than right hoping that the shallow bank of the airplane would make it easier to move cargo leftward into the doorway. But the effect was not enough. Larry turned around and saw by the anguish on Tom's face that he had pushed his strength to the limit and was about to give up. Once again, Larry climbed out of the co-pilot's seat and crawled into the rear. Working together, they got the second set of bags up on the first. Then they pushed the third cargo net near the doorway so that it could be quickly moved into position after the first two were toppled out.

Tom's next job was to secure the ripcords. One end of the bright yellow nylon line was fixed to the parachute packs. Tom attached the other to the floor bolts that held the seat belts. It was a static-line system. When the cargo nets were thrown out, the ripcord would tear open the parachute pack and release the canopy. Larry and I watched closely as Tom worked. There were a lot of lines in the cabin and we wanted to be certain that the ripcords were properly attached. A mistake would not only be wasteful but very dangerous to people on the ground.

Right after Tom finished, Billy's voice crackled over the radio. "Five-three-romeo and five-eight-romeo, this is four-one-juliet. The time is now four-forty-four. Acknowledge. Over."

It was the magic moment. I waited for Jim to go first, "Five-eight-romeo, roger," then answered, "Five-three-romeo, roger."

Our planes broke out of the circling pattern and started east, beginning to descend at the same time. We were at the point of no return. If any civilian traffic controllers or military personnel at the Air Force base near Rapid City were casually following our course on radar, they saw us leave the Denver-bound airway and make straight for the restricted zone over Wounded Knee. But what they saw no longer mattered. It was too late to stop us. We were going to get through, all three aircraft and the entire ton of food.

A feeling of relief washed over me as I realized that the final commitment had been made. My eyes met Larry's and we looked at each other with expressions of obvious satisfaction. I clapped him on the knee and turned around to flash a broad grin at Tom. Our planning had been right. We had done our job properly and we were ready to lean back, relax, and watch all the careful choreography come to life.

I took my gloved hand off of the throttle and swung my arm back over the seat to survey the duffel bags sticking out through the open doorway.

"The top two bags aren't out far enough," I shouted to Tom over the engine and the noise of the wind. "You won't be able to topple them unless they're out a little past the two on the bottom."

Tom went to work and I continued maneuvering into formation. We had lost 500 feet and were still 1,500 feet above the ground. The half-V formation was getting tighter, but at least 150 yards remained between the aircraft. Formation flying had become less difficult. I eased the throttle back and forth to narrow the gap between my plane and Jim's, while still performing the flight work for a coordinated descent. I felt confident, almost serene.

Without warning I heard a sharp noise, like a rope snapping taut. A split second later the aircraft was violently jolted. The nose shot upward into a steep climb. All I could see in front of me was the pale white bottom of the clouds above us. Instinctively, I pushed in on the control wheel, struggling to get the ship back down to level flight. But it didn't work—we were still pointed sharply up. Frightened and on the verge of panic, I suddenly understood that I was no longer in control of the airplane.

Tom moaned in the back, almost tearfully, "Oh no, no!" I whipped around to see why. He was up against the wall of the cabin, hand to his face, staring wide-eyed out the open doorway opposite him. Something was wrong back there, but I couldn't tell what. It all looked like it had the last time I turned around, yet it was somehow different. Then I knew. The top pair of duffel bags wasn't there! The two huge bags of food had fallen out of the plane!

I turned forward to fight the controls, stupidly thinking that I understood the problem. But I quickly realized that I understood nothing. The missing bags did not explain my inability to get the airplane back down to level flight. I turned around again, desperate, trying to choke down the fear. My eyes raced around the rear of the cabin, searching for some clue. I saw nothing. But then, amid the tangle of nets and ripcords lying on the floor, I saw a perfectly straight yellow line. Something was being stretched tightly. The bright yellow line pointed straight toward the open rear doorway. I followed it with my eyes, horrified, not believing what I saw. The line went up over the lip of the doorway and down out of view outside the aircraft.

It was a ripcord. I knew it was a ripcord. That was the only thing it could be. And it was stretched tight because something hung from it! That was the reason we were pointed up. The yellow ripcord had not detached from the two duffel bags that fell through the doorway. The bags were still out there. We were flying along with more than 200 pounds of dead weight suspended from the rear of an aircraft that itself had an empty weight of only 1,700 pounds.

As the weight of the duffel bags pulled down our tail, the nose was forced up in a steep climb. But the climb was too steep for the engine. The plane was gradually slowing down. If it got to 63 mph, the stall speed, we would die. Below that speed the wings couldn't provide enough lift to keep us up. The plane would act like any other metal object 1,500 feet in the air—it would fall, straight down. At 63 mph we would slip back into a tail-down stall, and there would be absolutely nothing I could do to get us out of it.

"The bags are hanging out there!" I shouted at Tom, almost screaming. "The ripcord didn't break. Get the knife off the wall and cut the ripcord. Fast."

Two nights before, Jim had taped knives next to the doorway of each plane after we had briefly discussed the possibility of the exact situation we were in. Then it had been almost too much of a long shot to take seriously. But there it was, actually, unbelievably, happening to us.

I looked down at the airspeed indicator—105 mph and falling. I was certain that if the duffel bags were still attached to that ripcord, the parachute was too. It was out there, partially or fully open, creating an enormous amount of braking drag and slowing us down even more drastically. Desperately, I went to work on the controls, reaching down between the seats to spin the trim tab for maximum nose-down position, pulling the lever that extended the flaps, punching the throttle all the way in, and moving the propeller speed knob to the fastest possible setting. The plane was adjusted for maximum descent power. Again I pushed against the control wheel with both hands, but there was still no way to get the ship even close to a horizontal flight position.

I looked back at Tom. He hadn't moved! He was all the way in the rear of the cabin, immobilized. Larry saw it the same instant I did and dove out of the co-pilot's seat into the back. He crawled over the third cargo net down to the open doorway, working his way toward the knife on the wall. It was a dangerous pursuit. He wasn't wearing a safety line, and with the airplane pointed up at such a sharp angle, he could have easily fallen out as he reached for the knife. But there was no hesitation. Larry pulled the knife down and stretched his body across the first cargo net that was still sticking out into the open doorway. The ripcord was on the aft side of it, out of his reach but just in front of Tom. Larry pushed the blade up to Tom's face and shouted at him to take it and cut the ripcord. Tom snapped out of his trance, grabbed the knife from Larry, and started struggling with the yellow nylon line. In front, I kept pushing on the control wheel. My eyes were riveted to the airspeed indicator, the measure of our life or death. Our speed was already down to 87 mph, and I could see the needle dropping one mph every second. We were more than halfway to 63 mph! I looked at the microphone on the instrument panel and thought of the other two aircraft. They were below and in front of us and couldn't possibly be aware of our predicament. But there was no point in radioing them. I didn't want to take my hand off the control wheel, and in any case, there was nothing they could do to help us. If we crashed in that position, there would be no survivors.

Behind me Tom still fought to cut the ripcord. He knew nothing about the stall speed. Helpless myself, I felt driven to tell him how important it was that he work fast, but there was too much engine and wind noise to be understood. A chilling fear began to drag me under. Barely on the sane side of complete panic, I could only yell, "Cut it! Cut it! Cut it! Cut! Cut! Cut!"

Eyes locked on the instrument panel, I didn't know what else to do. I sat watching our lifetimes run out on the dial of a speedometer. . . .85 . . .84 . . .83 . . . To die like that, seated, facing forward in the pilot's seat as the plane suddenly started to fall, backward. . . . 82 . . . 81 . . . 80 . . . To die falling backward against the earth . . . it was unthinkable. I continued to shout, "Cut! Cut! Cut! Cut! Cut!" . . . 79 . . . 78 . . . 77 . . . Yet, soaked through with the fear of death, I began to hear my voice almost from outside myself. . . . 76 . . . 75 . . . 74 . . . The cry of "Cut!" grew monotonous and tiresome. I stopped, suddenly furious at the absurdity of such a death. . . . 73 . . . 72 . . . 71 . . . I wanted to abandon the controls, climb into the back, and attack the yellow nylon that was killing us all. Then, as abruptly as it began, it was over!

Tom cut through the ripcord. The duffel bags and their trailing parachute fell down and away. The airplane's nose dropped below the horizon like a stone and we started picking up precious airspeed. Cautiously, afraid to believe it, I moved the control wheel in and out and the ship went up and down on command, just like it was supposed to. With the lifeblood of speed returning, I cut back the throttle, reduced the propeller speed, and returned the trim tab and flaps to their normal position. The other two planes were several hundred feet below us and a half mile ahead. Shocked and nervous, but anxious to rejoin them and continue, I increased the airspeed and sharpened our glide slope enough to catch up.

Larry crawled into the co-pilot's seat on my right and buckled himself in. Our eyes met briefly, but nothing was said. We were both too rattled to communicate. I was slowly swelling with anger, and I didn't know where to direct it. "How could something like that happen?" I asked myself. "How could we be so careless not to foresee it?"

At that moment, I realized Larry and Tom were more bewildered than anything else. Their experience of the emergency had not been the same as mine. Neither knew how close our escape had been. Tom didn't know enough about airplanes to understand a stall. He and Larry were both unaware of our speed and the fact that we were slowing down so drastically. My own near panic could have only confused and frightened them. (Larry would tell me much later that several times after that flight he was awakened by a recurrent nightmare in which he dropped the knife out of the doorway before being able to hand it to Tom.)

Tension hung in the air like static, but I was too upset and too busy maneuvering us back into the half-V formation to offer an explanation. Tom was in the extreme rear sobbing that he was to blame for the disaster. Larry got up again, compassionately making his way into the back to steady him. I kept my attention forward as my mind wandered, angrily searching for an explanation and for someone to blame.

Tom could not have pushed the duffel bags out far enough for them to fall by themselves. They were certainly too heavy to be sucked out by the wind. But the small parachute pack on top was not. It must have been blown out of the open doorway. Outside, it split open, releasing the parachute canopy, which in turn opened, inflated, and pulled out the heavy food bags. The ripcord must have then gotten entangled in the cargo net.

Blame was more difficult to determine. First, I cursed Tom for not holding the parachute pack down. Then I faulted myself for telling him to push the bags out farther. Next I went after Jim. It was his responsibility to anticipate everything that could go wrong with the equipment, and he had not stressed the importance of holding the parachute packs down when the cargo nets were moved. Yet Jim had most certainly saved our lives by taping the knife to the wall. Ultimately, I had only myself to blame. I was in command of the aircraft, and I had overall leadership of the airlift. Everyone's mistakes were partly my responsibility.

But assigning guilt was a waste of time. We had caught up with the other two planes, and I slid into a tight number three position in the formation behind Jim.

Still aboard were two cargo nets full of food bags—over 400 pounds. Billy had three cargo nets on his plane and there were four on Jim's. Only two duffel bags out of twenty-two were lost. The analysis could come later. We had work to do. I turned around, still on edge and impatient, and shouted back to Larry and Tom.

"Let's go, you guys. Get that third cargo net up on the first one. We're only twenty minutes from Wounded Knee."

The set of duffel bags lying next to the doorway had to go on top of the pair already in the doorway—to replace the two that had gone over the side. It was the same task that had gotten us in trouble before, but it had to be done. I tried not to further humiliate Tom by reminding him to hold down the parachute pack, but in the end it wasn't possible to restrain myself. Despite my abruptness, though, Tom and Larry got right at the work, obviously glad for something to do.

The three-plane formation was below 500 feet and continuing its slow descent. Tom and Larry, shaken by the trauma we had just gone through, were having a difficult time lifting the clumsy duffel bags. They took frequent rests. I was anxious they finish and several times tried to coax them on, but it was only badgering. When they did get done, Larry got back into the co-pilot's seat and Tom positioned himself next to the cargo so he could hold down the uppermost parachute pack. We were ready, for the second time, to make the drop. The strained atmosphere in the airplane subsided considerably.

It was then, with calm restored, that I slowly realized something was wrong with the control wheel in my hands. The aircraft was level and descending in a straight line, but subconsciously I had been holding the wheel turned far to the left. With the control wheel in that position, the airplane should have been in a steeply banked left turn, not level and flying straight. I wiggled the wheel around and the plane responded properly. I was more annoyed than anything else. In any case, I didn't expect the problem to be very serious since the aircraft was definitely under my control. Perplexed, I examined the instruments one at a time and then the other flight controls in a methodical search for the trouble. But I found nothing. With no place else to look, I turned in my seat to make a perfunctory check of the rear of the cabin.

Everything appeared normal. My glance aimlessly drifted out the open rear doorway where Tom sat next to the food bags. The door was six feet behind me, and looking through it on a sharp angle I had a fleeting glimpse of the tail. What I thought I saw so horrified me that for a moment I dismissed it as impossible and looked away. But erupting fear drove my eyes back toward the door. The terrifying image was real—part of the tail was gone!

I couldn't believe it. The left horizontal tail fin ended in a stump of bare and twisted metal. The outboard two feet had been torn off. I leaned over Larry to look out the window on the right side of the plane. It was true! The right side of the tail was undeniably longer than what remained on the left. For the second time in only a few minutes I fought down intense fears of death and desperately tried to clear my mind enough to think rationally about what to do. Airplanes can't fly without their tails. The horizontal part keeps the aircraft level. The rear section of it, the elevators, are the controls the pilot uses to go up and down. Without them, the plane would nose over and dive into the ground. But we were still flying. Elevator control was intact, and by turning the wheel to the left, I had unknowingly found a way to use the ailerons on the wing to compensate for the loss of stability in the tail. . . . at least for the time being.

Mustering what courage I had, I turned again to inspect the damaged tail. Normally, the horizontal part extends about six feet out from the fuselage. We had only a four-foot stump, and even it showed additional damage. Its entire surface, top and bottom, was rippled and bent by the impact of the lost duffel bags that had torn off the outboard section. Airflow over the remaining length was disrupted, reducing its stabilizing properties even further. Leaning over Larry again to check the right tail fin, I saw that its surface too was bent and rippled. Dizzy and nauseous with fright, I realized that the impact on the left side could have been strong enough to weaken the structural supports that held the entire tail assembly onto the fuselage. The possibility existed that any minute the whole tail would come off, leaving us helpless and quite unavoidably dead.

It was all I could do to maintain self-control. I told myself that if I let up, even for an instant, the fear would overwhelm me and we would be lost. I decided against telling Larry and Tom about the damage, at least for the moment. If either of them was to panic, it would be that much harder for me to swallow my own fear. In any case, there was no time to explain either the damage or the danger. I wasn't planning to stay airborne long enough to have a conversation.

The word "emergency" flashed on and off in my brain and I raced through the check list of things to do in a forced landing. I was preparing to crash land the aircraft on the prairie. "It'll only take a minute to descend from 500 feet," I thought. "If the tail stays on for another 60 seconds, we'll live."

The rolling rocky hills below were clearly visible in the predawn light. Suddenly I knew that it would take more than the tail staying on to bring us in safely. Landing on the rough terrain was certain to damage the plane even more, and if our luck didn't hold, injure all of us as well. I had second thoughts about what to do. The first wave of fear subsided, and I began to weigh our options more logically. The aircraft, despite its severe damage, was still under my control. There was no turbulence or gusty wind. If I kept the plane flying at a constant speed, with no bumps or swerves, the pressure on the tail could be kept to a minimum. Maybe it would stay on. It had, up to that point.

Over 400 pounds of food sat behind me. We had nursed it for days across a thousand miles of America. We had committed ourselves, utterly, to delivering it to Wounded Knee. In fifteen more minutes, we would be there. Fifteen minutes. I looked down at the uneven landscape. With a little luck, I knew I could land and not kill us in the process. But what of the tail? There was no guarantee it would stay on, even for the 60 seconds it would take me to make an emergency landing. "If it stayed on for that one minute," I thought, "why wouldn't it stay on for another fourteen?"

We had no choice but to risk death for the next minute. If we could endure it that long, we could endure it longer. I looked down at my hands and the control wheel I was turning so far over to the left, then back at the food and at the unknowing faces of Larry and Tom. We had to go on! No other choice was possible. I started undoing my preparations for the emergency landing and gently easing the crippled aircraft back toward its number three position in the formation.

Jim's airplane floated 150 yards in front of me. Billy's was beyond it and to the left. Still awash with fear and shock, I fidgeted in my seat. Every few seconds, like a nervous twitch, I jerked around to look through the rear doorway at the broken tail fin, magically trying to hold it to the plane with my gaze.

Our three-plane formation was descending to tree-top level. If I started to lose elevator control before we got to Wounded Knee, at least I would be in position to make an immediate emergency landing. Hopefully, it would not happen over rocks or a twisting creek bed. The other two aircraft did not know the danger we were in. If I made a forced landing, I would have to radio them to circle overhead until we were safely down. If medical help had to be summoned, the incident would alert authorities that unauthorized aircraft were in the vicinity of Wounded Knee. The two other planes would then have to abort the mission or fly over Wounded Knee at a time when nearly everyone below expected their arrival. There was a distinct possibility that none of the 2,000 pounds of food would get through. That only made me more determined to go on.

Several miles ahead and off to our right, the few street lights in Oglala stood out against the brown landscape. The old country road we were following curved south toward the small reservation town, but we continued flying east guided then only by our compasses. Again I looked back at the mangled tail, flexing fingers stiff from clenching the control wheel.

We were at the altitude we wanted, less than 100 feet above the ground. It was so low, Billy and Jim were going up and down with the terrain, gaining altitude over the small hills and descending into the washes and little valleys. I stayed at a constant altitude 50 feet above them, not wanting to put additional pressure on the tail by following the terrain up and down. For the first time in many minutes I felt the cold air rushing through the plane. The rocks, the crests of the ridge lines, the occasional trees, all sped past below us. In fantastic close-up I watched the two other planes sink down and away and then abruptly rise back up toward me. It was like flying over an ocean of land—there were no signs of life below, only the huge waves of barren brown prairie.

I looked behind me again. The missing part of the tail had been separately riveted to the rest of the horizontal stabilizer. The impact tore out the rivets as the heavy duffel bags sliced through. But I didn't know how many of the rivets holding the rest of the tail onto the aircraft had also been destroyed and how many might still be popping out as a result of the airplane's continued flight.

I was helpless. I had to sit passively by as forces outside my control determined whether the three of us would live or die, forces to which our lives were merely incidental. Powerless and afraid, I felt on the verge of being strangled by panic. To push it away, I tried to keep busy mentally. I literally forced questions into my mind so I could keep myself preoccupied looking for their answers. "What if we did get to Wounded Knee?" I asked. "What were the options then?"

I could land the airplane on a road immediately after we made the drop. Aeronautically, that was the safest thing to do, short of landing it right there where we were on the prairie. But if we got all the food into Wounded Knee, federal agents or vigilantes might be angry enough to shoot at us if we attempted a landing. They wouldn't know it was an emergency—and they might not care even if they did know. I could make the drop and land five or ten miles away. That would keep us from getting shot, but there would be no way to escape an arrest. We couldn't just walk away from an aircraft out in the middle of the reservation. And when federal officers got our registration number they could quickly trace it back to Midway Airport in Chicago and eventually get all of our friends as well. To make the drop and really have a chance of escape, we would have to risk flying far enough away to get the plane repaired without anyone suspecting it came from Wounded Knee. That would mean hours more of stress on the uncertain tail assembly, flying with the knowledge that at any moment the plane might nose over and dive the short distance into the ground.

While I filled up my head with various contingencies, Larry made small talk, trying to reduce the tension that remained from the ripcord-cutting episode. Through no fault of his own, he was unable to affect what was really troubling me. I answered him with an abrupt nod or a single word. When he asked what was wrong, I snapped back that everything was fine. I couldn't conceal my nervousness. At first, Larry was bewildered, then he began to resent it. I still thought it a mistake to tell Tom and him about the smashed tail. They were even more helpless than I, and that made a panic reaction all the more likely. If they knew the truth, they might insist on an immediate landing. I would disagree, and by the time we talked it out and voted we'd be at Wounded Knee. I'd tell them right after the drop.

The lights of Oglala soon passed under my right wing tip, off to the south. Wounded Knee was twelve minutes away. It was time for Billy and Jim to switch places in the formation. Billy's navigating work was over. Now it was the responsibility of hastily recruited Oliver, sitting in the co-pilot's seat next to Jim.

Since we had gradually slowed the 155-mph Cherokees down to 120 mph, they had plenty of speed left in them. Jim's plane seemed to jump out of the middle position in the formation. He banked to the right, passed Billy, swung back to the left, and throttled down to 120 mph. Billy accelerated slightly to come up just behind and to the right of him. When Billy was settled into the number two position, I started very gingerly inching my way forward to close the distance between our planes. When only two plane lengths separated my nose from Billy's tail, we were set. Crippled tail or not, we were going through with the airlift. Everything was still on schedule. Our three little planes formed a perfect diagonal as we skimmed along only a stone's throw above the ground. We flew as the birds fly—close to the ground and in the company of our own kind.

For a few minutes I was able to lose my fear in the stark beauty of our flight. Two events bracketed our existence: Wounded Knee in the future and the mid-air collision of duffel bags and tail in the past. But for those few minutes, the brackets seemed to stretch away from the present. The little hills rose quickly toward us, and then, as we flashed past their crest lines, they fell sharply away to the barren gullies below. Dull white rocks rushed at us out of the sides of some of the hills between patches of tall brown grass pushing their way up through the dusty soil. Crooked rows of stunted pine shot by the windows, revealing the pathways of the infrequent water. I let myself see the drama of the rugged land and the two aircraft in front of me faithfully following its every contour. It was a moment of intermission, a welcome escape from our terrifying vigil. I felt refreshed and even enjoyed being there in that sky on the way toward what we were doing.

Ahead, the lights of Manderson appeared in the distance. It was the last settlement before Wounded Knee, and it bristled with government forces. When we got within four miles, we had to make a half-right turn off our easterly heading in order to approach Wounded Knee from the northwest and remain adequately clear of Manderson. I looked again at the damaged tail fin. It loomed back there like a vision of death. I shifted in my seat and flexed my fingers still tightly clutching the leftward control wheel. Enjoyment and fear were swept away by intense concentration on piloting the airplane. Then, in front of me, Jim's plane banked into the half-right turn. A second later, Billy dropped his right wing and followed, and a second after that, I gently dipped to the right following Billy. The dance had begun.

Manderson lay off to the left, tugging at my attention. There were guns there, guns that could radio other guns at Wounded Knee to warn of our approach. We remained low, too far away to be shot at but close enough to be heard. In the early morning silence, the roar of the three 300-horsepower engines would carry for miles. At that moment, armed goons and federal agents sleeping in Manderson would be waking up and asking each other whose side our noisy aircraft were on. The little town

passed under our left wing tips. We were exactly eight miles from
Wounded Knee. Four minutes and thirty seconds to go.

I told Larry and Tom to ready themselves for the drop. Tom crawled
around opposite the inside ends of the duffel bags sticking out the
doorway. When we got the signal from Jim over the radio, he had to lift
them up and topple them out, two at a time. Larry crawled into the rear to
help if he was needed.

The hills and rocks and grass rolled by beneath us. I concentrated on
the engine and flight controls, making last minute adjustments in the fuel
flow and propeller speed and trying to maintain my position in the
formation as precisely as possible. I was completely absorbed by the work
of flying and the overwhelming excitement of being so close. No longer
afraid, every unit in my nervous system seemed focused on doing the job.
The minutes slipped by. Jim's plane began to rise out of the formation.
He was on his way to 500 feet, the drop altitude. His plane, pointed only
slightly upward, appeared to float vertically away from us. Billy responded on cue, leaning back and climbing in close pursuit. Nursing our
damaged tail, I eased in the throttle, very gently pulled back on the
control wheel, and followed them up.

The ground slowly dropped away and the landscape spread out before
us. At 200 feet, what had been a white spot in the distance became a
lonesome country church sitting on an otherwise empty hill some three
miles ahead. The low hill was cut by a dirt driveway that snaked up to the
steepled church building. From pictures I recognized it as the Sacred
Heart Catholic Church, built next to the grave of the 1890 massacre
victims. We were almost there. The tail had held and we were going to
make the drop.

We hit 500 feet a mile and a half from the church. On the far side I
could see the trading post and the small clump of buildings called
"downtown Wounded Knee." The Manderson road, one of the four that
led out of the "downtown" area, pointed toward us. We had been flying
alongside it, but off to the side, for the past few miles. Less than a half mile
out from "downtown," a dozen homes were built around a block-long
street that paralleled the Manderson road. According to the map drawn
for us in Rapid City, this cluster of homes sat just inside the northwest
corner of the defense perimeter. We were heading right at them.

The climb had slightly increased the spread in our formation. I started
slowly closing the gap between my plane and Billy's, trying not to pick up
too much airspeed. The slower we were the less the shock on the
parachute lines when the big canopies opened up. In a few seconds we
had a perfect 100 mph diagonal line. I shouted back at Tom to get set.

A half mile from the cluster of homes, I looked down at the Manderson
road. For weeks I had seen news pictures of government weapons at

Wounded Knee. For days I had prepared for a personal confrontation with those weapons. But when I looked down from the cabin of that small airplane and saw what appeared to be a tank only a block or so away from me, I could hardly believe my eyes.

In fact it was an olive drab armored personnel carrier with a big white Army star. Along with several cars, the APC was parked next to a barricade that stretched across the Manderson road. To the side of this barricade, several bunkers were dug out of the ground and reinforced with stacks of sandbags. It was a federal roadblock. A hundred feet farther away from Wounded Knee, a more ragtag roadblock consisting of two cars cut across the highway. It belonged to the goon squad.

Looking out at the entire panorama now visible before us, I saw Wounded Knee surrounded on all sides by APCs. Some were on roads, others loomed grotesquely over the tiny settlement from nearby hilltops. Each of the four roads leading out of the village was blocked, and next to every roadblock were satellite bunkers and sandbagged trenches. I was stunned. We had flown out of the United States and into a war! It looked like a piece of South Viet Nam, APCs and all, cut out of Indochina and dropped into the middle of South Dakota. TV footage and newspaper pictures were no preparation for the real thing—they never are.

I looked at my watch. It was exactly 5:06. Dawn. There wasn't a single person visible anywhere. It was just as we planned.

In the lead aircraft, Jim concentrated on the clump of houses next to the Manderson road. They would be his key point for starting the drop. With Oliver on his right and John in the rear ready with the cargo, Jim was wide-eyed and alert, his body a muffled explosion of adrenalin. The APCs distracted him for an instant, but his excitement kept him from seeing any other details. Except for one. Smoke was rising from a small fire in the center of town. For the past few days, expecting us to land a small plane on one of their roads, people in Wounded Knee had kept a smoking fire burning to show us the wind. Jim used it to confirm the .ight southwesterly breeze we had planned on.

For the past several minutes, Oliver had been excitedly bouncing up and down, saying that the village ahead was really Wounded Knee. As they approached the two Manderson roadblocks, Jim pointed beyond them to the cluster of homes.

"Is that what we want?" he demanded of Oliver. "Is that the key point? Is that it, right there?"

Oliver nodded so violently he had to hold on to the instrument panel with both hands. Jim flew past the roadblocks toward the clump of houses. As he got to the first one, he banked into a half-right turn, assuming a southerly course along the western edge of the defense perimeter. The Manderson road was off to his left. A split-second later, past the last house in the cluster, he snapped around and shouted, "Now, John, now!" Jim then pressed the button on the microphone he had been clutching and shouted, "Go, go, go, go, go."

Meanwhile, John grabbed the inside ends of the top set of duffel bags and tumbled them out. Then he reached down, took hold of the ends of the bottom set, and lifted them up and out. It took only seconds. As he hauled the third and fourth cargo nets back toward the rear doorway, Jim flew past the white church on the hilltop. He continued south to the trading post in the center of Wounded Knee, the halfway point in our right-angle drop run, then made a full left turn to an easterly heading. Banked into the turn, he was able to look back at the sky they had just flown through. One parachute had not opened. The big red canopy streamered in the wind as it trailed behind two falling duffel bags.

Flying across the southern part of Wounded Knee, Jim started hollering at John to get the rest of the cargo out the door. But John wasn't able to move the heavy bags fast enough. Anguished, Jim saw that John couldn't make it in the 15 seconds they had left in the drop zone. He thought about the streamering parachute, knowing that when the two duffel bags beneath it hit the ground, most of their contents would be destroyed. Still no people were visible below. No bullets had torn into the aircraft. With twice as much aboard his plane as he had safely delivered, Jim decided there was no choice but to make a second pass over Wounded Knee.

He rolled into a steep right turn and dove for the ground, planning to fly into one of the shallow valleys south of Wounded Knee. By keeping a hilltop or a ridge line between himself and the guns, he could work his way back around at low altitude out of sight and suddenly re-emerge at the northwest corner to begin the drop run all over again.

"John, we're going back for another pass," Jim yelled. "Get that load set up in the doorway, pronto."

"I can't move these damn bags. Send Oliver back here."

With an angle of bank over 50°, the G-force of Jim's steep turn doubled the weight of everything in the airplane, including the food bags. Oliver pulled off his seat belt and, struggling against his own body weight, also doubled by the steep turn, dragged himself out of the co-pilot's seat and worked his way into the rear of the cabin.

Meanwhile, Billy had been following forty yards behind Jim. Just before the drop, Billy was concentrating on keeping a safe distance from the lead plane. He was thinking very logically, like an engineer.

"All right," he said to himself, "the chutes are going to start coming out. That means the load's going to decrease. The airplane will get lighter. That means it's going to fly faster and start gaining altitude. So I've got to gradually ease off on the throttle."

Suddenly, the radio exploded with the words, "Go, go, go, go, go."
Billy saw a package flying out the door of the lead plane. His tottering
engineer's composure readily collapsed. "Strobe," he shouted, "get that
shit out of here!"

Strobe toppled out the two cargo nets prepositioned in the doorway.
The second grazed the tail as it fell away. Billy felt it as a slight jolt in the
control wheel. There was no damage, but Billy was left nervous and
uneasy. He knew nothing of the damage done to my tail assembly. As he
sped by the Catholic Church and then the trading post, Billy banked into
the left turn behind Jim and looked back to see Strobe still struggling with
their one remaining cargo net.

"I can't do it," Strobe moaned. "It's too heavy. It won't go over the lip
in the door."

There was no one else in Billy's plane to help. He could see that Strobe
had worked hard on the first two nets and was exhausted. As he came out
of the left turn, Billy knew that only a half mile of safe drop zone remained
in front of him. He thought about the second pass that he never wanted to
make. Just then, on the government side of the defense perimeter below,
he saw something move. An olive green car stopped abruptly at the
federal roadblock directly in front of him. Out popped a man in a light
brown uniform. The man put his hands on his hips, cocked his head back,
and stared up at the sky.

"Look at that fool," Billy thought to himself, "I bet he's wondering
what the hell is going on here." The uniformed man standing furious on
the barren hillside, lifted one arm and shook an impotent fist at the three
airplanes roaring by overhead.

But Billy felt like a sitting duck. He was sure that if he went around for a
second pass, the outraged officer would be waiting for him with a gun.
And by that time, the engine noise would have awakened every
sharpshooter in the area. He crouched low over the control wheel inside
the plane. All of a sudden, govenment M-16s and goon squad hunting
rifles flooded into his imagination.

He had already delivered two-thirds of his load. "No," Billy decided,
"it definitely ain't worth it for one more cargo net. I'm getting the hell out
of here."

Billy jammed the throttle all the way in and the little airplane shot
forward, overflying the federal roadblock. Worried that someone might
be shooting at him from behind, he stayed bent over the control wheel,
trying to coax more speed out of his aircraft. Past the roadblock, he
pushed the plane down into a valley, seeking the shelter of an obscuring
hilltop. He went very low. Suddenly, Billy thought he saw smoke pouring
into his cabin. He looked for signs of a fire but soon realized he was so
close to the ground that the propeller wash was actually throwing up a
cloud of dust as he flew along.

As the drop began, I was trying not to think about the danger back in our damaged tail section. I approached the cluster of homes in the northwest corner of Wounded Knee and looked down on the U.S. military might surrounding the Indians. It was a bittersweet moment —feeling myself disgusted with the government yet happy that I had decided to push the crippled plane on and do the drop instead of attempting an emergency landing back on the prairie.

"Forty seconds," I thought, "if the tail stays together for forty more seconds, we'll drop the food and be gone."

Gazing down through the side window as we flew into the drop zone, I saw no one on the ground. Only the smoke moved. It was like flying over a Hollywood set, except the sinister APCs lurked in every corner of the aerial panorama, looking convincingly real and thoroughly dangerous. Then the radio burst to life with the sound of Jim's voice.

"Go, go, go, go, go."

The command filled our airplane. As I turned in my seat, I saw Tom .already toppling the top set of duffel bags out the doorway. Seconds later, he lifted the other cargo net off the cabin floor and it too fell cleanly away. I laughed, thinking there was hardly any tail left for them to hit.

With all our bags out, I banked into a left turn just past the white church instead of flying all the way to the trading post. That way I was able to keep the angle of bank low and avoid undue stress on our tail. Meanwhile, Larry strapped himself back into the co-pilot's seat. We looked at each other and smiled our pride and sense of satisfaction. We had done it!

Tom lay down on the floor of the cabin and looked at the parachutes out the rear doorway. Larry and I watched through the side windows. As we swung through the left turn, we could see the trail of billowing parachutes left by the three planes. They looked magnificent floating gracefully toward the ground. Five open canopies formed a dotted line in the sky parallel to and slightly west of the Manderson road. In unison, they rode the light southwest wind toward the middle of the Indian-controlled highway. By the time I rolled out of the gently banked turn, they hit—almost simultaneously and right on target.

Abruptly, more than 50 Indians erupted from the ground on both sides of the road. They flowed in streams toward the five parachutes, collapsing the huge canopies and detaching the duffel bags from the cargo netting. In an instant, people were running all over in a scene of wild and exuberant pandomonium. Some jumped up and down and waved their jackets at us. Others danced around hugging anyone within reach. Wounded Knee, empty and deserted a moment before, was alive and bursting with energy. We could almost hear their shouts and touch the overwhelming joy we knew they felt.

For us it was a fantastic sight, a golden moment of intense gratification. But for me it lasted only a few seconds. Continuing eastward and beginning to lose altitude for our escape, I was quickly preoccupied with thoughts of our damaged tail and how far we could safely fly.

Ahead of me, Jim banked hard to the right on his way back to Wounded Knee. He lost altitude rapidly and was soon well south of the village, flying inside a shallow valley. As he sped through, heading back west, he was obscured by a hill and safe from both federal and goon squad gun positions. It took less than a minute to get to the Big Foot Trail, the highway that ran south from Wounded Knee toward Pine Ridge. Jim's plane flashed by it, then skipped over a ridge immediately to the west. On the other side he dropped below the crest line and turned north, keeping the ridge between himself and Wounded Knee. Unable to see the village, Jim couldn't tell when he was exactly opposite the northwest corner of the defense perimeter. He guessed the location, made a sharp climbing right turn, throttled down to a slower speed and burst over the hill into the sky above Wounded Knee.

John and Oliver had the two cargo nets still on board positioned in the doorway. As their plane raced back eastward over Wounded Knee, Jim shouted to drop the bags. The two men in the rear quickly tumbled out the food. They watched as the parachutes rippled out behind the duffel bags and spread into mushrooming hemispheres to float the short distance to the ground. The two new loads landed west of the crowd already surrounding the first five. They hit the ground inside the defense perimeter but closer to federal positions.

Jim saw the jubilant people for only a moment before he banked into a half-right turn, jammed his throttle all the way up for maximum speed, and pushed the control wheel forward to lose altitude. Levelling out on a southeasterly course at 200 feet and 160 mph, he made his getaway.

It was quite an aerial show and it was over in a twinkling. Three little planes darted about dropping parachutes and then scattered as quickly as they had appeared. Of the ten cargo nets we had, one fell out of my plane on the prairie, one never got out of Billy's plane, and one of Jim's crashed into the ground in Wounded Knee under a streamering parachute. Seven reached the besieged Indians—over 1,500 pounds of food.

For the most part, the drop had gone according to plan. So did the escape. Billy flew straight east, kicking up a cloud of dust as he went. Jim cut to the right toward the southeast. I made a very gradual left turn, guiding our damaged aircraft off toward the northeast. I was afraid to alter any of the forces acting on the airplane. Seeing no one outside the APCs or anywhere on the government side of the defense perimeter, and knowing nothing of the few shots being fired behind us, hostile gunfire did not concern me. I let the plane slowly settle down to an altitude of 200 feet and left the throttle where it was at 100 mph.

The time had come to decide how much farther to fly. The safest procedure was to get a short distance from Wounded Knee, away from all the guns, and land the mangled airplane on a road. But that meant almost certain arrest. The alternative was to fly completely out of the area to a major airport several hundred miles away and claim we lost our tail in a collision with a large bird. It was a choice between safety and escape. The sooner we put down, the safer we were. The longer we stayed up, the less likely any of our friends would be arrested by police or FBI agents or penalized by the FAA. I looked back at the twisted tail, asking myself how much longer it could last—and, at the same time, how much more strain I could endure. My eyes went down to the bleak hills and brown buffalo grass below. There was very little time to decide.

14

The Food
and the Fire Fight

"If a man loses anything and goes back and looks carefully for it, he will find it, and that is what the Indians are doing now when they ask you to give them the things that were promised them in the past; and I do not consider that they should be treated like beasts, and that is the reason I have grown up with the feelings I have. . . . I feel that my country has gotten a bad name, and I want it to have a good name; and I sit sometimes and wonder who it is that has given it a bad name."

—Tatanka Yotanka (Sitting Bull)
Medicine Man and Chief,
Hunkpapa Sioux, 1877.

April 17, 1973, was the 50th day of the occupation of Wounded Knee. Twelve days before, on April 5, a single delivery of food was allowed into the besieged settlement as part of the unsuccessful truce agreement signed on that date. It was the first open shipment in more than three weeks. Since mid-March, all the people in Wounded Knee had been entirely dependent for their food supply on daring overland backpackers infiltrating through the government lines at night. But the supply dwindled as fewer and fewer backpackers escaped arrest and armed assaults on the trail.

By mid-April, Wounded Knee existed in a state of semistarvation. A medical team, which also had to infiltrate through government lines, reported signs of "irreversible" malnutrition in the younger children. The risk of epidemic disease had become significant when the fresh water was cut off, disrupting sanitation facilities and forcing the use of contaminated water. The federal marshals and FBI agents were keeping fire fights to a

268

minimum and relying instead on isolation and starvation. They expected the occupation to collapse at any moment.

Dennis Banks remembered those days as the most difficult ones inside Wounded Knee.

"Part of my duties," he said, "had to do with keeping up the morale of the people. Every night we got together and sang and the medicine men led different kinds of gatherings and gave the people spiritual direction. But when food got really low, morale started going right down with it.

"At the point when we first started running short, we began to issue rations for food. We went down to two meals a day. We had been eating three meals a day there, before that, but we realized that food was getting short and we decided to make it two meals a day. Then finally it got down to one meal a day.

"We organized a food train going in and out every night. We had it staggered. Every night we would send out fifteen people and every night a different fifteen people would come in with food. But then the government lines began to tighten. Fewer got out, and fewer came back. Finally it was one or two people getting out and maybe one coming back in. The snow and the blizzard made it even harder.

"It came down to where we had to eat one meal every other day with just soup in between. It was tough. With all that hunger it was hard to keep up everybody's morale. Towards the middle part of the occupation, the APCs would warm up their engines every morning. Then they'd start the gunfire. Several times, F-4 Phantom jets from Ellsworth Air Force Base would zoom over about 200 feet above us. The morale was really getting low.

"At one point, when we still had a few backpackers going in and out, we tried to organize some food from the outside. We asked people for air support. We wanted them to come in and land a little plane full of food inside Wounded Knee. Then we would get word that at four o'clock the next afternoon, there was going to be an airplane coming in.

"Four o'clock would come and five o'clock would come, but there would be no airplane. Then they'd say, 'Well, it's going to be six o'clock tomorrow morning.' Six o'clock tomorrow would come and the plane never came. No food. Finally, it was at a point where there was just no food at all. We began to send out the old people.

"For two weeks before that I was putting a daily newspaper out to all the people in Wounded Knee telling them what was happening. We found this old mimeograph machine and we put it in order. I tried to write in things to keep the morale up. I'd write in little jokes every day. I kept that newspaper up for about two weeks, but it was getting very hard in there.

"The food was gone. It was exhausted and some of the people were wanting to give up. I know the government realized that we were out of food. Every time some people were trying to get in with food, they'd start a big fire fight. Sometimes they'd fire thousands of rounds of ammunition in one night. That would discourage people from coming in with more food. And of course the government was always saying that negotiations were about to bring an end to the occupation, that any day it would be over. This was also discouraging a lot of people from bringing in more food.

"It was getting pretty desperate in there. Then early one morning—I used to do the newsletter at night and I'd finish it up at about six in the morning—I was sitting there working on it just after it got light out. We had converted one of those old houses into our headquarters and I was sitting in there looking out the window trying to figure out what to write. I could see some of the warriors walk by and a few of them looked in to find out if any food had come in that night.

"Suddenly, I heard this real faint noise, humming-like. The day before that, and the day before that, we had heard on these radios that the marshals and the government were planning to move in on us in planes and they were going to tear gas us all out of Wounded Knee and they were going to use choppers and they were going to use these Phantoms, these jet fighter planes, and everything else.

"And that morning it was real quiet, and I suddenly heard this noise. It was way, way off in the distance. Then it was getting louder and getting louder. First it was humming and then . . . it was engines, we could hear engines!

"At first people started running into the headquarters there. They told us that the feds and the marshals were moving in, and that the Army was moving in. They said they could hear planes coming in and we should get ready for a gas attack and stuff like that. Then some people said it wasn't the Army because we heard a few shots up in the direction that the engine noise was coming from. They figured it must be somebody else because the feds wouldn't shoot at their own planes.

"People and warriors were moving in and out of the headquarters, but then everyone took cover just in case. The noise was getting louder and louder and louder. I ran outside to a bunker. When I looked up, I saw that these three planes were coming in and they were flying at such a low level that I realized it couldn't be the military, it couldn't be an attack; it was for us, it couldn't be anything else but a drop for us.

"Pretty soon we saw these bundles come flying out of the planes and then we saw a line of parachutes opening up. We knew it was a food drop. These bundles were coming down and everyone went running over to get them. People began hollering and screaming. Jeez, they were grabbing each other and screaming up and down and crying. The women started crying and the guys were just laughing and crying at the same time."

Half an hour before the airlift arrived over Wounded Knee, while Dennis was at the mimeograph machine working on the newspaper, Gladys Bissonette woke up and began her day's work. With the rest of the staff assigned to her kitchen, she prepared food for the people coming off nighttime security duty. The meal was simple—a bowl of rice sweetened with white corn syrup.

"That morning it was real early and we were all down in the kitchen talking," Gladys recalled. "All of a sudden I heard gunshots coming from the Manderson direction. I'd say we heard at least eight gunshots. So I said to my friend, 'Did you hear all them gunshots?'" And she said, 'Yeah.' I said, 'I don't think that it's our bunkers because it sounds too far off, too far in the distance.'

"About that time we heard an airplane and we thought that it was the government helicopter. You know, they had been harassing us with airplanes and helicopters. But they didn't dare come over our perimeter. So, I said, 'It's probably a helicopter,' and we ran outside to see.

"Well, we looked up and here come these three airplanes. We didn't know who they were because no one had told us. Not even the leaders knew. They saw those planes coming in that close and—these leaders that we had are pretty wise—they had a feeling, and they said that those planes just had to be for us!

"So the leaders told people not to shoot and nobody shot at those planes from our side. We got out there and watched them. Everybody ran outside to watch the planes, and they just came down and dropped all that food to us. Somebody hollered, 'Food! Food!' and all these people started running toward where the food was falling.

"Even the marshals ran down the hill from their bunkers. They were running toward the food drop, too. You could see them running down the hill with their guns aimed up toward them airplanes. But those little planes just pulled out and away they went.

"Then one of them come back around and dropped more food. The federal marshals kept running down that hill aiming their guns at that one plane. Why some of those marshals were almost down to our bunkers and our boys shot warning shots over them 'cause they were trying to get that food away from us. That made them go back, but then them crazy marshals started firing machine guns at some of the bags of food, trying to destroy them before we could bring 'em in. There was some we couldn't get right away.

"Well, anyway, all those people went after that food and I went back inside because I was afraid my rice would burn. I got to stirring the rice and after a while this guy comes running in and he says, 'Come on,' he says, 'they want you over at the security building right away.'

"So I turned the stove off and ran outside and we rushed over to 'security.' They were hauling all of that food on foot from where it was dropped back up to the security building so we could divide it all up. One whole bag had just busted outright and there was a lot of chocolate and stuff that was all messed up. But there sure was a lot of food."

Dennis Banks was in the security building at the time.

"We had to leave some of those bundles that were farther out," Dennis explained, "because the marshals opened up fire on us when we started getting the food. We eventually got the rest of it, except what they shot up, by sneaking out there at night. They couldn't shoot at us during the night and pick us off as easily, even using their nightscopes.

"But we managed to get most of that food in right away. You know, we'd been cut off from communications with the outside world. We didn't know what was going on out there and if anybody out there actually even cared about what was going on inside of Wounded Knee. We didn't know if people were organizing to help us or not. We didn't know what was going on.

"Then, all of a sudden," Dennis continued, "all this food from the sky came down. The people were crying and happy and I realized then that there was . . . that goddamn it, there was somebody out there that really cared for us.

"I think before the airlift, during all of the time that I was inside of Wounded Knee, that then I was almost on the verge of saying we surrender. It was at that point that I realized that we could never surrender because there were people out there that really cared for us. The airlift was like a new beginning for us, like a rebirth of Wounded Knee.

"Anyway, we got those bundles in and we started opening them up. We started ripping into the sacks and tearing them apart and we saw all the hams and all the food there and people were crying. The medicine men came over there and just, you know, I really can't describe the kind of feeling that went through all the people inside of Wounded Knee when we saw all that food coming down.

"Everyone got assembled about a half hour after the airlift. We prayed immediately. We had a Thanksgiving right there. Inside each of the food bundles there was a message and I read that message to all of the people that were gathered together there."

Manifesto of the Wounded Knee Airlift

To the Independent Oglala Nation and their friends at Wounded Knee:

Your struggle for freedom and justice is our struggle. Our hearts are with you.

To the people of America:
The delivery of these packages of food to the courageous people in Wounded Knee is being carried out by a number of Americans who have worked, and continue to work, to end American aggression in Indochina. We look on with horror and dismay as the U.S. government and President Nixon ignore the lessons of their failure in Viet Nam and once again attempt to block the road to justice and self-determination for a freedom-loving people.

It is ironic that our actions are occurring during the concluding days of the Pentagon Papers trial in Los Angeles. Just as those Papers expose the lies and deception of our secret policies in Indochina, Wounded Knee exposes the treacherous treatment of the American Indian. The fight against these policies is becoming a fight against an unyielding and brutal government that makes the poor of the world the victims of its search for power and profit.

It is the responsibility of every patriotic American to contribute to the common goals of dignity and freedom. Our brothers and sisters at Wounded Knee have shown us once again that the poor in America become the strong and the just in struggle. Those of us in the anti-war movement have much to learn from them.

One lesson is to realize that the frustration and disillusionment we may at times feel are only the result of a misunderstanding of our real ability to affect the course of this country's policies. Wounded Knee shows us that no matter what the setbacks, just struggles are not stopped by any president or any policy.

The buffalos that gave life to the Sioux were killed by American rifles, just as the rice that gives life to the Vietnamese was destroyed by American chemicals and bombs. But the people of Indochina are moving steadily toward freedom and independence, and so too are the people who were the first Americans.

"We read that message," Dennis went on, "and I think that everybody was crying afterwards, everybody. We realized that people out there were really working for us and that the Great Spirit was with us. The food came to us from the sky and we knew that the Great Spirit was with us. Black Elk's wife, she said, 'To those people that sent us this food,' she said, 'wherever you're at, we know you're here with us at Wounded Knee.'

"It was a good feeling when that food came. It was the kind of feeling that made us realize that there could be no kind of surrender at Wounded Knee, that we could never lay down our weapons like the government wanted us to do, that we would stay there until the demands of our Indian people were met."

Gladys Bissonette arrived at the security building in time to hear the message being read. Afterward, extra copies that had been stuffed into the duffel bags were passed around.

"We all read them," Gladys remembered, "and some people got copies. Everybody was just tickled over those messages, over what those messages read. Everybody was well pleased. That made us feel so much stronger. That made us feel that we were not so isolated. We felt at times in there that we did not have a friend in the world. You know, naturally that happens in a place like that.

"But that airlift was the most welcome sight I saw in Wounded Knee. Everybody was so happy over the airlift, and they appreciated it so much. It gave them that much more courage and that much more spunk not to give in. They were so thankful that I don't think that it bothered them to get shot at.

"Well, after an hour or so we got all of that food divided up. Our two big kitchens got four hams apiece and then the other three small kitchens each got two hams and the people from the Wounded Knee community got six hams. I'm not sure, it was something like that. Anyway, we divided everything up. There was a long list inside those big bags of all the food that was in the airlift."

Food Manifest

112 lbs.-cheese	11 lbs.-baking powder
300 lbs.-white flour	25 lbs.-salt
200 lbs.-pinto beans	100 lbs.-carrots
200 lbs.-white rice	26 lbs.-raisins
100 lbs.-converted rice	40 lbs.-oats
40 lbs.-lard	155 lbs.-ham
50 lbs.-powdered milk	20 lbs.-cornmeal
50 lbs.-peanuts	17 bars-soap
100 lbs.-white onions	5 cartons-toilet paper
30 lbs.-yellow onions	20 cans-cigarette tobacco
25 lbs.-sunflower seeds	71 bars-chocolate
30 lbs.-shelled peanuts	4 cartons-tampax
60 lbs.-prunes	2 packets-flower seeds
100 lbs.-sugar	2,000 tablets-water purifiers
1 lb.-instant coffee	

"While we were dividing the food," Gladys proceeded, "a little girl that worked on the radio, the police radio that we listened to the feds on, she just fainted away. She went into some kind of seizure, it had to be an epileptic seizure. The doctor came in and said that she was too nervous and upset from the fire fights and all that harassment and that she had forgotten to take her pills that morning.

"Well, we went along and got everything divided up, and then we started hauling it all home. There were three or four people grabbing food and hauling it back toward our kitchen, but it was far and it took a while to walk there. All during that time there was a government helicopter flying around and around way off to the side of us.

"I was the last one to get back to that little white building where our kitchen was and I no more than get into it when this helicopter came right over Wounded Knee.

"Just then this family of residents from the Wounded Knee community was hauling its food up that Manderson road. They lived in the cluster of houses near the federal roadblock up the Manderson direction there so they had a ways to walk. They had a lot of kids, too, a whole flock of small kids.

"Well, this helicopter come right over the Manderson road and as this family was dragging food in a little cart or wheelbarrow or something and their children were all walking with them, that helicopter opened up fire on that Indian family going up the road.

"That's when some of our boys started firing back, and that was the time that 'Snoopy' was hit and crippled. 'Snoopy' was what those feds called their helicopter. Those boys doing that shooting drove that helicopter off and that family all rolled into a ditch and was safe."

The incident Gladys described is recorded in a log of government radio communications kept by the U.S. marshals at Wounded Knee. The radio log was subpoenaed by defense lawyers several months after the end of the occupation. The entry for 7:02 a.m., exactly one hour and fifty-six minutes after the air drop, reads as follows, "0702—Red Arrow reports shots fired at FBI helicopter Snoopy. Snoopy advised to leave area." "Red Arrow" was the government name for their field command post just outside Wounded Knee.

Snoopy took at least one direct hit. The helicopter then fled, managing a safe landing on the other side of the government bunkers. Neither of the agents aboard was injured. But the FBI, angered and embarrassed by the successful air drop, had been openly fired upon. It was all the excuse they needed. From roadblocks, bunkers, and armored personnel carriers, federal officers unloosed what became a two-hour barrage of gunfire into Wounded Knee.

How does it happen that federal law enforcement officers riding in a helicopter come to shoot at two adults and "a whole flock of small kids" walking down a road beneath them dragging packages of food? Part of the answer lies in the government radio log. The following entry occurs twelve minutes after the air drop. (The code letters "WK" stand for Wounded Knee. The code letters "RB" stand for any of the six federal roadblocks surrounding Wounded Knee.)

"0518—3 light planes, 2 blue & white & 1 red & white, all 3 Cherokee, flew over WK and made parachute drop of 7 packages. RBs were able to describe 6 of same as being leather cases measuring approx 3 feet in length and round in shape."

The duffel bags under the parachutes were, of course, cloth duffel bags and not "leather cases." It may seem like a minor difference, but in this case it was not. The term "leather cases" implies that the cargo was guns, not food. Despite their distance from the scene (they were wrong about the color of one of the planes), federal agents were confident enough in their mistaken impression that the duffel bags were "leather cases" to announce their error over the radio. It didn't matter whether the mistake was intentional. Other federal officers who heard the radio communication, or heard about it, must have made the logical assumption that the airlift delivered weapons and ammunition. That assumption then colored their behavior.

An entry in the government radio log six and a half hours later bears this out. (Here, the abbreviation "Hdqts 2" stands for the man in charge of the FBI headquarters unit functioning in Wounded Knee. The head U.S. marshal was "Hdqts 1." The code letters "AG" stand for the attorney general of the United States, Richard Kleindienst. The name "Mr. Pottinger" refers to Stanley Pottinger, the chief Justice Department representative on the scene in South Dakota.)

"1140—Mr. Pottinger contacted Hdqts 2, and gave him message from AG. Hdqts 2 stated that they [WK] provoked this situation, they have opened fire on all of our positions, and that Washington has got to realize this. Mr. Pottinger asked Hdqts 2 to state reasons why he felt this way, and to give reasons. Hdqts 2 stated that first there was the early morning plane drop, which he feels was ammo . . ."

The chief FBI agent on the scene, the supposedly cool, experienced, professional law officer presenting his case to the attorney general in Washington, began his request for permission to use more fire power in the early morning gun battle with the entirely unfounded assumption that the airlift dropped ammunition. The FBI always favored a shootout at Wounded Knee. Their assumption about "leather cases" was so self-serving, given their tactical preferences, and their record for provoking violence was so extensive, that one is forced to ask if the "leather cases" mistake was in fact intentional.

Thus, in the helicopter "Snoopy," the two FBI agents who fired on the Indian family dragging their food up the Manderson road might have thought that the family was hauling ammunition. If so, why didn't the presence of the children stop them from shooting? That is a question only they can answer. Nevertheless, with most helicopter pilots being trained by the military, one is tempted to speculate that the two FBI agents over Wounded Knee might have had experience flying missions in Indochina. In such a case, the practice of hunting native adults and children from the safety of helicopters might not be unfamiliar to them. After all, for the past ten years it had been quite familiar to tens of thousands of Americans paid by the U.S. government to perform precisely that task in Viet Nam, Laos, and Cambodia.

Whatever their reason for shooting, the FBI agents in the helicopter provoked one of the most intense fire fights of the entire occupation. An entry in the government radio log states that the battle lasted from 7:12 a.m. to 9:23 a.m. The price that the government exacted for the few defensive shots at the FBI helicopter was the life of a 47-year-old Indian man, Frank Clearwater.

Recalling how the fire fight got started, Dennis Banks said, "Our own outposts reported that the government was actually sleeping when the airlift came in at five o'clock. I don't think they knew what was going on for the first fifteen minutes or so. Then about thirty minutes after they realized a drop had been made, we received sporadic fire from them.

"At about an hour after the airlift, they got this helicopter into the air. Then around seven o'clock, there was that shooting incident with the helicopter. That's when the government started literally spraying us. Some of the guys said that it was thirty-caliber machine guns they were using that morning. Of course, we have recovered a lot of ammunition that has shown us that they were shooting thirty-caliber weapons at some point.

"You know, they literally tore that church apart with fifty-caliber bullets—great big holes the size of softballs going in one side and coming out the other as big as a . . . a washtub. Anyway, I don't know what kind of bullets they were shooting at us that morning, but they sure intended to tear us apart, too."

"Leather cases" of "ammo" to the contrary, Wounded Knee was woefully low on ammunition. Few of the 75 or so people manning the settlement's defense bunkers had more than ten rounds apiece in their pockets. Yet after the fire fight, a government spokesman insisted to newspaper reporters that the Indians had actually moved out of their bunkers and gone on the offense. He claimed that the targets of this remarkable offensive were the bullet-proof armored personnel carriers and the federal bunkers bristling with M-16s!

Frank Clearwater and his wife Morning Star, 37, and three-months-pregnant, had hiked into Wounded Knee only the night before. Frank was part Apache. Morning Star is a Cherokee. They were not members of the American Indian Movement, but had driven to Wounded Knee from their home in North Carolina wanting to help in whatever way they could. Some time after the air drop, Frank went to sleep on the floor of the Catholic Church up on the hill. When the fire fight started, he bolted up just as a federal bullet came through the wall and tore off the back of his head. Morning Star found him in a pool of blood.

Pottinger, of the Justice Department, assured the press that government forces had only fired in self-defense. Another federal spokesman quietly admitted that U.S. forces had fired at least 4,000 rounds. Five others besides Clearwater were shot and injured. There were no casualties on the government side. The fire fight was entirely without reason. The government had nothing to gain by provoking it or participating in it. There was no one under attack, no laws to enforce, no lives to save, no property to protect. The whole incident was a blind and unnecessary show of force.

The government radio log states that at 9:23 a.m. the marshals received a radio communication from Wounded Knee requesting a helicopter to evacuate someone with a head injury. Bullets lodged in the other five casualties were removed by medicine men or physicians working in the Wounded Knee clinic. Although some of the injuries were serious, none of the five persons suffered any permanent damage. But there was nothing that could be done for Frank Clearwater.

At 9:26 a.m., "hdqts 2," the FBI commander, ordered that "no copter is to go into WK; if they have any wounded, bring them out under white flag to RB-1, and they will fly them from there." For some reason it was not until 9:43 a.m. that this order was relayed to the Indians in Wounded Knee. Clearwater was immediately brought to Roadblock #1. The radio log indicates that at 9:54 a.m. he was aboard a helicopter en route to the reservation hospital in Pine Ridge. Clearwater arrived at 10:10 a.m., but doctors in Pine Ridge were unable to treat him and he was flown in an airplane to Rapid City where neurosurgical facilities were available.

Before Frank Clearwater was driven to Roadblock #1, Morning Star requested government permission to accompany her husband to the hospital. A safe conduct was granted. Once outside Wounded Knee, she was arrested by the FBI. They dragged her away from Frank and threw her in the overcrowded Bureau of Indian Affairs jail in Pine Ridge. The FBI kept her there, in jail, while her husband was being operated on and for an additional 24 hours after that. Not until 36 hours after the shooting was Morning Star able to rejoin her unconscious husband in a Rapid City hospital.

On April 25, eight days after he was shot, Frank Clearwater died. He never regained consciousness. Morning Star asked that he be buried in Wounded Knee, in the traditional Indian way. Two days later, Chairman Dick Wilson announced that the Pine Ridge Tribal Council would not allow the burial to take place in Wounded Knee or anywhere else on the Pine Ridge Reservation. In fact, the restriction was Wilson's private edict. The Tribal Council had not had a quorum since early in the occupation when several members resigned in protest against Wilson's high-handed rule.

The people in Wounded Knee entered a solemn four-day period of mourning. In the two months that had gone by since the seizure of Wounded Knee on February 27, Frank Clearwater was their first death.

Crow Dog, the spiritual leader, responded to Wilson's announcement by saying that no further negotiations would take place with the federal government until Clearwater was properly buried.

A compromise was reached on April 30. Wilson and Justice Department officials allowed Clearwater's body to be taken to the home of Chief Frank Fools Crow, which was on the reservation but 20 miles from Wounded Knee. They permitted the body to remain there for a one-day wake. Then it was driven off the Pine Ridge Reservation and on to the nearby Rosebud Reservation where it was buried on land owned by the family of Crow Dog.

Looking back to those sad days, Gladys Bissonette was asked if the people in Wounded Knee thought that the airlift had caused Frank Clearwater's death.

"Oh, no! Oh, no!" she said. "That was the FBI and the federal marshals who were responsible for that. They wanted to starve us out and they intended to keep us from getting any food. But then this airlift come and got all that food to us.

"We knew that this was why they shot at us, because we had gotten that food. We had gotten some help from somewhere and that's what they didn't want. They didn't want us to get help from anywhere. You mustn't blame people that come and do some good on account of some others who do something evil right afterward. Why then nobody could do anything to change this government."

Gladys thought for a moment and then, with anger in her voice, she declared, "Time and again, I have said this, in negotiations with those government men, and I still say it today. When the U.S. government, the FBI, and the BIA think that any time at the drop of a hat or the twist of a finger they can snuff out one human life, why they must actually think they have the Great Creator overpowered that they can do such things."

15

AIRLIFT
Safety or Escape?

We were a mile past Wounded Knee, our lives depending perhaps on a few rivets which might be all that was holding a broken tail section to the rest of our aircraft. My only concern now was to begin taking care of ourselves.

I held the plane down to a slow 100 mph cruise speed. Below us the hills and prairie of the Pine Ridge Reservation rolled by with monotonous consistency. We were at 200 feet to keep below radar coverage and it was not high enough to see very far. The barren landscape visible around us looked too rough and hostile and too disturbingly similar. It was unnerving, like flying just above the surface of a lake, unable to see the accommodating terrain on all sides.

The control wheel was still twisted far to the left. The damaged tail loomed up behind us, taking on the look of a huge predatory bird threatening to kill at any moment. I turned in my seat for what must have been the fiftieth time, straining to examine the damage that had become so familiar—the missing two-foot section of tail fin, the entire warped and wrinkled surface of what was left of the horizontal stabilizer.

Tom sat behind me shivering in the cold air howling through the open doorway. I looked at him and then at Larry, both smiling and happy, thinking no doubt about the parachute drop and the sea of ecstatic people surrounding the duffel bags. Neither had the slightest idea that anything was wrong with the tail or that all of us were in mortal danger.

We had to decide whether to land or keep flying. It was a desperate choice between safety and escape. Part of me wanted more than anything to make an immediate landing on a road below and get the hell out of that airplane. But with the drop behind us, the temptation was to go on farther and not land in the middle of the prairie—certainly not that prairie on that particular morning. Our only real possibility of escape was to get out of the entire South Dakota-Nebraska region and fly to a place where the Wounded Knee airlift would not be a local news story. The only direction that made sense was east toward Iowa since our trail of false clues would presumably lead the FBI west into Wyoming. I knew without looking at a map that Iowa meant another two-and-a-half hours of uncertain, terrorizing flight. How could the tail last that long?

High overcast stretched out to the horizon in front of us. The thin layer of clouds thousands of feet above played an essential role in my tentative long-distance flight planning. With a fragile tail assembly about to come apart, our worst enemy was turbulent air. On a clear day, most low altitude turbulence is caused by thermals, rising currents of hot air. Different types of terrain (forests, farmland, lakes, concrete cities, etc.) absorb different amounts of heat from the sun. The air above them gets warmed to varying degrees. The result is different currents of air rising at different speeds because they are at different temperatures. Flying in and out of these irregular currents causes the bumps felt as turbulence.

So far that morning the air had been very smooth. The high overcast clouds were blocking the sun and preventing the development of any warm air currents at all. Those clouds were what stood between us and excessive strain on our tail assembly. With the overcast there, extending ahead out to the horizon, we could remain aeronautically stable. By not changing the balance of forces acting on the airplane's delicate tail, we might make it to Iowa. The aircraft had been flying adequately for 17 or 18 minutes. Conceivably, it could continue doing so indefinitely.

Ahead of us on the horizon, I could see a radio tower. Twelve miles northeast of Wounded Knee, the 309-foot antenna was the only obstruction for 30 miles in any direction. It was the first landmark on our planned escape route.

"How come we're up so high?" Larry asked, shouting over the engine noise and the blast of wind from the open doorway. "Aren't we supposed to be right on the ground and going a lot faster?"

He knew something was wrong. I still didn't want to tell him or Tom the truth for fear of causing a panic, but there was no longer any choice.

"Remember when those two duffel bags went out near Hot Springs?"

"Yeah, sure I remember."

"Well," I said, looking him straight in the eye and trying to grin cheerfully, "on their way out, they took off two feet of the tail."

"What!?"

"Look for yourself. You see the left part of the tail through the doorway? Now look out the window at the right side. Interesting, huh?"

"Oh, my god! Oh, my god!" Larry's voice was aghast. His head moved from one direction to the other in an incredulous examination of the tail damage.

Tom was no less upset. "Can we fly this way?" he asked.

"We have been ever since those bags fell out!" I tried to sound as nonchalant and confident as I could.

During the next few minutes, as Larry and Tom got over the initial shock, I explained how I had been turning the control wheel sharply to the left in order to compensate for the missing tail section. Trying to display confidence in order to instill it in them, I said that the chances of keeping the aircraft under control weren't bad as long as the air remained smooth and free of thermals. I admitted that we were in some danger, that I had seriously considered a forced landing before getting to Wounded Knee, and that none of our current options was very desirable.

Tom fought to contain his fear. "If we land here, you'd get arrested, right?"

"Not just us. Eventually they'd trace our numbers back to Chicago and be able to arrest everybody."

"It was so perfect," Larry said, calming down for a moment. "We delivered the food. Every detail worked out according to plan, except one. But if we could get away, the airlift would still be a complete success."

"There's only one way to escape—fly out of this whole area, land at a big city airport, and try to get the plane quietly fixed."

"Where's the nearest city?" Larry asked cautiously.

"Iowa—Sioux City or Fort Dodge."

"How far away are they?"

"Three hundred miles."

Larry and Tom winced when they heard the distance. They asked more questions about the cloud cover, the tail damage, and the various courses of action available to us. I was frightened, badly, but not wanting their decision to be influenced by my own fear, I kept acting more self-assured than I really felt. Finally Tom seemed ready to make up his mind.

"What would you do if you were up here alone?" he asked.

It was the critical question. I couldn't shirk a decision by hiding behind their less knowledgeable anxiety. My thoughts alternated between two unhappy images. In one, everybody on the airlift was in handcuffs. In the other, our tailless plane was nosediving straight into the ground. I hesitated a moment, ready with brave words and a trembling heart, and looked across at my two friends.

"I'd stay low and go on. If we ran into turbulence or the plane got the slightest bit harder to control, I'd land wherever we were, airport or no airport."

Tom mustered his courage and started slowly nodding in agreement. He leaned forward to meet Larry's eyes with his own. "Okay?"

"Okay."

We flew past the radio tower looking up a hundred feet to its apex. If the federal bunkers were still tracking our escape with binoculars, we were too low and too far away to be seen. I turned east onto our true course. The next landmark was a power line 28 miles ahead. The high voltage wires ran north and south directly across our path. I eased the throttle forward to take our airspeed up to 110 mph. With southwesterly tailwinds, that gave us a groundspeed of 120 mph, exactly two miles a minute, and meant the power line was 14 minutes away. I pushed the start button on my stopwatch.

We flew over absolutely desolate terrain. Between us and the power line, nothing independently recognizable could be used to tell us where we were—no towns, no highways, no rivers, not even any telephone poles. The radio navigation equipment was useless at such a low altitude. Time was the only way to monitor our position in space. I had to read the stopwatch in miles instead of minutes, and when the time came, we all had to watch for the wires with a sharp eye. Once we were there, our navigation problems would be over. The power line ran south for 16 miles, then turned east and quickly merged with U.S. Highway 18, continuing east for the remaining 275 miles to Sioux City, Iowa. Paralleling the highway, the wires passed ten small country airports on the way. It was a perfect course. If an emergency landing became necessary, we could go down on the highway or try for one of the little airstrips.

Larry spread the map out on his lap and I gave him a quick course in how to read an aeronautical chart. Once we got to the power line, I wanted him to keep track of our location on the map. The towns, lakes, and roads we would fly over were all indicated, and I was worried about being too busy at the controls to be able to carefully plot our position. Meanwhile, his eyes and Tom's had to help me find those wires.

The minutes dragged by slowly and tediously. I felt more and more cut off and afraid. One hill after another passed under us in a constant and unchanging vista. Again, we seemed lost at sea. I wanted to seize the electric life line that could tow us out of the strange and uncharted ocean. The more I thought that way, the more my fear increased. After twelve minutes there was still no sign of the power line.

"Do you see it?" I asked Larry, trying to control the panic in my voice.

"No."

"Well, what's past it on the map? Is there anything that's past it that's recognizable, so we'll know if we've gone too far? A lake or a river or something?"

Checking the chart, Larry hesitated too long and then said, "No," with too much uncertainty. I glanced at his lap and looked for myself.

"What do you mean, no?" I shouted, jabbing my finger into the chart. "Here's a road right past it. Goddamn it, Larry, I just got done telling you that the brown lines are roads."

"Okay, okay, I'm sorry."

"Well, did we pass any roads yet?"

"I don't know," Larry answered. "I don't think so."

"Shit."

I tried to shut up. I knew it was stupid to be angry at Larry. But another minute went by, and with all three of us staring intently out the window, there was still no sign of the power line. I was afraid we had missed it and that we were heading off into another hundred miles of barren South Dakota countryside. Reaching the breaking point once again, I started shouting at Larry just as we flew up to the line of wires extending off into the distance on either side of us. I banked into a very gradual turn which put the airplane on a southerly course alongside the power line. Much relieved, I knew then that whatever else might happen, we would not get lost nor be very far from a possible landing site. Five minutes later, I could see the wires making their right-angle turn toward the east. Beyond, Highway 18 was visible as it moved up from the southwest to merge with them.

The land flattened out slightly as we flew east with the power line. Occasionally, we passed over a cultivated field which reduced my fears a bit more. Planted acreage is comparatively easy to land on. The improvement in the terrain meant that we were well beyond the Pine Ridge Reservation. In the distance off to our right, I saw the large man-made lake in the center of white-controlled Bennett County, taken from the Oglalas for a bombing range during World War II and never returned. Farther along we crossed more of the harsh, hilly, eroded country that we had earlier left behind. Checking the map, I saw that we were flying over another example of government generosity to the Sioux people—the Brulé's Rosebud Reservation. The land was not as severe as that around Wounded Knee, but it didn't look any more economically viable.

The power line pointed straight east and the highway occasionally zigzagged back and forth across it. As we flew along, I could see minor roads coming in from the north or south to form intersections with the main route, as well as an occasional river or creek passing under it. With so many landmarks it was easy to keep track of our position and coach Larry's map reading at the same time. Knowing exactly where we were—basically how far it was to the nearest airstrip—did not help the damaged tail, but it was an important psychological comfort and might be critical in an emergency.

Halfway across the Rosebud Reservation, we flew over a small airstrip. It was the first one since Hot Springs, where we circled getting the duffel bags ready for the drop. For a moment I considered landing in order to make a close inspection of the tail. But I knew that once the aircraft was on the ground, we would never take off with it again. The Rosebud Reservation was no place to be looking for a ride home, so we continued following the high wires east. Periodically, Larry or Tom asked if everything was all right, usually just after one of my frequent over-the-shoulder glances at the tail assembly. I kept lying, assuring them each time that we were in good shape and that there was little to worry about. We left Rosebud behind.

The minutes crept by, not as slowly as when we were first looking for the power line, but slow enough. Larry was still understandably clumsy with his map reading and continued to make mistakes, but I was too tense to be understanding and I let his errors goad me into more impatient outbursts against him. The terrain beneath us had become less dry and rocky and had dropped to an elevation 1,000 feet lower than the country around Wounded Knee. I descended with the land, but no longer below 500 feet, afraid at that point of attracting the attention of a stray state policeman patrolling Highway 18. The flatter farmland gradually returned to the checkerboard pattern of the Midwest. The High Plains were dropping off into the Mississippi Basin. The roads were longer and straighter and the population somewhat more dense. Looking ahead into the distance, I could see widely scattered towns straddling the highway like so many saddles on a long stockyard fence.

Seventy tortuous minutes had gone by since the drop. We were approaching Winner, South Dakota, and as tiny as it was, it was the biggest settlement we had seen all morning. I guided the aircraft south of the southernmost house, but as we looked north beyond the town, we could see another small airport with two grass runways.

Unknown to us at the time, Billy and Strobe had already landed there and replaced their rear door. By the time we got that far, they were on their way back to Chicago. After the drop, Billy made a high-speed getaway at an extremely low altitude. Still nervous about being shot at, he left his throttle wide open and clung to the ground for cover. Making a good 170 mph groundspeed, he avoided highways and towns, kept his compass more or less on east, and flew up and down only a few feet above the terrain. It was more the path of a runaway jeep than the course of an airplane.

At one point, he popped over the crest of a hill and found a farmer at work on a huge combine just off to the side in front of him. Streaking by only 50 yards away, Billy literally had to look up at the astonished man who sat dumbfounded on the gigantic machine. Finally satisfied that he was safe from the guns around Wounded Knee, Billy "climbed" to 200 feet and flew to Winner. After landing, Strobe replaced the rear door, dug up some cactus plants to take back to Chicago, and they were off once again. With the cabin heater all the way up, Billy climbed to a normal cruising altitude of 5,500 feet and the two of them settled in for a long, ordinary flight home.

Meanwhile Jim had flown a southeasterly course immediately following the drop. He felt confident and secure after two safe passes over Wounded Knee and quickly turned east toward Chicago. Thirty miles later, he passed a dirt landing strip in Bennett County, between the Pine Ridge and Rosebud Reservations. Jim checked the field from the air, and saw no people or automobiles nearby. It was only 5:30 a.m. He swooped in for a fast landing and braked to a stop on the runway. John jumped out and went to work on the rear door. Three minutes later they were back in the air. Jim set a course for Omaha where he planned to put Oliver on a commercial airliner back to Rapid City. Oliver asked Jim where he was going from Omaha. Still not trusted, he was told that it would be safer for everyone concerned if he didn't know.

Winner, South Dakota, despite its small size, did have an air navigation radio facility. As Larry, Tom, and I continued our eastbound flight, I was tempted to call and ask how far the precious overcast extended out in front of us. If it started breaking up soon, there was no point in planning a flight to Iowa. We could land immediately and be done with the terrifying ride. But everyone had agreed the airlift would maintain radio silence after the drop, and it seemed wisest to abide by that decision.

Winner passed behind us. The small towns turned up more often, and there were little country airfields at 25- or 30-mile intervals. Grain elevators, railroad tracks, drive-in theaters, and other rural landmarks slid by beneath us. I used them to push Larry on his navigational skill, still planning against the contingency of being so occupied with piloting the airplane that I'd be unable to read the map at the same time.

With the aeronautical chart spread out on his lap, I told Larry to keep one finger on our current position and another finger on the closest airstrip. As we moved along, sandwiched between the power line and Highway 18, his second finger was supposed to jump ahead whenever we passed the halfway point between the two closest airports, fore and aft. That way in an emergency I could glance at the map and instantly tell what direction to fly in and how far I had to go if I wanted to try and make it to an airport. But my impatience made it hard for Larry to learn the complex markings on the chart. I was too absorbed flying the crippled airplane to bother controlling my temper.

We were an hour and forty minutes from Wounded Knee. The freezing wind roared into the cabin through the open doorway. Still turned far to the left, the airplane's semicircular control wheel was my only defense, the only tool I had capable of protecting us from disaster. Under normal circumstances, I could push, pull, or twist it and the plane would faithfully dive, climb, or turn. The connection was unfailing. But that morning I moved the control wheel with the utmost delicacy, reluctant to cause any sudden, unnecessary strain on the tail assembly. Pinned to the seat by the intensity of my caution, I was afraid that at any moment I might lose control. If the tail broke away from the rest of the aircraft, the precious tool I held so gingerly would become utterly useless. No matter how hard I pulled back on it, the airplane's falling nose would not come up away from the ground.

As time wore on, my fears subsided and increased, over and over again. It was almost impossible to sit there for so long victimized by the ebb and flow of fear, wondering whether we would live or die. The terror was slow and painfully drawn out, totally different than a situation of instantaneous fright, like skidding off an icy road, where the fear is fast and abrupt, suddenly there and suddenly over. I tried to distract myself by studying the landscape and making unnecessary minor adjustments in the engine speed or fuel flow.

I was trying not to watch the clock, trying not to think about how badly I wanted to be out of that airplane, or how our obituaries might read the next day. But the same terrifying image kept forcing itself into my mind —pulling the control wheel farther and farther back and getting no response from the airplane. I saw myself desperately yanking on the wheel as I sat there helpless, watching at the last moment through the front windshield as the ground rushed up at incredible speed and smashed us to pieces.

But we had to go on. Our course gradually merged with the Missouri River. At first, the big river was off to the left in the distance. Then it swung a little south and we were flying along beside it. Despite the fear and tension in the airplane, the river was magnificent, wide as a lake and in complete command of the countryside around it. Before long it carried us across the South Dakota-Nebraska state line where we exchanged U.S. Highway 18 for Nebraska State Highway 12, holding a course between the road and the enormous flowing river. With Wounded Knee an hour and fifty-five minutes behind, Nebraska's wide Niobrara River came up on our right to merge with the Missouri in a great confluence of swirling, muddy water and tiny, forested islands.

We flew on over the rich farmland of eastern Nebraska, past the silos and the crossroads towns, past the little country airports and the tottering municipal water towers. Ten minutes beyond the Niobrara fork, the Missouri River broadened into the Lewis and Clark Lake, formed by a dam three miles long. It was an awesome and peaceful scene, a multi-colored, serene panorama of land and water. How much we would have enjoyed its beauty had we been calmly returning in an undamaged airplane, happy with our success and confident of our safety.

All of a sudden I saw blue. With a shock I realized that for the past several minutes I had been staring ahead at a narrow band of blue sky just above the horizon. Somewhere, far in the distance, there was no more overcast, and sunshine would be bouncing thermals and turbulence off the countryside below. It was impossible to tell how far away it was, maybe 50 miles, maybe 100. We would have to go down soon. Larry unfolded the map so we could see farther east. Sioux City, Iowa, was 50 miles ahead, Fort Dodge another 110 miles beyond it.

Fort Dodge was halfway across Iowa and well outside Indian territory. I was sure its people would not be preoccupied with Wounded Knee, but 160 miles was out of the question. Sioux City, in the western-most part of the state, not only bore the name of the tribe still struggling at Wounded Knee, but sat on the banks of the Missouri River, facing a border shared by the two Indian-hating states of South Dakota and Nebraska. I could only hope that the city's concerns were more with the cornfields to the east than the grasslands in the west. We simply had no other choice. Even 50 miles might be too far. After more than two horrible hours, we had to face the agonizing possibility that it had all been for nothing. We might still have to land at some small country airport where repairing the plane would not be possible and as a result our role in the airlift probably uncovered.

I leaned back and told Tom to dig my flight bag out of the rear of the cabin. Inside was a large "Airport Directory." Every airport in the U.S. was listed and described. Tom retrieved it, carefully crawling past the open doorway. After explaining the symbols to Larry, I asked him to look up all the airstrips between our position and Sioux City and see if any had Piper Aircraft repair facilities. If not, I told him to check the places behind and to the side of us. We were 45 miles from Sioux City.

I couldn't give up the possibility of escape. If we could land at an airport with the proper repair services, we could still make up a convincing story about how the damage occurred, sit tight for a few days until the plane was fixed, and then fly back to Chicago with no one the wiser. It would be difficult if we had to land where we were, in Nebraska, or across the river in South Dakota, but if we found a spot with an authorized Piper maintenance shop, at least we'd have a chance.

Ten minutes passed. Larry continued thumbing through the thick book while I warily examined the band of blue ahead, unable to tell exactly where the overcast ended and the turbulent sunshine began. Sioux City was only 25 miles away, but it seemed like a hundred. I expected the worst and got increasingly nervous. From time to time, I leaned over to check Larry's work with the map and the airport directory. It flustered him, and my anxiety, which was right on the surface, made it harder for him to work.

The blue strip on the horizon gradually thickened. Larry finally determined that none of the little airports anywhere around us had an authorized Piper shop. Inside my head, the old debate between safety and escape raged on. The blue got wider. Ahead I could see the point where the overcast ended. If we flew out from under it, anything might happen, from continued stability to a complete loss of control. The big Sioux City Municipal Airport was only 20 miles downriver, ten minutes away. Should I land safely and risk capture or continue and gamble on escape as well? We had come too far to turn back—that seemed to be the wisdom of the day, and it still applied.

I stared at the clock. Five more minutes went by. The wispy border of the overcast was clearly visible above us. Beyond it was a deep blue morning sky. The aircraft emerged into the sunshine. Almost immediately we hit the first thermal. It was only a ripple, but it felt enormous. The little jolt in the control wheel sent shivers down my back and nightmare visions through my brain. We were ten miles from Municipal Airport. Downtown Sioux City was visible to the left of it. I flew on. Another minute went by with only a small bump or two. I flew on.

Suddenly it got worse. In a buildup that took less than 30 seconds, the air turned violently turbulent. The plane was pushed up and down in a rapid seesaw. The wingtips bounced above and below the horizon line. The nose was blown a few degrees up into a shallow climb, then just as quickly, the wind forced it back down. In a normal airplane it would have meant nothing, but in that one it was an emergency. "We shouldn't be up here," I thought, "goddamn it, we shouldn't be up here."

I looked at Larry's fingers on the map, checking for the nearest airport, then snatched the chart off his lap. Four miles straight ahead, half way between our position and Sioux City Municipal Airport, there was a small suburban airfield. Without hesitating, I cut the throttle back to a lower power setting and eased the bouncing ship into a shallow glide. I planned to land at the small field. If the air calmed down on the way, I could stretch out my descent and come into Sioux City Municipal at low altitude. Larry saw my eyes darting from the map to the ground. My head twisted around for another desperate look at the broken tail.

"Listen," he said, so nervous and intimidated by my previous impatience that he regretted even having to speak, "this is really getting bad, isn't it? I mean, are you open to going down, right here?"

"Look at the altimeter, Larry. We're already on our way down. Just help me find that damn airport. It should be dead ahead, three or four miles. Tom! Tie yourself down to the floor."

"Oh, god."

The bouncing got more severe and violent. I couldn't find the little airstrip. It was somewhere ahead lost in the farms and suburban tangle surrounding Sioux City. I wasn't able to concentrate on flying the plane and finding the runway outline at the same time. At least it was in front of us so I didn't have to subject the fragile tail to the stress of a sharp turn.

Then it happened—what I most feared. A strong gust pushed the nose down below the angle of a normal descent. I brought the control wheel back about a half inch to reduce the steepness of the glide. Nothing happened. We continued down just as steeply. I pulled the wheel back farther, but there was still no change. With the wheel three inches behind the neutral position, the nose finally started to climb back toward the horizon. Under normal circumstances, a wheel deflection of that size is enough to climb the airplane straight up or loop it all the way over. There was no longer any question about it, I was losing the ability to aim the airplane up or down. In a last vain search for an easy solution, I checked the airspeed indicator. Controls normally get mushy at slow speeds, but we were still making a brisk 120 mph.

The rolling and pitching got even worse. When the right wingtip was blown down, I couldn't get it back up. The control wheel already rested so far to the left, there was no room to turn it any farther. All I could do was wait for an opposite gust to blow the left wing down and correct the roll. But flying sideways wasn't so bad. It was not being able to control pitch, the climbing and diving dimension, that was really dangerous. We hit another down draft, and another. Each time I had to pull the control wheel back even farther to correct the angle of descent.

At that point I saw the little airport two miles in front of us. Luckily, one runway was lined up in almost the same direction we were flying. Without slowing down, I pointed the aircraft directly at it. We were blown down once again, farther than before. I pulled the control wheel back two inches. Nothing happened. Three inches. Nothing. Falling into a panic, I yanked it back as far as it would go, only another inch. With overwhelming finality, the wheel hit the stops preventing any further motion. That was it, but still nothing happened. We were going down too steeply. It was the beginning of a crash. Then, miraculously, we flew into another thermal and the rising air pushed the nose up into the angle of a normal glide.

The instant my hands felt the dull thud of the control wheel hitting those stops, everything changed for me. A dangerous situation turned into an almost hopeless trap. For one or two very long seconds, I had no way to bring us out of an ever steepening dive. All around me, the world was gray and hazy. A single clear spot stood out, a narrow cone of life in sharp focus extending out from my eyes down to the runway two miles ahead. We were one minute away.

The plane was forced down by another severe gust. Again, I pulled the control wheel back to the limit until the stops froze my motion into uselessness. But this time there were no rescuing winds. We kept going down. I pushed the wheel forward, returning it to the neutral position, then started pulling it and pushing it back and forth, each time working it a little farther to the rear. Milking the wheel like that started having an effect. The nose, in irregular fits and starts, slowly jerked its way up to the horizon. We were in a normal glide once again. But it didn't last. Seconds later the aircraft was pushed down and the wheel hit the stops again before I started milking it in and out. Just as the procedure enabled me to recover, another gust of wind forced us back down.

The plane was being blown all over the sky. I sat there slinging the control wheel back and forth and side to side, moving it across the entire limit of its range. It was more like riding a rodeo horse than flying an airplane. Half the time, at least, the aircraft was so totally out of my control I could not override the buffeting we were subjected to by the turbulent air. In the intervals of control, as soon as I managed to bring the plane out of a climb or a dive or a turn, another gust blew us back toward the ground or away from the runway. I had never been as tense and alert in my life, but for the first time in two hours, I was completely beyond fear. There was too much clarity in the situation to be afraid. The rectangle of runway in front of me was glowing with life—ours. It was all I saw or thought about.

We were half a mile away, than a quarter. Normal landing speed was 70 mph. We were descending at 120 mph and I didn't slow down. The wind was blowing from behind me in the wrong direction for a landing, but I didn't know it or care. I didn't see if there were any other runways at that airport, or which direction aircraft were landing in that morning. I didn't radio to tell the airport I was coming. I didn't ask about or look for other air traffic. I just tried to keep the apron of that runway directly in front of me, inside the cone of life, and I utterly ignored everything else.

Slowly the narrow gray landing strip got bigger and bigger. It was no wider than a truck and not very long and it danced across the windshield as the plane wobbled and swayed toward a landing. But it looked like we were going to make it! I kept the speed at 120 mph, planning to drive the airplane into the ground. Fifty feet from the primitive runway, I could see that it was made of gravel. I repeated to myself, "No brakes when we hit. No brakes when we hit. . . ."

The elongated rectangle reached up from the grass around it to meet our little plane. With a loud noise, the wheels slammed onto the loose gravel. Immediately I pulled the throttle out to idle the engine and pushed the control wheel forward to try to keep the Cherokee from bouncing back up into the air. The nose wheel stayed on the ground. We were down!

The airplane raced along the runway, but after several seconds we could see the other end of the landing strip coming up very fast. I reached under the instrument panel, grabbed the hand brake, and started pumping it, gently at first and then more forcefully. We skidded on the gravel, but the airplane kept going straight. An instant later, the tires held firmly. We gradually slowed down. At the end of the gravel, I managed to swing onto a paved taxiway and brake sharply to a stop.

It was over! Every muscle in my body went limp. I melted into the seat, quivering with relief, closing my eyes for the first time all morning. The heavy feel of solid ground beneath us drew tension out of me like a sponge soaking up water. There was nothing to watch, no task to perform with life or death precision, no fear squeezing my mind into a knot of concentration. I was ecstatic. I felt spread out, almost liquid. It was really over. We were down!

Luckily, Larry felt no need for such profound relaxation. He jumped out of the co-pilot's seat and ran around the plane behind the damaged tail. With Tom on the inside, the two of them quickly put the rear door back on its hinges and pinned it into place. As Larry crawled back in beside me, I opened my eyes and looked around. Nobody was on the field. We taxied to the front of the airport's one small hangar. Inside two men worked on an airplane. It was 8:45 a.m. Central Standard Time, one hour later than in Wounded Knee.

I cut the engine and the three of us got out. My feet touched the ground for the first time since our 4:00 a.m. departure from Rapid City. The two men came out of the hangar; one was elderly and the other middle-aged. They were father and son and they owned the airport. After a surprised glance at our tail, the younger of the two whistled and asked me what had happened.

"I'm not sure," I answered. "We were flying along just south of here, on our way up from Omaha. All of a sudden something slammed into the tail. This was the closest airport so I came right in. I guess it must have been a bird. I thought I saw something flash by just before the impact."

The older man looked at me with a knowing grin, holding his hands up about two feet apart. "Was she dark brown and about this big?"

"Yeah," I replied, "yeah, I think it was."

"Well, you fellas hit an eagle. There's a lot of 'em 'round this time of year. 'Sides, that's the only thing big enough to do that much damage."

I grinned at him and nodded very thoughtfully. "An eagle, huh? I guess that must've been it. Just a big old American eagle."

We gathered around the back of the plane to inspect the damage. Most had been visible from the pilot's seat, but walking behind the aircraft I saw for the first time what was actually the worst of it. In the rear of the airplane the fuselage tapers down to a narrow cone at the end of which the tail assembly is attached. At the narrowest part of the fuselage cone, just in front of the tail, there was a tear in the aircraft's metal skin, a tear that snaked around all the way from the top of the fuselage to the bottom. The rip in the metal was on the left side, where the impact had been, and it looked as if it had been gradually getting bigger and bigger.

We had been flying with the tail assembly attached only to the right side of the fuselage. The airport owners pointed out that the entire tail section had already bent two or three inches around to the right. They said the bending would have continued until the tail came completely off the airplane. I felt faint and leaned up against the plane for support. The younger man continued inspecting the damage to the horizontal tail fin.

When he finished, he looked up at me, scratched his jaw, and said, "You know, you three fellas shouldn't be alive. I can't see how this airplane here could've possibly been flying." It was the same conclusion the insurance adjustors would come to three days later after their examination of the damage.

We walked into the shack that served as the little airport's office. I asked where we were. "South Sioux City, Nebraska," one of them answered. Iowa was just a few miles away, across the Missouri River. There was no radio playing, and they seemed to know nothing about the airlift. Tom, already on the sixth day of a two-day assignment, wanted to get a taxi immediately for Sioux City Municipal Airport and take the next commercial flight back to his office in Washington. The younger airport owner offered to drive him to the nearest taxicab office, and they quickly left.

Larry and I remained with the old man. I asked if he had facilities to fix the airplane. He said he did, but that it would take a long time to order parts, probably weeks, since he was not an authorized Piper dealer. I explained that the plane was rented and that all we could do was leave it with him and ask the owner to call and discuss the repair work. The old aviator agreed, but before we could leave he asked me to fill out a form with my name and the name of the aircraft's owner.

"Larry, while I'm filling this out, why don't you go get all our stuff out of the plane. And clean it out real good, too. You know what I mean?"

Larry went out the door knowing that I wanted him to remove all the ripcords, ropes, buckles, and other signs that the aircraft had been used in a parachute drop. Instead of completing the accident report, I asked for the bathroom. I wanted more time to figure out exactly what information I was willing to leave behind. There was still some chance that we could get away without the FBI discovering who had carried out the airlift. If I left a false name and made some arrangement to pay for the repair work out of funds raised for the airlift, our chances of eluding them would improve, but would be far from certain. If I left my real name and the real name of the owner of the airplane, our chances would be worse, but still not zero. If I put down fictitious names and eventually got arrested, the FBI would have the option of charging me with the falsification of documents or fraud, a simple criminal act for which I would have no defense. Leaving my real name, even though it would increase the likelihood of arrest, would help box the FBI into the possibly embarrassing position of charging me with the "crime" of bringing food to the hungry. That was a political act, rather than a criminal one, and would allow me to mount a much more effective defense. I decided to take the increased risk in exchange for being in a better position if they ever did prosecute.

I picked up the form and wrote in the real names, still sticking to my story about colliding with an eagle. The younger airport owner returned after taking Tom to a cab, so his friendly father offered to drive Larry and me all the way out to the Sioux City airport where we could get a plane east to Chicago. The old man had been a pilot since the biplane days in the twenties. Driving along in his car, he thought to take our minds off the terrifying flight we had just been through by telling us stories about his own numerous crash landings. It didn't work.

At about that same time, Billy and Strobe were taking off from Fort Dodge, 115 miles ahead of us. They had just completed a leisurely refueling stop. Two-and-a-half hours later they landed at Hinsdale Airport in suburban Chicago. Earlier we had decided to rendezvous there, rather than fly the three rented aircraft back into Midway, just in case the authorities were waiting for our return. Billy called Bob Talbot, our friend in Chicago, who had agreed to drive to Hinsdale with two other pilots and ferry the planes the short distance back to Midway. It was all according to previous plans.

While Billy was calling Bob, Jim and John arrived at Hinsdale. They had let Oliver off in Omaha and given him enough money to get back to Rapid City. Oliver had departed quite happy with the day's events. Jim and John had been apprehensive about landing in Omaha, expecting an alert to be out for our aircraft. But nobody questioned them or did anything out of the ordinary, and soon they were back in the air on their way to Hinsdale. It was a happy reunion when they arrived. They made fun of Billy and Strobe for coming back with a cargo net full of food and good-naturedly boasted about their own two passes over Wounded Knee. The four of them opened the two duffel bags Billy had brought back and to their relief found mostly beans. None was upset about my not being there. They knew that any of a dozen harmless reasons could be responsible for the delay.

Bob Talbot drove up to Hinsdale bristling with rumors about the FBI snooping around Midway Airport asking questions about us. Since he didn't want to fly into Midway himself, he arranged for the two aircraft to be ferried by other pilots and then drove Billy, John, and Strobe back to their cars in the city. Jim was dropped at the passenger terminal on the commercial side of Midway where he took the next flight back to Albuquerque. They all got home quite safely.

Meanwhile, in Sioux City, Larry and I arrived at Municipal Airport. Tom was still waiting for his plane. The next flight anywhere east did not depart until 11:00 a.m., an hour-and-a-half away. It went to Chicago where Tom planned to get a connecting flight to Washington. Larry and I bought tickets on the same flight. Tom was off in a corner of the airport lobby busy writing the exclusive story he had earned by accompanying the airlift. Larry decided to do some publicity work himself.

He got into a telephone booth and placed an anonymous call to the Associated Press office in New York. He told a reporter there that he had flown with the Wounded Knee airlift and was with the airlift's chief pilot who was willing to be interviewed but would not give his name. Were they interested? They were. In a moment Larry was transferred to a senior editor. Their office had been called earlier that morning by our friend in Boston, following through on our plan to give the press our own version of the story immediately after the drop. Larry spoke briefly with the editor, then put me on the phone.

While I answered questions about the airlift, Larry ducked into the next telephone booth and called United Press International. He made them the same offer he had just made to AP, an interview with the anonymous chief pilot of the airlift. By the time I finished with AP, Larry had me set up to begin again with UPI. And so it went as Larry orchestrated my way from UPI to the Washington *Post* to the Los Angeles *Times* to the New York *Times*.

But in my conversation with the New York *Times* I learned more from them than they did from me—and it was all bad news. One of their editors said that only minutes before they had received a sketchy report that a major fire fight had taken place at Wounded Knee right after the airlift. No details were available, but some people had been seriously hurt. The editor invited us to call a *Times* reporter in Rapid City who might have more information and would want to interview me.

We called Rapid City immediately. The reporter said that one Indian was dead and six others were critically injured in a fire fight following the air drop. (It was many hours later before we learned that the fire fight did not occur until two hours after the airlift and that in fact one person was mortally wounded and five or six others were injured but not critically.)

Larry and I came away from the phone booth reeling. We were deeply shocked by the news of the fire fight. In a daze, we drifted to the end of the airport lobby away from Tom and sat down. The first thought in both of our minds was that we were at fault, we were responsible for people dead and dying. The airlift had caused the fire fight, and we had created the airlift. It was a cold and a profoundly sobering moment. There was no easy wisdom to wipe away our guilt, despite how we hung on each other's words in hopes of hearing it.

We had acted mercifully to help people fighting a battle we believed was just and correct. Men acting not on principle, but because it was their job, were angered by our action and decided of their own free will to shoot those people. Either we had to accept the ultimate blame for the shootings or we had to accept the responsibility of forcing the blame onto the government and the men who had pulled the triggers. But in that moment, we could only feel stunned by the fact that people were needlessly suffering or dead as a result of our actions. Not until much later in the day did we regain the composure to know that we were not to blame, that some battles do pit good against evil, and that morality does not lie in turning one's back on such struggles.

Meanwhile, at the other end of the waiting room, Tom was finishing his eyewitness account of the airlift for the Boston *Globe*. Little time remained before our departure. Seeing Larry and me in such intense conversation, Tom thought it best not to interrupt and ask either of us to read his story before he phoned it in to the *Globe*. It was a grave mistake on his part and one I should have stopped him from making. But Larry and I were absorbed by news of the fire fight and were not keeping track of what was happening around us. Our flight was called and we boarded the Ozark Airlines jet. As I buckled in, a little Piper Cherokee taxied past the window.

We sat three abreast on the jet. Tom was told about the battle at Wounded Knee, and for a long time afterward nobody said anything. The fire fight was all I could think about. No doubt the same was true for Larry and Tom. Then Larry started quietly crying. His sobs were wrenching and came from deep inside.

Tom leaned over and put a hand on Larry's shoulder. Very softly, he said, "It wasn't our fault, Larry; it wasn't our fault."

Larry drew away from Tom's touch. Choking back his sobs, he lashed out, bitterly. "Yeah, that's easy to say. But somebody's dead back there. Right where we were, somebody's dead. Just think about that. One Indian person is dead. Dead. And six more are probably going to die."

"I know," Tom murmured, "I know."

Larry calmed himself a little, then went on talking through his tears. "Look, I'm not trying to say we killed those people. But the airlift isn't isolated from Wounded Knee and what's happening there. You know, the main thing that went on today was the fire fight, not the little adventure that we were on. What we did was fine, but think about the seriousness of what's just gone down at Wounded Knee. People have had to die to show this fat, corrupt country what it's like to be an Indian."

The three of us were silent for some time. We wanted to make some kind of contact with the people in Wounded Knee to extend our sympathy and try to share their pain. But we knew all the telephone lines were cut. We decided to send a telegram to Rita in the Rapid City legal offices in hopes that she would give it to a backpacker who might carry it into Wounded Knee. We composed the message on the plane and sent it as soon as we landed in Chicago: TO THE INDEPENDENT OGLALA NATION. WE CAME IN PEACE TO BRING YOU FOOD. WE GRIEVE FOR THOSE WHO WERE SHOT TODAY AND PRAY OUR PEACEFUL MISSION WAS NOT THE CAUSE. IN STRUGGLE THERE IS LIFE. [signed] THE WOUNDED KNEE AIRLIFT.

With a stopover in Davenport, it was after 3:00 when we finally got to Chicago's O'Hare Airport. Tom left us for the press room. He wanted to start a follow-up story on the airlift while waiting for his connecting flight to Washington. Our farewell was a casual one, given how close we had been for the past six days.

Larry and I made several calls to notify people of our return and get an updated report from Wounded Knee. Bob Talbot told me about the FBI nosing around Midway. He didn't think it was serious, only a routine check of our activities prior to leaving the previous Thursday. We still had to finish paying the owners of the rented airplanes, as well as arrange for repairs on the damaged aircraft in South Sioux City. All things considered, it seemed best to get some rest first. I called a friend who lived on the north side of Chicago, far from Midway Airport. Larry and I took a cab to her apartment, showered, ate a huge dinner in a nearby restaurant, and slept for twelve hours.

Early the next morning, I arranged to meet Bob in a coffee shop close to Midway. On our way south, Larry and I stopped in the Loop at the out-of-town newspaper stand. The story of the airlift and the fire fight at Wounded Knee was on the front page of the New York *Times* and prominently covered in the Chicago and Washington papers. Larry's press work had succeeded. The stories were accurate. They all mentioned that the cargo was entirely food and that the airlift was carried out by people associated with the anti-war movement acting in solidarity with the Indians.

The New York *Times* story reported Stanley Pottinger, the head Justice Department official at Wounded Knee, discussing the airlift at an afternoon press conference. Larry and I laughed as we read about Pottinger's pompously placing the exact time of the drop twelve minutes too late, giving the wrong colors for one of the airplanes, and insisting that federal authorities had not been able to see our aircraft registration numbers because they were covered up. The dawn air drop really had caught federal forces unprepared, if not sound asleep. Through Pottinger, they had to lie to the press, embarrassed by their failure to see the large numbers clearly painted on the sides and wings of each of our planes. Their ineptness was both amusing and pathetic.

The newsstand did not have a Boston paper. Since we wanted to see Tom's story more than any of the others, I called the Medical Aid for Indochina office in Boston and asked them to read me the *Globe*. Tom's "exclusive" was on page one. Larry and I shared the earpiece as we listened to the story.

There was some good description and a long section of the message we had enclosed in the food bags, but also a disturbing number of minor factual mistakes. At the end of the article, Tom described our damaged tail and the long terrifying ride following the drop at Wounded Knee. The story got more and more personal. Then, in the next-to-last-paragraph, swept up by his own excitement, Tom told of our crash landing "near Sioux City, Iowa."

Larry and I were stunned. I hung up and we looked at each other in disbelief. "That fool," Larry sputtered, "how could he write that? Damn it, the agreement was that he wouldn't mention the names of any of the people or any of the places."

"Yeah, I know," I said, walking away from the phone booth and angrily throwing the newspapers into the back seat of the car we were driving. "He sure lost himself in that story, didn't he?"

"Well, he wasn't too good with the parachutes, either."

We got in the car and continued driving south to meet Bob.

I looked over at Larry. "You know there are only three airports near Sioux City. The FBI can find a plane with a busted tail just by making a few telephone calls. Once they get the aircraft number, they can trace it to the owner at Midway and then just ask him who he rented the plane to. That's it. A chimpanzee could solve this case without getting up from his desk."

"Right. Thanks to Tom."

"It's all up to the FBI now, whether they want arrests or not. Once they read that story, it won't take them four hours to get back to Midway."

Larry groaned. "Do you think Tom did it on purpose? I mean, do you think he intended to break the agreement all along?"

"No, I think I understand why he did it. Put yourself in his place. He's scared stiff of flying. He went through a terrible experience in the air. When he was safely back on the ground, he started thinking, 'My god, I could've gotten killed up there.' Then he had to write about how he had almost died. He was fascinated by it, lost in it, until he forgot about previous agreements and the words came spilling out, indiscriminately. He didn't do it intentionally. If it's anybody's fault, it's yours and mine. We shouldn't have trusted him to phone that copy in without reading it first. But we were too hung up thinking about the fire fight."

"So what are you saying?" Larry asked nervously. "Are we going to be arrested?"

"I don't know. I still think they'd look foolish arresting us for bringing food to starving Indians. But it's the FBI. They're crazy enough to do anything. Anyway, it'll just be me and Billy. We're the only names the owners have. The FBI's not going to assign agents to trace our path all the way out to Wounded Knee and figure out who the rest of you were."

"I think you're nuts. I think they're going to arrest all of us. But just tell me if you agree with this one thing. If either of us is arrested, it shouldn't be here in Chicago. It should be in Boston. We're known there. There are good lawyers that would help us. We should do what we have to do now and then get the hell onto a Boston flight as fast as we can."

"Sure, I agree with that."

Bob was in the restaurant waiting for us. He had just called the two flight services that had rented us the three airplanes. Earlier that morning, FBI agents had visited both places. At that time, Bob didn't know enough to ask if the agents were carrying copies of the Boston *Globe*. The aircraft owners, made aware of our difficulties, were anxious to get paid before we were arrested. The flight service that owned the damaged aircraft took the news calmly, having good insurance, but wanted to know the location of their plane and how badly it had been torn up.

Bob was visibly shaken. Despite a happy-go-lucky streak and his reputation as a daredevil pilot, he was still an ex-small-town chief of police, the father of four children in a strict parochial school, and a leading professional aviator who took his flying very seriously. He didn't like working on the wrong side of the FBI. We ordered some breakfast and tried to calm each other with a scholarly discussion about the aerodynamics of flying with only half a tail. Afterward, Bob talked about the flight service owner from whom we had rented only a single plane, one of the two safely returned by ferry pilots the night before.

"Look, the poor guy is scared shitless. I'm sure he told the FBI everything he knew, which luckily wasn't so much. But if you just waltz into his office to pay him, you might come out wearing handcuffs."

I knew Bob was right. "OK, but we've got some leverage over him. You can bet he wants the money we owe him a lot more than he wants to help the FBI. Get on the phone and tell him to meet us in a restaurant right away. Pick a place we can get to before he can. Tell him we want to pay, but he has to come alone or he'll never see us again."

Bob arranged the meeting in a nearby diner. The man promised to show up in fifteen minutes. We drove there immediately and parked a block away. Larry and Bob went inside to wait for him while I stayed in the car watching the entrance. If he was followed or accompanied by anyone else, I was ready to drive away from the diner and meet Larry later. The FBI would be after me, not him. If the owner came alone, Bob and Larry planned to stall him inside for five minutes to be safe, then bring him out to the car to be paid.

But he never came. Bob and Larry left the diner five minutes after he was due. "Let's get out of here," Larry said, "I smell a rat." We sped off, stopped at a phone booth about a mile away, and Bob called the man's office. He apologized for not coming, claiming an important customer had come in just as he was about to leave. Bob arranged another meeting, fifteen minutes later, in the greenhouse of a local garden shop. We used the same plan, with me in a parked car down the block. This time he came, on time and alone. He was very frightened. He assured me that he had said nothing to the FBI, which was a lie. Then, nervously clutching the money I had given him, he fled. Finished with one owner, we drove back to Bob's house to telephone the other and arrange a pay-off meeting with him. Larry and I retrieved the belongings we had left with Bob a week before. While we put on fresh clothes, Bob made the call from the kitchen. Suddenly he slammed the phone down and burst into the room.

"Get going, fast! The FBI is on the way over here. That guy gave my address to two agents who came in asking for it. They left his office about a minute before I called. I don't want you two here when they show up."

I barely had my belt buckled. The second owner's office was only three minutes away. I threw on a shirt and without stopping to button it, helped Larry scoop up all our stuff. Dropping socks and toothpaste, we dashed through the house, out the kitchen door, and across the backyard to the car. We threw what we had on the front seat, got the motor running, and pulled away, tires screeching. Several blocks away we parked the car and breathlessly finished dressing.

Larry wanted to drive immediately to O'Hare Airport and get on the next flight to Boston. I insisted that we stay and figure out some way to pay our last remaining debt. We owed the second flight service for two of our planes, including the damaged one in South Sioux City. They knew that Bob was a friend of ours and were apparently willing to implicate him in the airlift. Perhaps a prompt payment would reduce Bob's chances of being drawn into the whole mess and ease their anxiety about the damaged aircraft.

We waited a half hour and then telephoned Bob from a supermarket. As soon as he heard my voice, he said, "Hi, Cindy," and I knew the FBI agents must still be questioning him. Talking quickly, I told Bob that I wanted to pay the flight service and hopefully take the pressure off him, but I also wanted to get out of Chicago fast. I asked him to tell me where he would be that night so I could get a friend to bring him some money. Then he could pay the flight service owner the next day.

"Sorry, honey, I can't make it tonight," he said, "I'm lecturing on helicopter safety at the Fire Academy . . . .yes, from eight to ten."

"Good, Bob," I answered, "I'll give the money to a friend and she'll bring it to you tonight. That's at the Fire Department Headquarters Building, right?"

"Right."

"Okay, now listen. Do those agents have my name and Billy's?"

"Yes."

"Anyone else?"

"No."

"Do they have warrants?"

"I don't know."

"But I take it they're not arresting you, they're just trying to question you, right?"

"Yes, I'm sure that's true. Listen, I'm sorry but there are some people over here I want to talk to. I'll call you back later."

"Okay, Bob, good luck. I'll call you when I get back to Boston. Remember, policemen are your friends."

While I talked to Bob, Larry called the lawyer in New York who had agreed to help us if we got into trouble away from home. He explained the situation and gave the lawyer a list of friends in Boston and New York who could be called on for bail money if that was required. We crawled back into our rented car and drove to where the friend who had housed us the night before worked. Once inside her office, we described the Keystone cops episode that had just taken place at Bob's house. The story of how we had gone out the back door seconds before the FBI came in the front was funnier than I expected it to be. Soon the three of us were laughing and happy.

I told my friend that Larry and I wanted to leave Chicago right away and asked if she would deliver the money to Bob at the Fire Academy that night. She agreed. Then I called the flight service to get the amount of our bill. I told the owner that we had not seen the FBI and would try to avoid them for as long as possible. I described the damage to his aircraft and gave him the name and phone number of the airport in South Sioux City. I said that for the time being he would not be able to reach me, but that I would be in touch with him about anything we might still owe on the damaged plane. After counting out the money to be taken to Bob, Larry and I thanked my friend for delivering it and for putting us up the night before.

An hour later, we turned in our rented car and purchased eastbound tickets at O'Hare. Larry decided to go first to Washington, where he had two days of work to do for Medical Aid for Indochina. I was returning to Boston, fully expecting to be questioned by FBI agents there and perhaps arrested on minor charges. It was late afternoon, and we each had two hours to wait. Over dinner in the airport coffee shop we began to unwind. All the loose ends had been taken care of, and we would soon be safely out of Chicago. The restaurant was busy as the early rush-hour crowd filled the airport. The public address system was continually paging people and announcing flight departures and arrivals. In spite of the noise and the crowds and our uncertain situation, we felt better and better, especially when food arrived at our table.

But halfway through the main course, the loudspeaker said, "American Airlines, paging Mr. B. Zimmerman. Will Mr. B. Zimmerman come to the American information desk, upper level, please."

Larry dropped his fork. "Did you hear that?" he said. "They're here. They traced us to the airport."

"Take it easy, Larry."

"What do you mean, *take it easy*? We've got to get out of here. We can use phony names and fly to Atlanta. Then we can get up to Washington and Boston from there."

"Okay, we can do that if we have to, but let's finish dinner first and figure out if that's the best way to handle this."

"Finish dinner? Are you crazy? They're about to arrest you."

"Look, there must be fifty thousand people here. They can't just 'cover the airport' the way they do in the movies. The only way they're going to find me is if I walk up to that information desk and hand myself over."

We argued, but with well over a hundred boarding gates, to say nothing of the time necessary to assemble that many policemen and duplicate that many photographs, Larry quickly saw the logic of my position and we finished eating. Then, instead of answering the page at the information desk, we called American Airlines on the telephone. We planned to get on the next plane to Atlanta or Miami under assumed names if they continued to insist that I come to the information desk to get my message. But the American operator told me that the page had already been answered. It was a simple coincidence. Someone had the same name I did. We boarded our separate jets without incident and after a bizarre day as fugitives from the law, we happily left Chicago behind.

Later that night I was met at the Boston airport and taken home by the friend who had composed the original draft of the statement we had put in the food bags. The next morning, Thursday, I was back at work at the Medical Aid for Indochina office. When the FBI failed to appear by the end of the day, I assumed they had simply decided, all things considered, that we were not worth prosecuting. I spent a quiet evening at home and worked through half of Friday in the office. When the opposition still failed to materialize, I called Larry in Washington and told him that the whole incident was over; we were not going to be bothered.

But I spoke too soon. Late Friday afternoon, two short-haired men wearing the traditional beige raincoat knocked on our office door and asked to speak to me. As six of my fellow workers looked on, they identified themselves as "special agents" of the FBI. They wanted to talk to me alone. I explained to them that I knew too many people who had talked to FBI agents alone and then found themselves without witnesses when their comments were distorted by the same agents in courts of law. If there were going to be two of them, I insisted there would have to be two of us. They agreed. Reaching for a tape recorder, I invited the agents into the next room. They asked about the tape recorder, and I told them that if they had nothing to hide, there was no reason not to tape our conversation. At least we would not have to argue later over what had or had not been said. The two men informed me that it was against FBI policy to conduct an interview with a tape recorder present. The game had gone on long enough. I told them to produce a warrant or get out of the office. They left.

Once I refused to cooperate, I assumed they would get an arrest warrant and come back. I alerted lawyers and friends but did not see the FBI the rest of that day or night.

Shortly before 8:00 the next morning, Saturday, I awoke to simultaneous pounding on the front and rear doors of the house I shared with five friends. It sounded like an arrest just from the way they knocked. I got dressed, went to the front door, and pulled away the curtain. There were three of them, flashing badges up to the window and pulling their jackets aside just enough to reveal the guns on their hips. I asked for their warrant and the leader shouted back that it was downtown and that if I didn't open the door, they would break it in. It was a beautiful wooden door. I opened it.

They slammed handcuffs on my wrists just as one of my housemates appeared on the stairs in his pajamas waving a portable tape recorder and demanding to know what was going on. The head agent looked up. "Just who the hell are you?" he demanded. My friend gave his name, informed the agents that he was the newscaster for a popular local radio station, and told them that he was covering the arrest for the evening news. For a moment the agents were speechless, then they pushed him aside and threatened to arrest him for interfering with justice.

Meanwhile, the three agents who came in the front were joined by three others who had been "covering the back." Two of them started up the stairs to the second floor. They were met by two women who lived in the house. The women blocked their way, refusing to let them pass until a search warrant was produced. The agents tried to shove them aside, but the women shoved back. Since they were higher up on the stairs, they easily won the scuffle, and the government retreated back down to the first floor. To the delight of thousands in the Boston area, the entire incident was broadcast that evening on my friend's news program.

With an escort of six FBI agents I was marched in handcuffs out to an unmarked car. My housemates shouted questions from the porch about what progress the Bureau was making in the Watergate investigation. The officers had come in three cars. The one they put me in drove downtown sandwiched between the other two, just in case the FBI agent driving it tried to get away. The two agents on either side of me in the back seat apologized for not taking off my handcuffs but explained that the "rules" required them. I said that it was pretty heavy security for such a minor arrest. Little did I realize then exactly what the charges were going to be.

One of the agents complained about the hostility of the people in my house. I reminded him that the "rules" also required search and arrest warrants. Then I asked how it felt to have captured someone who brought food to hungry Indians. He said they didn't know much about the content of the case or the crime or what evidence there was against me. They had just received orders to bring me in and that's what they were doing.

The three agents riding with me complained to each other about having to report for duty at six that morning. One told of plans to spend his Saturday gardening and that my arrest would ruin his day. Another explained that he would have to break a promise to take his kids to the park. I sat there shocked, feeling completely objectified. My life was about to undergo a dramatic turn for the worse, and the human instruments of that turn talked about pulling up weeds and frolicking in the park, as though I weren't there at all. They were robots with no conception of protecting the community or upholding the law. They followed orders and just did their job, and that morning their job happened to be me.

The FBI office downtown was empty, closed for the weekend. All six agents took me in. It was a huge, spotless room with about thirty gray metal desks arranged in three long rows. There wasn't a sign of humanity anywhere, not a single sheet of paper visible on a single desk. Everyone had to put away all his work before leaving for the day. The telephone on each and every desk was placed squarely on the far right-hand corner. The place smelled of mindlessness.

One agent took me into a side room that contained a new automatic fingerprinting machine. He tried for ten minutes but could not make it work. Then another agent came in; he too was unable to operate it. Finally, the two of them called in their leader who, after failing himself, decided to fingerprint me in the orthodox inkpad fashion: The FBI didn't look too good that morning. In fact, they seemed rather mediocre, used to performing on command whether the job was boring or brutal. Four hours later the judge arrived. I was permitted a short conference with an attorney who had agreed to represent me. After we were all sworn in, one of the FBI agents took the stand. As evidence against me, he introduced a xerox copy of Tom's article in the Boston *Globe*.

The judge asked a few questions about my background, establishing to his satisfaction that I was properly middle class. He set bail at $1,000, unsecured. That meant no money was required, but I could not leave the state of Massachusetts without his permission. On the way out of the courtroom, my lawyer handed me a copy of the warrant. The charges were incredible.

I was under arrest for three separate federal felonies, each one punishable by up to five years in a federal penitentiary and $10,000 fine. The charges were: Count I—interfering with federal officers in the lawful performance of their duties; Count II—conspiracy to commit offenses against the United States; Count III—interstate travel with the intent to aid, abet, promote, encourage, and participate in a riot. All three charges were rendered in much greater detail. For example, the full text of Count I read as follows:

> On or about the 17th day of April, 1973, near Wounded Knee, in the District of South Dakota, William B. Zimmerman did wilfully, knowingly, and unlawfully commit an act to obstruct, impede and interfere with U.S. Marshals and agents of the Federal Bureau of Investigation who were then engaged in the lawful performance of their official duties incident to and during the commission of a civil disorder at Wounded Knee, South Dakota, which civil disorder obstructed, delayed, and adversely affected commerce and the conduct of a federally protected function, in that said defendant did participate in the execution of a plan to supply persons engaged in the civil disorder by parachuting supplies into Wounded Knee from aircraft flying over Wounded Knee,

in violation of Title 18, United States Code, section 231,
subsection a), paragraph 3.

The second and third counts, the conspiracy and interstate riot
charges, were the same two violations that the government had consistently but unsuccessfully used against its political enemies, from the
Chicago Eight to the Viet Nam Veterans Against the War. Meanwhile, as I
was being informed that the United States wanted fifteen years of my life,
similar warrants were issued for Billy and, surprisingly, Tom.

As a reporter, Tom's case was unique. The federal government occasionally subpoenas newspeople before grand juries where they are compelled to reveal information about stories they have covered. For the first
time, a reporter for a major metropolitan newspaper was indicted for the
"crime" he had been assigned to write about. It was another escalation in
the Nixon Administration's attacks on the press. But the *Globe* lined up
solidly behind their man, from the corporate president in Boston to
Tom's bureau chief in Washington, who said, "When the day comes that
you have to check with lawyers whether to cover a story, then Nixon's the
editor-in-chief."

The FBI had a bit of a hard time finding Tom to make the arrest.
Despite all of his *Globe* stories carrying a Washington dateline, they
conducted an early morning raid on a house in Boston he had not lived in
for two years. Agents roughed up the doctor currently living there before
realizing their mistake. Tom and his lawyer heard about the warrant
before the super-sleuths of the FBI managed to find his new address,
which was listed in the Washington phone book. The lawyer called the
local agent-in-charge and arranged for Tom to voluntarily surrender on
Monday morning.

Billy did not do as well as his two white co-defendants. He too was
awakened by federal knocking early Saturday morning and given a
handcuffed ride to the (Chicago) FBI office. But no judge was called in on
Saturday to set Billy's bond. He spent the weekend in jail. Monday
morning, instead of an unsecured release, Billy had to post $200 bail. As
he was walking out of federal court, Mayor Daley's city police arrived and
arrested him for $2,500 in unpaid parking tickets. He spent several more
hours behind bars before city officials realized they had the wrong
William Wright.

The following week, they got Bob, despite his earlier refusal to fly with
the airlift. The day that Larry and I ran out his back door just before FBI
agents came in the front, Bob gave them a statement including complete
details of his own involvement, but no names of any of the rest of us. The
agents impressed Bob with their politeness and understanding. Like most
people, he didn't think of FBI agents as mere cops. He accepted their

assurances that they were not after him since he had only helped in the preparation and had not gone on the flight itself. Naturally, they were lying. Bob's treatment was no different than that given to the rest of us, right down to the handcuffs and the felony indictment.

A few days after Bob's arrest, Chicago FBI agents came to see John's parents. It turned out that the airlift case did concern the government enough to justify teams of investigators tracking our path across the Midwest. In Huron, South Dakota, they obtained a list of all the long distance telephone calls we made from our motel rooms. It was a short list because we almost always used a pay phone. But one night John went through the motel switchboard to telephone his parents and tell them he would be a day or two late getting back home. John was there alone when the agents arrived. Disappointed that his parents were not in, they unsuspectingly asked him if he knew anything about a call from South Dakota the previous week. Convinced that he had done nothing the FBI would be interested in, John naively said, sure, he had made it. They thanked him for his help and left. The next morning they returned with a warrant for his arrest.

Somewhere along our route, the FBI got Jim's name from a motel register or a flight plan. Agents came to his house in Albuquerque, but Jim refused to talk to them. The following day, he was arrested. The charges were the same three federal felonies, and like all the other white defendants, Jim was released without posting any bail money.

But there was more to come. Two weeks after the airlift, we heard a rumor that the FBI was looking for Larry. He had been working at my side in the Medical Aid for Indochina office in Boston all of that time, but apparently they never thought to look there. A lawyer representing Larry called FBI headquarters in Boston. He questioned several agents, but all seemed unaware of the airlift. Finally, he asked the agent-in-charge to confirm or deny rumors that his client was wanted. According to the lawyer, the head agent then muffled the telephone with his hand and shouted, apparently to the entire FBI office, "Hey, are we looking for anyone named Levin?" After a pause of several minutes, the highly trained investigators discovered that a warrant was indeed out for Larry's arrest. He voluntarily surrendered the next morning.

Tom's case received a lot of publicity. Newspaper columnists and editorial writers came to the defense of their profession. Before long, Tom was the focus of a counterattack by the press at a time when the Nixon Administration was reeling under the sensational implications of Watergate. On May 22, a White House press spokesman admitted that President Nixon was personally following the Tom Oliphant-Wounded Knee airlift case. With U.S. Attorney General Kleindienst already forced from office by Watergate, his replacement, Elliot Richardson, decided that the

Justice Department had enough trouble without tackling Oliphant as well. On July 5, he ordered all charges against Tom dropped. In a move that came as a happy surprise, charges were dropped at the same time against Larry. The reason cited was "lack of sufficient evidence."

A year-and-a-half after the airlift, as I write these lines, Billy, Jim, Bob, John, and I are still under federal indictments and awaiting trial in Deadwood, South Dakota. The judge has yet to set a date for the proceedings to begin. Tom and Larry are both free and unencumbered. Strobe and Oliver were never apprehended, and to this day the FBI has not discovered who they are.[1]

+   +   +

Why did the government come down so hard on the airlift? Why did they risk the embarrassment of prosecuting—with triple felony indictments no less—people who had merely fed the hungry? Why did the FBI conduct a criminal investigation of the airlift that involved dozens of agents, the interviewing of witnesses in at least eight states, the services of fingerprint experts, photographic laboratories, local police departments, and enough stenographers and typists to grind out thousands of pages of reports? One lawyer estimated that the investigation cost over $200,000 of taxpayers' money, all spent before the trial had even begun.

Several answers to these questions have been suggested. Our delivery of food came at a very critical time. The people in Wounded Knee were forced to consider certain concessions in negotiations simply because they were being effectively cut off from supplies. Also, the exuberant morale and optimism that did so much to unify people throughout the occupation was just beginning to wither. The government was fully aware of these factors and expected a surrender at any moment.

Because of unfavorable publicity and the weight of public opinion, the government was anxious to get out of the Wounded Knee situation as quickly as possible. If that could be achieved without an armed assault, so much the better. Armed assaults are costly in terms of public relations. Only a year before, Governor Nelson Rockefeller had suffered massive

---

[1]By 1975, Attorney General Richardson had been replaced by William Saxbe, who in turn had been replaced by Edward Levi, the fourth attorney general in office since our arrest. On February 27, two years to the day after the seizure of Wounded Knee, the Justice Department finally dismissed all counts against us. Long before, in 1966, Attorney General Levi was provost of the University of Chicago. In May of that year, students seized and held the University's Administration Building in a prolonged protest against the war in Viet Nam and the draft. Levi and I argued with each other for three days as we negotiated the end of the occupation, he for the University and I for the students.

criticism after ordering a brutal attack on New York's Attica Prison, resulting in the needless loss of 43 lives. The Nixon Administration had enough blood on its hands. But just as they caught the scent of victory, the huge food drop destroyed their hopes. Evidently, they were quite angry.

The manner in which the food was delivered must have also been very hard for the government to take. It is one thing when the courts issue temporary restraining orders allowing supplies past their blockades. It is quite another when daring overland backpackers defiantly infiltrate food and ammunition through their roadblocks and all-night patrols. But a squadron of airplanes, employing techniques like parachuting and split-second navigation, was certainly a particularly bitter pill for them to swallow. The action clearly implied an opposition more competent than they like to admit.

Finally, the airlift was tied to an organized political force, the anti-war movement. The airlift came not as eight random individuals helping an isolated group of Indians, but as a bridge from one movement to another. While no longer sponsoring demonstrations that drew millions of people into the streets, the loose-knit anti-war movement exerted a power far beyond its diminished numbers, because the many small groups that comprised it were well organized and focused in their work. The Bureau of Indian Affairs and the Justice Department did not want the anti-war movement involved. An expression of unity between it and the American Indian Movement may not have amounted to much in and of itself, but it was another small indication that more profound friendship is possible.

In the airlift, some of the more "privileged" and "free" opponents of the system reached across wide class and racial barriers that separated them from some of the least privileged. The action suggested that seemingly large differences between people can be overcome, that united effort is a real possibility. The powers behind the government fear the development of any kind of alliance between an organized predominantly white force, like the anti-war movement, and an organized non-white force, like the American Indian Movement. Whenever such an alliance begins to flower—even in such minor episodes as the Wounded Knee airlift—the government will try to crush it with what often seems to be excessive fury. Thus the heavy charges leveled against us.

But despite our indictments, the airlift was a clear victory. It delivered much-needed supplies to the Indians at Wounded Knee, allowing the occupation to continue for three more weeks until a settlement could be worked out that was not influenced by hunger and demoralization. The airlift was a message to the government and to the Indian people of America that struggles like the one at Wounded Knee would not be fought by Indians alone. And, hopefully, the airlift showed sympathetic non-Indian people the importance and the ever-present possibility of acts of solidarity. The arrests, though they constitute a major disruption in our lives, in the long run will be worth these achievements. The legal problems are another battle to be fought and won on another day.

There were dozens of anti-war activists who played behind-the-scenes roles in the airlift by raising money, buying food, coordinating publicity, doing legal work, and performing numerous other tasks. But among those who actually flew on the airlift, only Larry and I considered ourselves part of the anti-war movement. The people on the planes were a very diverse group and each came to different conclusions about the meaning of his experience:

Larry Levin, 25, political activist, Boston.

"We had to take risks, but they always seemed very secondary to me. What we did could almost be equated with those people who tried to smuggle food, as well as guns, into the Warsaw Ghetto to Jews fighting against the Nazis. They were taking a risk, but it couldn't be compared to the risk the Jews inside the Ghetto were taking by sacrificing everything to try and re-create their own society and their own culture.

"I don't think physical danger and physical suffering are worth talking about. I've just seen too much of it in pictures of the B-52 bombing in Viet Nam, and first-hand with my own eyes seeing what British soldiers are doing in Northern Ireland. And the most common example of all, to millions of Americans, the violence done to the Indians in this country. It's just ridiculous to try and compare that to any danger or suffering that someone like myself might have to endure.

"In Ireland, I saw people of great sensitivity and intellect forced to resort to very inhuman and brutal methods of resistance that repelled them because a foreign power was trying to deny them their culture and their way of life. When your very existence as a people is threatened, there comes a point where you're forced to respond, where you can't back down anymore. I'm sure that everyone in the U.S., no matter who they are, feels that there is a limit to how far they'll back down to some other group or some form of authority.

"When the Indians took action, it was so unique in this country in our time that it demanded a response, especially from those of us who had been working on a more ordinary political level—going to meetings and demonstrations, handing out leaflets, doing educational work. Their action represented the feelings of myself and many others about the kind of stand that needed to be taken, some stand in preservation of the values that are being eroded in this country, the values of culture, of preserving a culture like the Indians had against the erosion of American materialism.

"The Indian action at Wounded Knee represented a deeper level of commitment to political activism. It was one step beyond anything that had happened in the U.S. in the sixties. It took great courage and desperation on the part of the Indians to take that step and put themselves on the front lines like that. What they did had great meaning, not only for the Indians, but for all of us."

Jim Stewart, 28, ex-school teacher, Albuquerque, one child.

"It was worth it. I really remember the feeling we had when we came over and made that drop right on the button, how elated we were that we helped out those people and brought that food to them. I think that was worth it right there, just the knowledge that we had really helped some people that needed the help badly.

"I don't think the fact that we got arrested would stop me from doing it again. It didn't surprise me too much to get busted. You know, something's really screwed up in the government. We didn't do anything wrong, but it was no surprise that they arrested us.

"Still, it's been worth it even going through the legal hassle. You got to live your life as you see fit, and if it runs afoul of somebody's funny rules, that's part of living the life that you believe in.

"The airlift hasn't changed me particularly. Oh, it might have helped some to get me out of the rat race, but I was on my way out of it anyway. I don't think it's changed my thoughts or feelings about the way this country is being run or about the way my life works.

"It was definitely a momentous thing in my life. I really did something there; I stood up to be counted. But I don't think it changed me a whole lot. I was the same way before. I'd do it again."

John Adelman, 21, fork lift operator, Chicago.

"I had a good time on the airlift. It was something new, something exciting. I didn't think of it as being on the other side of the law when I was doing it.

"If I had it to do over again knowing that I'd be arrested, I wouldn't do it. There's just been too much legal hassle. I'm not a political activist, just a student going to college and working to be able to fly.

"This is *their* country, man . . . mine, too, I guess, but you got to play by their rules."

Billy Wright, 28, professional pilot and flight instructor, Chicago, one child.

"The airlift was a far out thing to do, man. Really. The adventure wasn't so much, I mean, the adventure did mean something to me 'cause I like to do shit like that when the opportunity presents itself. But you know, for the first time in a long while, I said to myself, 'Well, damn, I'm doing something here that I ain't gonna collect nothing on, and it's gonna be something good.'

"But I'll tell you, nobody **ever** unloaded no food on no blacks, man. I mean, it's just so widespread a problem that it's hard to do anything for the people. But here we had a confined thing. We knew where to find the problem and we knew what to do about it.

"This may sound like a strange thing to say in America, but you know what was so good about the airlift? It was a legal opportunity to do something right."

Bob Talbot, 35, professional pilot and collegiate aviation instructor, Chicago, four children.

"I was proud of the airlift. It was a fun thing, for one. But it was also the first political thing I've ever really gotten involved in . . . other than trying to get the mayor indicted when I was chief of police down in North Carolina. I lost so miserably on that, that I just gave up on politics and started worrying about taking care of my own family.

"But the legal hassle is what made the airlift memorable. If I hadn't been arrested, I would have forgotten the whole thing; it would have been just another episode in my everyday life. I mean, a man doesn't ponder much about giving ten dollars to the poor. But when you have to fight like hell to do it, you tend to remember it.

"Actually, it is the arrest and the legal hassle that made the airlift worthwhile for me. It polarized my views. It made me take a different stand toward my government. It's not a government of the people anymore. It's a government of the top three percent. And I'm not in it; therefore, I don't like it. Maybe if I was in the top three percent, I'd be fighting as hard as they are to hang on to it. But I'm not really even sure of that anymore.

"Flying is my business and teaching people to fly is my business. I didn't give a shit what you were doing, if it was over Israel or over Jordan, it made no difference to me. As long as I got my money, I'd fly. But I think the airlift moved me a little bit toward some kind of morality that maybe a guy should have. . . . rather than just flying for the dollar that I'm so famous for.

"I hate that picture of myself. It's like the airlift was a mirror that I didn't want to look into, but it had a good effect on me. That thing with the mayor in North Carolina was the turning point in my life toward apathy. The airlift was the turning point into coming back out to giving a shit again."

In the end, the story of these people is in no way remarkable. They rose to the demands of a moment. They responded with a determination that released their best efforts and their best instincts. They are no different than millions of other Americans who, if presented with a similar situation, would have reacted in like manner. And neither is the situation particularly unique. The opportunity to stand with people struggling for a better world is all around us, and nowadays in America stories like the airlift are quietly unfolding in every corner of the land.

16
Another Broken Treaty

"It matters little where we pass the remnant of our days. They will not be many. A few more moons; a few more winters—and not one of the descendants of the mighty hosts that once moved over this broad land or lived in happy homes, protected by the Great Spirit, will remain to mourn over the graves of a people once more powerful and hopeful than yours. But why should I mourn at the untimely fate of my people? Tribe follows tribe, and nation follows nation, like the waves of the sea. It is the order of nature, and regret is useless. Your time of decay may be distant, but it will surely come, for even the White Man whose God walked and talked with him as friend with friend, cannot be exempt from the common destiny. We may be brothers after all. We will see. . . .

"And when the last Red Man shall have perished, and the memory of my tribe shall have become a myth among the White Man, these shores will swarm with the invisible dead of my tribe, and when your children's children think themselves alone in the field, the store, the shop, upon the highway, or in the silence of the pathless woods, they will not be alone. At night when the streets of your cities and villages are silent and you think them deserted, they will throng with the returning hosts that once filled and still love this beautiful land. The White Man will never be alone."

—Chief Seattle
Chinook, 1854

April 18, 1973, the day after the airlift, a crowd of people gathered at one of the federal roadblocks just outside Wounded Knee. All were permanent residents who had not been near their homes since the occupation began almost two months before. Dozens of their neighbors had stayed inside Wounded Knee from the beginning and had been incorporated into the occupying forces. Many who originally left later tried to return to Wounded Knee, but they were kept out by federal marshals and BIA police. With new supplies of food airlifted into the settlement, everyone knew the occupation would continue for some time. Many former residents gathered at the roadblock in another attempt to return home.

But the refugees were turned back once again. The last thing that Tribal Chairman Dick Wilson and the federal officers wanted was a stream of reservation Indians going *into* Wounded Knee rather than pouring *out* of it. They had told the press all along that the occupation was made up of off-reservation outsiders and that the real residents of Wounded Knee were strictly opposed to it. But the residents would not accept the blockade. Volunteer lawyers and legal workers tried unsuccessfully to work out a compromise. Finally, in a desperate bet that they would not be shot, fourteen Oglala Sioux women and children bravely ran through the government roadblock refusing to obey orders to halt.

The marshals were too surprised to react, and the blockade-crashers made it through to a warm welcome by the occupation. Frustrated by their inability to prevent the episode, the marshals angrily arrested everybody in sight, that is, all of those who had not tried to rush the roadblock, plus their lawyers. Twenty-one persons were taken into custody. In typical fashion, they were turned over to the BIA police who held them for 27 hours in overcrowded cells at the tribal jail in Pine Ridge. At their arraignment the next day, the legal personnel complained of being kicked and pushed by the tribal police. They were rewarded with a court order barring them from any further legal work on the reservation. The other defendants jailed in the incident, all Indians, ranged in age from 3 to 90 years.

That afternoon, April 19, the head Justice Department representative on the scene, Stanley Pottinger, acknowledged to the press that Wounded Knee was being subjected to periodic sniper fire. He admitted that Wilson's goon squad was responsible and that the forces of the U.S. government assembled there were somehow unable to stop them.

Three days earlier, just before the airdrop, Stan Holder, AIM security chief inside Wounded Knee, had voluntarily surrendered to federal agents. He sacrificed his own freedom in the hope of hastening negotiations. But on April 19, in an ironic twist, government men took Holder out of federal custody and actually brought him back to Wounded Knee. They wanted Holder inside to help implement the cease-fire in effect since the shooting of Frank Clearwater. After having accused AIM from the beginning of being responsible for the violence, the insincerity of the Justice Department was revealed as they turned to AIM to keep the peace.

With the exception of an occasional rifle shot and the persistent sniper activity, Wounded Knee remained calm for the next several days. Reflecting lack of interest in renewed negotiations, the Justice Department recalled Pottinger to Washington on April 20, leaving his deputy, Richard Hellstern, in charge.

Meanwhile, AIM leader Russell Means was out on bond and traveling around the country to encourage support for the occupation. In a Tulsa news conference on the 20th, he noted U.S. threats to resume bombing North Viet Nam in retaliation for alleged violations of the three-month-old Paris Peace Accords. Means admitted not having direct knowledge of the situation in Indochina, but pointed out that since the U.S. itself was such a specialist in treaty violations, the truth of their accusations against the North Vietnamese should be measured by their own treaty relations with American Indians. If the Indians used the same logic as the U.S. government, Means stated, they would be justified not only in taking Wounded Knee, but in blowing up Washington as well, civilian population and all.

Late at night on Saturday, April 21, federal officers captured close to 50 persons on the trail as they tried to hike through the newly fallen snow into Wounded Knee. They were jailed in Pine Ridge. The next day, Easter Sunday, 125 people from around the nation gathered at the nearby Rosebud Indian Reservation to show their support for the occupation. The group, composed primarily of clergymen, college students, and pacifists, began a five-day protest march intending to walk the hundred miles to Wounded Knee. Wilson's Tribal Council quickly barred the marchers from entering the Pine Ridge Reservation. The Council, however, still lacked a quorum since many of its members had resigned weeks before rather than continue to work under the personal dictates of Chairman Wilson.

Conveniently overlooking the illegality of the Tribal Council order, Hellstern announced that the Justice Department would support it. He complained to reporters that "at least 90% [of the protest marchers] are white." He saw no irony in the fact that almost all of his force of over 300 law enforcement officers were also white. The size of the protest march was relatively small. But Justice Department officials in Washington understood its significance. With the approach of summer, they feared that thousands of college students might decide to spend time at

Wounded Knee before going off on vacation or to summer jobs. The government had to buck massive public opposition in their use of armored personnel carriers and M-16 rifles against Indians. But the protests following the murders at Kent State and Jackson State had taught them how much more difficult it might be to deploy arms against college students.

Meanwhile, Tribal Chairman Wilson became increasingly belligerent. He stepped up his threats to launch an armed assault on Wounded Knee and continued to claim that there were only a few "real Indians" inside. Wilson was unaffected by the general attitude of restraint in the aftermath of Frank Clearwater's critical injury. When a reporter asked him how many casualties there might be if he did lead an attack against the settlement, Wilson calmly said, "Everyone in Wounded Knee."

More moderate elements on the government side—everyone, despite various positions, was more moderate than the FBI—had become impatient with Wilson, his sniper squads, and his constant attempts to sabotage any move toward a peaceful settlement. On April 9 Wilson's goon squad had established a roadblock only a hundred yards behind the federal roadblock on the Big Foot Trail, the highway that led from Wounded Knee toward Pine Ridge. The goons were ignored by U.S. marshals, but four FBI agents continued to work with them on 12-hour shifts helping to maintain the roadblock and organize patrols. In violation of federal firearms laws prohibiting automatic weapons in the hands of civilians, the FBI also supplied the goon squad with M-16s and ammunition.

On April 23, personnel from the Justice Department's independent Community Relations Service (CRS) tried to get into Wounded Knee to discuss the resumption of negotiations. They were stopped at gunpoint by eight men at the goon squad roadblock. The chief of the U.S. Marshal Service, in nominal command of federal forces, heard about the incident, went to the roadblock, and ordered the goons to let the CRS people pass. Wilson's men explained that they had been deputized by the Executive Committee of the Tribal Council, as well as the Chief Tribal Judge, as "emergency tribal law enforcement officers." (The Executive Committee and the Chief Judge were all appointed directly by Wilson.) The marshal was not impressed. He insisted the CRS people be allowed through. Angry words were exchanged and the eight deputized "emergency tribal law enforcement officers" leveled their guns at the chief marshal of the United States. A shootout appeared imminent.

The marshal backed off, temporarily, but the problem with Wilson had finally gotten out of hand. A while later, returning with adequate reinforcements, the chief marshal dismantled the roadblock, disarmed the eight goons, and placed them all under arrest. An FBI agent on the scene tried so hard to prevent the arrests that at one point the chief marshal had to tell the agent to cooperate or put his hands up. The arrests that night were the first against anyone on the Wilson side in the two months of the occupation.

In a matter of hours Wilson was on local radio calling for "all able-bodied Oglala Sioux" to meet him the next morning with their rifles in order to forcibly re-establish another Tribal Council roadblock outside Wounded Knee. Hellstern, speaking for the Justice Department, backed up the marshals and insisted that Wilson would not be allowed to erect another roadblock. So, while the actual occupation of Wounded Knee temporarily faded into the background, a major split opened between federal and tribal officials.

By 11:00 a.m. the next day, approximately 100 armed supporters of the Tribal Council, many of them neighboring white ranchers, assembled in Pine Ridge in response to Wilson's call. The tribal chairman led them in a 30-car motorcade across the bleak grasslands toward Wounded Knee. Seven miles from the settlement, they were stopped by 24 heavily armed U.S. marshals lined up across the road. The marshals, however, did not want a confrontation. Meetings were underway in Washington on the question of Tribal Council roadblocks and Wilson was urged to wait for the results.

At 12:15 p.m., a helicopter raced over the plains and landed in the middle of the armed standoff. Two senior FBI agents emerged with the news that high officials in Washington had given the go-ahead to Wilson's roadblock. Having made his point, Wilson sent most of his supporters back home. With the rest, he drove past the marshals to the outskirts of Wounded Knee and there, in cooperation with other FBI agents on the scene, he re-established his roadblock. Wilson then told reporters he had received assurances that all CRS personnel would not only stay out of Wounded Knee but leave the reservation entirely (thus making a negotiated settlement virtually impossible), and furthermore that charges would be dropped against the eight men arrested by marshals the previous night.

While all this was taking place just outside Wounded Knee, the Justice Department official supposedly in charge of all government forces in the area was completely in the dark. At a 2:00 p.m. press conference 20 miles away in Pine Ridge, Hellstern announced that the Tribal Council supporters would not be allowed to set up their blockade. He also insisted that CRS personnel would continue to mediate between the Justice Department and the people in Wounded Knee.

The episode was another example of how the FBI provoked situations to a greater level of confrontation than even their own superiors desired. Later in the day, an embarrassed Hellstern learned from reporters that

Four members of the airlift and two Oglala Sioux tribal leaders meeting on Pine Ridge Reservation a month after the occupation. From l. to r., Jim Stewart, Larry Levin, Chief Frank Fools Crow, the author, Billy Wright and Oscar Bear Runner. (*courtesy Peggy Stewart.*)

Treaty meetings between Oglala Sioux chiefs and White House r
resentatives following the end of the occupation. From l. to r., Ch
Red Cloud, Brad Patterson, assistant to Presidential Counsel G
ment and Chief Fools Crow. (*courtesy Ken Norgard.*)

Two U.S. Marshals operate an armored personnel carrier outside Wounded Knee. They've labelled a cattle skull "death machine" and attached it as a hood ornament to the APC. *(courtesy United Press International Photo.)*

the roadblock was already up. He tried to cover his tracks by claiming it was under the control of the FBI, not the Tribal Council. But back at the site, FBI agents would not say who was in charge, and Tribal Council supporters insisted that the roadblock was under their command. The poorly organized and misguided government mission at Wounded Knee was again split by rivalry within its ranks.

That same afternoon, Kent Frizzell returned from Washington. Weeks before, he had left Wounded Knee after serving as the head Justice Department negotiator. In the interval, President Nixon appointed him the Chief Solicitor of the Department of the Interior, of which the Bureau of Indian Affairs was a subsection. During the night following Hellstern's confused press conference, he and Frizzell and the chief marshal went together to the disputed roadblock. There was an angry and impatient confrontation. Frizzell demanded the removal of the blockade. Four of Wilson's men put their guns on the three highest government officials on the scene, who furiously got back in their car and left. Agents of the FBI looked on but did not interfere.

The next day Hellstern admitted to the press that the gunpoint confrontation had taken place and that the four men involved were not arrested. He said that for the time being Community Relations Service personnel would stay out of Wounded Knee and the Tribal Council roadblock would be allowed to remain in place. It was a complete capitulation to Wilson. When asked for his version of what had happened the night before at the roadblock, Wilson held his fingers a short distance apart and said, "We came this far from shooting Frizzell and Colburn [the chief marshal].

That same day, April 25, Frank Clearwater died in a Rapid City hospital. His wife, Morning Star, asked that he be laid to rest in Wounded Knee. Hellstern responded by announcing that the government of the United States would not permit the body to be buried at Wounded Knee because Clearwater was not an Oglala Sioux.

Meanwhile, the 125 non-Indian sympathizers who had been marching for three days were stopped halfway between Rosebud and Wounded Knee. Fifty BIA police and federal marshals stood shoulder to shoulder across the road and threatened to arrest anyone trying to pass. The crowd dispersed peacefully. But late that night 68 persons were captured on the prairie as they attempted to infiltrate through the cordon of federal officers around Wounded Knee. Most were from the march. It is not known how many got through.

Late the next day, Hellstern announced a deal between the Justice Department and the tribal chairman. A group of Wilson supporters, that is, the goon squad, would be trained by marshals and FBI agents and allowed to help patrol the area. Wilson would be given a voice in decision-making. In return, Wilson would dismantle the Tribal Council roadblock and lift the ban on CRS personnel in Wounded Knee. The huge fruit salad of lawmen was united and ready for action once again.

Also on April 26, an Interior Department official announced that $5 million had already been spent on law enforcement efforts around Wounded Knee, and unless Congress came up with a special appropriation, the money would have to be repaid to the Justice Department out of the budget of the Bureau of Indian Affairs, the equivalent of taking it out of the pockets of Indian people. It was a thinly disguised and ruthless attempt to turn Indians on other reservations against the people in Wounded Knee. The contemptuous official argued that it was proper for the national reservation population to suffer the loss "so that they will learn the price of choosing irresponsible leadership."

That night, April 26-27, encouraged perhaps by their successful showdown with the Justice Department, Wilson's goon squad triggered the most intense fire fight of the entire occupation. It lasted close to 24 hours. Before it began, goon squad members infiltrated themselves between government and Wounded Knee positions and fired in both directions to provoke the battle. A number of cease-fires were arranged over two-way radios, but during each one the goons fired on federal bunkers, often with the M-16s given them by the FBI. Law officers assumed that the shots were coming from inside Wounded Knee, in violation of the cease-fire, . and resumed their attack on the village. By the time it was over, government positions had fired an estimated 20,000 rounds into Wounded Knee, as well as innumerable gas projectiles from M-79 grenade launchers.

Gladys Bissonette recalled the goon squad's actions that night. "They came up the creek on both sides," she said. "They'd fire mostly on the offense to get a fire fight against the Indians going. The feds claimed that the Indians were shooting at them, but the Indians really weren't shooting at all. It was those goons in the middle; they were like a third party. Of course, the federal marshals all knew what they were doing. It was just an excuse to try and kill Indians."

At 9:00 a.m., after a night of almost constant rifle and machine gunfire, a man was injured inside one of the Wounded Knee bunkers. An M-16 bullet passed through the calves of both his legs. A ten-minute cease-fire was arranged over the radio and a lone medic volunteered to go to his aid. When she had gotten about half way there, the FBI in government Roadblock #4 falsely reported that she was carrying a rifle. They fired on her and she dove into a ditch for cover. The battle flared up again. Continuous firing kept the medic pinned down in the ditch for the next three hours.

During that morning fire fight, the government repeatedly denied using gas. But Indians inside Wounded Knee monitored federal radio communications and recorded the following words in the middle of the intense battle: "Throw gas into that bunker and flush them out so we can have good targets." Confronted with this evidence later, a spokesman for the BIA admitted that "a non-toxic" gas had been used.

"That day that they used gas on us," Gladys Bissonette remembered, "some of our boys only had five to seven rounds of ammunition apiece left. On that day, and this is the work of our Great Spirit, the wind changed seven times. Each time they shot at one of our bunkers with that gas, the wind would change and take the gas away. The wind changed seven times in that one day."

Finally, at 12:30 p.m., another cease-fire was arranged over two-way radios. The injured man was still not treated and the medic was still pinned down in the ditch. During the lull in the shooting, a warrior hiked into the Wounded Knee security headquarters from an outlying bunker that had been cut off from radio communications all morning. He reported that Lawrence "Buddy" Lamont, 31 years old, had been killed two hours earlier. As Lamont knelt beside the bunker, a bullet slammed into him from behind. It passed through his heart, emerged from his chest, and shattered the stock of his rifle. He died instantly.

Lamont was an Oglala Sioux who had lived on the reservation. He had served with the U.S. Army in Viet Nam. Two of his great-grandparents were killed in the 1890 Wounded Knee massacre. Before the occupation, he was employed by the Tribal Council. But when Lamont signed a petition calling for Wilson's impeachment, he lost his job. Lamont was not a member of the American Indian Movement. After the occupation began, he told relatives one day that he was "going down there to fight for my people's rights." He said that if he was killed, he wanted to be buried at Wounded Knee.

Word was passed to the government command post that a Wounded Knee defender was dead. They agreed to a sustained cease-fire. Some of Lamont's relatives who were with him inside Wounded Knee obtained radioed permission from the FBI to accompany the body as it was removed from the settlement.

Lamont's mother said later, "His sister and her little baby and some other people—they [the FBI] told them it was all right to bring him out in an ambulance. And when they came out with the body, they put them all in handcuffs and threw them all in jail."

The baby, Lamont's nephew, was taken to the BIA jail in Pine Ridge with his mother. She asked from her jail cell if she could telephone her own mother to inform her of the death, so that she would not have to learn the tragic news over the radio. Permission was denied by a BIA policeman who said she "could rot" before he would let her use the telephone.

Buddy Lamont was his mother's only son. Asked after his death if she could still support the American Indian Movement, she replied, "I'm with them all the way now."

The cease-fire established after Lamont was killed lasted for the remainder of the occupation. Sporadic sniper fire continued, but there were no more massive gun battles. The following day, April 28, negotiations resumed for the first time since the abortive agreement signed April 5. Dennis Banks and Leonard Crow Dog were the principal negotiators for Wounded Knee. Frizzell, a signer of the earlier agreement, represented the government. A two-hour meeting was held in the "demilitarized zone" between the opposing bunkers. Despite some progress, negotiations were cancelled the next day when Frizzell became involved in the growing controversy over the burial of Frank Clearwater, the first victim of the government siege.

But Frizzell indicated to reporters on the 29th that time was "running out." He warned that if an agreement was not reached in the immediate days ahead, the government might be left with no alternative but an armed attack. Meanwhile, the Justice Department brought in extra marshals. A U.S. Army helicopter capable of laying a thick cloud of nausea gas was moved to Pine Ridge. Other equipment and ammunition were flown in from army bases around the country. Word was leaked that the government had developed a combined helicopter-and-armored-personnel-carrier assault plan and was ready to launch it on short notice.

The night of the 29th, a child knocked over a kerosene lantern inside the Wounded Knee trading post. Since the water supply had been cut off, the fire that started could not be kept from spreading. The entire building was destroyed. The trading post had served the occupation well as a main barracks and meeting hall, but most of the press the next day accepted government accusations that the fire was an act of arson.

With events quickly moving toward a crisis, Frank Fools Crow, a 78-year-old Oglala Sioux chief and medicine man and one of the most respected traditional leaders on the Pine Ridge Reservation, issued an invitation to all chiefs and headmen of the various tribes of the Sioux Nation scattered throughout the eight reservations in North and South Dakota. He asked that they come to a council on his land, 15 miles from Wounded Knee, and help him bring about a peaceful settlement of the occupation.

On April 30, Frizzell allowed Chief Fools Crow and two other Oglala Sioux chiefs, Frank Kills Enemy and Tom Bad Cob, to pass through federal roadblocks into and out of Wounded Knee. Inside, they spent several hours talking to their people and to AIM advisors. It is believed that the chiefs also delivered an ultimatum from the government—that this round of negotiations would be the last chance for a peaceful solution before Wounded Knee was taken by force.

That night, on coast-to-coast television, President Nixon took the lid off the worst scandal in the history of the United States. The two highest Presidential advisors, H. R. Haldeman and John Ehrlichman, the head of the Justice Department, Richard Kleindienst, and Presidential Counsel John Dean were all removed from their positions, effective immediately. Three days before, the Acting Director of the FBI, Patrick Gray, resigned after disclosures that he had purposefully destroyed Watergate evidence. Gray and his superior, Kleindienst, who would eventually become the first Attorney General in history to be convicted of a crime, both played a central role in decision-making that had affected Wounded Knee.

The extraordinary council of the elders of the Teton Sioux Nation, called by Chief Fools Crow, lasted four days. Over 50 chiefs and head-men from across the Great Plains gathered to discuss a solution to the impasse at Wounded Knee. The council received no publicity. Yet, these were the authentic leaders of the full blood and traditional Sioux Indians. They had no officially sanctioned titles. They generally boycotted the elected tribal councils on their reservations, just as their people generally boycotted the elections. But among the Sioux people they commanded enormous respect, and as a body they were immensely influential.

At the end of their deliberations on May 3, the old chiefs announced that Wounded Knee had delegated them the power to negotiate a settlement with the government. The chiefs revealed that they had been advising the occupation from the beginning. They dispatched a proposal to Washington that called for a Presidential Treaty Commission, the firing of corrupt BIA officials, and the suspension of the Tribal Constitution in order to provide the people on the Pine Ridge Reservation with an opportunity to vote Wilson out of office and return to a form of self-government more in keeping with Indian traditions. Except for minor compromises, this proposal held fast to the occupation's original three demands. Also, the chiefs and headmen commended efforts by the American Indian Movement to protect the Oglala Sioux people.

Finally, the elders said, "There is great sorrow among all the Indians at the loss of brothers Clearwater and Lamont who have unselfishly made the supreme sacrifice in a quest for recognition and rightful sovereignty. It is tragic that men have to make this sort of sacrifice to recognize inequities allowed to exist in this so-called civilized society."

Contrary to government hopes, there was no generation gap among the Sioux.

That same day, a hundred miles away in Rapid City, Darald Schmitz was acquitted of second degree manslaughter. He had been charged in the stabbing death of Wesley Bad Heart Bull, which had touched off the protests in Custer three weeks before the seizure of Wounded Knee. The jury, none of whom was Indian, deliberated for an hour-and-a-half before finding the white defendant not guilty.

On May 4, Frizzell announced that a reply was en route to the Sioux chiefs from Leonard Garment, the newly appointed Special Counsel to the President replacing John Dean. Hank Adams, an Indian activist and treaty expert, was asked by Garment to hand-deliver the letter to Chief Fools Crow in South Dakota. But Adams, who had participated in the Trail of Broken Treaties demonstrations in Washington, had been banned from the Pine Ridge Reservation by Dick Wilson, so on May 5 a meeting was held 50 miles north of Wounded Knee on the boundary of reservation land. There Adams, acting as an emissary from the President of the United States, stood just outside the reservation line and handed the letter over a barbed wire fence to Chief Fools Crow. About a hundred people were present to witness the ceremony. The tall, stately Fools Crow wore buckskins. A headdress decorated with white, black, and red-tipped feathers covered his long braids. He said he would deliver the offer from Washington to his people in Wounded Knee.

In his letter Garment volunteered five White House representatives to come to the home of Chief Fools Crow during the third week in May to discuss treaty issues with the Oglala Sioux. The government insisted that Wounded Knee be evacuated by May 11 and all people with outstanding warrants submit to arrest prior to that date. The White House also offered to authorize an extensive investigation of the operation and finances of the Pine Ridge Reservation, including both Tribal Council and BIA activities, and to protect people against unlawful abuses of power by tribal authorities. The talks during the third week in May would cover implementation of the 1868 Sioux Treaty and would set the stage for further negotiations later in the summer.

It was significant that the government offered to send representatives to meet with Sioux elders on Chief Fools Crow's land. In so doing, federal officials recognized for the first time in 30 years that the traditional chiefs and headmen were the real leadership on the reservation, not Dick Wilson and the Tribal Council imposed by the Indian Reorganization Act of 1934. Nevertheless, the demand for a vote on Wilson's removal from office was ignored.

A month earlier the Oglalas had submitted a petition to the Department of the Interior requesting an official referendum on the question of dissolving the tribal government and the Tribal Constitution. The petition was signed by more than the necessary one-third of the 3,104 registered voters on the reservation. Suddenly, on May 5, the same day Garment's letter was delivered to Fools Crow, Frizzell announced that the number of signatures on the petition fell far short of the necessary one-third. He claimed that the Interior Department was figuring on the basis of 9,518 eligible voters, not just the 3,104 registered voters. The mathematics came as a shock to the Oglalas. How could there be 9,518 voters over 21 on a reservation where the total population was less than 12,000 and the number of children very high? The question was never resolved.

Despite the shortcomings in the government's offer, the chiefs decided to accept it in the interests of peace. Talks were held inside Wounded Knee on May 6 to resolve the delicate issue of the laying down of arms. Some Indians were simply afraid that as soon as they gave up their rifles, the FBI and the goons would shoot them down. Other disputed questions concerned arrest procedures, the availability of lawyers, who would have access to Wounded Knee after the disarmament, and the definition of legal versus illegal weapons. The Oglalas were also determined that the end of the occupation be a dignified and simultaneous laying down of arms, not a surrender.

Final agreement came at 11:00 p.m. on the night of the 6th. The actual disarmament was to be delayed for three more days, until May 9, to give the Indians time to raise bail money. On the morning of the 9th, when the Oglalas signaled they were ready to begin, the Justice Department would withdraw its armored personnel carriers to a point several miles from Wounded Knee. An Indian elder would then be invited into each government bunker to act as an observer. At that point, the people in Wounded Knee would evacuate their bunkers, assemble in the center of the settlement, and stack their weapons. All legal weapons would be processed by the Community Relations Service of the Justice Department and returned to their owners within 24 hours.

The plan called for CRS personnel to divide everyone in Wounded Knee into three groups. Those with outstanding arrest warrants would be taken to federal cells in Rapid City, not the BIA jail in Pine Ridge. Wounded Knee residents would be immediately returned to their homes. Those that remained would be escorted off the reservation and released. The stacking of weapons and all searches of individuals or buildings would take place in the presence of defense attorneys. Anyone arrested would have the right to consult with lawyers during questioning and booking.

The final agreement was drawn up by the negotiators. On the government side, it was signed by Frizzell for the Department of the Interior, Hellstern for the Department of Justice, and Colburn for the U.S. Marshal Service. Those signing for the Indians were Chief Frank Fools Crow, medicine man Leonard Crow Dog, Chief Frank Kills Enemy, Sioux treaty expert Matthew King, and seven other Oglala Sioux people, including Gladys Bissonette. Dick Wilson was not a party to the agreement. He was handed a copy during a press conference and stormed out without reading it. Neither Dennis Banks nor Carter Camp, the two AIM leaders still inside Wounded Knee, signed the agreement.

In a written statement, Banks said, "I have reviewed the agreement and find that the document falls outside the protection of the U.S. Constitution. I will submit to the arms laying down because the chiefs and headmen have agreed. Also, AIM's job is done here. It must be understood that AIM was called on to aid these Oglalas in their struggle against repressive government forces."

On May 7, Camp and Crow Dog voluntarily surrendered to federal authorities. Warrants were out on each for a variety of charges, including larceny, arson, breaking and entering, and assaulting federal officers. Their bonds were set at $70,000 and $35,000, respectively. A legal worker, present at their arraignment in Rapid City, said, "The bonds were outrageous. Either the entire amount or collateral had to be posted. For Crow Dog, who never lifted a gun in his life, for a spiritual leader, it was an outrage. They would not have done this to a white minister. Both men were led around in chains, shackled and handcuffed."

At the request of the people inside Wounded Knee, the disarmament took place a day early, on May 8. Several minutes after 7:00 a.m., on the 71st day of the historic occupation, the U.S. armored personnel carriers withdrew from sight. The first signs of betrayal were evident shortly afterward when lawyers for the Indians were not permitted into Wounded Knee. The actual stand-down began at 7:45 a.m. The Oglalas emerged from their bunkers and stacked their weapons for CRS personnel inside the settlement. Twenty minutes later, the first two people wanted on federal arrest warrants were placed in a car by the CRS and driven to an FBI post one mile away. But when the next wanted person emerged, he told government officials that no one else would come out unless attorneys were allowed in. After a bitter argument, Justice Department representatives permitted a single lawyer to enter the village. Over the course of the next hour, carload by carload, the 120 people remaining in Wounded Knee were ferried to the FBI post. Warrants were outstanding for only 15, and they were taken into custody. The others were released. Forty were permanent residents of Wounded Knee. In violation of the agreement, the residents were prevented from returning to their homes for another 24 hours. At 9:51 a.m., U.S. marshals received a radio message that Wounded Knee was empty. They advanced down a hill from the west in a skirmish line and began a sweep of the settlement.

Contrary to the signed agreement, the government sweep of Wounded Knee took place with no defense attorneys present. The armored personnel carriers, which should have been withdrawn from the area, went only as far as the other side of the first hill. The BIA police and Wilson's goon squad, who were supposed to be barred from the settlement, sped into it as soon as it was cleared. The promise that Sioux elders would be in government bunkers as observers during the disarmament was "kept"—they were all, as a group, put at a single roadblock three miles away.

Medicine man Wallace Black Elk was in Wounded Knee during the stand-down. The sacred articles of the Sioux religion belonging to him and to Crow Dog, who had surrendered the day before, were stowed in Black Elk's car. These objects included irreplaceable pipes, medicine bags, and other artifacts handed down from 19th-century leaders like Crazy Horse and the first Black Elk, who in turn had obtained them from their own ancestors. The head CRS official inside Wounded Knee made three separate promises that Black Elk would be allowed to drive his car out of Wounded Knee after being processed at the FBI post. But the promises were broken. Black Elk was not permitted back into the area. His car was destroyed and the religious articles smashed or stolen. To the Sioux, these objects were equivalent to the holiest relics of Christianity, like pieces of the True Cross. The Sioux religion, which had already endured so much, suffered another incalculable loss.

At 10:19 a.m., the skirmish line of U.S. marshals broadcast over government two-way radios, "Gentlemen, the village of Wounded Knee is clear." For several hours no one was allowed in—other than marshals, FBI agents who were presumably carrying out a criminal investigation, officials of the Justice and Interior Departments, and the BIA police and goons of Dick Wilson.

Law enforcement officers were not very happy with what they found. Of the 120 people left inside Wounded Knee, there were only 15 subject to arrest warrants. Thirty-five others with outstanding warrants had voluntarily surrendered during the preceding three days. But that left over 40 people still wanted by the FBI who were missing and unaccounted for. One of them was Dennis Banks. Unknown to federal agents, Banks had secretly led some 60 people out of Wounded Knee two nights earlier. Fourteen were apprehended with a variety of weapons as they worked their way through government lines. But Banks and the rest disappeared without a trace.

A week before the May 8 disarmament, Russell Means was speaking around the country on behalf of the occupation. A federal judge revoked his $25,000 bond. He was re-arrested and held under a new bond of $125,000. Means was still in jail at the time of the disarmament, and it was clear that AIM would have trouble obtaining the money necessary to release him. Dennis Banks knew that he could expect similar treatment. He had already spent a lot of time in jail cells, and he believed a quarter of a million dollars was too high a ransom for just two individuals. So Banks slipped out of Wounded Knee and went underground. He successfully eluded the FBI for the next several months. When AIM had finally raised the bail money later in the summer, Banks surrendered voluntarily and was released in a matter of hours.

At the disarmament, federal officers were also disappointed when they examined the stack of weapons left by the occupation forces. Besides eight old and decrepit twenty-two caliber rifles, they found a bow and arrow, a couple of plastic M-16s, and several carved wooden replicas of guns. Hellstern, irate over the fact that no other weapons could be found, said, "These guns are a lot of crap."

Almost as soon as they announced the end of the occupation, newspapers across the nation ran stories "exposing" vandalism that had allegedly taken place. There were pictures from Wounded Knee of garbage in people's homes, household articles smashed to bits, windows broken, obscenities scribbled on walls, and so forth. Dick Wilson said that the mess was to be expected from "these hoodlums and clowns—that's the way they live." Unfortunately, most of America uncritically accepted that interpretation.

But weeks later a team of defense lawyers presented a very different picture of the vandalism at Wounded Knee. They revealed that immediately after the disarmament, marshals and FBI agents ransacked the village, kicking down doors and destroying furniture under the pretext of looking for weapons. Afterward, Wilson's men were allowed in to loot and deface what remained. When the wanton destruction was over, government press spokesmen invited a carefully selected group of reporters and television film crews on a guided tour of the damage. Other members of the press, lacking clearance from the government information officer, were barred from Wounded Knee.

Subsequent investigation uncovered the scope of the vandalism deception. People inside Wounded Knee the day before the disarmament testified that at that time the village was intact. The damage could only have occurred *after* the occupying forces left. Several of the destroyed homes displayed by the government turned out to be behind their own lines, not within the Wounded Knee defense perimeter. Highly publicized fire damage in the village was primarily the result of government flares. Water to put out fires had been cut off from the outside. During the occupation, the government had refused to allow lime to be brought into Wounded Knee. Thus, garbage piled up instead of decomposing. Finally, the destruction of personal property in people's homes or the loss of the sacred articles belonging to Black Elk and Crow Dog was certainly not in the interests of the people who seized Wounded Knee. On the contrary, the opposite was true.

Three trailer homes were destroyed during the occupation. They collapsed because of huge holes made in them by high caliber government machine gun fire. After showing these trailers to the press in the quick guided tour following the disarmament, federal agents moved in with bulldozers and buried them. They also plowed under the trenches and fortifications dug by both sides in the conflict. They claimed it was all part of a clean-up attempt. In fact, they were trying to hide evidence. The cartridges and shell casings lying about were proof that for the first time in history, fifty-caliber machine guns had been fired by government forces engaged in actual combat inside the borders of the United States.

The day after the disarmament, Russell Means made the following charge from his jail cell in Rapid City. "The United States government delayed the return of the original residents by 24 hours in order for their forces to vandalize and steal from the original residents of Wounded Knee in order to make it appear that the occupiers had done these terrible acts to their own people, thereby creating further division among our people."

But Means went unheard. That day the mass media carried the more dramatic footage and pictures of the destroyed reservation village. The result was an important public opinion victory for the beleaguered Justice Department. Since the press and the American people were so distracted by the astounding revelations of the Watergate story, interest in Wounded Knee faded before the record could be set straight. It was a major turning point. From then on, the government grew more confident that the American people would not be able to keep abreast of continuing events on the Pine Ridge Reservation, and federal officials became much less restrained in their dealings with the Indians.

After the disarmament on May 8, the White House decided that treaty meetings would take place at Chief Fools Crow's on May 17 and 18. The dates were timed for maximum public invisibility. Only the day before this decision, Senator Sam Ervin had announced that his Senate Select Committee on Watergate would begin televised public hearings that same day, May 17.

But the White House and the Justice Department were undergoing successive shock waves because of Watergate. Two days after the treaty meetings announcement, on May 10, a federal grand jury returned a felony indictment against former Attorney General John Mitchell. This came only ten days after Mitchell's successor, Kleindienst, had himself been forced from office. The next day, May 11, Justice Department prosecutors lost the Pentagon Papers case following the disclosure that Daniel Ellsberg's psychiatrist's office was burglarized by agents under the direction of White House staff members. Only nine days earlier, the judge in the case revealed that President Nixon's chief assistant, Erlichman, had offered to bring him into the Justice Department as Director of the FBI, and this only two weeks after the Acting Director, Gray, had to leave his post for destroying government evidence.

It was unprecedented, but these massive internal convulsions did not deter the Justice Department from prosecuting the people responsible for Wounded Knee. There were 428 who had been arrested during the two-month occupation. Slightly over a hundred were under indictment for their direct participation. The remaining 300 or so were accused of

federal felonies because they tried to bring food or other supplies, including arms and ammunition, into Wounded Knee. However, the arms
cases were a distinct minority of the 300. If all 428 cases went to trial, they
would constitute the most massive and complex series of legal proceedings in the history of the United States.

In the aftermath of the occupation, Hellstern, the chief Justice Department official in South Dakota, seemed unaffected by the new-found
humility Watergate was stimulating among some of his colleagues in
Washington. He described to newspeople how he would handle any
future incidents like Wounded Knee. "The major thing we learned about
it is that it's a law enforcement problem, primarily. You cannot sit down
with people like this and work out arrangements successfully. If I were in
control in the future, I'd handle it as a law enforcement problem, treating
them the same as bank robbers and plane hijackers."

While Hellstern was contemplating future shootouts, the marketing
director of a five-state western tourist promotion group commended Dick
Wilson. The white businessman said that he thought the Indian people
had a good spokesman in Wilson and he urged all "tourist-oriented
individuals" to support the tribal chairman. In Rapid City, Clyde Bellecourt of AIM called for a tourist boycott of the Black Hills in South Dakota.
He asked people not to trade in or visit the area until the U.S. government
"fulfills the treaties made with the American Indians."

Meetings to discuss the fulfillment of those treaties began as scheduled
on May 17. The chiefs and headmen present on Fools Crow's land wore
traditional dress and eagle feathers. Behind his house, on the sandy soil
of the reservation, they had constructed a canopy from freshly cut pine
bows suspended on ash logs. Two large helicopters dropped onto an
adjacent pasture and deposited the delegation from Washington. They
were accompanied by an armed guard of U.S. marshals in full battle gear.
The 20 to 30 Indian elders were disappointed at the relatively low stature
of the five officials sent by the United States, but the delegation was
invited to sit under the canopy. It was headed by White House Special
Counsel Garment's assistant. Also included were two Interior Department attorneys, a BIA official, and a part-time White House consultant on
Indian affairs.

Chief Fools Crow opened the meeting with prayers and a speech. The
78-year-old leader spoke only in Lakota, the native language of the
Sioux. His words were translated by Matthew King, Oglala interpreter
and treaty rights expert. Throughout the two days of meetings, the Oglala
chiefs and headmen reaffirmed the need for a referendum in which the
Sioux could vote to live under traditional, treaty-recognized law, or under
the elected Tribal Council. They insisted on a Presidential Commission to
examine violations of the Treaty of 1868. Their demand was endorsed by

chiefs attending the meeting who represented the other tribes of the Teton Sioux, as well as the Cheyenne and Arapaho tribes, all signers of the original document. Indian treaty rights were the most important issue at stake, locally and nationally. A Presidential Commission would not solve any real problems, but it was an effective way to mobilize widespread concern about the treaties and just compensation for violations.

But the two-day session was unproductive. When it was over, the head of the government delegation promised to return for another meeting on May 30, at which time he would deliver a written reply to each of the Sioux requests. Before leaving, he told the press, "This country is one that gives minority groups a hearing."

And, as usual, a hearing was all they were given. When White House decision-makers noticed that the historic meeting at Chief Fools Crow's attracted almost no attention in the press, they decided not to bother holding the second meeting. The May 30 session was abruptly cancelled by White House Counsel Garment, who also declined to respond to the Sioux proposals.

In a May 29 letter to the Teton Sioux chiefs, Garment said that another meeting would not be useful since "the days of treaty-making with the American Indians ended in 1871." He noted that 1871 Congressional legislation barred the President from negotiating any new treaties with Indians as sovereign nations. Furthermore, he said, changes in existing treaties must be taken up with Congress, not the White House. So, despite his "sincere" desire to help, Garment's hands were tied.

The letter was a cynical public relations stunt, intentionally worded to confuse the issue. In a June 9 reply, the Sioux elders stated, "We are not asking for the negotiation of new treaties or the changing of any existing treaty; we are merely asking that the treaties that already exist be enforced." The chiefs also made reference to the 1871 Congressional legislation mentioned by Garment, which is contained in Title 25, Section 71, of the United States Code. The chiefs quoted a passage from Section 71: "No obligations or any treaty lawfully made and ratified with any Indian nation prior to March 3, 1871, shall be hearby invalidated or impaired." Neither has any subsequent legislation invalidated or impaired the Treaty of 1868. According to law, the Treaty is still in force. In their letter the Sioux chiefs insisted that as a result, the Teton Sioux Tribes are still a sovereign nation and must be recognized as such by the United States. All other questions hinge on the issue of sovereignty, and the Sioux approached it with the utmost seriousness.

In closing their reply to the White House, the chiefs declared, "Hope is the fountain of youth for all mankind, and we Indian people are the proud owners of the deepest well of hope in the world, but that well is almost dry. We are a people who can maintain our dignity in spite of poverty and other extreme social ills, but even the most dignified people in the world cannot live on hope alone."

No further meetings between the traditional leaders of the Oglala Sioux and officials from the White House ever took place. No Presidential or Treaty Commission to look into the 1868 Treaty with the Sioux Nation, or any other treaty, was ever appointed. No referendum giving Indian people a choice between traditional and Tribal Council forms of self-government was ever held on the Pine Ridge, or any other, Reservation. No changes in the practices of the Bureau of Indian Affairs office at Pine Ridge were ever instituted. From the point of view of the U.S. government, Wounded Knee was over.

Management of the Indians at Pine Ridge was returned to the corrupt BIA and the remnant of the Tribal Council headed by Richard Wilson. Press coverage was nonexistent. Indians in general, and the Oglala Sioux in particular, again became invisible. But as relieved government officials and law enforcement agents returned to other concerns, a long stream of commentators and intellectuals from the press and various universities began to interpret the events at Wounded Knee. In a string of magazine articles and interviews with "experts," conservative apologists for the government and naive liberals rewrote the history of the confrontation. All agreed that the real villains were the "outside agitators," the American Indian Movement. Many argued the absurd notion that AIM had "staged" the event with almost no local support.

Closest to the scene was a history professor from the University of South Dakota named Joseph Cash, a white "expert" on the Sioux people. He said, "In the case of Wounded Knee, you essentially had a group of urban Indians in opposition to an elected tribal government." Cash believed that the TV coverage was biased in favor of the occupation because the mass media are "conditioned to take the side of minorities in almost any situation, whether it is justified or not."

Cash's history colleague at the University of South Dakota, Clyde Dollar, published a long article in the magazine, American West. He described the airlift as follows: "Hired sympathizers flying dawn missions of mercy air-dropped supplies, and food intended for the noncombatants still in the village found its way into the stomachs of the combatants."

But Dollar's distortions were more than ridiculous mistakes. They were vicious attacks against the Indian people of his state. He chided the Sioux for living with "many more material possessions than at any other time in their history," claiming that their "wealth" was responsible for the decline in their religion, since their religion could "flourish only in the 'poverty' of material possessions." The white and Indian taxpayers of South Dakota were paying the salary of a "historian" so infected with anti-Indian racism that he was able to write this sentence about the fire fight in which Frank

Clearwater was fatally injured: "One of them died a few days later, thereby providing *the much desired* first martyr from the take-over." (emphasis added)

A *National Review* writer named Victor Gold joined the chorus. He used to be the Vice Presidential press secretary before his boss, Spiro Agnew, had to leave office for being a crook. Gold called the óccupation "extended political theatre" and "an over-exposed political art form." He called the AIM leadership "the PR pros at Wounded Knee who, given a dull day, could always count on a publicity hype from some member of the usual gang of protest pilgrims . . ."

Cash, Dollar, and Gold—apt spokesmen for the United States! One cannot help but remember the early years of the Viet Nam War when, despite what was being officially said about the reason for U.S. involvement there, the truth was laid bare in the name of the general they sent to command U.S. forces in the area: West-more-land.

But the prejudices of the critics were hardly worse than the sophisticated analyses of some of the well-intentioned liberals. No one, it seemed, wanted to believe that the confrontation had its origins on the Pine Ridge Reservation. It was all AIM's fault, they said, arguing the well-known "outside agitator" theory of social unrest. An article in *The Nation* called Wounded Knee "a media *coup d'etat.*" It claimed that the essential element in this new political strategy "is that it makes a direct and powerful appeal to the public through the mass media." The confused newsman author declared, in all seriousness, "From start to finish, it was a staged event, different in degree but no different in kind from the group theatre of the Black September men." (a reference to the shooting of Israeli athletes at the 1972 Munich Olympics)

In a *Harper's* article with the chic title, "Bamboozle Me Not At Wounded Knee," a smug newswoman author called the occupation "a pseudoevent" performed as "political theatre." *TV Guide* published an unprecedented four-part series on the media's role during the confrontation entitled, "Was The Truth Buried At Wounded Knee?" The series was authored by a journalist claiming to be sympathetic, but it carried such subtitles as, ."How the siege was staged for TV," and "An inquest into a political confrontation in which television was the primary weapon."

The authors of these articles, who covered the occupation for shorter or longer periods of time, were entirely caught up in their own role and importance at Wounded Knee. They leaned toward that new trend in journalism in which the story of writing the story becomes, itself, the story. They neglected to research the complex events that led up to the seizure. The people of the Pine Ridge Reservation were forgotten as the microphones were characteristically jabbed only into the faces of the visible leadership personalities. As a result, the truly significant stories of reservation life and the fundamental causes of the unrest were lost.

The self-important "media coup" notion convinced large segments of the working press that they were somehow taken in at Wounded Knee. Editors and reporters were reluctant to provide Indians any more news coverage. A virtual blackout resulted which prevented the American people from following the aftermath of the occupation on the Pine Ridge Reservation. Thus, the "interpreters" of the event did a tremendous disservice to the grass roots Indian people who had felt compelled to seize Wounded Knee in the first place.

Unfortunately, there were numerous tragic and newsworthy events on the reservation in the months following the occupation. It will never be known how many of these disasters could have been avoided if the press had not turned its back so completely on the Wounded Knee story. Two irreconcilable camps consolidated after the disarmament, those who supported AIM and those who supported Wilson. But since Richard Wilson was in complete command of the tribal government, and since the press had focused national attention elsewhere, a reign of terror began in which AIM sympathizers were often the defenseless targets.

It started with severe beatings and multiple rapes; then it rapidly escalated to shootings. In July, three AIM supporters were caught one night asleep in a parked car. As the BIA police arrested them, two were shot and Maced. One died a few weeks later. Toward the end of the summer, in one of the outlying villages that had supported the occupation, a well was poisoned causing an outbreak of stomach disorders. In September, a nine-year-old girl and her father were fired on as they drove past a house where a Tribal Council meeting had just taken place. The girl was shot in the face and lost one of her eyes. The BIA police, brought to the house immediately afterward by the girl's father, found three Wilson supporters inside. There were no arrests.

A flurry of violence occurred in November, just before a primary election in which Wilson was pursuing his second term as Tribal Council Chairman. On November 10, an AIM supporter was beaten to death, and someone from the Wilson side was charged with manslaughter. On the 15th, another person who had associated with AIM was gunned down by a sniper. He lived. But five days later, on the 20th, a 15-year-old AIM supporter was discovered dead in a ditch with a bullet through his heart. All this took place against a months-long backdrop of brutal beatings, shootings that missed, and drunken rapes of AIM-associated women on lonely reservation roads and in the BIA jail in Pine Ridge.

During that same period, defense attorneys were working on behalf of the 428 persons arrested in and around Wounded Knee. At one point, they were able to subpoena the man who had headed the Justice

Department during most of the occupation, Kleindienst. Forced to testify at a pretrial evidentiary hearing, the former Attorney General stated under oath that federal forces fired approximately 500,000 rounds of ammunition at the "militants" in Wounded Knee—presumably in self-defense. It was probably the largest concentration of small arms fire in any battle ever fought on the North American continent. Yet, more people were killed and injured by the duly constituted authorities and their henchmen in the months of "normalcy" and "peace" following the occupation than were hurt on all sides by a half million bullets during the "war." None of these incidents of violence was covered in any significant fashion by the press.

Typical of the violence was the killing of Gladys Bissonette's nephew, Pedro Bissonette, five months after the Wounded Knee disarmament. Pedro was 33 years old. He was a founder and leader of the Oglala Sioux Civil Rights Organization, the group that originally invited AIM onto the Pine Ridge Reservation to help in the impeachment of Dick Wilson. Pedro was well liked on the reservation, a natural leader and a prominent figure during the occupation, but he was hated by Wilson. When the BIA police issued an arrest warrant, Pedro went into hiding, fearing what might be done to him in the Pine Ridge jail. The night of October 17, 1973, he decided to turn himself in, and the police were, unfortunately, notified to that effect.

As he drove toward Pine Ridge to surrender, Pedro was stopped by two BIA policemen on a desolate reservation road and shot to death. The police claimed he went for a gun and they were forced to shoot from 50 feet away. Lawyers working with the Wounded Knee defendants insisted that the seven bullet holes in Pedro's chest were made by a gun fired at point-blank range. They presented autopsy evidence indicating that he was held down and murdered in cold blood.

Pedro Bissonette was going to be a star defense witness in the upcoming trials over the occupation of Wounded Knee. He would have been able to give competent testimony about the corruption in Wilson's administration, about fixed elections and bribed officials, about kickbacks on tribal contracts and secret deals with white ranchers. More than anyone else on the reservation, Pedro had the experience to document how the tribal government, the BIA, and the Justice Department had illegally worked together to discredit AIM and protect Wilson. Pedro's death was no great loss to the tribal chairman.

Two thousand people came to Pedro's three-day wake. Tribal officials tried to get a court order banning AIM leaders from attending the funeral, but even the local federal judge would not hear of that. However, BIA police were able to bar Dennis Banks, a Chippewa, from setting foot on the Sioux reservation. Pedro's funeral procession then made a long detour to the edge of reservation land and there Banks sat for a few moments by the side of the road gazing at the body of his comrade before the line of cars moved slowly on.

During the first month of the occupation back in March 1973, a group of lawyers, legal workers, and nonprofessional volunteers, Indian and non-Indian, joined together to form the Wounded Knee Legal Defense/Offense Committee. On their shoulders fell the massive job of coordinating the defense of all those arrested in connection with the seizure of Wounded Knee. Volunteers came from all over the country, including some nationally prominent attorneys. Some stayed for over a year, others only a month or two. All worked, and are still working today, for no salaries, both lawyers and nonlawyers alike. They take what they need for a meagre subsistence out of money sent in by contributors across the nation. On their office wall there is a poster with Pedro Bissonette's words: "Once all I thought I could be was a drunk. Now that I found out I can fight for my people, I feel like a man."

A number of minor victories were won by Indian people and tribes in the months following the historic occupation of Wounded Knee. But all of these successes had to do with narrowly defined specific issues in the judicial and legislative arenas. No advances were made on the fundamental issue of treaty rights, and there were no changes in the functioning of the executive branch of government capable of easing the burden of suffering for the vast majority of American Indian people.

In the winter following Wounded Knee, when Dick Wilson came up for re-election as the Tribal Chairman of the Pine Ridge Reservation, Russell Means, a native of the reservation and a leader of the American Indian Movement, ran against him on a platform of disbanding the tribal government immediately upon election. Russell's candidacy in the primary was one reason for the intense anti-AIM violence around Pine Ridge in November 1973. The first round of the election, in which twelve candidates ran, took place on January 22, 1974. The results, announced by Wilson's own election workers, were: Means, 677 votes; Wilson, 511 votes; and Gerald One Feather, 367 votes. AIM supporters claimed that Wilson's election workers had altered the results and the true totals were Means, 930; One Feather, 624; Wilson, 540. In any case, a run-off election between Means and Wilson was scheduled two weeks later. AIM members were understandably dubious about its fairness. They felt that if outside observers were not brought in, Wilson's corrupt administration would simply steal the votes. As a result, AIM contacted the White House staff person who had led the U.S. delegation to the post-disarmament treaty meetings at Chief Fools Crow's and asked him to send a team of impartial observers from Washington. He refused. After a half million bullets, two Indian deaths, and a 71-day siege, he had the gall to say that the federal government did not want to "meddle" in the tribe's affairs.

During the run-off election on February 7, 1974, Means had to campaign from a courtroom in St. Paul, Minnesota, where he and Dennis Banks were on trial facing close to a hundred years in federal prison for their "crimes" at Wounded Knee.[1] The election was a predictable fiasco. Oglala supporters of AIM insisted that Wilson had enrolled non-Indians to vote for him. AIM voters and officials were physically barred from some of the polling places. Wilson's BIA police were given the job of bringing ballots into Pine Ridge from the outlying districts. They stuffed the election boxes without signing register books. One district, Potato Creek, showed 83 votes but only had 40 registered voters. Out on the street, local alcoholics showed new $20 bills to their friends, money earned by voting for Wilson.

The final count was 1,709 for Wilson and 1,530 for Means. It was a clear election fraud, but AIM had little faith in a recount. No way could be found to keep Wilson's election officials from repeating their crooked performance.

After the election, a new outbreak of beatings and violence was directed against those friendly to AIM. People who had supported Means were threatened at gunpoint and told to leave the reservation. Nonetheless, Means pointed to the positive side of the election results. Despite all the obstacles put in their way—his own heavy criminal indictment, the crooked election officials, the violence of Wilson's police and goon squad—Wilson's apparatus was forced to admit that 1,530 people had voted with AIM. It was a clear indication of the massive support AIM must have really had on the reservation. The federal officials, the prejudiced authors, the liberal news commentators, everyone who had claimed that the occupation of Wounded Knee was the work of a few outsiders, or that it was an unwelcome imposition upon the "real" reservation Indians, or that it was some sort of sophisticated media manipulation, were all proven wrong. Wounded Knee had been a grass roots movement all along.

The costs of the armed occupation were high, but a great deal was at

---

[1]Seven months later, the case was finally dismissed by a federal judge who accused the government, the prosecutors, and the FBI of "misconduct," "deception," and "negligence." But a year later, in 1975, Banks was put on trial again, this time in a South Dakota state court. He was charged with riot and assault for participating in the Custer Courthouse demonstrations just prior to the occupation of Wounded Knee. The all-white jury found him guilty. Rather than submit to sentencing, Banks jumped bail and went underground.

Dennis Banks is one of the authentic Indian leaders of our times. When called upon by his people, he endured grave personal risk and assumed awesome responsibilities with intelligence and passion. He is not the first great chief to be wanted by the U.S. government—nor will he be the last.

stake. The seizure of Wounded Knee electrified the Indian population of America. It unleashed a new wave of Indian militancy still unfolding before us. It reawakened a cultural heritage and spirit of resistance that are the cutting edge of a movement to change the lives of hundreds of thousands of Indian people. The occupation taught non-Indians more about the real-life problems of their Indian neighbors than any other single event in the 20th century. It focused national attention on the critical and unique issue of Indian treaty rights. According to the U.S. Code, the treaties are still the law of the land and the tribes are still sovereign bodies. As such, they legally own vast tracts of land, and they insist that whenever this stolen land cannot actually be returned to them, the U.S. government must provide adequate financial compensation since it permitted the original thefts to occur.

+   +   +

From the first moment that white men set foot on the eastern edge of the North American continent, they made war on the native population. For four centuries, they pushed west in bloody battle against the Indian people they encountered. The last armed confrontation, the symbolic securing of the continent, was at Wounded Knee in 1890. But the continent was not enough. Driven by a ruthless economy that must expand or perish, the dawn of the 20th century saw the same westward movement pushed out into the Pacific Ocean when, in 1898, the U.S. annexed Hawaii and fought Spain for the Philippines. After spending the first half of the 20th century securing the Pacific islands, the American Empire used the second half to push even farther west, attacking the Asian mainland itself. Today, in Viet Nam, half a world away from Wounded Knee, that same war for imperial expansion has been finally turned back—a war that made Westmoreland the most American of all names.

The Vietnamese people, united in resistance, have stemmed the bloody westward tide. At the same time, progressive change like that inspired by the American Indian Movement is evolving inside the United States. Progress, however, is not measured by changes in the laws and governmental bureaucracies alone. Progress ultimately depends on the developing consciousness of people who will change the laws, the governmental bureaucracies, and the economic injustices that distort their lives and needlessly limit their human and productive potential.

That consciousness is exploding all around us as active, vital organizations, of which AIM is only one, spring up among women, blacks, Chicanos, tenants, rank and file laborers, Puerto Ricans, welfare recipients, Asian-Americans, farm workers, homosexuals, ecologists, students, prisoners, the elderly, consumers, and many, many others. The progression is inevitable. It will continue and fan out in every direction in the coming years as one political action triggers another, one person's grasp of how he or she is oppressed provokes the understanding of another, one glimmer of a liberated moment nourishes the desire for a life in the embrace of authentic struggle.

Two questions remain unanswered about Wounded Knee. First, will the people who fought there, who were not massacred on the field like their ancestors of 1890, now be massacred in the courts and in the prisons? Second, and more importantly, how many more armed and unarmed confrontations will be made necessary before there is real change in the deplorable condition of Indian life in the United States? One thing is clear—the solutions will never come from above. The answers to both questions are up to us, the Indian and non-Indian people of America.

"*My heart is a stone: heavy with sadness for my people; cold with the knowledge that no treaty will keep whites out of our lands; hard with the determination to resist as long as I live and breathe. Now we are weak and many of our people are afraid. But hear me: a single twig breaks, but the bundle of twigs is strong. Someday I will embrace our brother tribes and draw them into a bundle and together we will win our country back from the whites.*"

—Tecumseh
Chief, Shawnee Tribe, 1795.

"*To wage a long resistance war, the entire people must be united and single-minded. It is the same with our people as with a bundle of chopsticks. If the chopsticks are bound together it is difficult to break them. But if they are separated, nothing is easier than to snap them one by one until the last.*"

—Truong Chinh
Chairman, National Assembly,
Democratic Republic
of (North) Viet Nam, 1947.

Afterword

by Mark Lemle Amsterdam,
the author's attorney

The tale of the Wounded Knee airlift should have been merely an exciting adventure story, not the subject of a criminal trial. It should have been a tale of daring exploits, of well-planned maneuvers, of make-shift equipment, and of action based on concern for human suffering, not of arraignments, courtrooms, pre-trial motions and bail pending trial. That the adventure story turned into a courtroom story was in itself a contemporary drama.

It is indeed a shame that people in this country cannot respond to human need without running afoul of the law. The law is supposed to be the fountainhead of justice, a majestic tribute to human intelligence, morality, and concern. It was not designed to blockade food from starving Indians. It was not created to threaten with imprisonment those who would run the blockade. Nor was it created to thwart struggles for legitimate freedoms and for basic necessities. The travesty is that the law now is wielded for just these purposes.

As a result of the narrative told in the pages of this book, Bill Zimmerman and his companions, who in another age would be the subject of ballads sung by itinerant minstrels, were indicted by a federal grand jury sitting in South Dakota. Instead of being glorified by balladeers in splendid multi-colored costumes, they faced a stern judge in a somber black robe. The people of the community will not hear these ballads. They almost had to sit as a jury, deciding the future of men who dared bring food to the hungry.

The charges against these men were threefold, two substantive counts and that symbol of a political trial—a conspiracy count. An examination of each count reveals the present level of degradation of our government institutions.

341

Interfering With Federal Law Enforcement Officers

The first count of the indictment charged the airlift participants with interfering with United States Marshals and FBI agents "who were then engaged in the lawful performance of their official duties . . . by parachuting supplies into Wounded Knee. . . ." This charge stated an incredible proposition: that the dropping of supplies interfered with the official duties of the FBI and U.S. Marshals! How can that be so—unless, and this is truly amazing—unless the official duty of the FBI and marshals was to starve out the inhabitants of Wounded Knee. Yet a policy of starvation is exactly what the indictment implies.

What type of government do we have that can intentionally starve a group of people they have already shamed and beaten and robbed? The government not only did this, they had the audacity to publicly take credit for it by spelling it out so clearly in the airlift indictments. It was, therefore, the *official duty* of the FBI and marshals to starve the inhabitants of the besieged village of Wounded Knee. Interfering with that duty was the "crime" Bill Zimmerman and the others were charged with committing.

One would think—or at least hope—that starvation as a punishment even for the most "hardened" criminal would be barred by the Eighth Amendment to the Constitution, which forbids the infliction of cruel and unusual punishments. At Wounded Knee, where people had not been convicted of anything, or even charged with committing a criminal act, forced starvation was a totally improper, illegal, and immoral act. When the victims are innocent people, whether they are children, men, or women, infants or elderly persons, forced starvation becomes a crime against humanity. For interfering with an attempted official governmental policy of forced starvation, Bill Zimmerman faced five years in a federal penitentiary.

The Rap Brown Act

Bill and his friends faced an additional five years imprisonment for violating an infamous statute known as the Rap Brown Act. Count III of their indictment alleged that the airlift participants traveled to South Dakota (across state lines) "*with the intent* to promote and encourage and participate in a riot. . . ." That the *intent* of the airlift participants was totally humanitarian is clear from reading the statements of Bob Talbot and the others who took part in this heroic event. But aside from the reasons the airlift took place, the mere existence of this statute is a continuing offense to the American people and to our concept of justice.

The statute received its name from the desire of its authors to deal with the militant leaders who were traveling throughout the country in 1967 and 1968 supposedly trying to "agitate" the black community. The purpose of the statute was to suppress the "rabble rousing" and "hate mongering" ideas and speeches of national black spokesmen such as Dr. Martin Luther King, Stokely Carmichael, and H. Rap Brown.[1]

Despite the Kerner Commission's report that ghetto violence was caused primarily by "white racism" and not by black "agitators," the Rap Brown Act did not disappear. In the summer of 1969 the government used the statute unsuccessfully against the Chicago Eight. Four years later at Wounded Knee, it was still their major offensive weapon. While the particular circumstances at Wounded Knee concerned American Indians, the significance of the event affected people everywhere. While the struggle by Native Americans to regain some of their homeland is not the black liberation struggle that the statute originally sought to control, the similarities were not lost on the government.

The statute is so dangerous a threat to our liberty because it seeks to prohibit not an act but merely a thought; it is crossing state lines (or the use of interstate facilities such as the mail or television) with a specific state of mind that the statute classifies as an offense. Since the state of one's mind is so difficult to prove, the government is free to make its allegations, cause an indictment to be returned, and force an individual or group of individuals to a costly criminal trial. Even though the prosecution is unable to prove beyond a reasonable doubt that an accused person had a particular *intent*, they can succeed in dragging him/her into a legal battle, causing a shift in his/her attention into the courtroom and away from the struggle for liberty outside the courtroom. The mere threat of a criminal trial is sufficient to chill support for a struggle such as Wounded Knee.

During the government's siege of Wounded Knee, this statute was used to an unprecedented degree in an attempt to control the support the public was permitted to show for the Indians. People were arrested all over the country for trying to go to Wounded Knee. Some arrestees had not even left their home states when they were arrested for violating the statute. It should be noted that under the statute it is a criminal offense for a T.V. newscaster to say in an editorial that the Wounded Knee struggle was important and that, in the opinion of the announcer, the Indians should continue their struggle. Such remarks could be construed (by the government) as encouraging the "riot." On the other hand, the same announcer is perfectly free to declare his support of the marshals and FBI agents in their plan to starve innocent people. This is thought control and should be abhorrent to the "American Idea." Instead, it has become a bullwark of the American legal system.

---

[1] For an outstanding analysis of this statute, see Kinoy, Schwartz, Peterson, *Conspiracy on Appeal* (Center for Constitutional Rights, New York, 1971).

THE CONSPIRACY COUNT

No political trial would be complete without the prosecutor's favorite weapon—the conspiracy count—and the airlift indictment was no exception.

Conspiracies are beloved of prosecutors for very good reasons—they are easy counts to prove, and even if they are not proved they are extremely prejudicial to the defense. Some judges define a conspiracy as engaging in a common plan or scheme, even without formal agreement to do so. Added to this loose definition is the broad scope of conspiracy which holds one co-conspirator liable for the acts of all other co-conspirators committed in furtherance of the conspiracy. What this all amounts to is that anything done or said by one alleged co-conspirator may be introduced as evidence against any other co-conspirator even if the latter person did not want that act to be done. Regardless, then, of whether the prosecution is able to prove the conspiracy, the mere presence of a conspiracy count permits a great deal of possibly prejudicial evidence to be introduced against a defendant who may have no responsibility for the acts for which he/she is being held responsible.

As a result of the three counts pending against them for almost two years, each airlift participant faced a total of fifteen years imprisonment and/or $30,000 fine.

CUSTER IS NOT DEAD

But the airlift people were obviously not the only victims of the government at Wounded Knee. Over 400 were arrested and formal indictments finally returned against well over 100 of them. In addition, numerous state charges are still pending as a result of the earlier police riot at Custer, South Dakota, and subsequent courtroom disturbances in Sioux Falls, South Dakota.

The most common federal charge is interfering with the marshals and the FBI agents by trying to enter Wounded Knee during the siege. Recently, two federal judges in separate cases dismissed charges under this statute on the grounds that federal law officers were not performing a lawful duty at Wounded Knee. The basis of this conclusion was the illegal presence of U.S. Army officers and materiel. The Pentagon is barred by law from performing any domestic police functions in the absence of a state of emergency declared by the President. Hopefully, these few dismissals will eliminate many of the Wounded Knee charges, but at present the government is persisting in its efforts to maintain them.

Defense efforts in all of these cases have been hampered by the size of the task and the lack of personnel and money with which to perform it. Changes of venue have scattered trials from South Dakota to Minnesota to Nebraska to Iowa, requiring the volunteer defense committee to split its meager resources among several different headquarters. This decentralization places tremendous strain of the defense efforts. The lack of operating funds has interfered with the adequate preparation of cases and has added to the personal financial burdens borne by the volunteers. While some money has been donated and many legal workers and lawyers have volunteered a portion of their time, these resources have never been sufficient to meet the overwhelming need. The government, funding these prosecutions through tax dollars, does not have the same problem. Washington claims that money is not available for improved medical care, jobs, welfare, and other necessities of life, but there never seems to be a shortage when it comes to prosecuting people fighting for those very necessities.

CONCLUSION

It is truly outrageous that major crimes have been committed against the people of the United States, indeed, the people of the entire world, and the distinguished perpetrators of those crimes are now freely walking the streets. Some live in oceanside mansions, some are becoming millionaires through the publication of their memoirs, some have slipped into quiet but comfortable oblivion. The same government that permits those men to remain free now seeks prison terms for other people who, starting at the bottom of the American class structure, came together in a brave attempt to regain their land and heritage. Such action is consistent with prosecuting war resisters while making heroes of mass murderers, with a policy of enforced scarcity and malnutrition at home while burning food supplies of people abroad. The major difference between the bombing and spraying of Viet Nam and the policy of starvation at Wounded Knee is the speed with which the U.S. government tried to kill its victims.

Some people think that ridding the White House of Richard Nixon has cleansed the country of the oppressive mentality of its leaders. Such thoughts are, indeed, naive. The Ford-Rockefeller Administration is wedded, perhaps even more firmly than Nixon's, to the oil companies and other corporations who profit from war and exploitation—whether at home or abroad. Until power is wrested away from this handful and returned to the many, no change in the White House can be more than temporarily meaningful. While the short-term actions of one Administration may have differed from another, long-term strategy has been the same, regardless of the name of the individual who holds the reins of government.

The parallels between Wounded Knee and Viet Nam are eloquently drawn in this book—they were obvious at all times to many people, including the Indians at Wounded Knee and the government in Washington. Just as a statute aimed at suppressing black liberation was utilized to suppress the rights of American Indians, a military force designed to fight abroad was utilized against Native Americans at home. Just as the government sought to suppress dissent over the war in Viet Nam, so it sought to silence those who would support Wounded Knee. In neither case were they successful. Nonetheless, it is our responsibility to prepare for their continued attempts. The overt and covert warfare now waged by the U.S. government against people struggling for their national liberation is no longer thousands of miles from our shores. The empire is collapsing and the war has been brought home.

New York City
July 1975

Notes

The Foreword (pp. 2-3) lists the books that served as sources for the quotations (from Indians and some whites) used throughout the text. More detailed references are cited below:

Text page	Source
12	Jacobs, *et al.*, I, 4
17	Brown, 1
18	Armstrong, 1
19 (eyewitness)	Jacobs, *et al.*, I, 45
19 (Miantunnomoh)	Armstrong, 3
20	ibid., 12
21	ibid., 24
22-23	ibid., 31-32
24	Jacobs, *et al.*, I, 51-53
25-26	ibid., 53-56
26	ibid., 57-60
26-27	Armstrong, 47
28	Jacobs, *et al.*, I, 31
37 (Bent)	Brown, 88
37 (Conner)	ibid., 89
38 (Sheridan)	ibid., 166
38 (Sheridan)	ibid., 165
38 (Crook)	ibid., 209
40	ibid., 118
41	ibid., 140
42	Armstrong, 92-93
43 (Crazy Horse)	ibid., 101
43 (Long Mandan)	ibid., 100
44 (Treaty)	Burnette and Koster, 305
46	Armstrong, 105
47	Brown, 413
48	Neihardt, 276

57	McLuhan, 120
61 (Senate Subcommittee)	Burnette and Koster, 49-51
66-67	ibid., 181
69 (U.S. Secretary)	Hayden, 105
69 (U.S. general)	ibid., 75
71	*Focal Point,* Vol. II, No. 8, January 7, 1975, Santa Monica, California, 2 [re South Vietnamese visit to BIA]
110	McLuhan, 134
147	ibid., 53
195	Armstrong, 42
224	McLuhan, 45
268	Brown, 415
314	Armstrong, 79

THE AMERICAN INDIAN MOVEMENT

"We're trying to regain what we had in the past, being human beings and being involved in society."

—Stan Holder, AIM

WE REMEMBER

1890-1973

WOUNDED KNEE

The American Indian Movement is working across the country, from Boston to Los Angeles, from New Mexico to Minnesota. AIM people are involved in Indian cultural revival, anti-alcoholism programs, job placement, self-help projects.

We work where our people live — in the big cities and on the reservations. At Pine Ridge, still under the heel of Dick Wilson and the FBI, AIM people have their hands full just staying alive.

Attempts by the government to discredit us have failed. Among Indians in need or embattled, AIM has appeared to help. We were with the Menominees of Wisconsin during the seizure of the Alexian Brothers Novitiate in 1974. We were in the Fairchild Camera factory in New Mexico when Navajos took it in 1975.

Whether it means teaching our people to publish a community newspaper, organize a survival school, administer a fund-raising drive, or defend themselves with arms, AIM has been ready, both to build and to struggle.

We need your help. There is very little money in the Indian community to support us. Give what you can.

_____I can make a monthly pledge of $_____.

_____I am enclosing a contribution of:
$10___ $15___ $25___ $50___ $100___ Other___

Send to: National Office, American Indian Movement
P.O. Box 3677, St. Paul, Minnesota 55101

Name_____

Address_____

City_____State_____Zip_____

Make checks payable to American Indian Movement

•WOUNDED KNEE
LEGAL DEFENSE/OFFENSE COMMITTEE

SOUTH DAKOTA

PIERRE

RAPID CITY

• SIOUX FALLS

The courtroom struggle to free the Wounded Knee defendants *still* goes on. The Wounded Knee Legal Defense/Offense Committee, now over two years old, is *still* hard at work.

Four trials are scheduled in the summer of 1975 — in four different cities across the Midwest. Over 60 defendants *still* have outstanding cases.

For two years, we have worked under an almost total news black-out. Our resources are *critically depleted*. We need money desperately. Please contribute and help us keep Wounded Knee alive.

_____Enclosed is $1.50 for Wounded Knee info booklet, including text of 1868 Treaty, May 5, 1973 Agreement, and more.

_____I can make a monthly pledge of $_____.

_____To help with legal expenses, I have enclosed:
$10___ $15___ $25___ $50___ $100___ Other___

Send to: Wounded Knee Legal Defense/Offense Committee
P.O. Box 2307, Rapid City, S.D. 57701

Name_____

Address_____

City_____State_____Zip_____

Make checks payable to Wounded Knee Defense